Lucky Alex

*Aluminum box engraved for Alex by an Ambonese POW
from a sketch completed in POW camp by Sid Scales.*

Lucky Alex

THE CAREER OF
GROUP CAPTAIN A. M. JARDINE,
AFC, CD, RCAF (RET'D),
SEAMAN AND AIRMAN

ADVENTURES AT SEA, ON LAND AND IN THE AIR,
FROM HARD TIMES TO COLD WAR, 1929–1965

Colin Castle

Design and production by Alaris Design, Victoria.
Illustrations by S.E. Scales OBE

Printed in Victoria, Canada

National Library of Canada Cataloguing in Publication Data

Castle, Colin, 1936-
 Lucky Alex : the career of Group Captain A.M. Jardine,
 AFC, CD, RCAF (ret'd), seaman and airman
 : adventures at sea, on land and in the air,
from hard times to cold war, 1929-1965
Includes bibliographical references and index.
ISBN 1-55369-054-0
 1. Jardine, A. M. (Alex Myles), 1914-
 2. Canada. Royal Canadian Air Force--Biography.
 3. Military attachés--Canada--Biography.
 4. Air pilots, Military--Canada--Biography.
 5. Merchant marines--Canada--Biography. I. Title.
UG626.2.J37C37 2001   358.4'0092   C2001-903629-9

TRAFFORD

This book was published *on-demand* in cooperation with Trafford Publishing.
On-demand publishing is a unique process and service of making a book available for retail sale to the public taking advantage of on-demand manufacturing and Internet marketing.
On-demand publishing includes promotions, retail sales, manufacturing, order fulfilment, accounting and collecting royalties on behalf of the author.

Suite 6E, 2333 Government St., Victoria, B.C. V8T 4P4, CANADA

Phone	250-383-6864	Toll-free	1-888-232-4444 (Canada & US)
Fax	250-383-6804	E-mail	sales@trafford.com
Web site	www.trafford.com	TRAFFORD PUBLISHING IS A DIVISION OF TRAFFORD HOLDINGS LTD.	
Trafford Catalogue #01-0231		www.trafford.com/robots/01-0231.html	

10   9   8   7   6   5   4   3   2   1

For Alex, for his family, and for all who served with him.

CONTENTS

FOREWORD
by
Lieutenant-General R. J. Lane DSO, DFC & Bar, CD, CF (Ret'd)

This is a remarkable book about a remarkable airman. Before he joined the Royal Air Force he had already had two careers as a seaman, first with Canadian Pacific in the Pacific Ocean and then with Donaldson Line between Vancouver and Glasgow. He was a very restless young man, always seeking new challenges without the benefit of a university education. While this may have bothered him in the RAF it did not in any way affect his progress once he had joined that great service.

Becoming a prisoner-of-war of the Japanese early on in the war with that country, while serving with the RAF in the Far East, had a more lasting effect on his career in the Royal Canadian Air Force, which he joined at the end of World War II. His age and the time spent as a POW meant that he had to prove himself at every opportunity. This he did. His hard work and leadership qualities stood him in good stead as he progressed from one position to another, being promoted along the way.

One of his great strengths was his insatiable love of flying. Even in positions where aircraft were not readily available he would find the means to get one even if it meant using his leave to do so, and in this way kept his qualifications as a pilot constantly to the fore. In so doing he was an exceptional officer and not many others made such an effort. In this way he satisfied, as far as it was possible, his extraordinary love of flying.

The author is to be commended for the research necessary to write such a detailed and fascinating story. He was assisted in part by the large number of letters Alex sent to his mother, which are now in the BC Archives. They permitted the author to add a personal touch to the biography, bringing out the strong and determined personality that brought Alex through the horrors of the Japanese POW camps. These experiences helped him in his career when he filled positions requiring such leadership abilities in the peacetime Air Force.

Although Alex and I are from Victoria it was not until we were on the same RCAF Staff College course that I met him for the first time. Our careers never caused us to be in the same area at the same time although we came close. For example, when Alex stepped down as the Air Force Honorary Aide-de-Camp to the first Canadian Governor General, Vincent Massey, I had the honour of replacing him. I am sorry I did not have the opportunity of working more closely with this remarkable gentleman. This book is a great read.

11 APRIL 2000
VICTORIA

AUTHOR'S PREFACE

In the 1990s, when governments stopped providing hotel rooms for provincial exam markers, I was faced with a choice when I came to Victoria to perform that little-valued public service. Either I could go slumming in the University of Victoria dorms or I could scrounge a bed from Alex Jardine, a cousin of my wife's whom I knew slightly and whose story intrigued me. My Scottish ancestry won, Alex was most hospitable – providing bed, board and bicycle – and I came to know him well. Over several marking sessions, while drinking beer at Spinnaker's or walking it off on the trail around the golf course, he told me of the sea-chest full of his letters that his mother had kept – and of other items of interest that he had. Could I recommend a history student at U. Vic who might make a university project out of writing his life story? It was a good question and I tried to find one, but without success – the material was too much for any student actually taking courses.

When I stopped teaching, in June 1998, I had already decided to start writing books. I worked during the fall on a children's history of Canada but, around Christmas, decided to put it on hold in order to start on Alex's biography. One thing that convinced me to do so was the order that he had meanwhile brought to his papers: he had hired an archivist to reduce the contents of the sea-chest to a large number of meticulously referenced files. Apart from the fact that he had deposited most of them in that intellectual Fort Knox, the BC Archives, it now looked like a manageable task. I started work in the Archives in February or March 1999 but realised immediately that, even with the new filing and reference system, the job was enormous. The prospect of spending most of the year living out of a suitcase in Victoria was not appealing, in spite of Alex's welcoming hospitality. If I was to do the job the Archives had to be persuaded to part with five or six boxes of the letters, dating from 1928 to 1956. Their initial rejection of my request forced me to bring up reinforcements in the form of Alex himself. That did the trick; his well-known charm brought about the release of the files to the care of Randy Manuel at the Penticton Archives. There I did most of the research during the summer, substituting a daily drive down the valley for a weekly commute to Victoria. The first draft was finished by October. After a millennial break I returned to the book in February 2000 and completed the editing and re-writing by May.

It has been an experience from which I have learned much. I must thank Deirdre Mills, Alex's youngest sister, and her husband Bob for reading the manuscript with great care and filling my e-mail inbox with suggestions for changes, most of which I adopted. I have to thank my wife Val, my Emperor's Clothes department, for reading chapters hot off the printer and for giving me the sort of advice that only a wife can get away with. I need to thank Kathryn Bridge of the BC Archives for being accommodating and Randy Manuel and his staff at the Penticton Museum and Archives for giving me a desk, pleasant company and a quiet place to work for a few months. I must also thank David Erskine, Sid Scales, Michael Taylor, Lionel Johnston, Pam Robertson, Diana Castle and John Kelly for reading the manuscript and offering feedback. Thanks go to Sid Scales, creator of marvellous cartoons, for giving me permission to use them and for being a most helpful source for the POW years. Others, whose own writings I was permitted to quote, include Talbot Knight, John Jackaman and Hugh Campbell. I learned interesting details about Alex from his goddaughter Robyn Dangar, from his cousins Robin Johnston and Mary Johnston (late of Tunbridge Wells), from his sisters Deirdre and Ruth and from Ann's cousin Derek Lukin Johnston – many thanks to all of them.

Thanks go to Dianne Greenslade of Kelowna and her colleague Maggie Charlton of the Annapolis Valley who defied space and time in providing advice and expert copy-editing of the manuscript. Thanks also go to Arifin Graham of Alaris Design in Victoria; not only did Arifin produce a fine artistic product but his advice helped to keep Alex and myself – both literary neophytes – pointed in the right direction during the long process of producing a book.

Most of all I must thank Alex. Working with him has been delightful. It cannot be easy to have your life dissected before your eyes, to have your own memory repeatedly called into question. When he saw some of the early chapters in manuscript I am sure that he felt he had bitten off more than he intended to chew. He had hoped for a no-fuss book dealing extensively with aircraft, ships and events. Most of that he got, but he had not bargained for his love life as a young man being given front page treatment! I hope that the interest of such pages for those who know him best will compensate for any discomfiture that they may have caused him. I certainly found that part of his story fascinating and continue to marvel at his emotional strength. Here is wishing him long life and happiness!

COLIN CASTLE
KELOWNA
JUNE 2000

ACKNOWLEDGEMENTS

The author wishes to make the following acknowledgements: to the Wylie Agency (UK) Ltd., for permission to quote from Ian Buruma's *Wages of Guilt* (London: Jonathan Cape,1994); to the Random House Archive and Library for permission to quote extensively from Laurens van der Post's *The Seed and the Sower* (London: Hogarth Press, 1963) and from *The Night of the New Moon* (London: Hogarth Press, 1970); to Lionel Lacey-Johnson, copyright holder and publisher, for permission to quote from *Global Warrior, the story of G/C Jeudwyne* by Alain Charpentier, et al.(Eastbourne:Kall Kwik,1999); to Grub Street Press for permission to quote from *Bloody Shambles* by Christopher Shores, Brian Cull & Yasuho Izawa (London: Grub Street, 1992); to Penguin Books (UK) Ltd. for permission to quote from V.S. Naipaul's *Among the Believers* (London: André Deutsch, 1981); to Lonely Planet for permission to quote from *Indonesia,* by Robert Storey et al, Lonely Planet series, (Victoria, Australia: Hawthorn, 1992); to Penguin Books (Australia) Ltd., publisher, for permission to quote from E. E. Dunlop's *The War Diaries of Weary Dunlop* (Melbourne: Thomas Nelson, 1986); to Ken Stofer, author and publisher, for permission to quote from his book *Dear Mum* (Victoria, BC: Kenlyn Publishing, 1991); to Curtis, Brown, literary agents for the works of Noel Barber, for permission to quote from *The Natives Were Friendly …So We Stayed the Night* (London: MacMillan 1977); to Penguin Books, (Toronto) for permission to quote from Ernest Hillen's *The Way of a Boy* (Toronto: Penguin Books, 1993); to Hugh Campbell for permission to quote from his *History of the Tungsong;* to John Jackaman for permission to quote from his unpublished autobiography; and to Sid Scales for permission to reproduce his magnificent POW cartoons. The author wishes to apologise to the holders of the copyrights for John Gunther's *Inside Asia* (New York: Harper and Brothers, 1939), Hugh Popham's *Sea Flight* (London: William Kimber, 1954) and G.S.Richardson's poem *Singapore Soliloquies* whom, in spite of his best efforts, he was unable to trace.

ILLUSTRATIONS, PHOTOGRAPHS AND MAPS

"Alex's World"

*Alex and his sisters, circa 1928 (left to right): Ruth (7), June (10), Theo (11), Alex (14),
Deirdre (5), Marjory (13).*

1

EARLY DAYS

1914–1929
In which we examine Alex's ancestry and
in which he grows up in Vancouver and Victoria, BC.

"... and we all have bene good ..."
— ALEX, AGED 7

Alexander Myles Jardine was born in Vancouver on the 16th of March 1914, avoiding the ides by a day – surely the first demonstration of his motto, "Lucky Alex." And it is perhaps a demonstration of his optimism that he would consider himself lucky being born in such an ill-fated year. His parents, Harold and Agnes Octavia Squire Jardine, rejoiced in the event. They brought rather different baggage to their alliance and it is perhaps another piece of luck for Alex that later events make it appear that his Squire genes predominate. He was the most recent of a long line of wayfaring and sometimes eccentric members of this family who made the whole world their territory, as much at home on any continent or ocean as they might have been on their ancestral island, England.

Agnes's maternal grandfather, the redoubtable Admiral J. Wylie East, RN, had seen active service against Russia during the Crimean War, receiving the Baltic medal in 1854. Later on, as agent of the expanding Raj and in an attempt to forestall French and Germans in the Scramble for Africa, he commanded two of Her Majesty's ships, HMS *Lynx* and HMS *Pioneer*, in a 400-mile expedition up the River Niger. The flag having been planted and the Africans duly subdued by demonstrations of gunfire, then-Commander East became aware of a Sub-Lieutenant Mountjoy Squire, also serving on the *Lynx*. It was a small wardroom; the few officers saw a good deal of each other and the two must have hit it off. When now-Captain East was made commander of the naval station on Ascension Island between 1873 and 1877 he had among his officers this same Mountjoy Squire. That young man may have agreed to accept such a godforsaken posting for reasons of professional ambition. It may also have been because of a certain fancy which he had taken to the boss's daughter. Whatever the case, Lieutenant Mountjoy Squire married Ruth East, presumably on Ascension, and probably in 1876.

Captain East left Mountjoy and Ruth on Ascension. His last active-list posting was as captain of HMS *Comus*. In this capacity he commanded the Royal Navy's China Cruising Squadron in 1881. Then, for the following three years, he was a sort of Naval 007 with licence to roam, projecting power in the Pacific as Her Majesty's representative. *Comus* was not exactly the *Victory;* according to that year's census she had fifteen officers and petty officers, including three engineers and a gunnery officer – but no crew. The crew must have been non-British, probably recruited in Hong Kong.

To begin with, by means of the threat of his guns and a stern dressing-down, Captain East managed to extract without bloodshed a 'fine' from the islanders of Pelau in the Solomons. Their crime was to have committed an "outrage on British subjects." Next he sailed to the rescue of an American merchant ship in distress, for which he was awarded a gold medal by the U.S. Government. That took him to San Francisco where he encountered the Marquis of Lorne and Princess Louise, themselves en route to Vancouver's Island (as the *Times* called it, and as it was still known). The Marquis was Governor General of Canada; in those pre-CPR days he and the Princess had reached the western end of the American railway system and needed transportation to Victoria, BC, which Captain East was happy to provide. He attended them for three months on the west coast and returned them to San Francisco. Next, he busied himself with the security of British subjects endangered by the War of the Pacific between Chile and her Bolivian and Peruvian opponents. Finally, from Santiago, Chile, he sailed home via Cape Horn, to retire from the Navy in 1884 at the age of fifty-four. He became Inspector of Coastguards and was promoted Rear Admiral in 1888. In 1893 he died, much appreciated by a grateful nation.[1]

Agnes Octavia was born to Mountjoy and Ruth Squire in Tokyo in 1889. She was 'Octavia' because she was the eighth child. She and her brother Lionel were fortunate to be born in Tokyo although it was not the most medically advanced place in the world in 1889. They might have been born on Ascension Island, a windswept, goat-populated, equatorial rock halfway between Africa and South America, as were their two oldest brothers, Tom and Bill. Or they might, like sister Marjory, have been born on Perim, an island with the climate of an oven in the middle of the Red Sea, where the Royal Navy stockpiled coal – a sort of infernal Robert's Bank. The thought of Marjory's birth, in a place where the average summer temperature is 95 degrees, and at a time before air conditioning and electricity, makes a modern reader respect those tough old Victorians. Ruth Squire was only able to bear three of her eight children in England: DeeDee, Winnie and Ruth Eliza – all born in Liverpool. Such was the life of a Royal Navy career officer's wife when Britannia ruled the waves.

Ruling the waves made exiles of thousands of similar families in lonely and uncomfortable places. Ascension, where then-Lieutenant Squire was posted during the 1870s, strategically controlled the mid-Atlantic. If Britain was to control the sea lanes, which she knew she must, she could allow no other power to hold Ascension. Its harbour was an anchorage and supply depot for RN ships engaged in suppressing piracy and the slave trade. It also ensured the safety of India-bound traders and passenger ships, for which it was a port of call. Perim became important after 1869 when the Suez Canal opened; the shortest route to India now lay through the Red Sea and the Royal Navy was beginning to rely on coal rather than sails. To enable Britain to project power, Perim became as undramatically vital as Ascension was. It was here that Mountjoy Squire was posted in 1883 to manage the RN coaling station. His family spent two years of heat, coal dust and flies on five square miles of rock, marooned five miles from Arabia and fifteen from Africa.

Thereafter, life became immeasurably better. The year 1886 saw the family in Tokyo where the Meiji modernisation was in full swing. Japan was determined to become a modern power on the principle of "if you can't beat 'em, join 'em." Both Britain and Germany saw it in their interest to assist with the formation of Japan's modern navy and merchant marine; after all, Russia was the only conceivable enemy for both countries while Bismarck still ruled Germany. And Japan, harbouring Manchurian and Siberian ambitions as she did, was a natural ally against Russia. Perhaps more importantly, a modernising Japan represented a tantalising market and Commander Squire found himself appointed Assistant Superintendent of the Mercantile Marine Bureau in Tokyo, responsible to the Japanese government. He and his family were to live in Tokyo for the next five years.

In 1891 he retired from the Japanese service and for his efforts was rewarded with the Order of the Rising Sun, the highest award open to a foreigner. He moved his family to Shanghai in 1892 and took up an appointment with the Chinese naval service. He was working there when the Sino-Japanese War erupted in 1894. After a lopsided war and a Japanese victory, Mountjoy returned to Tokyo in 1895, to a new position as adviser to the Japanese Harbours Board. His recent work in China, however, had offended Japan's aroused nationalism. Upon arrival, not only was his Order of the Rising Sun confiscated but he himself was thrown in jail. Happily the trouble seems to have been short-lived; his liberty and his medal were soon restored[2] and he continued to live and work in Japan throughout the 1890s.[3]

When Mountjoy and Ruth first arrived in Japan, their six children ranged in age from nine to one. The youngest needed nannies and the two boys needed to go to school. One imagines their house filled with short-statured Japanese servants and nannies and maybe tutors. As representatives of the world's greatest imperial power, they could be forgiven perhaps for adopting a somewhat patronising attitude towards the Japanese. For them the Japanese qualified among Kipling's 'lesser breeds'. But Japan was also fascinating and absorbing. Bill, the eight-year-old, certainly learned fluent Japanese. With the exception of the Shanghai interval his upbringing and schooling were almost entirely in Tokyo. Lionel and Agnes were born there. They were baptised at Tokyo's St Andrew's Church and Marjory was confirmed there. It was also in Tokyo that their mother Ruth died in 1897 at the age of forty-one.

Bill, because of his father's mercantile responsibilities, knew Yokohama well and was familiar with the shipping from all over the world, but mostly from Britain, which called at the port. He must have felt Britain's effortless domination. He may have dimly remembered the bustling docks of Liverpool, one of the world's busiest ports in the 1880s, but he felt at home in Japan and in its maritime environment. One imagines that Bill was always a hero for little Agnes. By the time the bereaved family left Tokyo, Agnes was nine and Bill twenty. She would have picked up his attitudes to Japan – admiring, but a little patronising. And she would have thought it the most natural thing in the world when Bill later decided that Japan was where he wanted to live and work.

When he retired around the turn of the century, Mountjoy and his family went to live in England where five of his children married and settled down. As a morose widower who drank more than he should, Mountjoy was unable to attend to the schooling of the youngest, who were boarded out. During this time Agnes suffered torments in the household of a strict female relative and, after their father's death in 1910, Marjory and Agnes came to British Columbia to start a new life – probably under the protective eye of their older brother Bill. It was to be in Vancouver that both would meet their husbands.

On his father's side Alex was possibly remotely linked to the Jardines of Jardine, Matheson, of Hong Kong and Singapore. However, big business did not appeal to Harold. He was an intensely private person, obsessed with a desire to be his own boss, but possessing none of the business acumen that would convert self-employment into a decent living for himself and a growing family. Alex considers him "one of the unluckiest people on earth; everything he tried simply did not come off as a money-making project." Harold was born in Scotland in 1880 and went to school in Helensburgh. At school he was senior to Logie Baird, later the inventor of television. In 1897 he emigrated to Canada on the three-master *Loch Ryan*, with his mother, his sister Floss and a brother whose name does not survive. For a few years the brothers farmed successfully in Manitoba. As a youth Harold was an exuberant athlete. In Manitoba, he loved to swim or skate all day; he was always first on the ice in winter and first in the water in summer. However, his brother deserted them, attracted by the siren call of the United States. One hopes he did well thereafter but he lost contact with the family. Harold would have had difficulty running the farm single-handed so he and his mother sold up and headed for Vancouver.

Ironically, in later years a farm would have been an ideal occupation when Harold was married with a large family to feed – and to assist him. But the lure of Vancouver was too strong; it was an Eldorado which was to grow from Gassy Jack's disreputable hamlet to a city of 100,000 people between 1885 and the First World War. There were fortunes to be made in real estate and finance but Harold seems not to have had much luck in making one. In fact the tricky real estate market could easily ruin the unwary – and unwary he certainly was. The details are difficult to establish because of Harold's love of opaque language but in 1911 he seems to have become involved in property development with Floss's husband, Tom Plumb, as his partner. Alex relates an unsubstantiated family legend that Harold and his lawyer friend Roy Johnston, who had arrived from England in 1910, not only knew but together courted Marjory and Agnes Squire. All four were athletic, liked to play tennis and make their own musical entertainment. Although both sisters lost their hearts to the genial, outgoing Roy, a star cricketer with a well-paid CPR land conveyancing job, it was Marjory who carried the day when Roy proposed to her. This left the field clear for Harold to continue to pursue Agnes.

In a letter to Tom on the 18th of December 1911 Harold described his early relationship with his future wife. Guardedly he wrote:

> "I have had several good times of a different sort, both fortunately and unfortunately, with the little girl [Agnes was twenty-two to Harold's thirty-one; maybe 'little girl' because she is the younger sister] ... The worst features with me being that I have lost my head, and it won't come to my rescue, so I can only hope that some outside influence will save me. And to make matters worse Xmas is coming along and up till yesterday we are still the best of friends. I did not try to see her today but will be sure to ring her up tomorrow, and have tea or go to the theatre. If she would only do or say something I don't like or agree with it would not be so bad, but she generally does the opposite of what I expect. Well? Anyhow, I am still free; I will let you know developments later."

Looking after their mother, apparently an extremely difficult old lady, had become too much for Harold. His sister Floss, with two little boys to raise, could not help. He told Tom: "I have made a firm resolve at last, with no turning back this time, that I will take her home [to Scotland] as soon as I have several hundred dollars together ... I will leave her and come back by return. You will no doubt be glad to hear of this as it will be a relief to Floss and yourself." He seems to have been as good as his word. He was hoping to rid himself of one responsibility, which he found unbearable, whilst postponing making a decision about another. However, leaving his mother, presumably with her own family, was easier said than done. He told Tom later: "After my awful experience in Edinburgh ... I was on the verge of a breakdown." Later in life, when pursued by the Jardine Clan Society of Scotland, Alex told its president and founder, Sir William Jardine, that the Jardines of British Columbia had only gone there to forget their ancestors and past history! Presumably he had absorbed this attitude from his father.

In 1912, back in Vancouver, Harold resumed his hesitant courtship of Agnes. It was as if he was both attracted and repelled by the roles of husband and father. No 'outside influence' saved him and, for richer or poorer, they were married in May 1913. What did Agnes see in Harold? Because she was twenty-three in an era when girls of that age were 'on the shelf', she was under some pressure to marry. She was also, doubtless, attracted by this good-looking older man, by his reticence, his carefree air and mysterious references to business dealings which would make them rich!

Agnes and Harold started married life in Vancouver, where Alex was soon born. Fourteen months later, in May 1915, Marjorie was born, to be followed in April 1917 by another girl, Theo. From the beginning, the family had money difficulties. In August 1913 Harold confessed to Tom that he had been naively trusting of an Englishman's word in a real-estate deal. He was seriously in debt with but eight dollars in the world, and consequently was unable to pay Tom and Floss money that he owed them. He was horrified to discover that they were counting on this money to live on and his relationship with Floss suffered permanent damage as a result. Harold told Tom, for transmission to Floss, that in 1913 he had had a personal crisis from which he was lucky to escape with his reason. "Though I appear on the surface as if I never had any real care in the world," he wrote, "I know what real cares are, and knowing, keep them to myself."

This silent and vulnerable man continued to eke out an existence for the next four years on the edge of the real estate market and the house-building industry. Although a hopeless businessman, Harold was a talented builder who could build good houses. His problems were with financing and partnerships. In the spring of 1918, with a fourth child on the way, the family went to live in Port Alberni, hoping that a change of scene might bring better luck. This was hard for Agnes because her sister Marjory continued to live in Vancouver, after marrying Roy Johnston in 1914. She could certainly have used Marjory's help and advice and it would have been nice for their two families to grow up near each other; Marjory's son, Robin, was born in 1916.

For a fellow who had a hard time putting bread on the table, he was soon needing a great deal of it; in June 1918 June was born. With six mouths to feed and presumably seeking a big fix for his financial embarrassments, Harold entered a partnership with another man to cut spruce for the Imperial Munitions Company of England. Together they had a contract to supply the company with enough wood to make them both a lot of money – and to pay the wages of a Chinese cook they hired for the camp. But it meant a move to the cutting site at the mouth of the Toquart River, on the west coast of Vancouver Island. As Agnes had recently suffered a tragedy in the family – her oldest brother Tom had been killed in France on the 30th of June – she was probably glad of the distraction provided by this adventure.

In a pre-dawn downpour on the 3rd of August 1918, Harold and Agnes heroically loaded children, luggage and mattresses onto a 32-foot fishing boat in Port Alberni. With them went an eighteen-year-old girl, June Paynter, to help with the children. Agnes was showing the spirit of her ancestors. After an eerie journey down the Alberni Canal, watched by sentinel bald eagles from cloud-shrouded trees, they swung north through Junction Passage. Passing inside the Broken Islands they reached journey's end in Toquart Bay. Here they set up house in a one-room cabin at the water's edge. They also had access to an oyster-packing float connected to the shore by a plank. This had on it a shed, divided into two rooms, and there they all slept, leaving the cabin for eating, cooking and living. Meanwhile Harold commuted daily to his work camp, three miles away, by dugout canoe. He returned each evening after dark, completely exhausted.

All went well through the fall. The timber was being cut and the partners' boom was growing. June would take Alex and Marjorie to pick berries in the bush, which was so thick that there were no roads or trails. It was too late in the year for hucks and salmonberries but the blackberries were good. One can imagine June reaching down the high ones for Alex to pick, occasional squeals of pain when bare arms met thorns, whoops of delight when they found a new patch and the gradual purpling of two little faces as they sampled their crop. Each day they came back to the cabin with enough for the family for supper. Agnes must have had her hands full with the diaper-washing for the little ones. She found the cabin's attic "a godsend to dry clothes." It was reached by way of a pull-down ladder – which kept Alex and Marjorie from risking their necks.

In November their world started to fall apart. First June, probably suffering cabin fever, returned to civilisation. Then the war ended, followed at once by the Imperial Munitions Company cancelling its agreement to buy the wood. Next, Harold's partner decamped with his wife and as much of their joint property as he could manage, leaving the wages of the Chinese cook for Harold to pay. Harold, with a few locals who were trying to help the family, began fishing for salmon to fill an American order. As he had no gear except a pair of hip waders, his contribution was gaffing fish, illegally, in the river after dark. Between them they filled an ice-filled scow with salmon and hoped to make a killing. This time it was disease that scuppered the plan; the 1918 killer flu hit Port Alberni and the American buyers stayed home and reneged on their promise to buy. The sky was dark with gulls when they dumped the fish. Notwithstanding the outcome, the locals paid Harold thirty dollars for his efforts; Agnes recognised charity when she saw it but Harold seemed not to.

As if things were not bad enough, the partner then sued Harold for some breach of their contract. He was subpoenaed to appear in court in Nanaimo. Agnes never did understand the issue and Harold probably never did either. He left Agnes to look after the kids while he went to Nanaimo, telling four-year-old Alex that he was now the man in the house. One can imagine Alex's dutiful expression when he was told – the same one he was wearing for his picture when he went to sea in 1930. In Harold's absence great-hearted neighbours kept things going, bringing water, mail and firewood daily. But when Harold came back a week later, "having lost out," they were down to a few dollars.

Desperate times call for desperate remedies. Harold's good neighbours who owned lots on the shoreline allowed him to cut as much of their timber as he could manage to get into the water. As the trees were big and not easily handled, they suggested that they would turn a blind eye if he were also to cut accessible trees on the adjacent crown land. Now this was serious lawbreaking in broad daylight for which the penalties were much more severe than those for gaffing a few fish. What was needed was teamwork in the Jardine family. While Harold was cutting on public land, Agnes kept a sharp lookout for boats entering the bay. At the first sign of unfamiliar visitors – potentially forestry inspectors – Alex and Marjorie were out on the porch of the cabin. They marched up and down singing "Ta ra ra boom-dee-ay!" at the top of their voices, banging the daylights out of old kerosene cans strung around their necks. Hearing this shindig, Harold was out of the woods in a flash, for all the world an innocent beachcomber looking for driftwood!

That winter they spent Christmas at the cabin. Surprisingly, the children were not disappointed by Santa Claus. Harold had given June money for presents for the children when she left and the conscientious girl had sent presents for all. What is more, when she left they had abandoned their floating bedroom. Agnes on her own could not possibly keep an eye on four children at once; there was too much possibility of adventurous tykes falling into the water. So a lean-to at the back of the cabin became their bedroom.

In due course Harold completed the boom. They were able to leave Toquart when the wood sold and were helped by a legacy of eighty pounds which Agnes received when her grandmother Ruth East died. Some time in late winter they moved to Victoria and so ended what Agnes always called "our west-coast interlude."

In Victoria they lived at 426 Niagara Street. Robin vividly remembers his first sight of his cousins on a family visit to the Jardines when he was four. Under the back verandah, Alex, Marjorie and Theo, aged six, five and three, were marching up and down between the posts, lustily singing "God Save the King." Their household was full of music. Agnes was a fine pianist and Harold sang well. Often they would invite friends in for singsongs and Agnes loved to play concertos – her favourite being Grieg's Concerto in A Minor. They were both good athletes and played tennis well enough for the children to consider watching them a treat. The family, though still living in rented houses, was sometimes fairly comfortable when Harold managed to sell houses. During the next few years he designed and built two large houses at 1710 and 1720 Rockland Avenue, and Alex's notebook tells us that they sold for $11,250 and $10,250. His favourite occupation was helping his father and he was fiercely proud of the houses that were built. Unfortunately, there were long periods between houses when the family had little to live on and Alex little to do. In one of these times Harold built for his children a swing and a merry-go-round in the back garden.

Alex would never say it but Harold seems to have found it hard to be a good father to his son. The absence of his own father when Harold came to Canada may mean that he had had little fathering himself. Whether or not this was the case, from early days he managed to waste opportunities for developing a strong bond with Alex and occasionally either hurt or humiliated him. Alex recalls his father taking him on a biking and camping trip, an experience that every Canadian boy looks forward to; but when Harold went for a dip in the freezing water of Juan de Fuca Strait he derided Alex for hating the cold of it. On another occasion, when Alex was twelve or thirteen, Harold had promised him wages for his summer holiday's work on a building project. At summer's end he gave Alex a cheque but suggested that he not go to the bank with it. "I have a vague feeling of upset about having been paid with a worthless cheque," Alex recalls. Seventy-three years ago the feeling was no doubt more painful.

Alex tells a happier story of summer work at about the same age.

"One summer Dad operated a logging camp on Saltspring Island and I was taken on as 'whistle punk'! From the felled tree to the water's edge a skid road was built; a wire hawser leading from the donkey engine at the water's edge to the felled tree hauled the tree out. Alongside the skid road a wire was rigged and attached to the donkey engine's whistle. The whistle punk ran alongside the road within grabbing distance of the wire. If a log jammed, the whistle punk grabbed the wire, which triggered the whistle, and the engineer running the donkey engine would stop the machinery! I fell once and twisted my ankle. Unknown to me a large Aboriginal was following me. He came up to me, plonked me on a tree stump and with huge hands felt my ankle. 'Not broken! You go home!' he advised. I had sprained it. Later Dad sent me to take telephone messages. I was sitting on a stool when the telephone rang. I jumped off the stool to pick up the telephone and promptly fell down; my ankle had swollen to the degree that I could not walk on it. After a long time Dad came and piggybacked me to the cabin we were sharing."

Harold was a good father to his daughters. He used to tease them by plunging his hand into his pocket and pretending to have found a mouse. When they had become suitably hysterical he would pull out his hand and open it, slowly, to reveal ... a handful of candies. When taking the girls for a walk he would chase them among the trees outside the Empress Hotel. On such occasions Deirdre and Ruth remember him tripping them up with his walking stick – which they all considered great fun. After Alex had gone to sea, Harold would take one of his daughters to help him when he was building houses. Theo, in particular, would ride to building sites in style on the handlebars of his bicycle.

The first school that Alex attended was Craigflower, followed by the Beacon Hill School. He was a most attentive student and quickly learned a mature-looking copperplate script which was to stay with him for a lifetime. However, six-year-old Alex came home from Craigflower with more than his share of nosebleeds and black eyes. Agnes discovered that other boys were picking fights with him because of the English accent he had learned from her and which he was showing no signs of losing – a tendency rare among children who usually adopt the accent of their peers. So Agnes found her youngster a boxing instructor, twenty-year-old Chuck Morris who lived nearby. Morris, later a well-known Victoria printer, taught his charge to box by shadowboxing with him while kneeling! Alex learned a life skill and the black eyes became less frequent.

Agnes had two more babies after June. Ruth was born in August 1921, when Alex was seven, and Deirdre in March 1923, when he was approaching his ninth birthday. It was probably when Agnes was in hospital for the birth of Deirdre that Alex wrote her this letter.

"426 Niagara Street. My dear Mummie. Yes! I would like to have our birthday together very much. Then you would have your birthday too? [His was the 16th of March, hers the 2nd of April.] So am I waiting to see you very much. And we all have bene good and I hope you were having a nice time their. And we all give you kisses from Alec your boy and I am so very glad she is a girl. And ? so glad it is a girl. For all who love you I love you the most. And I wrote you this letter when I was in bed, but I got up lit the fire and came back to bed."

This was a pretty good effort for a nine-year-old, especially a lad who was writing in bed in a freezing bedroom and who was missing his mother. Agnes, good mother that she was, was afraid that her hospital stay would cause her to miss his birthday and had come up with a marvellous solution. We also see a nine-year-old already adept at masking his feelings and aware of the need to consider the feelings of others. It was to become a lifelong discipline. A typical boy of nine would wallow in his own unhappiness and bemoan the fact that he had another sister instead of the brother he must have craved. He would take his mother's equanimity for granted. But not Lucky Alex. He just focused on the silver lining – the upcoming doubleheader birthday – and put the clouds behind him.

Alex was soon old enough to travel to Vancouver on his own to stay with his cousin Robin. There he suffered from homesickness, in spite of all the love and care he no doubt received from his aunt and uncle. An undated letter survives, written by Alex to his mother from Robin's house.

"Dear Mummy: I hope you are feeling well. I feel as if I was at home. And Robin and I are going to stay with Aunty Bertha. [This would be Bee Lukin Johnston, wife of Rufus, Roy's brother – no relation to Alex, but Robin's aunt.] And one night I cryd because I wanted to come home. And a very nice thing to do is to loos my knife of course. Lots of love from all of us to my dear loveing Mummy."

This sounds like a school holiday visit to Robin, to give both boys some male company and to allow Alex to escape the 'monstrous regiment' at home! The trip to

Bee's house suggests that Alex was having his first lengthy spell away from home. It was perhaps on this occasion that he first met Derek, son of Bee and Rufus, though Derek remembers their meeting being in Victoria. A studious boy a year older than Alex, Derek was dismayed by the apparently 'tough' lifestyle of the younger boy. In particular he remembers being entertained to tales of gang warfare in Victoria streets – Alex no doubt enjoying the effect that his wildly exaggerated description of a fight at school was producing on his audience!

When he was ten Alex went to South Park School, a few blocks further north on Douglas Street. Next year at eleven and a half, he joined the Sea Cadets, which opened a new window on the world for him. He was soon preoccupied with pieces of rope and knots – clove hitches, sheepshanks, bowlines, timber hitches and other mysteries of boyish lore. Maybe the knife was a sign of the times, no doubt the kind with a spike, really intended for splicing rope – a thing which sea cadets had to learn. Even at that age he never did things by halves. Very quickly he was not only a sea cadet but the best sea cadet in the whole Rainbow Sea Cadet Corps. For two of the three and a half years he was a member he was Chief Petty Officer, the highest rank open to him. At twelve he also joined "C" Company of #388 Army Cadet Battalion, based in South Park School, and his 1926 certificate of qualification in 'cadet semaphore' survives from this period. Naturally, Alex also became the senior cadet officer in Army Cadets! Obviously he relished the discipline and structure of both organisations and his future direction was really no longer a mystery. The only mystery, in fact, was the form it took: nothing in his cadet life suggested that he would eventually take to the air.

Decisions about careers were still a year away in the summer of 1928. This was to be his chore summer, when he would spend the entire vacation working at the Natural Bridge Café and Guest House at Field, BC. He did not realise it at the time, but he was testing his wings. This would be nine weeks away from home, much longer than the couple of weeks with Robin. It was an eye-opening experience from which Alex returned a different person, a change reflected in his diary. He was interested in everything that he saw and experienced. On the crossing, on a Canadian Pacific (CP) steamer from Victoria Inner Harbour to Burrard Inlet, he recorded his visit to the bridge and concluded: "I learned some new things today." In Field he was initially homesick and anxious to get letters from home but was treated like family by Daisy Swayne, the owner of the guest house and a good friend of Agnes's (they wrote to each other as "Swaynee" and "Jardinee"). She gave him definite tasks to do and he very soon forgot to be homesick. It was to be a lifetime cure and homesickness never afflicted him again.

He relished the hard work and the fact that he was trusted to get on with things. Most days he spent hours chopping wood for the kitchen and for winter heating. In fact the chopping included taking down many whole trees – he had to be careful because he was not supposed to be doing it (memories of his father at Toquart!). Once some of the railwaymen brought him a couple of hydro poles to cut up; this robust teenager did the job with a bucksaw, complaining only to his diary that it was pretty hard work! He would proudly record the size of the stack. He must have been in amazingly good physical shape because the summer was a hot one and wood-chopping an exhausting activity. He made a particular friend of George Forbes, a carpenter, who taught him some basic carpentry and provided him with pieces of lumber on which to try out his new skills.

Alex also had floors to scrub and tables to wait on. Waiting tables brought him a few tips and he was very uncritical of people's meanness. On one occasion towards the end of the summer two different men from a large party each handed him a quarter which he pocketed with thanks. However, when the second tipper found out about the first he demanded that Alex return his quarter! He paid up and recorded the event without comment. A big event was his stetson. Having admired and tried on Bill Cunningham's stetson – Bill drove a large Buick touring car for Brewster Brothers – he was bowled over with gratitude when Bill and his girlfriend Gertie came back from the Calgary Stampede with a new one for him to keep. And not only that but, as he recorded with some degree of anticipation, "tomorrow Bill will show me how to wear it."

Quite early on he became familiar with a bear, whom he christened Benjy, but with whom he was not always on the friendliest of terms. Predictably Benjy was really only interested in the garbage outside the café and of course it was Alex's job to clear up the mess when Benjy had eaten his fill and burped his way back into the forest. At first all was well; Alex was quite excited to see the bear, often enough that he could record "he came back today; he has been away for two weeks." Daisy Swayne decided to tame the bear and even Alex believed that she was succeeding when it ate from her hand. But she was probably a fortunate woman because quite soon he was telling his mother: "Benjy doesn't like me; I have to be careful." What that meant was that Benjy would fix him with his eye and walk aggressively towards him. He didn't growl, but Alex learned not to relax his naturally cautious attitude to the animal. He made himself scarce and solemnly told his diary: "I don't wear my stetson when the bear comes!"

He had a good deal of spare time and, thanks to the Eaton's mail-order catalogue, became the proud owner of a mouth organ which he taught himself to play. Later an American tourist, impressed by this friendly lad, sent him a much more elaborate one from Seattle. He had soon graduated from *Hinky Pinky* to *A Long Trail A-Winding*, *Rule Britannia*, *Wherever I May Roam*, *Tipperary* and *I Love a Lassie*, returning home as an accomplished party musician! It was a skill that would stand him in good stead for many years at sea and later make him both loved and loathed in various air force messes.

His diary records, without explanation or description, a couple of fights that he had with Betty Allan, a girl of nineteen who was also working at the guest house. He was clearly not too happy about them. Probably Alex, used to riding herd on his sisters, had been a bit too free with his advice and we know that she needled him, hiding his stetson on one occasion. As she was going to normal school and training to be a teacher, one of her jobs was to give Alex lessons, so there were plenty of potential causes. He was not a large boy at the time, about 5 ft. 4 in. in his socks, and Betty was probably bigger. The fights did not worry Daisy Swayne – in fact the reverse; she wrote to Agnes that Alex was always cheerful – a bottomless pit and the family garbage pail. "Alex is the friendliest youngster I've ever seen; he's palled up to all the drivers and is friends with everyone in Field as far as I can see. He and Betty are real friends – scrap and fight, which is a good sign."

He also had an accident. George Forbes had sharpened an axe for him and Alex was amazed at how much more efficient it was. Too efficient; one careless stroke and he chopped his foot quite severely. The doctor in Field put in a line of stitches and Alex was the centre of attention for a couple of days, lying around with his leg up, being waited upon. However, unable to tolerate idleness, he was soon back to wood-chopping. He made two more visits to the doctor to have the stitches removed and the doctor then proceeded to bill him, much to the indignation of the adults. There was no health insurance in 1928. The incident appears in his diary, but not in his letters to his mother or sisters – even at fourteen he was keeping his troubles to himself.

Everybody spent the last day of the summer in a great assault on Mount Burgess, the mountain behind the town. From there the party of fourteen walked to Emerald Lake and then to Summit Lake. It must have been a pretty tough walk but Alex and another boy delighted in scampering ahead like mountain goats, then waiting in mock exasperation for the older people to catch up. A couple of days later he went up to Lake Louise where he met his two cousins – presumably Floss's daughters up from Calgary. His comment: "Very nice, very pretty."

Before leaving for home he wrote a final letter, instructing his sisters to "leave some of the blackberry jam, please." He returned via Vancouver, on a train full of beery loggers, admitting years later that he had allowed them to press beer upon him which no doubt made the journey pass more quickly. He arrived in Victoria just as school was starting, little richer but wiser and more confident. Among the lifetime habits which he had begun was that of letter-writing. He had started a regular correspondence with his Mum, who matched him letter for letter. In fact so frequently did she write that Alex had politely suggested that she could write a little less often and he would still be okay! Nevertheless her letters were to be the key to his future equanimity when he was roaming the oceans and the continents.

Whatever tricks fate played upon him, he could handle them calmly as long as there was regular news from home. Victoria would always be the calm centre of his turbulent universe.

At this time Alex was reading quite a bit, usually the kind of books of which a parent or teacher would approve – Dickens, Jules Verne and Henty, stories of action and adventure, stories about faraway places. He also enjoyed drawing and sketching. At school he had been a good student. In 1929, aged fifteen, he had completed eighth grade at South Park and the principal, Mr A. A. Campbell, wrote of him: "He possesses good ability, is diligent, obedient and gentlemanly. As a student he acquitted himself very creditably, passing into High School by recommendation in June of this year." Undoubtedly the principal expected him to continue in school until matriculation. However, Alex considered himself a man of action rather than a scholar and the prospect of further years in school filled him with doubt.

He spent his last month at South Park in the woodwork shop, finishing the desk for his mother that he was making. In his spare time he was puttying and painting the family boat with his friend Dave Kirkendale. He had a variety of odd jobs which brought in a few cents – taking the boss's lunch to Emery's store was worth ten cents a day, twenty cents if he delivered a parcel for them and up to thirty-five cents if he stayed long enough to work in the store. He kept going to cadets for cutlass drill and when his cousin Frank Plumb, Aunt Floss's son, came to visit from Alberta, he showed him around after school. He took him over to Esquimalt to visit HMCS *Thiepeval*, whose engine room they explored, and went aboard the ship *Otterpool* down at 'the wharves'. Frank became too much of a good thing when he stayed out fishing until 11:00 p.m. – "Dad was mighty mad" – and Alex was dispatched with Frank to find the lad lodgings in town!

Alex had been presented by Mr Campbell at South Park with an honour roll certificate for holding "the First Rank in Regularity and Punctuality" for the second year running; also with a certificate entitling him "to be admitted into any High School in the Province." However, his interests and abilities and the economic situation of his family all pointed towards the same decision: leave school (most boys did at fifteen), take a job on a ship and aim to rise through the ranks. So far in life rising through the ranks had seemed to be the reward for just being Alex – diligent, obedient and gentlemanly. Surely this would continue.

And so the die was cast and his childhood came rather suddenly to an end. Instead of taking a place at high school Alex threw himself upon the job market – a somewhat quixotic action in the fall of 1929 but one that was to have satisfactory results.

2

GONE TO SEA

1929–1931
In which Alex becomes familiar with the Pacific Ocean
as a bridge messenger on the *Empress of Canada*.

"a damned fool to go to sea"
— A.J. HICKEY, FIRST OFFICER OF THE EMPRESS OF CANADA

Once the decision had been made that Alex was not going to high school, the decks were cleared for action to find him a job. Through July the references were arriving. Colonel A. G. Vincent, ex-Royal Marines, recommended Alex for employment "in any capacity for which honesty and steadiness are requisites"; he had "always shown great keenness with regard to a seafaring life." His Army Cadet commanding officer (CO), Lieutenant Waldo Skillings, found him "smart and efficient" and added that Alex had received the compliments of the inspecting officer for his excellent work at their annual inspection. Mr Campbell, in addition to his educational comments, wrote that Alex "has always been a trustworthy and reliable boy ... [who] I am sure will use his talents to the very best of his ability in any position he may occupy." It looked like a winning portfolio in spite of the fact that the key document, a reference from Lieutenant Percy W. Tribe, CO of the Rainbow Sea Cadet Corps, had not yet arrived. It was certainly enough for Alex. On the 27th of July, in his best letter-writing style, he wrote to Captain Aikman, General Superintendent of CP Steamships, Pacific Service, applying for a place as Officer Cadet. He wrote an identical letter to Captain Tedford who held the same position with Canadian National (CN) Ships. On the 6th of August Harold wrote to Captain Aikman (and presumably to Captain Tedford as well), supporting Alex's applications and indicating that Alex had parental support.

Aikman's reply, written on the same day as the long-awaited Sea Cadet reference, was like a bucket of cold water. "Our cadets," he wrote, "are drawn from the cadet training ship *Conway* which is stationed near Liverpool, where they receive two years' specialised training prior to appointment to a ship. We have not at present any vacancies [presumably for cadets on CP ships] and do not anticipate any before next year." The reference from P. W. Tribe was rather disappointing when it finally appeared and surely would have made no difference. For his exceptional, two-year chief petty officer, all Tribe could manage was a statement of that fact and a compliment on efficiency and smartness – all in five lines. If Captain Tedford replied, his answer must have been similar to Aikman's. Anyway, Alex decided that August was no time to be sitting around, waiting for the mailman – he would try something more promising.

First he tried every boy's summer standby, fruit picking. He started picking strawberries with Agnes – she would go on her own if he was not coming with her and on those days Alex got supper ready. He also went fruit picking with Harold and was able to make two dollars a day, pretty good money in 1929. When the fruit ran out he signed on as deckhand for the late summer on a millionaire's yacht, his first job afloat. This job paid the same as fruit picking and was a great deal more enjoyable; but even millionaires go back to work and this one did in the middle of September. There was something shady about the man and his boat and Alex was advised to keep his mouth shut about what he had seen on board – it was, after all, the age of rum-running.

Alex next worked for three weeks near Powell River, as chainman with a surveyor, thanks to his parents' knowing Mr Arthur Collins, a senior government surveyor. Spending the fall days, often in heavy rain, marching along a sighted line, dragging a steel tape until he reached the end of his 'chain' and then waiting for the surveyor, a Mr Moffat, to reach him, was at least different. It involved a lot of tramping through fairly open country and some burnt-over areas. A hard day, like the 3rd of October, was a strip of "30 chains of the most damnable swamp ever," about two miles or more. One day he renewed his acquaintance with black bears in a very frightening way: he looked up from making a blaze on a tree to see not one but two black heads inspecting him from twenty feet away. The smaller one, a cub, ran away but the mother "started to grunt and come for me – it ain't a comfortable feeling! Anyway, she came to about ten feet away from me – I still held my ground. Then, for some reason or other, she ran away. Sighs of relief from me!" Alex felt a bit guilty because Moffat, being an adult, had to carry more than 50 percent of their gear when they moved camp; this might have been okay if Alex had been experienced – which he was not. As it was, the packboards that they used were "damned heavy" and made his shoulders sore. But it paid him fifty dollars for three weeks' work while he waited, Micawber-like, for something more permanent to turn up.

And turn up something did. Alex took up a position as office boy for the BC Electric Company in downtown Victoria. Once again the position had been obtained by his parents and he made a serious effort to start a great business career.

18 LUCKY ALEX

His goal was nothing less than to become chairman – after all, had he not always risen to the top? Well, maybe not quite always. No doubt he seemed to his co-workers to be as amazingly friendly as he had to Daisy Swayne at Field. His cheerfulness and willingness to help as a roving office boy – he always had a horror of idleness – won him pals in every department. It was not long, however, before Alex, at first so full of determination to make a success of business life, was finding it increasingly difficult to imagine himself in such a career. In spite of his speedy acceptance into the office – and he made some friends that lasted a lifetime – there is a limit to the number of teacups a fellow can wash, to the number of inkpots he can fill, even to the number of fascinating errands to the offices down the street he can run. At least it gave him time to think and he thought more and more of his original plan of going to sea.

Now that he had sampled some of the alternatives he was more certain than ever that this was what he wanted. The Navy League had begun to stir the pot; the president of the Victoria branch, Mr MacMullen, had first of all written to support Alex's applications. Then MacMullen planted the idea in Alex's head – and in the heads of a few other top cadets – that they should apply for positions as bridge messengers rather than as officer cadets. It would not be so grand but the possibilities of getting hired were much better. Not only that but he got CP's Captain Aikman to agree to select boys alternately from the Victoria and Vancouver branches.

So, terminating his business career with few regrets on his part but with considerable sorrow on the part of his co-workers (Alex visited them faithfully whenever he was in Victoria during the next few years), on the 17th of December Alex wrote again, very correctly, to Captain Aikman. "With reference to my letter of the 27th of July, 1929, in which I applied as Officer Cadet; having been informed that you do not accept applications in this manner, I herewith apply for the first vacancy that occurs as Captain's Messenger." It sounds as though the BC Electric experience had polished up his business-letter style. He had to wait for a reply until after the holiday season and while he waited a Christmas card arrived from the staff at BCE. They had passed round the hat for him and enclosed the proceeds, the card being signed by the workers at Langley Street, Douglas Street, the ticket office, the line and meter room, and the substation. It must have made him feel appreciated and on the 8th of January he heard something that made him feel even better: CP Steamships would accept boys alternately on the recommendations of the two Navy League branches and advised him to see the secretary of the Victoria branch. Alex was top of the list in Victoria and MacMullen gave him the nod. He was appointed Bridge Messenger on the *Empress of Canada* and sailed on her from Vancouver on the 5th of February 1930.

Alex said his farewells to his parents and sisters as he boarded the CP steamer in Victoria harbour. His diary records that he had a good night in a fifty-cent berth. Stepping ashore at 6:00 a.m. in Vancouver, he walked over to Pier C and stood on the dock, staring up at the *Canada*. He could hardly believe that this immense steel ship, with its hundreds of portholes, was to be his home. As he humped his kit into the crew quarters he was overwhelmed by the smell of the alleyway, a smell unique to ships with Chinese crews at that time, compounded of Chinese food, incense, opium and unwashed humanity. It was not particularly pleasant, but it was definitely Oriental and it thrilled him! This new seaman was still a boy. Aged fifteen and a half and 5 ft. 6 in. tall, he had brown hair, hazel eyes and a dark complexion. He was bunked with two other bridge messengers, Red and Doman – his companions until the end of May 1931. Dave Kirkendale, his friend from Sea Cadets and South Park School, would join the ship after Alex's first trip.

The ports of call of the *Empress of Canada* from her headquarters in Vancouver were: Victoria, Yokohama (the port of Tokyo), Shimidzu, Kobe, Shanghai, Hong Kong, Manila and Honolulu. During his two years aboard, the *Canada* made twelve voyages, each of approximately six weeks with port time in Vancouver in between. The ship's officers, including two officer cadets from the *Conway*, were English, Scottish or Canadian, as were the petty officers, craftsmen and bridge messengers. The crew were Chinese, and at first Alex and the messengers had little contact with them – only meeting the Chinese cooks when they visited the galley to collect the duty officer's meals. Occasionally they had to thread their way through or over the crew in the alleyway outside their own cabin whenever there was a Chinese concert or a crew meeting. After Dave Kirkendale joined the ship, the four messengers were together for about a year and, considering the lack of privacy of a four-bunk cabin, they were good shipmates. Whenever they were in port the off-duty messengers tended to go ashore together in whatever combination the duty roster dictated. In addition there was a good deal of filling in for each other to allow one to spend a night ashore.

As on any ship, on the final leg of a voyage 'channel fever' gripped the crew, an impatient excitement when any delay, such as fog, could seem unbearable. Nothing mattered except getting home. Alex and the other messengers would be eagerly straining their eyes at the crowd on the dock whenever they called at Victoria. Those were red-letter days for Alex and his family. His mother and five sisters lined the dockside, cheering wildly as the great white ship tied up. After excited hugs, if there was time he would give the girls a tour of the ship, where they liked to play in the gym. Then they would rush home for a game of blindman's buff in the garden. A blindfolded Alex, roaring good-naturedly in his new man's voice, would try to catch his sisters. Their aim was to lead him into the holly bush, from which he would extricate himself painfully, amid hoots of excited laughter. Sometimes they would climb trees. Once Alex passed the point of no return on a sumac branch, breaking it and crashing to the ground. Afterwards, Agnes would provide a triumphant supper before they all escorted him, happy and probably sore, back to the ship. When ashore in Vancouver Alex stayed at his Aunt Marjory's house at 649 Keith Road East, North Vancouver. He had shipboard duties to perform each day but returned to Aunt Marjory's – which he took to calling home – when off-duty. At some point during the Vancouver stay he would be granted two or three days' leave to see his family in Victoria; but he also disciplined himself to write a long letter to his mother between trips. On his visits he had a marvellous time, chatting with his sisters and his father, going to the movies with his mother, looking up his BCE friends. On summer visits he enjoyed beach supper picnics round a driftwood fire when he would play his new squeezebox and everybody would sing. After one such evening, when everything had been just right, even the sunset, he wrote in his diary: "Got home around eleven feeling gorgeously tired and happy."

Dave Kirkendale joined the *Canada* after Alex's first voyage. Alex, of course, knew him well; the two boys had had a good time over New Year 1929 while Agnes was away – among other things, laughing uproariously as they beat the dust from her sitting room carpet on the clothesline. Now Alex was the 'old hand' and spent so much time telling tall stories of his exploits, some of which must have seemed

Alex's sketch of the messengers' cabin, Empress of Canada, *1930.*

shocking, that Dave thought that Alex was 'bad'! In case Agnes should hear about his 'badness' from Mrs Kirkendale, damage control was called for; he assured his mother in a letter that his badness was only on the surface. Why, he explained, he had had no cigarettes for the whole trip, had said his prayers every day and only had booze once (aged fifteen)! Possibly he had picked up some choice language which did the trick with young Dave but which Alex failed to mention to his mum. Or maybe he fed Dave with myths about his amorous exploits which were no doubt mainly imaginary. He certainly met girls when he went ashore but Agnes may have been happy to read "so far I have not met a girl that I really cared for. Which I'm rather glad of in a way." Dave's father was the Victoria harbourmaster and Dave must have felt confident that he could always get a job at sea, unlike Alex who had no such advantage. For Alex every minute had to be employed learning something new and he was surprised by the easygoing lifestyle of the other messengers who behaved as teenagers do when given the opportunity to put their feet up. Alex's surprise is more of a comment on his own extraordinary maturity and focus when it came to bettering himself and directing his own life.

The first officer was a Mr A. J. Hickey whom Alex admired. Interestingly he did not find him a nice person: Alex considered him sarcastic and inconsiderate – he had told Alex that he was a "damned fool to go to sea." But he was a thoroughly competent professional who showed coolness under pressure; he was a man "who does not get flustered." And for that this youngster, whose own 'steadiness' had been recognised by Colonel Vincent, admired him. He also mentioned the chief officer, Mr Claxton. From the start they had taken a liking to each other and Claxton had gone out of his way to smooth Alex's path. Later on, he was to be picked out by Claxton for cadet responsibilities, principally the supervision of cargo stowage in the hold by the longshoremen. This promotion occurred when Alex rejoined the ship after a home leave. Claxton summoned him and sternly told him he was fired as a messenger! Alex's jaw dropped in dismay. Claxton laughed, then told him of his promotion to cadet duties. Huge smiles of relief! What Alex liked was his thoughtfulness. When the *Canada* visited Victoria after his first voyage, Claxton had arranged an opportunity for messenger Jardine to go ashore to see his sisters. "I thought it was jolly decent of him to have thought about it at all," wrote Alex. "You see, I am getting used to not having any notice taken of me, and so when a little bit of thoughtfulness like that comes along, it is certainly appreciated." The school of hard knocks was teaching its pupil well. Actually Claxton had given Alex permission to spend two nights off the ship on that occasion though Alex did not realise this. After supper and a long chat with his family he caught the overnight coast steamer to Vancouver and reported on board the *Canada* in the morning to find that Claxton had not expected him back until the next day! "Oh Gawd, but wasn't I peeved!"

On the 27th of February 1930, during his first trip, the *Canada* called at Yokohama, the port of Tokyo, where his mother had been born and had spent her childhood. It was also where her brother, Alex's uncle, still lived and tried hard to make a living – unfortunately with declining success. Uncle Bill, meeting Alex for the first time, took him to lunch. He wrote to Agnes: "He struck me as being a very nice boy indeed and I feel, my dear, that you are to be very highly congratulated on the results of the care and love you have expended on him under circumstances which have always been so unhappy." What a snapshot of Alex's family life to that point! His mother's circumstances, though clearly often difficult, have never so far seemed unhappy through Alex's eyes. He wanted so badly to admire his father that he was unable to see him as his uncle could. Bill, as his mother's only living brother with whom she corresponded frequently, was in a position to know. Apart from her sister Marjory, who else offered Agnes a shoulder to cry on? At any rate, it helps us to understand the great consideration with which her son had treated her from the age of nine.

It was at about this time that Alex received a letter from his third sister, June. She had decided, like the first officer, that her big brother ought to be at school; so she wrote to suggest that he change his mind and return to school in the fall. He gave two reasons why he was unwilling to consider the idea: first, he told her, he was not "of a scholarly mind"; and secondly he would not be able to behave like "a good little boy" and would get "flung out." He went on: "I've learned more of life and people and places at this game ... so the answer is a doubtful <u>NO</u>." Then, as if to demonstrate the truth of that statement, he went on: "Sometimes life will not be very enjoyable. That's natural and to be expected. There are very few people in the world absolutely satisfied with their lot; the better they're off, the better they want to be. And really that's what one ought to be like. Otherwise if, say, the majority of the people were satisfied to carry on as they were, the commerce of the world would stop. There would be nothing done to make things better."

Alex was proud to be aboard the fastest liner on the Pacific and it was a real cause for sorrow when the *Canada* lost that title to Canadian Pacific's new *Empress of Japan*. Even the *Canada*'s fastest-ever crossing, in May 1931 at 21.47 knots, was no match for the *Japan*'s April record of 22.27 knots. On the *Canada*, and later on the *Gracia*, he was frustrated by the unchallenging nature of the work he was hired to do. Being an intelligent person with great curiosity about how things work, he treated the world as his university. Everything was worth examining, quantifying, comparing, even if that meant work. All his life he has had a horror of idleness and in his diary he criticised others for this. He was always keen to learn the skills of navigation and seamanship and his record speaks for itself. His boat was usually the best and fastest in the boat-drill competitions – probably largely thanks to him. On the 8th of May 1930, when he was just sixteen and had been at sea for only two months, he took the wheel of the *Canada* for thirty minutes when they were leaving Hong Kong. When on lookout on the bridge in the small hours he was the first to sight ships on the horizon and, if the occasion warranted, to communicate with them in Morse by Aldis lamp. He and Red studied Morse code and wired their bunks so they could communicate in Morse to practice their skills. He was jokingly rated 'nautical instrument manufacturer' after doing a good job on cleaning Mr Claxton's sextant. He learned how to use a sextant from his friend Jonesey, a cadet, then took shots on the sun and worked out the position of the ship – one foggy day in the Inland Sea, he was the only one on board who DID know where they were! He learned logarithms and trigonometry from a book and from the officers on board, and was once horrified to find that a navigational problem completely stumped the officer to whom he took it for help. And he seized every opportunity to handle small boats, being appointed coxswain of the ship's motorboat on several occasions, though this also led to his worst embarrassment.

He and another messenger were in charge of the ship's launch, taking Mr Claxton and other officers up the Pasig River close to Manila. The officers went ashore and Alex was left in charge of the launch. Nobody had thought to remind him that the river was tidal and when the officers returned the launch was firmly stuck in the mud. Their only remedy was to wait six hours for the tide to float her off. As a result the ship was delayed and Mr Claxton was in the doghouse. Looking back Alex remembers: "I think there was a small feeling that Jardine should not have let it happen." He certainly suffered a good deal of ribbing and Claxton never let him forget it. "God, but I felt cheap!" he commented to his diary at the time.

He had a lot of fun with other small boats. He took the ship's motorboat around Vancouver's much more deserted Burrard Inlet on several occasions. In Hong Kong, when the *Canada* was in dry dock for three weeks, he adopted a sailing dinghy called the *Betty*. He worked out that he could have a great sail with a "keen breeze", ending up miles away from the docks, but as Hong Kong was (and still is) the busiest port in Asia, he could always sneak a tow home by getting a line onto an incoming junk! In return for borrowing the *Betty*, Alex spliced some frayed ropes that he found on board her, a skill he had recently learned.

When not sailing small boats he was visiting any vessel that would allow him aboard. He explored the German ships *Gsar* and *Derflinger* – "the Germans were very nice to us" (which usually meant they gave them food!), the U.S. ship *President Jackson*, the Japanese *Chichibu Maru* – "the finest ship I have ever been on – absolutely wonderful" – and the *Tatsuta Maru* from which he "swiped writing paper!", the CP *Empresses of Russia, Asia* and *Australia*, unnamed French and Blue Funnel ships and the Royal Navy submarine HMS *Odin* – "one of the largest subs in the world – simply wonderful!" He also "saw a whole fleet of Japanese warships manoeuvring in the Inland Sea. Certainly was a wonderful sight. There were fifty-two, I was informed – battleships, dreadnoughts, cruisers, light cruisers, an aeroplane carrier, destroyers, submarines and aeroplanes, with a hospital ship to boot." Had he known it, this was a preview of future events but at the time he was all enthusiasm.

On duty he was alert, efficient and obedient. Off duty Alex reverted to the normal pastimes and behaviour of a teenager in a rough-and-tumble world. Maybe it was because of his early boxing training but for whatever reason he was always 'scrapping'. Hardly a week went by without the laconic diary entry: "One h – l of a scrap with Doman" or with Red. They were pretty brutal affairs, apparently, but there were no hard feelings and they seem to have fought as a release from the tensions of living at close quarters. On one occasion he "thought that murder was going to be the mildest outcome of it" but nobody was seriously hurt. He had a fight with Robin in North Vancouver which "tore a large hole in my grey trousers." He and Red had boxing gloves and boxed with each other, sometimes drawing blood, but it was considered good clean fun. One week he missed his diary entries and so summarised, finishing up with: "Did I have a fight with Doman? Most probably, but I cannot remember!"

In his second year on the *Canada* Red and Doman left the ship, to be replaced by "two new messengers, very meek and mild persons," named Bradley and Patterson. Alex exulted "I can easily clean the cabin up in a scrap, I think!" He was clearly confident of his ability to look after himself if an argument came to blows. He recorded two such occasions: once when he nearly had a fight with a stevedore in Manila; and another occasion when he rescued a Chinese boy on the crew who was being choked by a Filipino. As time went by on the *Canada*, Alex began to work off his animal spirits in less aggressive ways. He took to going to the gym before duty for gymnastics or other physical training. He took any opportunity to play deck tennis and, when he could get away with it, to run laps around the promenade deck.

In addition to his physical toughness he experimented with 'tough' attitudes; he was trying out teenage loutishness and it was soon abandoned. This normally considerate bridge messenger once compelled a Japanese street-trader, who had set up his stall on the ship for a few hours in Shimidzu, to part with one of his trade items, a lacquered tray, in exchange for Alex helping him to pack up and get ashore. "A dark thought filled my mind – why not ask him at this critical moment for a present for helping him?" Having seemed to get the trader's consent, "I picks up the tray and 'ops it, informing him that I was needed elsewhere on important business" in case he changed his mind. "Maybe that was not quite the thing a clergyman would have done, but then a sailor is a sailor. And if fate will put such a chance in his hands, what can one expect, especially when he is broke?" On another occasion, when visiting a lady in North Vancouver for whom he had brought a package from her husband in Hong Kong, he and a friend sat in her house while she tried to give them coffee, making "bad breaks" and giggling uncontrollably. Delivering another parcel he picked up a football and wanted to prove to his friend that the football would not go down the chimney of the house. He threw it and it fell right down the chimney! First he tried using fishing line to bring it up again and then tried dropping stones down to push it into the fireplace. Eventually he left the football still in the chimney. But such behaviour was not his style and his true nature soon reasserted itself.

He always had a hobby which kept him occupied. From the beginning he had owned a mouth organ and found a musical companion in Cadet Jones, who was a few years older. They would get together for concerts in the cadets' cabin. He moved on to the accordion or squeeze-box, at which he became proficient and which would be one of his social skills for many years. The 1930s were the heyday of the wind-up gramophone. The cadets bought one in Hong Kong and would spend evenings listening to music or the droll humour of the Two Black Crows – every three minutes leaping off the bunk to rewind the machine and turn the 78 rpm record. For a period of several months Alex and his friends hoarded empty bottles, popped mysterious notes inside them and sealed the necks with hot tar, which they heated in the galley – much to the annoyance of the Chinese cooks. Then they heaved them over the side. It is not recorded that they ever made contact with another human in this way. Throughout his sea service Alex took plenty of photographs. He was good at composing his pictures, many of which have a professional look – he even took a picture of blood in the alleyway after a fight! Tanaka's in Hong Kong did a good job of developing and printing, but for a while Alex and Jonesey took to developing their own, with mixed results. As his snaps suggest, Alex was quite artistic. He enjoyed drawing, usually ships and landscapes with ships, but after his first meeting with Muriel Fardel he found that he just wanted to draw women's faces from magazines. He was also adept at whittling wood, that old seaman's standby, and spent a considerable part of one voyage carving a Turk's head, even taking his carving with him onto the bridge.

Cards were popular with his friends but Alex never really took to them. He liked to learn a new game, like German rummy which he thought was fun, but big-time gambler he was not. He usually lost when they played for money although he was to have one stunning success later on the *Gracia*. In spite of the fact that he once told his diary: "I am getting much better at cards" the measure of his interest was established when he followed that with: "Had a thrilling game of Snap!" And bridge? Well, that was the trouble with Uncle Bill who liked to play!

Increasingly, books became his way of passing the time. He managed to read a phenomenal number, only some of whose titles he included in his notebook. Whilst on the *Canada* he records thirty-two that he read, apart from the mathematics texts which occupied a good many hours. He seems never to have had a focus on a particular author. Probably this was because he acquired his reading as he could. For example, once he saw a pile of books in the mail room and absconded with them, with the chief officer's permission. He liked stories of adventure, war, action and mystery and was not much interested in the classics that he might have had thrust upon him had he been at school. He read biographies of sailors and explorers – Amundsen, Magellan, Nelson and Cook – also stories by Edgar Rice Burroughs, Sapper, Zane Grey, Conrad and W. W. Jacobs; and he included such well-respected books as T. E. Lawrence's *Revolt in the Desert*, Remarque's *All Quiet on the Western Front*, P. C. Wren's *Beau Geste* and Robert Graves's *Goodbye to All That* (which did not meet with his approval).

Alex's love life on the *Canada* was fairly low-key. Although he saw many different girls, there was only one in whom he showed signs of being interested and she was no doubt the least affected or made-up of them all. He had a horror of 'paint' which invariably put him off. His disapproval is apparent when he coldly notes: "Red had a very muchly painted female in the cabin; she was introduced as his girlfriend." He sounds reluctant to admit that she is human. He tells the tale of meeting two girls when he was ashore with another messenger. At the time, they were on their way back to the ship to go on watch, so made a date with the girls for the following night. At the appointed time, surveying the crowded square where they had agreed to meet, Alex was horrified to see the girls made up like ladies of the night. Hoping they were not observed, they slipped quietly away and stood them up.

He tells a funny but rather sad tale of a young woman he met in Honolulu. He had the phone number of a couple to call, given him by friends of his Aunt Marjory. These people were kind to him and drove him out to Waikiki Beach. On the way back Alex was aware of a whispered conversation between the lady and her daughter, whose name was 'Baby Girl'; Baby Girl was pressing her mother to invite him to dinner. This she did and he was happy to accept – never being known to refuse a meal. After dinner, tickets for the movies were produced and "Jack, the son, who is about twelve years old, takes out the car and drives Baby Girl and self to the theatre. Lord, to see the change in that girl was absolutely a scream – from nice girl to the so-called hot flapper: oh, oh! After having seated ourselves she hauled out the smokes and we finished damn near the whole package between us. I'm going to the dogs!"

Alex first met Muriel Fardel on the 27th of July 1930, on a motorboat trip from the ship to Bowen Island, which had been organised by Mr Claxton. They seem to have clicked immediately and the next day Muriel, with a friend, came aboard the *Canada* where Alex squired her around, allowing Cadet Fawcett the honour of entertaining her friend. Three days later he was able to spirit her away in the *Canada's* motorboat for a picnic on Indian Arm and later spent hours talking to her on the phone. But sailing day arrived and he had to leave. Not surprisingly, for a young fellow who has fallen for a girl for the first time, he wrote in his diary: "Did not like leaving Vancouver and home this trip at all."

He may not have realised it but his own wanderings and those of Muriel would limit them to letter-writing for the next three months – and ultimately forever. He saw her again, briefly, in October; the *Canada* was anchored in thick fog off Victoria when out of the murk loomed the *Salvage King*, bearing Agnes and Muriel who came aboard for a visit. Clearly Muriel had his mother's approval. The Fardels had a house in Victoria, a place to stay in Vancouver and a house in Yokohama. It was there that he saw her next, ten months later on the 1st of August 1931: she came aboard during a brief stop and they arranged to meet again later in the month on the return trip. Inevitably, events conspired. When the *Canada* returned, Alex received the sad news that Aunty Jim, Bill's second wife, had died, so all his time ashore was spent with his uncle. In late September he met both Muriel and her mother. He spent a day with her, including a visit to the Grand Hotel. He met her again with Uncle Bill in October and the last time that he mentions meeting her, for half an hour "at the [seamen's] club" in Yokohama, was on the 23rd of November. After that, he sailed on the *Gracia* in 1932, never again visiting Japan.

Muriel was obviously a special person for him but events and distance were at work against them. Many people would be driven to despair by such a situation, but not Alex. He had a lifesaving ability to live for the day; every day held great possibilities for enjoyment which he accepted with both hands. Brooding was just not in his nature; he accepted disappointments as bad luck and made the best of things. And his friends were always friends for life, with whom he kept in touch by constant letter-writing.

Life at sea produced its moments of high drama; it is impressive how calmly Alex reacted to them. There were storms – one memorable one with 160 kph winds and 50-foot waves: "Dave and I went out on the foc'sle where the water was coming over in tons; consequently a big wave nearly did away with us ... completely swallowed us up in a swirl of green water for about ten seconds!" On another occasion, early in his career, a communications error saw the *Canada* go full ahead instead of full astern while docking in Kobe; two cranes were smashed and the ship damaged – "lots of fun," commented Alex. The more terrifying incidents involved murder and mayhem. In the mildest of these incidents Alex noted: "About 3:30 there was a mutiny of sorts; the carpenter [European] got cut up kind of badly; the [Chinese] saloon boys started it." That's all! But there were worse

incidents, including a couple of murders. In Shanghai the ship's Chinese interpreter had been shot and killed while ashore; he recorded that he "stayed up for a
while to see what was going to happen about our interpreter getting shot." Disappointed, he had to continue: "Nothing happened ... they had detectives on board."
The other murder affected him directly but he was even less impressed. While in
dry-dock in Hong Kong, a soccer game, in which he was about to play against the
Russia, was cancelled because Mr Harrison, the *Russia's* plumber, had been murdered. The match was postponed for five days, at which time, in spite of holding a
collection for "Harrison's people" and the issue of new boots, the *Canada* lost 3-1.

The bloodiest occasion, which must have had Agnes fearing for her son, occurred at sea after leaving Honolulu. "A Filipino steerage passenger went 'bugs',
killed two Chinese crew and wounded twenty-nine others – Chinese crew, a
Japanese passenger, two ship's petty officers, Mr Campbell and Mr Coldwell, and
also the European plumber and the steward's 'Stores'. Alex went along to the ship's
hospital and saw many people with various wounds. Feeling a bit insecure, he
hightailed it to the bridge, only to be put in charge while the mate and officers got
revolvers and went after the killer! "I didn't like being on the bridge on my own,
apart from the helmsman. What if the man headed for the bridge? He was found,
after a bit of a search, down a trunkway leading to the engineroom. 'Stores' fired a
couple of shots at him but he was behind a bulkhead door so he couldn't hit him.
The Filipino gave up after that and he certainly seemed sane enough then. I went
along to the doctor's office later on and the mess was terrible – blood all over the
place. You simply slid along the alleyway in blood. He did most of his stabbing in
the working alleyway," the alleyway outside Alex's cabin. Had Alex chosen to
step outside to investigate the noise he might have been a victim himself. "He only
used an ordinary scout knife with two blades. The crowd that came down to the
wharf when we arrived in Hong Kong was something terrible. You couldn't see
the wharf for Chinese. The police had quite a time getting him through the crowd,
but managed after much prodding, shoving and pushing." For Alex it was all in
the day's work apparently; it was certainly not worth worrying about his own
close shave!

Violent incidents may well have been connected to drug smuggling. In
Honolulu Harbor, a few days before the Filipino passenger ran amok, Alex had
seen packaged opium being hurled off the afterdeck, which was immediately picked
up by fishermen. From the upper deck he was unable to see the thrower on the
deck below – presumably in the crew quarters. When the ship's bar was broken into
and a bundle of money stolen a few months later he took part in a fruitless search
of the Chinese crew quarters. And after leaving Yokohama for the last time in
December 1931 the messengers took part in a search for opium in the lifeboats.

There was another danger of the times: Chiang Kai-shek's China was neither united nor at peace and the southeast coast, between Shanghai and Hong Kong, harboured pirates. Their technique was to put to sea in two junks and position themselves, as though fishing, on either side of the course of an approaching victim. The pirate vessels were connected by a floating grass rope and when the victim ship passed between them she snagged the rope on her bow, swinging the smaller pirate junks alongside. After a minute's work with grappling hooks pirates were swarming over the ship and it was 'game over' for passengers and crew. Lloyd's of London considered this an unreasonable risk and insisted on an armed guard. Consequently, every time the *Canada* sailed, from one of these ports to the other, she took on board a guard unit of fifteen to twenty lugubrious White Russians, all armed to the teeth. Everything of value on the ship was locked up; the Russians were fed but otherwise left strictly alone on the boat deck. Alex's friendliness nearly proved fatal: wanting to chat with the newcomers, he bounded up the companion-way to the boat deck, to be halted at the top by a rough challenge and a Russian bayonet inches from his stomach! For this he received no sympathy, just a "bawling out" from the first officer.

There were other, more natural dramas to record. When the ship was leaving Japan for home on one occasion he recalls that "we passed through schools of dolphins, porpoises, whales and whatnots all day". Natural history was not his thing. On another occasion, en route to Manila from Hong Kong, they had a whale stuck across the stem of the ship. There was great excitement on board. "Had to stop engines and go astern, the captain issuing orders from the foc'sle head. I believe every living thing on board was up forward." It took the ship fifteen minutes to free herself from the unfortunate whale, presumably dead and almost cut in half – a victim of one of life's less equal games of chicken!

Alex was also able to widen his acquaintance with the human race. As a BC boy he had little experience of non-whites, with the exception of Chinese, Japanese and native Indians. His experience of blacks came from *Little Black Sambo* and of East Indians from reading Henty. He was therefore fascinated and maybe horrified to find himself among both these races. In December 1930 his sociable nature delivered to him a short course in race relations, as recorded in his diary, which changed his thinking. One day he talked on the afterdeck to "a Nigger, a Hindu, a Swede and a Canadian" – all passengers. A few days later he "watched a Nigger and a Filipino play Spanish checkers; got a great kick from watching the expression on the Nigger's face." Obviously, to him 'niggers' were still comic, alien beings. Later, he was impressed when "a Nigger did, or rather gave us, a little bit of tap dancing. Mighty good too!" Finally he "talked with a Nigger and a Hindu for an hour." The word 'nigger' is still there because everybody used it; it was the usual word used by whites. But in the course of an hour's conversation he had broken through the stereotypes and had moved towards an acceptance of equality. In this he was ahead of his generation.

Teenage boys are always hungry and there were few moments when Alex and his friends were not thinking about food. Consequently he soon had a mental map of the ice-cream parlours of the Pacific Basin. Manila was really the best; there, any place served good American pie and ice-cream, but the best of the best was the Rainbow lunch counter. In Shanghai nothing would do but the Palace Hotel on the Bund; on one occasion Alex was obviously overwhelmed by its delights: "lucivious [sic] Peach Melba and also a pineapple soda." Shanghai in the 1930s – "one helluva burg!" as Alex once called it – seemed very Western, with its British police and its European hotels, shops and parks along the Bund; so much so that Alex, shopping for a bargain, once wrote that he had visited the "native quarter." In Hong Kong, the best soda fountains were on Queen's Road and worth going out of your way for.

In the teenage hunt for food, Alex found that the cooks on the ship were bribable – "three pieces of chocolate cream pie in exchange for three cigarettes!" Drunken third-class passengers had their uses; when they were "three sheets in the wind" – a favourite expression – they could be persuaded to buy ginger beer for penniless messengers. On every trip there was a fancy dress ball for the passengers which the messengers were allowed to watch, if not on duty. Alex developed a regular business lending his uniform to female passengers, for a price – two dollars being his best take. But the real reason to go to the ball was that "we were able to help ourselves from all the trays as they passed us!" His mother always sent him to sea with a chest full of good things which he took to calling "tuck"; Alex used to 'issue' cake at regular intervals to his drooling companions – maybe as a guarantee of their good behaviour. Perhaps it was the extras they had that made Red and him pretty choosy about the 'chow' they were served on the ship; food was to be the only subject about which they tangled with the officers.

There were two ports where Alex, and sometimes his chums, could be sure to eat like kings: these were Hong Kong and Yokohama of which the first was by far the more reliable. On his second trip Alex met Captain Thomas, a friend of his Aunt Marjory, who worked in Hong Kong though his wife lived in North Vancouver. The captain was a truly generous man who liked nothing better than to show Alex and his rascally friends a good time. After their first meeting in May 1930, Alex wrote in his diary: "Captain Thomas took Dave and me for a wonderful motor ride, way into the hills, up to the reservoir. It was the most wonderful ride I have ever had. We came back and had a scrumptious dinner." The following day Captain Thomas organised a motorboat ride to Stonecutters Island where they had a swim; and on their third and last day, after a fine dinner at his lodgings, he drove three of them to Ten Mile Beach where they swam, meanwhile consuming six bottles of ginger beer between the three of them. The next day the ship sailed, but not before Alex had been ashore to thank and say goodbye to the captain at his office. Thereafter he treated them in much the same way every time they were in port, which was twice a voyage and sometimes for long periods when the ship was in dry dock. In return Alex ran an unofficial courier service between the captain and Mrs Thomas in North Vancouver, usually being entrusted with a parcel to deliver on which he sometimes had to pay duty. Among themselves aboard ship the messengers could always raise a delighted laugh by imitating the captain's constant question: "More ginger beer, boys?"

Yokohama, home of Uncle Bill Squire, was another home from home for Alex. He usually met his uncle, who would come down to the ship and would sometimes arrange for Alex to stay with him overnight. At other times he would take the electric streetcar to the village where his uncle lived. On New Year's Eve 1930 Bill took him into Tokyo in a hired car for what Alex described as "a dinner and a half – simply gorgeous!" Alex was impressed because the restaurant "was on the street Mum was born on" which must have made the meal even better. Bill always filled Alex up, often at his club, and took him to visit his friends, the Helms or the Mosses, who also fed him. Yokohama had a surprisingly large European population although Alex also met and liked Mr Nakomoto, a great friend of his uncle's. Visiting Uncle Bill always held the possibility of a meeting with Muriel; but it also had its perils, particularly the danger of being asked to play bridge, which he did not enjoy.

Two incidents on visits to Yokohama allowed him an insight into the role of the military in Japanese society. Riding a crowded streetcar he witnessed an old woman give up her seat to a scruffy young soldier. And on another occasion, as senior messenger, he had to show Japanese naval cadets around the ship. They were arrogant and rude, so much so that he found it hard to be polite. They told him that each evening in barracks they would take turns beating each other – a training in bearing pain without flinching. Had he known it, these were omens for his own future.

By the end of his fourth voyage on the *Empress of Canada*, Alex was beginning to look for ways of improving his prospects. In his own words: "Life on board a huge liner was easy and really not much of a challenge." Given the *Conway* system of cadets used by the CP ships, the future did not seem to hold out much hope for rising to the top. How could the company allow him to bypass those fellows who had put in their time on *Conway*? On the 12th of December 1930 he penned a letter to the Blue Funnel Line – on Canadian Pacific letterhead! "I am presently employed on RMS *Empress of Canada* as a bridge messenger," he told Blue Funnel, "which position does not give me sufficient training in seamanship. Therefore I would be grateful for an early opportunity to become articled in your steamship company." He added his statistics – height: 5 ft. 8.5 in.; weight: 135 lbs.; chest: 34 in. He had grown two and a half inches during the year, maybe thanks to his fights with Red and Doman. Blue Funnel did not bite; in Yokohama on the 11th of March he received his rejection letter. Philosophically, he wrote in his diary: "my unlucky day – no letters, and one hope fallen through!"

But he had another iron in the fire. His interest turned towards the Donaldson Line of Glasgow and on the 17th of July 1931 he was writing to Captain Clark, their agent in Vancouver, applying for an apprenticeship in the Donaldson Line. In addition to his previous problem with Canadian Pacific, he pointed out that he had no chance of advancement. He had called on Captain Clark at his office, but had been told he was away until the 24th, so would call again in early September after his next voyage. He was beginning to discover the difficulties of a rolling stone which would like to gather a little moss. It was to be the story of his life until he finally came ashore. The outcome of his September visit to the captain, as it turned out, was very satisfactory. After negotiations and the presentation of his references, Alex arranged to complete the current year with CP and to sail with the Donaldson Line as an apprentice when their ship, the SS *Gracia*, called at Vancouver in January 1932. He would sign his apprenticeship papers when the *Gracia* reached her Glasgow headquarters in March.

How did he manage to get himself hired on a British ship at a time when the British unemployment rate was into double figures? Alex would say it was Lucky Alex. Captain Clark, almost certainly, was impressed by this confident seventeen-year-old who already had a fine service record with CP, who presented himself so well and who exuded seamanship and enthusiasm. His hiring was certainly not on account of the very complimentary reference letter which he had received from Captain Hailey of the *Canada*, because this was not written until December, by which time Alex already had his new job. He wrote in his diary for the 28th of October: "One more trip, then I leave the *Canada*!" In fact, in spite of Alex's seafaring virtuosity, his references and his good interview with Clark, nothing would have allowed him to 'jump ships' in the depths of the Great Depression without the good offices of a certain Mr Albert Evans Black. This gentleman had two important virtues: he was the brother of Alex's uncle and also a director of John Black and Company, shipowners and managers of Donaldson South American Line. Albert Black had received a letter from his brother Arthur, married to Agnes's sister Ruth. Arthur asked for Alex to be employed at Donaldson Brothers and Albert replied that he would ask Captain Clark to see him and report. He sounded doubtful: "Donaldson's are rather averse to taking on apprentices in Canada as from experience they frequently chuck their indentures. But if Jardine is serious about staying in the Mercantile Marine ... they will do what they can." Albert Black must have been impressed by what he heard from Captain Clark in Vancouver and have decided to do his best for this colonial relative. He was to become a key figure in Alex's future, his main support throughout his time with Donaldson Brothers and during his later efforts to come ashore and become an officer in the Royal Air Force.

Things were left hanging until the last minute. On the 20th of December the *Canada* called at Victoria. Agnes and Harold were on the dock to tell him that he had his job with Donaldson's. Full of joy and relief – he had outgrown the messenger job – Alex spent the next day on the ship in Vancouver arranging his discharge, obtaining a letter of reference from the captain, collecting his pay and then visiting Captain Clark. On the 22nd he collected his gear from the ship, said his goodbyes, made sure that he had everybody's address in his little notebook and caught the 10:30 steamer for Victoria where he was met triumphantly by the whole family at 3:00 in the afternoon. He brought presents for everybody from Japan. For the girls he had kimonos, money-boxes and little Japanese shoes – also a form of badminton called Battledore and Shuttlecock, which they played endlessly in the garden in spite of the time of year. He had six weeks ashore before he must join *Gracia*. He made the most of his mother's willingness to cook him 'lunchy breakfasts', saw plenty of his friends and on the 7th of January, in a special service in the Cathedral, was confirmed into the Anglican Church by the bishop. Alex, one feels, was only half convinced; it was probably Agnes's wish that he do this, perhaps seeing this commitment as a moral shield for him in the tougher life that lay ahead.

3

BEFORE THE MAST

1932–1935

In which Alex 'jumps ship' to the freighter *Gracia* as a midshipman apprentice
on the Glasgow to Vancouver run; in which he passes his Second Mate's exam;
and in which he comes ashore to join the Royal Air Force.

"for the wander-thirst is on me, and my soul is in Cathay"
FROM "THE SEA GYPSY" BY RICHARD HARVEY

Alex sailed from Vancouver on the *Gracia* on the 10th of January 1932. He
reached Glasgow after stops in London and Liverpool, on the 10th of March.
A week later he signed his indenture which locked him into an agreement to serve
for two and a half years as a midshipman apprentice. In this mediaeval document
he undertook faithfully to serve his master (Donaldson Brothers), to obey his
lawful commands, keep his secrets and account for his money. In addition he agreed
not to damage his master's property, embezzle his goods, be absent without his
leave, "frequent Taverns or Alehouses nor play at Unlawful Games." In return,
Donaldson's agreed to teach him the business of a seaman, feed, house and pay
him, for two and a half years' work, the princely sum of fifty-two pounds and ten
shillings. This was signed by officers and witnesses for the company, by Albert
Black on behalf of Alex's parents and by Alex. It was an exceptional hiring: a Canadian apprentice was being taken aboard a Donaldson ship. Alex remembered: "For
a long time I was considered a 'foreigner' by the other men, most of whom came
from the outer islands – until an English cadet joined the ship and he became the
'foreigner'!"

In Glasgow he received a letter from his old friend Captain Thomas of Hong
Kong. It was a letter of farewell, for they were unlikely to meet again, but he also
offered some paternal wisdom and encouragement. "Take my advice and leave the
booze alone," the Captain wrote. "I have been through the mill and know what I
am talking about and also realise how difficult it is for a young man to keep straight
when he is so far from home." Alex remembered fondly his 'more ginger beer,

boys?' "Buck up my lad, put your shoulder to the wheel and keep your eyes on the bridge with a fixed determination to arrive there as quickly as possible." Thomas was not to know it but Alex adopted this last admonition completely – it was in line with his own thinking and was to govern his life, not only at sea but throughout his career.

Gracia ran a regular general cargo route between Vancouver and Glasgow, calling at Victoria, Seattle, Tacoma, Portland, San Francisco, San Pedro (Los Angeles), then through the Panama Canal to London and Liverpool, sometimes also visiting Rotterdam and Hamburg. Although a cargo ship she occasionally carried a few passengers. Alex objected to female passengers because he felt compelled to shave more often! The ship's time in various ports was longer than for the *Canada* because cargo takes longer to load and unload than people, so Alex was able to develop a social life along the way. Thus he could see family and friends in Victoria and Vancouver, including those at BCE, and also have a large circle of people to see in both London and Glasgow. *Gracia* made three round trips a year, being in Glasgow every March, July and November and in Vancouver in January, May and September. Fortunately the bulk of the eastbound cargo was destined for the Port of London, which meant that three times a year Alex might have up to a week in that city. And the turnaround time in Glasgow lasted seventeen or eighteen days, so he was able to set up an extensive visiting list. But this pattern, though it had its delights, meant it was impossible to have a normal business or social relationship with anybody, as he had discovered in his *Canada* days when trying to meet Captain Clark.

The move from the *Canada* had been equivalent to a move from a junior school to a high school. Instead of running errands to the bridge and supervising others' work in the cargo holds, he found himself in a much tougher environment, expected to work eight-hour days doing hard, boring, physical work, outside in all weathers. And whereas on the *Canada* he could leave at the end of any voyage, the indenture which he had signed with Donaldson's bound him to continue 'before the mast' for two and a half years. His *Gracia* diary started well but soon petered out, restarting sporadically. He was, he claimed, tired of the repetitiveness of his *Canada* diary.

A more likely explanation for his lagging diary-writing was fatigue and boredom. Eight hours chipping old paint from a steel ship was hard on the ears and exhausting. Re-stowing bales of cotton that had shifted in a storm was not only exhausting, it was dangerous. That is a mild description for the perils of re-lashing lumber deck cargo in a gale. When the pumps broke down in heavy seas, bailing out the forepeak with a bucket, to put it mildly, was "no fun." 'Soogeeing' the paint on the outside walls of the cabins with a mixture of soap and caustic soda was a thankless, boring and a frequently assigned chore. His diary tells us that he spent the 8th of October 1932 "Soogeeing in the after well deck all morning. She was taking them over the starboard bulwarks 'cold green'. We got soaking several times – 'wet going in the waist', as a romantic sailing ship painter put it." Polishing brasswork in salty sea air sounds like the sort of thing reserved for souls in purgatory. For sheer hard work holystoning wooden decks took some beating: wet decks were sprinkled with sand; then a large stone attached to a wooden handle was dragged backwards and forwards across the sand for hours until the wood gleamed white. And painting, painting, painting, every time the bosun could think of nothing better – always dirty and smelly and always with the risk of kicking over the pot and having the deck to clean as well. Sometimes he got a break: painting allowed you to sit down, if you were not afraid of hanging over the side of the ship, painting the rusty spots while dangling on a stage; and splicing wire cables, which sounds like a quick way to injury, became one of his special skills, earning him both the leisure to do it and a certain respect. But after a day's work at any of these tasks, sleep would have been more attractive than writing a diary.

Every other week the chores regime gave way to going on watch – when he would either be on lookout, at the wheel or on standby. It sounds more interesting, and obviously was, but after the *Canada*, holder of the trans-Pacific speed record and able to steam from Victoria to Yokohama in eight days, the *Gracia* was a wallowing tub which averaged 240 miles a day, taking eighteen days to cross the Atlantic from Panama to London – not a great deal faster than the *Santa Maria* or the *Mayflower*. Neither being on lookout nor taking the wheel was normally a stimulating duty, although occasionally either one could become downright exciting.

Once in the Pacific, a day out from the canal, the ship was approached by a waterspout -"a queer-looking thing, with a rather evil and grabbing look about it!" Unwilling to be 'grabbed', the captain took drastic evasive action and it passed them by. At anchor at Panama Alex and friends had baited a huge wrought-iron hook and optimistically put it over the side; lo and behold, they caught a huge shark. They brought it alongside but a dozen men were not strong enough to raise it. When they began to lift it with the cargo winch, that mother of all fishing rods, the weight of the unfortunate beast straightened out the hook and it escaped – surely the fishing story of all time! Alex had noticed that Captain Cook of the *Gracia* was not as fussy about the exact course as Captain Hailey of the *Canada* had been. However, there were limits; on one occasion he came on watch to discover the helmsman asleep and *Gracia* busily steaming a course nearly 180 degrees from their intended direction. Maybe as a reward for saving him from embarrassment the captain allowed Alex to take the ship, with the pilot in charge, in and out of San Juan, Puerto Rico – a task assigned to no other apprentice. At first Alex was nervous but was enjoying himself after five minutes. Some days later he came onto the bridge to discover the second mate in a panic, their only means of determining longitude, the chronometers, having stopped because he had failed to wind them – an unheard-of sin! Alex was sworn to secrecy while that gentleman restarted them, though with approximate time. When this same officer was sick in December 1933 Alex was assigned his watch and for four hours, while the company slept, nineteen-year-old Alex was in sole charge of the ship.

On the *Canada* it had been acceptable to while away hours on the bridge with reading, writing or whittling; now that he was doing an adult's job such activities would have been a breach of his indenture as well as fireable offences. Moreover, 'Lackey' Campbell, bosun of the *Gracia* and a confrontational Scotsman, would not tolerate them for a minute. In fact, in so far as life on the *Gracia* became increasingly oppressive and dull, Lackey was part of the problem. Not only was he given to delivering constant, repetitive, long-winded and obscene verbal abuse to any seaman at any time; as bosun, he had, within limits, complete authority over the seamen and could make a man's life miserable with unpleasant work. He got both mad and even for any misdemeanour. Alex noted early in his time on *Gracia*: "I had rather a furious argument with Lackey about a most silly thing. Have never met a man so ready to argue as he is." It was just not worth crossing him, however much in the right one felt. Alex tried it later, soon after signing on as an able seaman and having completed his indentures. The ship was in Vancouver and the crew sitting down to breakfast when Lackey ordered all hands on deck to move the ship along the dock. They had already moved the ship twice and Alex suggested to Lackey that, as it was not an emergency and as lamb chops would become cold and greasy if left, they would eat quickly and then do the job. Incensed, Lackey rushed off to fetch the first officer. Ten minutes later he reappeared with that officer, by which time the crew had eaten their chops and were happy to comply. That ended the incident but not the mean-spirited consequences for Alex, which followed him, on and off, for his remaining months at sea. In his diary he observed that life on board for seamen was like being in a jail without the bars. "I do wish it were possible to make a little bit of excitement without making it bad for yourself. I feel sometimes that I must get away from all obligations and know that I need not worry what the consequences are. It must be heaven to say 'to hell with you' whenever you feel like it."

Sometimes Lackey himself provided light relief. Alex had found early on that dripping paint 'accidentally' onto the deck, whilst hoisted up the mast on a bosun's chair, was a way of driving the man into contortions of rage, but at a safe distance. They had all enjoyed the spectacle of Lackey trying to prevent gulls from pooping on his paintwork by hurling apples from the cargo at birds on the stays – and being beside himself with rage when he kept missing them. The man did lay himself open to ridicule: the *Glasgow Herald* had carried a picture of a Chinese actress trying on a Campbell tartan kilt; Lackey was loudly indignant and was ribbed about it for days. One evening the bosun, tiring of the petty officers' mess, descended upon the seamen's quarters and for two hours proved that there was another side to him by telling the most chilling ghost stories in his gentle West Highland accent. Eighteen-year-old Alex, while he had never experienced such things, was half-convinced, half-sceptical. True tales or not, he enjoyed the evening in spite of himself. In fact Alex discovered a way to neutralise the cantankerous Lackey. This was a satirical newspaper, the *Gracia Gurgle*, launched by Alex and other apprentices in April 1934. In a disciplined environment such a venture is tricky, but Alex was sufficiently well thought of by the officers for the *Gurgle* to become part of shipboard routine. It was posted weekly on the alleyway wall and in its second week members of the crew could be heard anticipating that such and such a misadventure would "be in the *Gurgle* next week". It was not a coincidence that Lackey began calling him 'Alec' for the first time that same week! Not that he antagonised the man – rather the reverse; his long-term policy of politeness under provocation was bearing fruit, Lackey had been giving him the 'soft' jobs and now the bosun's instinct for keeping out of trouble did the rest.

What did Alex do with his off-duty time at sea? His experiences had made him grow up quickly; although he had enjoyed horsing around with Red on the *Canada*, by the time he came aboard *Gracia* he was nearly eighteen, his outlook more mature, and this is reflected in how he kept himself occupied. With no formal high school education he educated himself. In his notebook, apart from sailing times, calculations of average speed, lists of cargo, he wrote: "Get textbook on algebra, etc.; also on writing." "Get book of Canadian poets." There was a list of Canadian authors and poets: Bliss Carman, Merril Dennison *(The Unheroic North),* Norman Duncan, W. A. Fraser, J. W. Garvin, F. C. Haliburton, E. P. Johnson, Marion Keith, W. D. Lighthall, Charles Mair, Charles G. D. Roberts, Duncan Campbell Scott, Robert Service, Bertrand Sinclair, Robert Stead, J. W. Tyrrel, Robert Watson, Beckles Wilson. In other places the names of books or authors are jotted: *The Cruise of the Cachalot –* Frank S. Bullen*; The Broad Highway; Burning Daylight –* Jack London*; Beau Geste; Twenty Years After; Sir John Dering; The Little Minister.* He had pages of 'useful data' including information on celestial bodies, on the dimensions of the planet, on the minutiae of the Panama Canal, distances to Shanghai and Yokohama via Siberia, via N. America, the history of Curaçao, statistics on Vancouver Island.

In the Panama Canal there was always something of interest happening. Once he noted: "usual crowd of darkies aboard to manage the ropes" – presumably to the donkey engines in the Gatun locks. One of them, an older man, was an authority on English history and Alex "could not catch him on one question, especially about present-day politics. He could tell you the last words of all the great men of history!" He found this much more interesting than the ropes! It looks as though Alex had access to the radio room on the ship and could contact a ham in Salt Lake City. And there is an intriguing page where he has set himself various commercial investigations. Most likely this was information needed for articles he was planning to write for the *Colonist*. This included: "Yellow cedar samples, one foot square; find out what wood suitable for veneer on cabinets and 3-ply; see about merchantable lumber; chances for farm equipment; ask GB [G. Beggs, Summerland] about apple organisation; what types of cars; canning of all goods; also about 3-ply wood, mills and doors; enquire about cycles and motorbikes; get a list of dutiable goods, also cost of shipment; find out best paper for Canadian affairs, Canadian shipping – Mr Ingers, BCE, Mr Collins, Forest Dept."

When he felt the urge to beat the daylights out of somebody, there being no Red or Doman on board, he would content himself with "punching a punchball like hell; came up sweating some!" But he had exams to write at the end of his apprenticeship – for his second mate's certificate and for his certificate in navigation. Consequently he usually studied in the evening or felt guilty if he did not. In his time off on Sunday he would "take a sight and a bearing of the sun" and then work out the ship's position, checking his results on the bridge later. He had both an accordion and a mouth organ with him. The accordion was his favourite and he learned the songs which the mostly West Highland crew liked to sing. Except for the Glaswegians, worldly to a fault, his fellow sailors were unsophisticated, untouched by civilisation as that term is understood outside the Highlands and Islands – the annual fair at Oban being their cultural mecca. These 'heelanders' were physically tough but sentimental and friendly; they loved to sing, usually about their other two loves, whisky and women – scarce commodities on board.

In spite of the frustrations Alex had moments when he loved the ship and the sea and being part of it, but always with a hint of longing to be finished with it. In October 1932, in the Atlantic northeast of Bermuda, he wrote in his diary: "… It's simply a gorgeous night – bright moon shining, the sea, wind and swell have all gone down wonderfully. The weather is rather like home, just a tinge of cold. Oh, how I love it. Feel as if I could stay outside and enjoy it instead of sleeping …" Again, in September of 1933, this time in the Pacific between Los Angeles and the canal he wrote: "It's a great night out, absolutely wasted?! Slight ripple on the sea with a gentle swell. Beautiful clouds near the horizon and around the moon, a slight breeze keeping things comfortably cool. It would be so wonderful to have one of one's friends for company on a night like this – and I do not mean a male

friend – far from it." There were some less spiritual perks which came his way
from time to time. When they were loading fruit they had to work all day in the
refrigerated hold, which was miserable, even in the Californian climate. However,
in those pre-container days fruit was packed in small boxes, some of which could
be relied upon to slip 'accidentally' from the sling and break open on the deck or in
the hold. Alex records separate occasions when the apprentices were able to gorge
themselves on pears, oranges and peaches, to the point of admitting that he was
feeling sick.

In affairs of the heart his will-o'-the-wisp sailing schedule was pretty devastat-
ing; no girl likes to be abandoned for four months just when things are warming
up. She might be forgiven for singing a different tune at their next meeting. Alex
was to have a taste of this in early 1933, at the end of his first year with Donaldson's.
In London the previous March, just before his eighteenth birthday, he had met for
the first time his Aunt Ruth (one of Agnes's older sisters), her husband Arthur
Black and their niece Daphne. Daphne was twenty-one, three years older than he;
he had corresponded with her since she first wrote to him in December 1930 –
presumably as an act of Squire family support for 'poor cousin Alex' instigated by
their mothers. Daphne was a stunning young woman with a riot of auburn hair
and a bubbly sense of humour. In what must have been a retrospective note on a
special page in his address-cum-notebook, he wrote: "First met Daphne on March
1st, 1932 – only for an hour or so, with Aunty Ruth and Uncle Arthur." An hour
maybe, but in springtime this was long enough to turn a young man's fancy. Clearly
he was smitten. He goes on: "Spent an afternoon together in London on June 28th
1932, Daphne and I." It had been magical. After lunching in Lyon's Popular Café
in Piccadilly, for which he paid two shillings and threepence, they walked through
Green Park to the Palace. They waited a few minutes in an expectant crowd, to be
rewarded by Queen Mary waving regally to them from a royal Daimler, while they
cheered themselves hoarse. Then, after strolling up Birdcage Walk to Hyde Park,
they sat on the grass to talk and compare palms. Wonder of wonders, Daphne's left
palm bore the same straight line across as Alex's right palm!

A week later, en route for Glasgow, Alex read a poem by Richard Harvey in the
Liverpool Echo of the 5th of July. Into the same notebook he copied it out. It seemed
to catch his situation.

> *The Sea Gypsy*
> I am fevered with the sunset, I am fretful with the bay,
> for the wander-thirst is on me and my soul is in Cathay.
> There's a schooner in the offing with her topsails shot with fire
> and my heart has gone aboard her for the islands of Desire.

I must forth again tomorrow! With the sunset I must be
hull-down on the trail of rapture in the wonder of the sea.

Alex had written his own poem beside this, picking up terms which he liked
from Mr Harvey and incidentally revealing his own talent:

My heart is in the sunset as it tints the sparkling sails
of ships, hull-down and racing to fight the lashing gales.
For I'm tired of living on the steady and sober shore,
And the roving spirit comes o'er me as of yore.
I hear the sea a-calling, with every wave that breaks.
To sail beyond the skyline the urge within me wakes.
But I'll come to rest again, and rest awhile some more
before I hear the message to leave again the shore.

The last two lines seem to indicate that he would really like a little more time 'on
the steady and sober shore'.

His note on the special page continues: "From Oct 18 to Oct 23 in London had
heavenly time. Saw Daphne nearly every day." Then after a space: "First letter
Daphne sent me on 6/12/30. D's birthday Feb 24." Before the *Gracia* reached the
Port of London on the 16th of October 1932 Alex had spent five shillings and
threepence – a huge sum on an apprentice's wages – for an extravagant twenty-
three-word cable to Daphne arranging to meet. His Scottish ancestry was no doubt
satisfied when he won four shillings of that back from 'Sparks', the radio operator,
in a card game, thus reducing the cost of his cable to one shilling and threepence.
In his diary he records four meetings with Daphne on this, his third visit to
London. She was teaching in a residential convent school and had to be back every
evening before 9:30. They met twice at the Shepherd Market house of Captain
Hunt, a family friend who seems to have encouraged them to meet there. On other
days they met at Oxford Circus or Piccadilly Circus tube stations and went to a
movie – "Harold Loyd, it was awfully funny" – or to Lyon's Popular Café for tea.
On Sunday the 23rd Alex went to the service in Saint Paul's Cathedral. Afterwards
he met Daphne at the Carrvicks' and "had tea and lots of fun. They are awfully
jolly." After dinner at Captain Hunt's he "took Daphne back to the convent,
arriving there at 9:45. For the last time we said farewell." He was deeply affected by
the parting and continued: "Daphne and I get on wonderfully together. I think it
must be our both having Squire blood in us. Certainly she is the first girl that I
have ever really liked in every way. I do love her but what kind of love I cannot tell:
time alone will settle that." His entry for the 24th of October reads: "Leaving

London today. What would I not give to be staying! ... have not felt awfully cheerful all day." There is another poem in the notebook; it looks to be Alex's own and
is more specific to his 1932 situation:

> Farewell to thee,
> farewell to thee,
> thou charming one who dwells among the bowers.
> One fond embrace before I now depart, until we meet again!

It is evident that there was a romance and that Alex, anyway, was starry-eyed!
But the sea had snatched him away.

When they met again in March 1933 things had changed. While Alex's heart
had grown fonder during his absence, Daphne had had time to reflect about the
'fond embrace' and had decided she wanted just a brother-sister relationship. They
met at Swan and Edgar's and Daphne wanted to go to Brighton by train to visit her
sister Ruth, a Roman Catholic nun in a convent. This was expensive and Alex had
left his money, such as it was, on board ship. To his diary he confided humiliation
over that but seems to have concealed it and cheerfully described the day in Brighton
in a letter. They seemed to be having as much fun as ever and Alex had no inkling
of a change. He met Ruth for the first time and concluded: "She is a proper sport,
no more a nun than I am." The three of them spent the afternoon telling risqué
jokes – " they were both afraid that I should be very shocked!" Then, having said
goodbye to Ruth, they went to the Royal Albion Hotel, where Nancy Preston, the
manager's daughter, was a pal of Daphne's. Harry Preston, her father, was famous
for his somewhat mindless skill in dancing the length of a table set for dinner
without touching a single item. Alex wrote that he "seems to be very well known by
all the famous people. As a matter of fact Prince George was down there – saw him
several times and had a good look at him." Another royal presence had to be a good
omen! Daphne, Alex and Nancy went on the pier, where there were huge crowds,
and shrieks of delight over peepshows like 'What the Butler Saw'. Then they
returned to the Royal Albion for a "scrumptious dinner" before catching their train.

It was probably during a brief meeting next day that Daphne broke her decision
to Alex – and only then because he was showing no sign of reaching a similar
decision. He was blindsided and heartbroken. Neither his original feelings nor his
heartbreak appeared in his letters home and for a month he could not write in his
diary. Only in April did he make a retrospective entry blaming himself for his
earlier emotions: "That's how I felt then; since, I have learned differently – a cousin
and three years older than I! Besides, what on earth made me think of such a thing
when I must have known her feelings were entirely different to what I thought
mine were."

The situation must have been torture for him but he refused to be its hostage. Daphne was not the only iron in the fire; on the same page and written at the same time he notes: "Muriel's birthday is Feb 23rd. Met Muriel on August 3rd 1930." Muriel Fardel, though he would not admit it, was already part of his past. She lived in Tokyo and Alex was not to see her again until she passed through Singapore with her Royal Navy husband in 1941. But in March 1933 just thinking about her made him feel better. And although Alex, during that time and later, could never find a girl to match Daphne, he did not allow his feelings for her or for Muriel to interfere with having fun. In the month of his emotional turmoil over Daphne, the *Gracia* was stormbound in Liverpool. Alex and shipmate John Tierney went to a pub and then to a 'flick'. Outside the Met cinema they picked up two girls and asked them to the show. Whether the result of good beer or a bad film, Alex made so much noise in the cinema that they were nearly thrown out. "We had quite a time," he confessed to his diary. They took the girls home and returned to the ship. The next day the storm still raged; nothing daunted, the pair took the girls out again – hopefully to a better film. It was an enjoyable two days and an example of Alex's ability to seize the day and not allow reverses to depress him.

Daphne must have played her cards well and he must have shown the emotional resilience which would keep him cheerful in any situation. In spite of his heartbreak, they continued to be constant companions whenever Alex was in London during the thirties – indeed they were to remain lifetime friends and confidants. They continued to have fun, but it was understood that things would go no further. In July they met in Piccadilly for a couple of hours; in November 1933 he noted "letter from Daph saying they've a flat. Hooray! Went to see Daph. Met Aunty DeeDee for the first time." After enjoying DeeDee's cooking he and Daphne went to watch her brother Tom (or Connie) play rugby. He barely saw Daphne in February 1934 because she was spending her time at the hospital where Captain Hunt, now their lodger, was very sick; this provoked Alex into uncharacteristic teenage petulance, noting that Hunt had seemed earlier to have "every intention of dying, but hadn't, worse luck!" He was thrilled that she had had some success on the stage and in bit parts in movies but she was becoming less important to him. In July the ship had a short stopover and he had not phoned as "I could not stick seeing Aunt DeeDee or Captain Hunt, etc." However Daphne knew that *Gracia* was in, phoned him and they spent an evening together. In November 1934 Alex had only two days in London for his job search and saw no relatives at all; and on his final visit on *Gracia* in March 1935 he phoned, but her line was disconnected. He was not to see her until the fall when they could resume their relationship with fewer time constraints.

His address book contained no fewer than 111 addresses, among them many relatives, but the majority were of people, young and old, whom he had met on his travels. He had a full social life even if he did keep disappearing for four months. Stopovers in Glasgow always threw him on his own resources as he had to plan for a minimum of two weeks and usually longer. Glasgow was not an impressive city for a stranger in the 1930s; "rather a dirty place and terribly busy" was his first impression. The city was "far behind the times in living conditions. There are people living in unbelievable living conditions. The filth is almost intolerable – one cannot wear a white shirt more than one day" in an age when a man expected to change his shirt only once or twice a week. It was always raining, and fog was common in the fall and winter, so thick that it disrupted even horse-drawn transportation. In the November-December layover in Glasgow he needed lodgings as a refuge from an unheated ship but in March or July he could stay on board if not staying with friends. On his first voyage he had evidently made his mark with the crew, no doubt helped by his accordion-playing and 'foreigner' status, and had several offers of lodgings from crew-members who lived in Glasgow. On that trip he had six weeks there and stayed with the mother of his friend Willy MacFarlane in Pollockshields.

Mrs MacFarlane gave him a key and allowed him to come and go as he pleased so he was not dependent upon them socially. Alex treated her rather like his own mother, getting up first in the morning, making her breakfast, doing odd jobs and cutting the grass. Over the years he was a regular visitor, in spite of Willy no longer sailing on the *Gracia*. He also spent much of his time at the Beadsworths, friends of his parents, on his first time in Glasgow; they had two daughters, Olga and Audrey, who were "great fun and real sports". Alex enjoyed the company of the whole family and visited them often at their house in Scotstown, Glasgow. Initially Alex was also entertained once a week by Mrs Walker and Mrs McCallum, two ladies who lived in Kirkintulloch and whose address Agnes had given him.

On his second trip two new men joined the ship, John Tierney – already mentioned – and Sandy Baxter. Both were to become good friends and their houses his homes from home. A weekend with the Baxters in Kirkcaldy or at their holiday house at Abernethy, north of Perth, was the high point of a stopover in Glasgow. When she first brought Sandy aboard, Mrs Baxter had been impressed by Alex and had asked him to keep her son out of trouble and to look after him. She and her sister would spare no expense to give Sandy and Alex a good time when they were in port. They must have thought that Alex had done a good job of watching out for the lad because they would have him to stay, feed him up and drive both boys around the beauty spots of central Scotland. Later in his time on *Gracia* Mrs Baxter would even insist on Alex coming to stay every weekend of the stopover. Then

Albert Black, his mentor and signatory of his indentures, invited Alex often to his house at Rhu. Black lived comfortably and Alex could be assured of good meals either at home or at the North British Hotel, and often of a trip to the theatre. On one occasion Black begged off having Alex for the weekend because his maid was away — such were the limitations of *homo suburbis*.

On subsequent visits to Glasgow this young sailor, still the 'friendliest youngster' who had so impressed Daisy Swayne in Field, BC, was able to spread his visiting as he got to know people. Apart from those mentioned already, he saw Dave Kirkendale whenever his ship came in; he became friendly with David Lister, a friend of Sandy's who lived in Glasgow, and there were many others. Many were 'friends of friends' such as John Brown, Sandy Baxter's cousin. Alex had met him on a trip to Abernethy. Later, while docked in Liverpool, Alex spent weekends with John at his house in Wigan in industrial Lancashire — a place made notorious by George Orwell for everything but fun-filled weekends — where he played golf, rowed and swam in the canal, noting only that it was very muddy. On weekdays while in port the ship kept him busy during working hours, whether he was staying ashore or not. As time passed he found that his friends filled his evenings and weekends for him. In fact he had more invitations than he could handle.

While *Gracia* was at sea, much of his spare time was spent writing letters in addition to studying. Apart from the weekly letters to his mother he had a regular correspondence with others. The last page of his notebook, overflowing onto the second last page, has a list headed: 'People I've to try and keep in touch with'. This contained no fewer than thirty-seven names. As a rolling stone, he had found that keeping in touch was both hard work and important. To his youngest sisters Ruth and Deirdre, Alex was a slightly romantic figure about whom they loved to tell their friends. He obliged by writing funny letters, likely to give them grist for their mill. One contained warnings about 'Devil-fish' — "very horrible things; if they catch a hold it is hard to make them let go. If you can find their 3rd rib down on the starboard side of his No. 6 tentacle, tickle it with the tail feather of a seagull which has flown over a thousand miles and he will let go. Of course, sometimes you might not manage to get the right kind of feather, so the next best thing is to spit in his eye." He signed off with a picture of seagulls and "look out below!" He knew how to play to the gallery.

His life on the *Gracia* was limited by routine but it also provided him with a roving platform from which he witnessed major events of the thirties. The ship made two trips to Hamburg, in March and November 1933. His first run up the Elbe, when Hitler had been chancellor for just five weeks, allowed him only a morning walking round Hamburg. He liked the city's wide streets and the "clean, well-built people. All the Germans we had any dealings with were jolly decent and very polite. On the whole one could not help being favourably impressed ... They are in a bad state financially – one could not help noticing that things were not as cheerful-looking as they might have been." Six months later he had several evenings ashore and was able to see the changes that Hitler had brought about. No effort was spared to convince the crew of the *Gracia*; when the Elbe pilot came aboard he distributed pamphlets in English entitled 'Germany Declares Peace', quoting a recent speech by Hitler. "It was the usual," wrote Alex, "equality of rights, shameful treatment of the German people by the rest of Europe, their humiliation after the war, etc." As Alex and his friends were leaving the dock area they asked a watchman for advice on where to go. He directed them to the Café Vaterland, as no doubt he had been told to do.

The meal that they were served there was gargantuan even by Alex's standards. They ordered roast beef and when it came it was on a tray, not a plate. "There was beef, yes, but also ham, bologna sausage, hard-boiled eggs, lettuce, tomatoes, pickles and a crab and potato salad." They washed it down with beer, followed by cake and tea. "It made you believe that life was not real and this was a different world!" – which was probably Dr Goebbels's intention in the first place. The Vaterland also had a band and a dance floor. Hunger satisfied, Alex turned his attention to the girls and watched how young Germans asked for a dance. "I did as I had seen others do – rise, walk over to a lady, click my heels and bow very slightly." The results were gratifying and he and his friends danced the evening away, heel-clicking in their un-Prussian clothes. Their fun was spoiled by the tiny dance floor and the oddly static idea of dancing which still afflicts Germans – "sardine-style dancing," Alex called it. Two Spanish girls came and sat with them, then some German men. One of these was quite bombastic, insisting they throw away their cheap cigarettes and buy good German ones. They discussed politics and before leaving this man insisted, earnestly, that "Hitler is a good man." Later another revealed he was Jewish; he lowered his voice and looked around theatrically before telling them about atrocities against Jews and that he kept his job only because he was deemed essential. Alex and his friends eventually left and prowled the "street of entertainment," probably the Rieperbahn. They were not interested in the real fleshpots, and nights clubs like the San Pauli had little to offer except more sardine-style dancing. However, they found that they could watch the show in a cabaret for the price of a beer and the risk of being subjected to the music of Beethoven, Mozart and Wagner. Next day they explored the city on foot. "Some of the streets amazed us by the number of flags displayed from windows." There was an election campaign afoot, the last that Germany would see for twelve years. "The swastika was everywhere and hundreds and hundreds of shops have huge posters with *"Hitler Ja!"* across a swastika flag in their windows." On billboards Lloyd George praised Hitler for stamping out communism. The main square of Hamburg was now the Adolf Hitler Platz. "Everywhere one goes Hitler is more or less thrown at you. Everybody's for Hitler – invariably their argument is 'already he has put two and a quarter million to work – so remember this, people may talk but Hitler, he *good* man!' " Having murdered or locked up the communists and frightened any still-legal opponents, Nazi candidates were to win 92 percent of the votes cast on the 12th of November, a few days after Alex sailed.

He was not to know this at the time, but his visit to the Reich had immediately preceded that of Rufus Lukin Johnston, European correspondent for Southam newspapers and uncle of his cousin Robin. Johnston saw the Reich as a much less benign institution than the young sailor had. His questions to Hitler, in the first interview the 'Fuhrer' had granted to a Canadian, reflected that. Though he had filed his story by phone, Johnston, together with his briefcase, was to vanish from the Hook-to-Harwich ferry on the night of the 17th of November. It is tempting to believe, as most contemporaries did, that Hitler's thugs were responsible.

Communism was little understood and few foreigners really felt sorry for the German party. There was much talk of communists in the American press in May 1934 when the *Gracia* found herself in the middle of a fight to the death between striking stevedores and strikebreaking 'scabs' in San Francisco. The scabs were working the ship, loading and unloading cargo. They were living on two ships anchored nearby and commuted to the *Gracia* by motorboat with a police escort, each scab armed with a pickaxe handle. The city traffic was snarled because all police were at the docks keeping the two sides apart. Armed police on horseback protected the ship and, when the strikers charged, a man was shot dead and several injured. There had also been trouble uptown and police, who generally favoured the strikers, as did the general population, claimed that 4,000 communists were at the bottom of the trouble. "Boy, what a time we're having," Alex wrote: "Most of them have never been on a ship before, let alone worked cargo. The first day Dalgliesh and I had to drive the winches as the men dropped a sling which cost about $350 in damages. Things are still in a bad way; several fights have taken place and quite a few men injured. The strikers won't touch us – it's the scabs they're after." From Los Angeles, a few days later, he wrote: "Left Frisco Wednesday night and jolly thankful we all were! The trouble had not abated an atom, in fact if anything it was worse. Although it was the Communists that caused most of the rioting, the stevedores really have done very little physical damage – although if they ever get their hands on the scabs their lives will not be worth very much."

It is a measure of the failure of the communists, if indeed they were involved in the stevedores' union, that the strikers' cause rang no bells on board *Gracia*; the stevedores' actions were treated by her unionised crew as a hazard to be managed, like any other. There seems to have been as little sympathy for British unemployed men who demonstrated in Hyde Park, London, in February of 1934, when *Gracia* was in port. Alex simply reported that there had been 3,000 bobbies deployed there to keep tabs on 1,500 unemployed. Next year, at a time when London was 'Jubilee-mad' about the Silver Jubilee of George V, socialist Glasgow seemed less than enthusiastic and in fact Alex expected rioting between communists and royalists on the big day. However, communists were unable to make real headway in Glasgow, with its appalling living conditions, even on such a symbolic occasion.

The Panama Canal had been built with American money and technology. It was five months younger than Alex, having been opened to traffic on the 15th of August 1914, and its strategic raison d'être was to enable the U.S.A. to transfer warships between her two coastlines. It was not possible to traverse the waterway without being aware that you were on Uncle Sam's patch, if only from the constant air activity from Canal Zone military airfields, with occasional formation flying overhead. In May 1934 the *Gracia* was forcefully reminded of the reason for the canal's existence. Approaching the Pacific entrance to the canal, *Gracia* found herself required to anchor for forty-six hours while "the Yankee fleet came through – 111 warships of all sizes had to pass through the canal and so all the merchant vessels were held up to let them go. It was rather a wonderful sight to see so many warships at one go. I was told that it was the largest gathering of warships that the United States has ever had – without a doubt a very impressive sight." He was also impressed when taken by his cousin Walter, Uncle Bill's son by his American ex-wife, to San Francisco to see the *Makon*, touted as the largest airship in the world. Both were demonstrations of the dormant power of the U.S.A. which Alex certainly absorbed, allowing grudging respect to begin to balance his automatic and extreme Yankee-bashing attitude. A year previously, for example, the *Gracia* had crossed a US Navy submarine at Panama; Alex had been critical of the crew "standing or sitting all over the place and looking very slovenly." On another occasion, when *Gracia* called at Olympia, Washington, Alex visited the legislature and the so-called Temple of Justice; his comment was that 'justice' was rather a strange word for Yankees to use!

However, Americans did the right things in his opinion when the Duke and Duchess of Kent flew into San Juan, Puerto Rico, in an Empire flying boat in February 1935. The royal aircraft was accompanied by six U.S. military aircraft flying in formation with it. When the royal aircraft alighted in the harbour, HMS *Dragon* fired a 21-gun salute and all merchant ships, mostly American, sounded their whistles – that is, all except *Gracia* who made a thick cloud of black smoke which blew towards the royals, much to the indignation of her crew. America was forgiven everything when cousin Walter took Alex out in his stepfather's new Packard

Roadster – about the most desirable vehicle on the roads in the mind of a twenty-year-old; when Walter casually let Alex drive it and showed him a few tricks, Alex was in heaven! "Boy, oh boy, I learned to drive the car; did 55 miles an hour!" he wrote. "Gosh, I loved it!"

The time that he had available to him, and the experiences which came his way, had Alex thinking about a career as a journalist. In 1934 he made a serious attempt to write articles which he hoped would interest Mr Nicolas, editor of the *Colonist* in Victoria. He wrote articles on Nazi Germany, Empire trade, shipbuilding on the Clyde, ice hockey in Scotland, the U.S. west coast stevedores' strike and U.S.-Japanese hostility. He put considerable time and effort into the shipbuilding article – the story was about the soon-to-be-launched giant Cunarder, *Queen Mary*, set against Clydeside unemployment and the silence of the riveting guns along the world's foremost shipbuilding river. His Japanese article was based on stories in the American papers: a Japanese admiral had accused Lindbergh of espionage when he and other pilots delivered aircraft to Japan; and the record-breaking voyage of the battleship *Lexington* from San Diego to Honolulu in seventy-four hours had set the rumour mongers speculating on the large Japanese population there and whether Japan had her eye on the islands.

In an effort to write an interesting piece on London Transport, he marched into LT headquarters and interviewed the publicity manager, who gave him statistics and treated him respectfully as a journalist. Emboldened, he took his article on the west coast strike to the Daily Telegraph on Fleet Street. He was again treated with courtesy by a sub-editor; his work was declined but the sub-editor – at his request – gave him writing tips and escorted him to the door when he left. Nevertheless he had no luck with Mr Nicolas who did not even acknowledge receiving his several articles. Alex wrote to him in November 1934 to ask why – " 'for it canna' dae ony hairm', as they say aboard here." Unfortunately Mr Nicolas's continued silence put paid to a promising career; and other things were intruding in Alex's life which gave him no time for scribbling.

He found himself less and less satisfied with his life at sea. Increasingly he was feeling, in the modern idiom, 'been there, done that'. His 'real' life was his life ashore between trips and this is apparent in changes in his language – he was using P. G. Wodehouse expressions like "awfully jolly" which would have sounded odd in the seamen's quarters. Diary entries became spasmodic. One of his last recorded the sad end of Donald McInnes who "fell down No. 5 hatch from the tween-decks to the lower hold, in Vancouver about January 4. The horrible bit was that he lived for 5 days and was entirely conscious. All the 'heelan' men took it rather badly – simple folk usually do." Once the indenture expired Alex made one more voyage, this time as an able seaman. The change in status cost him one hard-earned pound, to join the National Union of Seamen. Although by 1934 the call of the sea was faint while that of the 'steady and sober shore' had become well-nigh irresistible, "the pay for an Able Seaman [AB] was eight pounds a month; I had learned that it was possible to live in Glasgow for about one pound a week." After three months as an AB he had twenty-four pounds, enough to keep the wolf from the door for five or six months. Finally, on the 10th of March 1935 he left the *Gracia* with the captain's letter of reference in his pocket. Captain Cook wrote: "He has conducted himself to my entire satisfaction, being strictly sober, diligent in his duties and in every way a capable man. He now leaves the vessel to sit for his examination as second mate, for which I wish him every success."

In the fall of 1934 Agnes had been working on Alex to come back to Vancouver or Victoria to sit this exam. Why must he do it in faraway Glasgow? Alex was adamant: the Glasgow ticket was considered the best available and, once successful, his chances for a job in Britain were "infinitely better than in Canada." In November 1934 Alex wrote that Albert Black had more or less guaranteed him a Donaldson job; "Influence is absolutely necessary these days and I certainly have it as far as Donaldson's is concerned." Agnes worried he might find himself unemployed in Britain but Alex was certain that if the worst came to the worst, he could get an AB's job any time. He had no Canadian connections; but in Britain, in addition to Albert Black, W. A. McAdam, BC agent general at BC House in London, was keeping an eye out for jobs for him. He ended decisively: "I know how you feel but just now is a critical time and I must find my feet and get settled into something first."

With his saved-up AB wages to finance him Alex became a landlubber. "The big adventure is on!" he wrote. His friend Dick West, at the Canadian government offices in Glasgow, helped him find affordable lodgings. He enrolled at the Royal Technical College in Glasgow and took a room in West's own boarding house at 50 Kelvingrove Street for ten shillings a week. Everything about his new situation delighted him: the other tenants were as poor as church mice, but good souls who accepted him as one of their own; from his lodgings he could hear the university bells; and he could walk to school with his suitcase of books in half an hour, though he sometimes spent a halfpenny on a tram fare for part of the distance.

He caused a sensation when he went shopping; no male Glaswegian ever shopped for groceries. He was mistaken by a terrified butcher for the dreaded meat inspector. "No doubt you can picture me and my half-disregard for convention doing these sorts of things in the most conventional and narrow-minded town in the world!" He had to be careful with his money. The receipts which he kept, from the Charing Cross Lipton's, explain how he managed to live on a pound a week. He could buy a white loaf for twopence, a brown one for twopence ha'penny, eggs for a penny each, a half pound of cheese for fourpence ha'penny, a can of baked beans (the 1930s' equivalent of Kraft Dinner) for threepence and a healthy luxury like a grapefruit for eightpence.

He worked really hard, exulting in his bohemian lifestyle. People at school and in his lodgings thought he was doing a marvellous thing; "I get quite a kick out of their astonishment – I don't know why it should seem so fantastic to them." All went smoothly until he spent a weekend with newly married Dave Lister and his wife Tina. With them was Babs MacLean, their bridesmaid. Alex seems to have let his hair down and indulged in a wild flirtation, in the process falling for Babs. "I suppose to outsiders it would have appeared that we had known each other for years. She upset me mentally. I had managed to get myself into a groove and all I had been doing was study. She smashed it – well the whole atmosphere did to be truthful and I've had a job getting back to the same old routine. Luckily Babs stays in Fyfe, at the other end of Scotland; by the time you receive this I shall have got over it, I hope." And of course, he did get over it. In the particular circumstances, a month away from exams and nearing the end of his money, many people might have tried to do the same thing; however, refusing to allow himself to feel emotional attachment was becoming a habit. It was not to be the last time.

His rigorous regime was soon back in place. Studying with fellow student Colin McKellar Young, their only relaxation was walking for miles in the countryside. He wrote exams for his navigation certificate and his second mate's certificate, foreign going, in late May. He passed the navigation certificate, signals and the written section of the second mate's certificate; however, amazingly, he failed the oral seamanship. But not for long. The retake was set for the 17th of June but Alex wangled an early exam by twisting the clerk's arm at the board of trade. His telegram to Agnes, dated the 5th of June, read: "Passed everything." He was set for a climb up the mercantile marine ladder. Had he stayed with Donaldson's, in the course of time he would have had his own ship.

However, it was not to be. As international trade was still much reduced by the Great Depression, seagoing jobs for second mates were hard to come by, in spite of Mr Black's guarantee. Donaldson's had a list of forty qualified men waiting for second mate's jobs and many ships were sailing with overqualified crews. Fortunately, this twenty-one-year-old, now a man of 5 ft. 11 in., had other plans and none included spending more time at sea. It was time to stop rolling and to be going back to Canada. Turning his back on the sea he took a temporary job canvassing for a newspaper, at two pounds a week plus commission, while he considered his career options.

An earlier plan had been to go back to work for the Canadian Pacific Company, but this time on land. As already mentioned, he had recruited the BC agent general in his 'find a job in Canada' campaign. In November 1934, while Alex was ashore from the *Gracia*, Mr McAdam had set up an interview for Alex with representatives of the Canadian Pacific Railway. However, in spite of his two years with the company on the *Canada*, the interview failed to produce a job offer. McAdam promised to keep his eye open for other possibilities but did not sound optimistic. Not that Lucky Alex was discouraged; within six months, from Glasgow, he was asking the agent general to help him with another plan, this time to find a job in the Royal Canadian Air Force (RCAF). The harassed official seized his escape route: the RCAF was a federal responsibility and he was passing Alex's letter to Canada House. But McAdam had not completely escaped. Alex thanked him politely for his efforts, told him that he had applied to the RCAF and that he had included him as one of his references! Squadron Leader Higgins, from Canada House, was at first encouraging but backed off when he found that Alex was only interested in entering with a commission. He informed him that the RCAF only accepted officer recruits who had passed through the Royal Military College, Kingston, or through the officer-training facilities at certain universities. It was the *Conway* all over again, another bucket of cold water!

Meanwhile things had been moving internationally. Hitler's unveiling of the *Luftwaffe* caused the British government to announce a huge expansion of the RAF in May 1935. Seventy new squadrons were to be created and 2,500 pilots trained, many of them on four-year, short-service commissions. The timing was providential but the seeds of Alex's flying career had been sown long since. He admired his cousin Tom Constantine, Daphne's brother, who was an officer in the RAF. 'Connie' was a graduate of Cranwell, the RAF's regular officer training centre. An outstanding and courageous pilot, he was well known as the leader of the RAF's Tiger Moth 'Upside Down Formation'. Alex had been inspired in June 1932 when he and Daphne went to a news theatre; to their delight, on the screen they saw Tom leading his flight and flying upside down at the air pageant at Croydon. Within a month Alex had made his own first flight; he paid his three shillings and sixpence at an air show at Craigandorran near Helensburgh and went up for fifteen minutes, the pilot reaching 80 mph. He felt no fear and loved it. Almost certainly the example of Connie, just then completing a two-year tour in Iraq with the RAF, encouraged his younger cousin to join. Then, just before Alex's exam, Aircraftsman T. E. Shaw, better known as Lawrence of Arabia, had died in a motorcycle accident. Lawrence had long been a hero to both Agnes and Alex and both had read *Revolt in the Desert*; his later incarnation as an airman and his belief in the new service was another direction post for Alex.

Mr Black must have been delighted when Alex announced that he wanted to fly, for it allowed him to escape his rash guarantee of a job at sea. No doubt Alex told him much the same thing as he had written to Agnes on the 7th of June: "My plans now are: into the air, either commercial or RAF!" The person who made up his mind for him was Hokey Sinclair whom he had met at the Royal Technical College and with whom he had studied from time to time. Hokey had been accepted by the RAF and not only encouraged Alex to do likewise but also gave him an application form. There and then, in June 1935, Alex filled it out and mailed it to the Air Ministry.

At the end of June Alex was peddling Hoovers in Glasgow, after a false start as a Jeyes' Fluid salesman. He was pleasantly surprised to receive an acknowledgement of his application from the Air Ministry. Their letter informed him that his application "will receive attention. I am, Sir, your obedient servant, M. Boddington." Although originally tickled pink to have the obedient Mr Boddington for a servant, he became daily more impatient as weeks turned into months, with nothing more from him. Alex found it no longer possible to endure when his wait had lasted for two months; "I must be doing something all the time", he complained. Dick West's sister was a friend of a sister of the late Sir Ernest Shackleton and she had often talked about the famous explorer. As a merchant seaman and man of action, Shackleton was much admired by Alex: "He must have been a wonderful man – how I envy such men as he! How I hope that one day I shall be able to say 'I have done something which few men, if any, have done!' " After changing his job yet again, this time to canvassing for the *Daily Herald*, in early September he quit, spent four guineas of his savings on a new suit and left for London. He travelled by train on the all-night bakers' special, the cheapest way to get there. Arriving early at Euston station, he went straight to the Air Ministry to force the issue. He told the white lie that he had two weeks' holiday before having to return to Glasgow and asked for an interview and medical exam to be arranged in that time. The bureaucracy grumbled but seemed willing to oblige.

In the next few days two influential men were to take a hand in his life. The first was Major R. H. Mayo, OBE, MA, AMInst.CE, FRAeS, with whom Albert Black had arranged a meeting for Alex. He was a director of the Mayo Composite Aircraft Company with offices in Pall Mall, a Fellow of the Royal Aeronautical Society and a person of substance in British aviation. He had that year invented and patented the MAIA, a float plane combination in which the smaller and fully loaded Mercury, when launched at altitude from a piggyback position on an empty Empire flying boat, could fly the Atlantic nonstop. Mayo took an instant liking to Alex, no doubt impressed by his courageous treatment of the Air Ministry; both then and later, he would be most generous with help, encouragement and advice. He pointed out that airlines did not train green young men to fly but normally hired pilots with expensive private flying experience or, more usually, air force training and experience. If Alex were to take a four-year short-service commission with the RAF, at twenty-five he could leave the service with enormous numbers of flying hours and have airlines falling over themselves to hire him. He was thinking of Imperial Airways; Alex was thinking of Trans-Canada Airlines (TCA), the forerunner of Air Canada.

It seemed a reasonable long-range plan even if intensely disappointing in the short term. There would be no imminent return to Canada; but the silver lining shone so brightly that the pain was all but eliminated. As Alex had already applied to be a pilot in the RAF, Mayo insisted that he also sign on as a student of the Royal Aeronautical Society. In addition, Mayo speeded things up with the Air Ministry by arranging an interview for him with no less a person than the RAF's director of recruiting. Alex heard again from the obedient Mr Boddington, asking him to come for an interview at 10:00 a.m. on Monday the 23rd of September. All went well; as anticipated by Mayo, the director overcame his doubts about Alex's educational qualifications when he saw his second mate's certificate and his certificate in navigation. On the 26th Alex was provisionally accepted for flying training, not anticipated to begin before January 1936. He was given a list of books to study meanwhile: the *Manual of Flying Training*, the *Manual of Rigging*, *Applied Mechanics* and *Mathematics for Engineers*, *part 1*, costing him twenty-five shillings that he could ill afford. A month later on the 25th of October Boddington wrote that his date of joining had been brought forward to the 25th of November.

The second influential person he met was F. R. Bradbrooke. In 1932, through BC House, Alex had met Eustace Bidlake, a Canadian member of a large import-export firm. Bidlake had also taken a liking to him, had invited him to stay in his house and had kept in touch. He was to be an invaluable friend at several junctures in Alex's career. On his arrival in London in September 1935, Bidlake introduced Alex to Bradbrooke, an aviation enthusiast whose capacity for love was divided between his wife Joan and aeroplanes. He was the editor and publisher of a new aviation magazine, *Aeropilot*, on which Joan was the only other full-time employee. Bradbrooke and his wife ran it on a shoestring with the part-time help of A. V. (Bert) Bellamy, a photographer whose other job was at Napier Engines. The Bradbrookes were impressed by Alex's navigational and maritime knowledge because flying boats seemed to be the way of the future in civil aviation. They hired him as circulation manager at the princely wage of one pound ten shillings a week. His duties consisted primarily of travelling round the bookstalls in the London area for two weeks each month, dealing with correspondence concerning circulation and helping the rest of the staff near press day.

His association with Bradbrooke and *Aeropilot* was to be rewarding for Alex in all sorts of ways: his wages gave him the marginal ability to support himself in

London while awaiting the Air Ministry's pleasure, and his work introduced him to aviation from the inside. In addition Bert Bellamy and his wife Doris became firm friends with whom Alex went sailing on the weekends on their 35-foot yacht. Also Bellamy helped him with the study of engines, about which he knew nothing but on which he was taking an evening course, to be better prepared for the RAF. Perhaps most important of all, because they ignited Alex's own lifelong romance with aeroplanes, 'Brad' took him up on flights in the course of their work for the magazine. On Friday the 18th of October he felt the wind in his face during a fifteen-minute flip in a De Havilland Moth. Later the same day he spent fifteen minutes in a Heston Phoenix which reached the thrilling speed of 142 mph – faster than many service aircraft he would later fly. A week later he was up again, for forty-five minutes in a twin-engined Monospar. Finally, some days before his November joining date, Bradbrooke took him down to Reading by air to look the place over and on the way back Alex took the controls for the first time. Bradbrooke told him that he "plunged about the sky, but on the whole did not do too badly!"

Living in London was more expensive than in Glasgow and Alex was unable to afford much of anything on his wages. Thanks to introductions by BC House, he teamed up with Ginger Hotham and two other BC lads to rent a three-roomed flat at ten shillings a week each. It was not much of a place: washing-up, when it was done at all, had to be in the bathtub, located in the room where they ate. Through the late summer and fall of 1935 they lived a bohemian existence. Food shopping involved haunting the meat market late in the day and offering "tuppence for that piece of meat, mister!" just as the place was closing. Usually the lateness of the hour or the staleness of the meat made it an offer the butcher could not refuse. When the weather turned cold in mid-November they decided to light a fire in the fireplace. Alex found his flatmates chopping up the drawers from the chest in the room for firewood. Once lit, the fire felt wonderfully warm – until its smoke drove them, coughing and spluttering, out of the room. They had destroyed the furniture in vain; the chimney had been bricked up long ago and four young men found themselves suddenly homeless. As things turned out it hardly mattered; Alex stayed with friends in Harrow for a few days and, on the 25th of November 1935, as a new member of the RAF, reported for instruction to the Civil Flying Training School at Reading. Luckily for him he could not know that it would be ten long years before he was to see Canada again.

Grandfather Mountjoy Squire, about 1888, aged 41.

Agnes Jardine, Alex's mother, in 1913, aged 24.

Harold Jardine (left) with Tom Plumb at Hooper's Lake, Manitoba, 1904.

Sea Cadet Chief Petty Officer Alex Jardine, 1928, aged 14.

Alex (left) with other messengers on board the *Canada*, 1931.
Clockwise from Alex: Kirkendale, Bradley, Baker, Patterson.

Alex with Uncle Bill Squire, near Tokyo, 1931.

Alex in a rickshaw, in Shanghai, 1931.

The *Empress of Canada*

Alex and Muriel Fardel in the *Canada's* motorboat, Vancouver harbour, 1931.

SS *Gracia* in a storm, painted by Agnes Jardine.

Daphne Constantine.

Alex (left), with fellow apprentices, holystoning decks on board *Gracia*, 1932-35.

Donaldson apprentices, Liverpool 1934. (l to r): Alex, (aged 20) W.S. Marshall, L.C. Hammond and Sandy Baxter.

4

INTO THE AIR

1935–1937

In which an able seaman learns to fly and becomes a flying-boat pilot.

"The Flying Tar"

— COL A. G. VINCENT, THE 'BLUE-FACED, RED-NOSED MARINE'

For the next sixteen months Alex was in Britain. First he attended the Civil Air Training School at Hawkhurst, a large country house near Reading. As he put it, "We had been tentatively selected for a four-year short-service commission; however, before being commissioned, they had to establish that we could fly an aircraft and learn basic navigation." He was learning the basics of flying from the private firm Phillips and Powis. The sudden decision to expand the RAF to face the emerging *Luftwaffe* had introduced an atmosphere of crisis; when Alex walked into his room, the walls were newly decorated and he was asked to stay in the centre of the room until the paint was dry! He had already had enough experience with 'Brad', in three types of aeroplane including a De Havilland Moth, to free him from the nervousness that other students felt about flying. However, the schoolish atmosphere of Hawkhurst filled him with apprehension – apart from his recent short time at the Royal Technical College he had not been in a classroom since he was fifteen. After three days he wrote to Agnes: "Lord knows whether I shall be able to make a go of this as there is really quite a tremendous lot to be known and some of it seems miles beyond me." A week later he was still not sure that he was suited for it.

Once training began he was back in a Tiger Moth, a relic of World War I and a standard, open cockpit, biplane trainer. The course, between November and February, must have been a little chilly even in the English climate, though no doubt the student pilots were warm enough; each was issued with fleece-lined flying boots and gloves, leather helmets, goggles and fur-collared oilskin coveralls. Initially, he had difficulty with landing but flew his first solo in a Moth on the 10th of December and loved it. His confidence increased with every flight. With six hours' solo to his credit, Christmas 1935 was on him before he knew it – he had had neither time nor opportunity for Christmas shopping for his family. He was finding it harder to keep in touch with friends, both in England and abroad, than it had been when he was at sea. Hawkhurst was miles from anywhere, as would be his other English bases. Living on his pay and lacking a car, he had to rely on other people for local transport, while buses and trains were too expensive to permit weekly jaunts to London.

He spent Christmas in London with his family's Victoria friend Colonel Vincent, whose adult children, George and Claire, both older than Alex, were good fun to be with. He did well for presents: Agnes sent him moccasins which delighted him – he had found that being a Canadian was very acceptable socially and a great icebreaker. Mary Johnston, his Uncle Roy's half-sister, sent him a sweater which he thought sweet of her, as they had not yet met; and the colonel gave him ten shillings addressed "to the Flying Tar from the blue-faced, red-nosed Marine!" In spite of the general jollity he was embarrassed and shocked when the colonel offered a toast to the king; Alex leaped to his feet with his glass, but George and his sister, followers of the British fascist Oswald Mosley, refused to drink. On Boxing Day he saw Daphne and Aunt DeeDee and was back at work on the 27th. "New Year's Eve was rather hectic; we all went out on the razzle dazzle and arrived back feeling 'sort of, sort of' at 3:00 a.m. Marvellous to relate New Year's Day I did exceptionally well – it almost encourages me to continue these debauches!" He claimed that the 1st of January 1936, when he was considered safe to fly a Tiger Moth for his first solo loops and spins, was the most exciting day in his life; "I really feel that I can do something with an aeroplane" he told Agnes. He was a good pupil and "created almost a record round here" by earning his 'A' licence on the 10th of January – in a mere six weeks. Any doubts he may have had simply vanished – he was in his element. Later in the month he went on his first cross-country flight to Hamble, near Southampton. There, the chief flying instructor, before completing his logbook, asked whether he had made a good landing. Alex modestly pleaded ignorance. The instructor asked: "Well, did you taxi the aircraft to the terminal?" Alex replied: "Of course." "Then," said the instructor, "you made a good landing." He was told that a 'medium' landing would involve damage to the aircraft and after a 'bad' landing the pilot left the scene on a stretcher. Alex thought these standards a trifle easygoing!

He and the thirteen others in his class were inspired by the high profile of aviation and the almost missionary attitude within the RAF. Aircraft and pilots were always news items in the 1930s. It was a time when the RAF was pushing the limits, partly to create headlines – to make it harder for the government to underfund it – and partly to test and demonstrate the potential of new technology. Between

1927 and 1931, in three successive victories for Britain in the Schneider Trophy race, RAF pilots pushed the air speed record from 281 mph to 340 mph. The 1931 winner, F/Lt John Boothman, became an instant celebrity, as did his colleague on the RAF High Speed Flight, F/Lt George Stainforth. He became the first pilot to fly faster than 400 mph a few weeks later. Both were flying the sensational-looking single-wing Supermarine S6 float plane, ancestor of the World War II Spitfire. With these exploits and the 1935 expansion programme, RAF morale was sky-high. In this humming organisation the future held promise of interest and excitement.

Before going on to an RAF flying training school, on the 3rd of February Alex and his intake were posted to the Uxbridge depot to learn how to march – otherwise known as square-bashing – the seemingly pointless marching up and down with which military organisations occupy and exhaust their recruits. He and his classmates were then commissioned as 'acting pilot officers on probation' – the RAF demonstrating little confidence in their civilian-trained flyers. However, the uniform was more important than the person wearing it; "We have it endlessly embedded in us that we are officers and gentlemen, representing the king!" Probation or not, they were despatched, with an allowance of fifty pounds each, to the best tailors for the finest uniforms that money could buy. Alex, a colonial from distant Vancouver Island, betook himself to Fulcher's of Saville Row. 'Taffy', a Great War officer on the depot staff, was charged with overseeing the quality of uniforms purchased by these fledgling officers. He inspected every item, his stammer making it difficult for him to explain to an indignant tailor that this item or that was not "up to ssuss, ssuss ... snuff." The uniform itself still spoke of mud and horses; only its colour was 'ad astra'! Alex found himself staring in the mirror at an apparition dressed in puttees, breeches and a stiff white collar.

At first he had been amused and puzzled by his encounter with the English upper class – very different from his maritime friends who were pretty down-to-earth. His intake at Reading were all from English private schools – 'public' schools as they are confusingly called. He thought it comical that a servant would wake him with a cup of tea and tell him that his bath was ready – things which his colleagues took for granted. That was but the tip of the iceberg; he had to learn an entire social code to survive as an officer. The need for formal evening wear was his first discovery on his Christmas break. Especially at RAF Manston, in the fall of 1936, he found the insistence on 'dressing for dinner', with other time-consuming traditions, to be ridiculous when he was hard-pressed to find studying time. Later he was to be repelled by the aloofness of many people he met.

Nevertheless, he loved parties and meeting new people and usually was able to have fun on his own terms – because people, and especially women, found this

extremely good-looking and well-travelled Canadian, with his RAF moustache*
and the casual air of a man of the world, to be quite irresistible. He even sounded
like one of them; the educated English accent absorbed in the cradle and never lost
on the playing fields of South Park Elementary, easily took on board the colourful
slang of the 1930s. But Alex scorned the aimlessness of their lives – the Bertie
Woosterish conversations about tennis and society events – and was exasperated
by their inability to let themselves go at a party. As time went by he played the
Canadian card more; this allowed him to make social faux pas – mixing himself
sherry and soda at a party or inquiring about the bedpan (a warming-pan) on the
wall – which set off gales of laughter and actually added to his appeal. Also, it
allowed him to flirt with every girl in sight and still be indulged by their mothers.

From Uxbridge, he was posted to No.11 Flying Training School at RAF Wittering
on the 17th of February. At Wittering he had a batman** and his first impression
was "all we do is go around studying flying and saluting airmen – the latter rather
gets my goat!" Both batmen and being saluted were shocks to his democratic nature.
But at Wittering square-bashing was forgotten; instead Alex learned to fly real
military aircraft, the Hawker Hart and the Hawker Audax, the latter equipped to
cooperate with the army. He flew his first solo on a Hart after just ten days. "Marvellous machine!" he wrote in his diary; compared to the Tiger Moth it was indeed
and, with streamlined fuselage and sloped-back wings, it was beautiful to look at
and fun to fly. However, in spite of such virtues, it was an obsolete biplane with a
serious flaw which made it incapable of dogfighting and therefore only useful as a
light bomber. Having a water-cooled Rolls-Royce engine, it had a radiator; this
automatically closed once the pilot started to throw the aircraft into loops and
rolls. It reopened only when the pilot returned to level flight and released the catch
holding the radiator in. In combat conditions the cooling water boiled in a matter
of minutes and the pilot was blinded by steam. One student pilot, unfamiliar with
this problem, mistook the cloud of steam for smoke, thought the engine was on
fire and bailed out – which was embarrassing, to say the least. The Hart was also
unable to reach 200 mph on the level – which was just as well because its pilot
was as exposed to the elements as he had been in the Moth. The RAF had many
squadrons of these aircraft still in service just three years before the country would
be fighting for its life against the *Luftwaffe*.

Alex at first had no use for his intake at Wittering whom he dismissed as "very
dull, simply not my type and they do not interest me." Fortunately, he had friends:
Hokey Sinclair, from Royal Technical College, was in the senior class; and he found
a kindred spirit in Michael Crossley, who wanted to work as hard as Alex did and

---

*Agnes hated it!
**usually an airman-servant, though the batmen were civilians at Wittering

who joined him studying while their colleagues were roistering at the pub. Alex was stunned by the amount of work that had to be done: in addition to mathematics, his particular bugbear, he had to pass exams in navigation, photography, bombing, the theory of flight, three different types of machine gun, engines, airframes, administration, drill, meteorology and signals. The theoretical subjects were to be mastered by the beginning of May and exams written as they went. His studying paid off and his first results were excellent. Encouraged, he and Michael decided to shoot for a Distinguished Pass for which they would need, among other things, an overall average of 80 percent. Before they all left for their summer holiday, three weeks in May, he was able to write triumphantly to his mother: "The world is a very good spot at the moment." He had received his last results and they gave him an average of 81.35 percent, second only to Crossley's 81.43 percent. It was a huge boost to his confidence. To have felt so intimidated at the beginning, to have set himself a difficult goal and to have reached it so convincingly wiped away the mental handicap caused by years of not going to school. The 'Flying Tar' had beaten the public school boys at the game of education. Halfway through his holiday he wrote: "Before, you wondered whether you were on an equal footing with some people – now I feel that I am!" It was a realistic piece of self-awareness from which he never looked back. Henceforth he relaxed, enjoyed life much more – and gradually became the life and soul of his group at Wittering.

Actually, his social life at Wittering had been improving even before he finished his exams. He had four invitations for the four-day Easter break, and any number for the three-week summer break in May, which cheered him up. He spent Easter with Michael Crossley's family at their large house outside Banbury. The family was wealthy and closely associated with the Crossley Motor firm. To Alex they seemed to live in the lap of luxury, a thing to which he would become accustomed as many officers came from well-off families.

Between them, Michael and his father had built their own aircraft from a French kit, a terrifying little monster called the Flying Flea (or *le Pou du Ciel*). It had a wingspan of six metres, was three and a half metres long, weighed 100 kg without the pilot and had a maximum speed of 100 kph. It had no ailerons, but the whole wing could be pivoted which, in inexperienced hands, would cause the aircraft to stall and crash. Attempts to fly it in France had proved so often fatal that the French government had banned it – but it was legal in Britain. Alex spent some time helping the Crossleys finish building the Flea, which he greatly enjoyed; then they were ready for a test flight. They pushed the little aircraft out of the shed and along a lane, on the way to their chosen field. However, the wind caused the wings to bang about so much that Alex climbed into the cockpit to control them with the stick while the Crossleys continued pushing. Once at the field, Alex, already in the pilot's seat, was elected test pilot. "I must admit that, at the time, I do believe I was not very keen," he remembered. They started the engine and he taxied around the perimeter to get the feel of the controls. Fortunately for everybody, a closer inspection showed the field to be shorter than the required one hundred metres and the test flight was called off. Alex thought it best to say nothing of all this in his letters home.

After Easter the senior term finished their course and left Wittering. That meant saying goodbye to Hokey Sinclair, his Glasgow chum. As the weather became more springlike in March and April, Alex and Sinclair had gone for long walks along the footpaths and lanes of the East Midlands; they liked to end up having tea in some crumbling hostelry, their favourite being the Haycock, an Elizabethan inn in Wansford, where an enormous tea cost one shilling and sixpence. Hokey became a flying-boat pilot like Alex, but flew Sunderlands for Coastal Command. He was later to make a name for himself rescuing British troops in the evacuation of Crete in 1942.

During his long leave in May Alex was able to visit most of his many friends in Britain. He spent time with the Crossleys, and then with George Vincent in London. There he saw Daphne and described her as "hale and hearty," which is probably how he wished every woman was – with none of this entanglement nonsense! One is reminded of Professor Higgins's complaint: "Why can't a woman be more like a man?" However, he confessed to having met a Montréal girl in London, probably the Miss McMaster he was to describe to sister Deirdre. "She is almost all that one could wish. George pulls my leg about it a lot. Dear knows how long the infatuation will last. It's very nice at the moment; however I'm cynical enough to realise that in all probability it won't last long! Probably until she finds a nicer man! Am afraid that at times I live very much for the moment." Having torn himself away from her, a week later he was visiting his Uncle Roy's father, a retired vicar living at Bures in Suffolk. The old man plied him with questions about his son, but Alex stoutly refused to let on that Roy, a lawyer, had fallen on hard times and that they had had to move house because of that – not wishing to become involved in Roy's family affairs. He came away very impressed by the peace that the old man had found, noting that he had never felt "so near to God". In Scotland he stayed with David Lister and his wife Tina in Kirkaldy and also with Sandy Baxter's family. He was blithely unaware, as he helped with housework, of the effect of his visit on poor Tina who, in spite of herself, was attracted to him. With Sandy he visited the Donaldson ship *Letitia* on which Sandy was sailing; he recorded, as though it surprised him, that he was the envy of quite a number of the officers on the *Letitia*, most of whom he knew. "In fact I seem to be the envy of everybody I meet," presumably, if for no other reason, for the change in his circumstances.

Then it was back to work at Wittering. In June and July he did plenty of flying and for the first time really had fun there. He pushed a Hart through the 200-mph barrier in a 5,000-foot dive and enjoyed flying above the clouds. The flying culminated in their August camp at Grimsby, on the east coast, where he and his fellows were aloft all day, each person either flying, bombing or machine-gunning, with live bombs and ammunition. Some of his less scrupulous chums "were in disfavour for shooting at livestock or dropping bombs outside the range!" Off the bombing range Alex was having a more varied social life. Many friends had cars in which they visited local pubs, or went off to rent boats on the rivers. He managed, cleverly, to return some of the hospitality he had received by escorting different families to the Royal Aeronautical Society's garden party or to the RAF display; and he managed to explore parts of the southeast that he had not seen.

The big moment of that summer was the visit of the new king, Edward VIII, on the 8th of July. A fervent monarchist from his Sea and Army Cadet days, reinforced by the pageantry of George V's funeral, Alex was beside himself with delight when the king asked to speak to Dominion pilots, of whom there were only four. Alex chatted to Edward for five minutes, being amazed that the king knew the lieutenant-governors of BC, although neither of them could name the incumbent. It was a high moment from which he took a long time to come down and it caused his stock with his classmates to soar. With them he traded on his Canadian roots; people lined up for a look at the 'funnies' (mostly American!) in the *Colonist* that Agnes sent him from Victoria; at camp he organised baseball, making up any rules he had forgotten. In the end he was genuinely sorry to say goodbye to his maligned Wittering class but was thrilled when he was posted to the General Reconnaissance (GR) course at RAF Manston. He had to leave camp early to fly himself back to Wittering. He took his leave by frightening the rest of the class out of their wits: early one morning he "did a spectacular takeoff and then dived on the tents and shook them all rather. As you can imagine I was feeling very much full of beans!" In six months of training on the course Alex had put in seventy-one hours' flying time on Harts and was now an accomplished pilot.

He had found the time and the means to go to London fairly often from Wittering and in mid-July was still talking in a current way about his Canadian girlfriend, whom he described on his sister Deirdre's insistence. If she was the girl with whom he admitted an infatuation in May she had been on the front burner for two months; he described her as a brown-haired, blue/grey-eyed twenty-year-old, neither a beauty nor plain, with a good sense of humour who used lipstick sparingly – "removes same if I do not like it, ditto with anything else (don't let your minds run riot!), likes walking, is not expensive (i.e., no gold digger), comes of a well-known Canadian family, the McMasters, also comes into money at 21! She does not use rouge as her cheeks are naturally rose-pink – hooray, one up for me, and that's about all. Oh yes, makes all her own clothes, very well too."

However this was the last time he mentioned her and her place was taken by Jocelyn Thomas, another acquaintance of George Vincent's, whom he had also met in May. He was to see his Wittering class again, many weeks later at a formal ball in the mess, for which they all returned to Wittering from their new postings. The belle of the ball, by popular consent, was a stunning young woman, fox-trotting the night away with an older student who was trying hard not to step on her toes, himself a top pilot of exotic charm – none other than Jocelyn Thomas with Alex Jardine! After berating him for his aerial stunt when leaving camp, his friends demanded to know where he had met her.

August 1936 found Alex in Kent at RAF Manston, a future key airfield in the Battle of Britain. Here he took the GR course at the School of Air Navigation. For three months he hit the books, though also flying to practice navigation and search skills; he was at first delighted to fly in an "enclosed machine with comfortable seats" and before long he piloted one, unofficially. But he was mainly attending lectures and passing exams – all the things he had told his sister June that he was unable to manage. As at Wittering, he showed himself definitely to be "of a scholarly mind" when it suited him, and in spite of the temptations offered by the pubs of Thanet, he managed not to get "flung out." He had an advantage over his expensively educated classmates in the learning of marine reconnaissance techniques – it certainly helped to have passed his second mate's and navigation exams. His notebooks contain solved problems in trigonometry, statics and dynamics, algebra and geometry; meticulous geometrical constructions and meteorological drawings; also detailed recognition notes on the ships of the British and the Japanese navies; on British fleet tactics, coding, photography, signalling to ships, maritime searching, antisubmarine patrols, the duties of flying-boat crews – and a good deal more. It is interesting that in 1936 the RAF was aware that the Japanese had six fleet carriers and that only the *Hermes* had been built as a fleet carrier for the RN. There was no mention of the types of aircraft which these ships might carry – something which would also be important to Alex later on. It was a thorough academic grounding in his new career, for it is clear that he had already chosen to become a flying-boat pilot. He passed his GR course with 75 percent, which might have been higher had he done better in mathematics.

It did not matter. In October he heard that he, Michael Crossley and one other pilot had received the coveted Distinguished Pass from Wittering; for this they had had to demonstrate not only marks over 80 percent but also a "high degree of skill as a pilot" and a high rating for possessing the "qualities of an officer." Not bad for South Park Elementary and six years before the mast. The payoff was his pick of assignments (flying boats), exemption from the future exam for promotion from Flying Officer to Flight Lieutenant and an extra pound a month in salary. Perhaps more importantly, he earned a reputation as a star performer in the RAF. He was right to remark, "so again I'm sitting atop the world!"

Flying at Manston provided him with his first maritime experience from the air. The pilots played cat and mouse with destroyers from Chatham, shadowing them and radioing their position, course and speed back to base. Later they went aboard the destroyer HMS *Veteran* for a day at sea. As an old *Gracia* hand, Alex found the seventeen-year-old destroyer's 25-knot manoeuvrability exciting and noted that her narrow beam made her hard to hit from the air. Near the end of the course they took off from Manston to intercept and shadow the Home Fleet which was making a rare venture into the North Sea; having found them, they stayed about ten miles away, aiming to observe without being seen. He was able to identify the capital ships *Nelson, Leander, Orion, Cairo* and *Neptune* and about ten destroyers – a thrilling sight as they manoeuvred at speed. He was no doubt the only one aboard to have observed the British, the American and the Japanese fleets at sea. On their way back to Manston Alex felt sorry for the tramp steamers below, pitching and rolling as they beat their way into the Thames estuary – a thing he had been doing himself just eighteen months before.

Being at Manston, two hours from London by train or car, allowed Alex to keep up with friends there, though not as often as they would like. He complained bitterly about people being disappointed that he would not come to stay more often and also being upset when he went elsewhere. He pleaded poverty and pressure of work but nobody listened. "I'm very glad that I have not a lot of money – otherwise, socially, I should be in a hell of a mess. It's bad enough now. I love meeting lots of people and making new friends, but it gets horribly complicated at times." In spite of his lack of money his immediate success in the RAF made him an excellent marriage prospect – 'Air Vice Marshal' was written all over him. Mothers and daughters of the upper class were much taken by his looks, his charm and his explosive sense of humour – and even more by his golden future.

His own plans for that future did not include marriage for quite a while. First, when he did marry he wanted to be a good provider, which he could not be for years; his own father's failure to provide had made him set his sights high. Secondly, the RAF forbade marriage for officers under twenty-six. And thirdly, he had set himself serious career goals and marriage or engagement would interfere with their achievement. He liked to quote Cecil Rhodes: "So little done, so much to do." Socially, he just wanted to have fun, to flirt with attractive women, to behave uproariously and make a lot of noise – and not to be 'stuffy'. He wanted to go on doing those things whenever opportunity presented itself and was quite happy to continue a relationship on that basis after a woman gave up on him and married another man. In fact, later on, he seemed to prefer to socialise with married women because they would not, or should not, be trying to ensnare him. He believed that his head ruled his heart and adopted the simple discipline of not thinking or daydreaming about that which he could not have. Alex never saw why his female companions could not just treat him as an amusing guy and enjoy his company for the moment, as he did theirs. It is fine if you can do it but most of us are weak.

Nevertheless, in spite of fine words he was not consistent and gave mixed signals to girls – he probably did to Miss McMaster. He mused to his mother that he would like to experience the kind of love portrayed by Hollywood but in the next breath is back with Rhodes: "It's just as well I have not encountered it, as I expect many of the things I have simply got to tackle to get anywhere here might go by the board." Maybe his relationship with Daphne had spoiled him. After his heartbreak over her when he was eighteen he had done the impossible: he still saw her as often as any woman he knew. And she had done the same; still single, and maybe because she too was a tough old Squire, she had converted him in her mind from Romeo to a person it was fun to be with. They took great pleasure in each other's company whenever they met.

One suspects that first Miss McMaster and then Jocelyn gave up on Alex. In October 1936 Jocelyn gave a dance and asked Alex. He knew most of the assembled company and took pride in having "danced with every young lady there and was accused of flirting by one or two which is more than likely!" – probably not what Jocelyn had hoped for. She may have been even less thrilled when Alex, who had a cold, came round to her house next day and allowed himself to be stripped to the waist while his chest was rubbed with Vicks ointment by any of several young women in the house. He chortled: "I had the time of my life, being fussed over by all and sundry!" Jocelyn remained a friend after Alex had moved to Calshot. She told Alex in early December that their mutual friend George, the cynical fascist, had fallen violently in love with a girl of eighteen and was going to marry her in two years. Jocelyn and Alex laughed about it, not sure whether to take it seriously. Poor Jocelyn – she probably hoped to jog Alex's elbow but it was not joggable. Ruth Elliott, one of his dancing partners at Jocelyn's party, also tried her luck with him; she took his flirtation at face value and invited him to stay the next weekend with her family at Chilham, a village twenty miles from Manston. Alex accepted, enjoying the prospect of a comfortable weekend without the cost of travelling to London. In spite of his delight in finding a girl who liked long downland walks and drinking beer with him in the Woolpack, Chilham's mediaeval pub, and in spite of the fun they had raking leaves and lighting bonfires, Ruth was to be another puzzled and maybe hurt young woman. He returned her hospitality the next week by asking her to a mess dance and she complimented him on his improved dancing. Again they had fun but when Alex went to Calshot in late November he probably never saw her again.

While at Manston he saw a little of Mary Johnston, his Uncle Roy's half-sister, who was seven years older than himself and a nurse at Ramsgate, two miles down the road. She had kindly sent him a Christmas present and he was glad to meet her, finding her most interesting and a link with his Uncle Roy back home. Mary was very keen for his cousin Robin, her nephew, to join the RAF too; Alex was noncommittal, realising that it should be Robin's decision. Besides, he himself was still considering Canadian flying options: in September he asked his mother to investigate flying for the Royal Canadian Mounted Police (RCMP); it seemed that trans-Canada airmail would not start for three years but he was keen to apply when it did. He was also hoping to jump in when a regular Canadian transatlantic air or mail service developed.

The final part of his training happened at RAF Calshot on the Solent where he was posted at the end of November. Here Alex was to learn to fly flying boats, a natural transition for an experienced seaman. Major Mayo was delighted with Alex's decision to go in for flying boats. Imperial Airways was just switching over to them for their main routes; they seemed the long-range passenger machines of the future and he considered that Alex had greatly improved his chances of flying commercially when his four years were up. Even without such encouragement, to be posted to Calshot was pretty exciting for an enthusiast like Alex. Among young pilots, flying boats were considered the top of the heap and Alex had kept his second mate's certificate (foreign going) and his navigation certificate always available to impress anybody who had influence in his posting! Also it was at Calshot that the RAF high speed flight had been based and it was from there that Boothman had won the trophy in 1931.

Almost before he had unpacked his bag Alex and other new pilots were loaded into a 25-knot powerboat for the ride to Portsmouth. There they took part in a revisitation of the Battle of Jutland with models of ships on a large floor, moved by sailors with pool cues. They were talked through the battle, stage by stage. In attendance were a number of older RN officers who had been at Jutland and who gave their view of events as they unravelled. The young pilots were fascinated and appalled: "To see the ghastly mistakes made, which resulted in our losing ships and in losing touch with the enemy, made one realise how little they [the Navy] seemed to know about modern warfare." It was a healthy insight, but for junior officers it simply made them more aware of the likelihood that such things could happen again – not a cheerful note on which to start their cooperation with the Navy.

At Calshot the trainers were Saro Clouds, twin-engined monoplane amphibians whose hulls, with sharpened bow and clinker-built appearance, really resembled boats. By comparison with the big machines – Singapore IIIs, Catalinas or Sunderlands – the Cloud was not easy to fly. It was while landing on his first solo on a Cloud that Alex came the closest he ever did to writing off an aircraft. Misjudging his height on approach, he allowed the aircraft to hit the water with a tremendous bang! Miraculously, it held together and was bounced upwards. "Grabbing the throttles and pushing them hard forward, the engines responded and the aircraft staggered back into the air. After a deep breath or two I assessed the situation and settled down to a proper approach." So loud had been the bang that the whole base heard it; people came pouring out onto the slip to watch him really destroy the thing next time. Every eye was on him as he made his second approach but he made a "perfect landing which always happens if one makes a perfect approach," much to the disappointment of the crowd which was holding its breath in anticipation. During the four months at Calshot he flew twenty hours on Clouds and thirty on the more user-friendly Supermarine Scapas, biplanes which looked less boat-like but which had an open hatch for a gunner-observer right in the nose where the observer's body was exposed to the elements from his waist up! However, their two Rolls-Royce Kestrel engines and their flying characteristics were good preparation for the Singapore IIIs he would be flying in the Far East. He recorded his first solo on a Scapa on the 6th of January and his landing was "as near perfection as it was possible to be." His first flights in a Singapore III came on the 19th and 20th of January; as an exercise they shadowed the Home Fleet on its spring cruise down the Channel to the "Meddy." Each day they were aloft for five hours and after his second flight he noted that he was "much better at it." He was intrigued by the aircraft's size and by the domestic arrangements on board, assuring his mother that yes, there was a toilet!

By far the most alarming part of Calshot had been the officers' mess, where Acting Pilot Officer Jardine and another 'colonial', Acting Pilot Officer Ainslie, felt rather out of their league. On meeting Group Captain Saul, their CO, who looked "fairly old – must be at least 45," Alex was astonished that so ancient a man be allowed in the RAF, let alone to command a flying-boat base. He was also surprised that the CO's wife was a girl a few years older than himself from Montréal. She turned out to be a useful contact, finding Canadian girls to meet him, protecting him from the unwanted attentions of a local rich girl who "had her claws into" him, and probably falling for him herself – to the extent of "feeling crazy ... laughing at the slightest thing," while Alex was spending the evening at the Sauls' house. Mrs Rice, wife of the second-in-command, dubbed the two colonials 'my black troops,' which they thought was quite a hoot. Needless to say, he and

Allan Ainslie were kindly treated by the officers on staff, who bought them drinks and invited them to parties.

As Christmas approached, self-respect demanded a return of hospitality. They talked to Mr Swain, the Jeeves-like mess steward, about holding a cocktail party in the mess, to which about twenty people were to be invited. They explained they had little money and asked him to arrange something within their means. When the day came they were horrified to see the lavish spread at the buffet, the number of open bottles and the rich food. Drink was literally flowing and their guests, including the Sauls and the Rices, had a marvellous time. It was a huge success and Alex crowed "we must be the first acting pilot officers to invite both the group captain and the wing commander and their wives to a party and get away with it. We are laughing like the devil as we most certainly have placed our two feet well in here; the houses for miles around are ours for the asking!" After an agonising wait of some weeks their mess bills arrived and the 'black troops' were astonished to see that they had been billed just one pound each for their party. Mr Swain assured them that he received a great many free samples from liquor merchants and was himself a teetotaller, so the party had paid for itself!

The black troops added to their popularity by volunteering for duty over the Christmas holiday, enabling the 'natives' to take leave. Needless to say, 'the houses for miles around' came to the rescue to prevent them from feeling left out. Thrown together by circumstances, Alex and Allan Ainslie became good friends. Another person who appeared on Alex's horizon at this time was Max Farrar, another Calshot student; he lived in the neighbourhood, was a great source of lively young women and enjoyed a rowdy party; they were later to be much better acquainted.

One social event at Calshot that left Alex dumbfounded was a beagle meet. The local beagles and their followers gathered for drinks in front of the officers' mess and, although he intended to remain a spectator, he got roped in much against his will.

"We followed those damn dogs all over the Common while they chased hares; good exercise! They are still at it as I write, but I'm afraid the idea soon palled with me and, along with a number of others, I came back. Extraordinary-looking people – in black velvet hunting caps, green coats and white breeches! They blew horns at intervals to let the stragglers know where the hounds were. Personally I don't think those hounds will ever catch anything. The number of people who seem to get a tremendous kick out of it is amazing – to watch dear old ladies and gents dashing through gorse and swamps towards the baying of the hounds struck me as rather amusing. However, I guess it is one of those 'things that are done' and it helps to make England what it is."

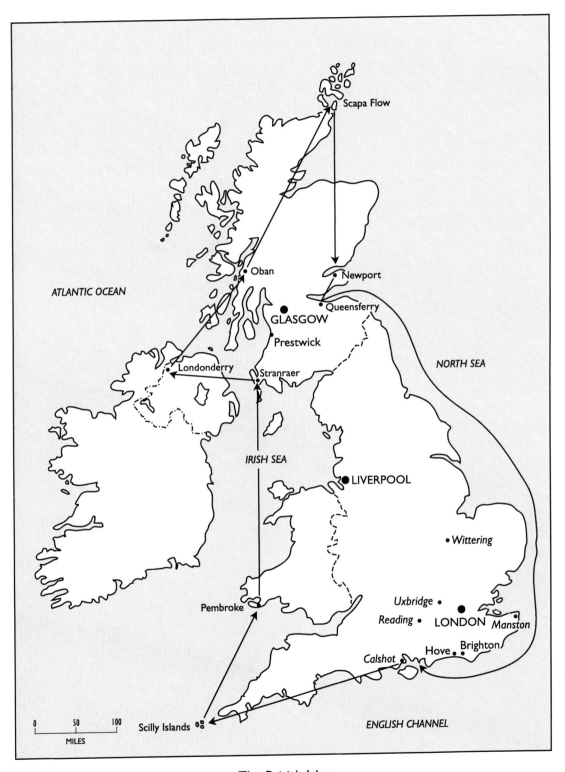

The British Isles

Exercise was a preoccupation with Alex and he was always a volunteer for any form of organised sweatiness. At Calshot he became a regular with the Rugby XV. Inexperienced compared to public school-educated officers, he was keen to improve and worked hard, usually in the front row of the scrum. He found the game provided wonderful release of tension and he turned out whenever possible, once captaining the side as the only officer and leading them to a 25 to 0 win.

His course ended with a cruise of England, Wales, Northern Ireland and Scotland. The student pilots left Calshot flying Scapas, calling at the Scilly Isles, thence up the Irish Sea in hops: to Pembroke, to Stranraer, to Londonderry, to Oban. Next they flew up the Caledonian Canal to Scapa Flow, returning by way of Newport-on-Tay to spend several weather-bound days at Queensferry on the Forth. The whole event must have seemed dreamlike: not only was Alex living on borrowed time before leaving for Singapore, of which posting he heard while at Stranraer; but he and his friends were treated like lords of the universe wherever they went. In Stranraer the owner of the King's Arms insisted on opening an ancient bottle of port so that Alex, he of the sherry and soda, could give his opinion. In Londonderry, after being wined and dined by the mayor and corporation, they had to refuse further liquor on the grounds that they had to fly. Later, they found themselves boozily cheering on pugilists at the police boxing championships from courtesy ringside seats, not an entertainment they would have chosen for themselves. The only difficult flying was provided by snowstorms on the way to Oban, though they arrived to see the town in sunlight with snow on the hills around. Later, forced to mark time on the Forth, Alex visited an RAF station where Wittering classmates gave him a noisy welcome, then visited Glasgow friends and finally made the five-hour flight back to Calshot. He had passed the course with 80 percent and, with effect from the 26th of March 1937, was posted to 205 Squadron in Singapore.

His feelings about leaving England were much more positive than his mother's. She realised that his posting to Singapore meant that he could not expect home leave for three years. Alex, on the other hand, had had his fill of England. Try though he might, he was unable to enjoy living in an atmosphere of moneyed gentility that he found suffocating. He was anxious to move on, see more of the world, advance his career, develop the skills, experience and seniority which would ensure his return to a flying career in Canada. He assumed he would be unlikely to see British friends again so undertook a lap around the country making his farewells. He had visited the Vincents in Beaconsfield before the cruise. Now he spent four days in London, staying in DeeDee and Daphne's flat. He visited Daphne's new office on Regent Street – she was making good money working for a corset company, which must have given them both a good laugh. Major Mayo, now a director of Imperial Airways, guaranteed him a flying job if he would sign on for a further two years with the RAF – he would have to sell that one to his mother. He saw Jocelyn Thomas twice, taking her to a show; and met with both Bradbrooke of *Aeropilot* and Bidlake who had introduced them. On a night out with Michael Crossley they were absorbed in a soulful and inebriated mouth-organ duet in Princes on Piccadilly when the manager interrupted them with: "Sorry, sirs, but we have no music licence"! Appropriately, on his last night in London he took Daphne to the theatre, trickling home with her at 2:00 a.m. having had a great evening.

Then he was off to Glasgow where he saw Dick West and stayed with the Listers and with Albert Black. He confessed: "Tina Lister, I'm afraid, means quite a lot to me and we were saying that it is just as well we did not meet before they were married. I know she feels very much as I do about the whole thing ... I think it's a good thing that I shall not see her for a while!" Difficulties in paradise – it seems the trusted head was having problems with the heart! Alex accepted a moving loan, at 3 percent, from Albert Black and then had to sidestep this same benefactor's request for his opinion on a bottle of wine. He took the money and ran, first to Calshot, then to Southampton, where he boarded the *Rawalpindi* a day before she sailed. He seemed to be shaking the dust of England from his feet.

5

SINGAPORE

1937–1939

In which Alex joins 205 Squadron, RAF, in Singapore and has certain
adventures during the locust years of Britain's eastern empire.

"What we do for England!"

Alex sailed for Singapore, on the P & O Royal Mail Ship *Rawalpindi*, on the
26th of March 1937. The *Pindi* was a "rather decent old tub, but getting on
in years, with no gym and a smallish outdoor swimming bath." However, he was
travelling first class and his cabin was one deck below the public rooms and on the
port side. This old *Canada* hand considered it "an excellent situation." He brought
his luggage on board on the 25th and made his mark by holding a noisy tea party
for Max Farrar and two girls who had come to see him off, upsetting some
"pompous, elderly passengers." For him it must have been sweet to frequent those
areas from which he had been excluded on the *Canada* all those years ago. As one
would expect, he quickly made friends – so much so that he was to arrive in the
Far East with a ready-made social group and his address book was to run to another
couple of pages with the names of the people he had met on board. He was
delighted to find the celebrated John Boothman, winner of the Schneider Cup race
in 1931, imperial heartthrob and now a squadron leader, at his table in the first
class dining room. They shared the table with F/Lt 'Batchy' Carr, his wife Ann and
two-year-old Paddy – plus an RAF dentist, F/Lt Guyler. All of them were bound
for Singapore, Boothman to Airforce HQ, Far East (AHQFE) and Carr, another
Calshot man, to 230 Squadron.

The band played on the first evening at sea and Alex, already acquainted with
the best-looking girl on board, got up to dance with her. The other passengers were
a bit 'sticky' and very English so Alex and 'Topsy', roaring with laughter, hauled
them onto the floor, "after which all went well." Within days a group of young

people formed a sort of good-time gang whose core included Topsy and Alex, with others dubbed Daddy Longlegs, Pam, Beetle, Jumbo and Menace – all devoted to having as much fun as possible on the voyage. For them, and for their many part-time followers, there are memories of a gorgeous month-long blur of good fellowship, horseplay and loud laughter, deck games, long drinks, languid cigarette holders and dancing under the stars, while Europe and then Africa blended into the haze over the stern.

Topsy was not her name; on the passenger list she was Charmaine Jenkinson. She was "going to Penang to marry a policeman, was tremendously in love with him and bubbling over the whole time." Alex, who could not manage 'Charmaine', christened her Topsy on the first evening, and the name stuck. He had just received a nickname himself – Boothman labelled him 'Canada' and Canada he remained for the voyage. At Gibraltar, the first port of call, Alex and his room-mate Jumbo Hills (a solicitor) went ashore with Topsy and a Mrs Stuart Lewis ("very good fun and jolly"). Ashore, Topsy, who had not been abroad before, was "frightfully enthusiastic about everything and seemed very happy indeed." No doubt Alex responded in kind. From the photographs taken on board, Topsy and Alex seem the best of companions. For Alex, whose working life had been spartan, the experience must have seemed like a reward. Maybe there was a little justice in the world after all. This was exactly the sort of relationship with a woman that he claimed to want – good, clean fun with no commitments. Between Gibraltar and Marseilles Alex penned a letter to Agnes. He wished she was with him to share the experience: "So far this has been a very welcome and lovely holiday. Topsy has just come into the writing room and asks me to send her love. I'm rather laughed at by our gang as I've taken on the job of chaperoning Topsy, Gawd knows why." Even in his own eyes the situation seemed to need justification and one hopes that Topsy was as proof against Cupid's arrows as Alex believed himself to be, though his experience with Tina Lister had cast doubt on that.

Alex in Marseilles reminds the author of his father on honeymoon in Biarritz, where his refrain at the entrance to any restaurant had been: "A bit too much garlic – let's go somewhere else!" After Alex's first encounter with French women, he declared: "They are certainly chic, but their make-up is too artificial!" By this time the dance band had exhausted its repertoire and they were sounding a little stale, poor fellows. Regardless, Alex was in heaven: "It's impossible for me to say how much I'm enjoying the whole thing." After Suez they expected fierce heat in the Red Sea; instead, a head wind kept things cool, even off Perim Island. Alex, unaware of the doings of his ancestors, spared no thought for his remarkable grandparents who had lived, worked and produced his Aunt Marjory there just fifty years before.

The expected heat broke upon them off Aden, "a more desolate, sun-dried place I have not seen – all slag heaps and chicken coops." Once into the humidity of the Indian Ocean life on board *Rawalpindi* became less comfortable, games of deck quoits less energetic, drinks longer and with more ice cubes. Alex later claimed to have drunk so much on board the *Pindi* that he was in serious danger of alcoholism before journey's end. Instead of dancing at night they congregated around the pool. But they did have a gala dance at which Alex gave true meaning to his constant urgings to partygoers to "let themselves go." Dressed as a prehistoric man, his face covered in greasepaint and with realistic cardboard fangs, he entered the ballroom shouting and howling and brandishing a huge club which, being slippery with perspiration, flew out of his hand towards the captain's table. Fortunately it was stopped by a crockery trolley "which collapsed with a really delightful crash. Everybody thought it great fun!" Except the steward, no doubt.

The *Pindi* called at Bombay, whose slums he visited in a taxi with Batchy Carr and F/Lt Lewis. In Colombo, Ceylon, Alex took a taxi 100 km to Kandy with Boothman, Beattie and Lewis, stopping to photograph elephants on the way back. Alex was grateful for the chance to see so much of the country as he could not imagine himself ever being in Ceylon again; in fact, he would come to know it well. Early in the morning four days out of Colombo they arrived in Penang, where Topsy left the ship. Mysteriously, Alex slept on until she was gone; he claimed that he had not been called – or maybe this was his way of ending their four-week idyll. Whatever the reason, he would hear later that Topsy had been 'pretty sore' about it.

The ship was soon running southeast through the Straits of Malacca where both heat and humidity began to feel familiar to an old *Gracia* hand. They brought to mind the steaming forests of Panama, black butterflies floating over the decks and the mountainous thunderheads exploding into afternoon lightning and rain. Unlike most of his fellow passengers who were travelling daily further from home, arriving in the Far East had a 'coming home' feeling for Alex. The Pacific and the tropics were familiar territory. This was reinforced by a chance remark as the ship was docking in Singapore. He was leaning on the taffrail with Anna, one of their group who was continuing to Shanghai. Alex asked whether she knew Mary Turner, with whom he had corresponded since 1931. Anna hooted with delight; Mary Turner was her best friend!

While the ship was under way the breeze disguised the appalling truth; but once docked in Singapore an ancestral spirit at his shoulder might have said: "Alex, welcome to this steam bath. Apart from the occasional escape into the upper atmosphere you are going to be living in this sticky temperature of 85 degrees, never feeling completely comfortable, day and night for the next EIGHT YEARS." Singapore is like that. Close to the equator, day and night are the same length all year. Night falls quickly and darkness brings only slight relief from daytime temperature. Sea breezes and gales during the monsoon also bring relief. But in spite of both wind and rain, a resident of Singapore very rarely has the common Canadian experience of feeling chilly. If Alex thought about this at all, he might have consoled himself with the parallel between the life that was beginning for him and that endured by both his grandfather and great-grandfather. All three would make sacrifices to guard outposts of Britain's Empire. Small consolation indeed when his fondest wish was to return to the forests and rivers of BC, themselves a world away from Britain.

The American journalist John Gunther, in his *Inside Asia* published in 1939, wrote that the naval base was at Seletar, on the north shore of the island and about twelve miles from Singapore city. Immediately to the east, below a small inlet, was the air base. There were three designs for Singapore, written variously by the Army, the Navy and the Air Force. 'Singapore Base' was the term used to embrace all three. Touted as a fortress, the keystone of Imperial defence in the East, its value, even at that time, was debatable. Gunther reported that there were two schools of thought among the British. One, largely that of the British Army, claimed Singapore to be as nearly perfect a fortress as geography and the mind of man could contrive, stronger than Gibraltar, and that no enemy could possibly attack it with success. They saw no land threat and would deny sea access by big guns. The other school of thought, while admitting that the defences were good, wanted a large RAF force of torpedo-bombers to sink attackers before they could land; it assumed that this might be to the north.[4] This view had originally been put forward in 1925 by Lord Trenchard, the first chief of the RAF, but he lost out to the Big Gun argument. The decision between the rival views was a political compromise, struck by the pig-farming Prime Minister Stanley Baldwin, that there should be some of each, which meant that there would not be enough of either![5]

Ironically, Air Vice-Marshal (AVM) Arthur Tedder, as Air Officer Commanding (AOC) Far East, was invited to fire the first shot from the first completed big gun in 1938, an honour he declined.[6] With huge naval guns set in concrete emplacements covering all the sea approaches, the best military opinion was that the island was open to attack only from the mainland to the north. To take Singapore, an enemy would have to land infantry detachments somewhere in Malaya, or possibly in Siam, and march south. Trenchard's proposal would have made such a landing impossible, but the British Army thought it impossible anyway, for no army could fight its way through all that jungle. So confident were they that they refused to construct northerly defences.[7] As a result, the RAF establishment in Singapore was never large and never equipped with the latest aircraft. The first-line fighters for Singapore's defence were not Spitfires or even Hurricanes but lowly Buffaloes, known to members of the Singapore Flying Club as 'peanut specials'. Hurricane ground crews, arriving from Britain after the Japanese had attacked, thought the Buffalo to be "short, fat ... like an overfed bulldog, loath to leave its kennel ... the noise from whose engine didn't seem to justify the results!"[8] In spite of the fact that the authoritative magazine *Aeroplane* wrote in 1938 that the air defence forces of Singapore were a laughing stock to any intelligent Asiatic,* Air Vice Marshal Brooke Popham gave his opinion that "we can get on all right with the Buffaloes here. They are quite good enough for Malaya."[9]

By serving there, especially in a flying-boat squadron, Alex was 'projecting power' no less than Captain East had been in HMS *Comus,* notwithstanding the faint overtones of comic opera apparent in this situation. However, as a hijacked Canadian, whose interest in imperial defence reached no further back than his classes at RAF Manston, and no further forward than the end of his four-year commission, he could never accept such isolation simply as his duty, as those old heroes had done. He was not immune to imperial feelings and, after listening to the band of the Gordon Highlanders, was moved to observe that such things were the glue that held the Empire together. But loyalty had its limits; he hailed an upcoming and certainly tedious official reception with: "What we do for England!" Basically he had got himself into a jam and, being Lucky Alex, he was not about to brood over it; rather he would look upon it as a stroke of fate and extract every advantage from a cloudy situation which had several silver linings.

The aircraft were the first of these. 205 Squadron flew Singapore IIIs. This delightfully obsolete aeroplane was manufactured by Short Brothers and was the ancestor of the Sunderland. To an acting pilot officer who had flown several small aircraft – even the Saro Cloud being tiny by comparison – the Singapore III was the most gigantic machine. It was a four-engined biplane flying boat, with two engines pushing and two pulling; at the time it was also the largest aircraft flown by any air force in the world. Its military value was small however; it could land any-where there was sheltered water but could stay aloft for only ten hours at a cruising speed of 105 mph (90 knots or 168 kph), giving it a range of only 1,000 miles. Its value for reconnaissance was consequently limited. Essentially, it was not a war-plane at all and had little hope of defending itself against hostile aircraft. But it was a comfortable, slow and forgiving aircraft – an ideal introduction to operational flying. And it was the greatest fun to fly. As with most other equipment procured by the RAF between the wars, it was definitely an 'economy model.' Its instrument panel was large and bare; it contained an altimeter, an airspeed indicator, four rev counters, a turn-and-bank indicator – and a compass on the floor. Its cockpit was

---

*Brad, working for *Aeroplane* after the demise of his *Aeropilot,* had visited Singapore in July 1937.

like the cab of a big truck, complete with large rear window. Alex recalls walking back into the aircraft whilst airborne; he would just look around in amazement, saying to himself: "And all this can fly! What a wonder!"

In spite of their aircraft's shortcomings the squadron trained seriously, hoping to be equipped with Sunderlands, already flown by 230 Squadron who shared their base. From the beginning Alex found himself regularly practicing air firing and bombing – both high-level bombing and dive-bombing. When dive-bombing, the big biplanes must have been a terrifying, possibly ludicrous, sight from below. They used practice bombs filled with a chemical which made smoke when in contact with water; their target was towed by an armoured sampan, of which Alex the Tar was in charge, and from which he would calmly write letters home, assuring Agnes there was no danger – belied by the vessel's battered appearance! Alex was determined to achieve the best bombing record in the squadron – a distinction he eventually achieved. There were also long marine searches and antisubmarine patrols. In August and September 1937 they used HMAS *Canberra* as their target, approaching her without being detected, then shadowing her at a range of ten miles, reporting her movements by radio. They cooperated with any submarines in the neighbourhood. After a day on board the submarine HMS *Rover* – a stifling experience when submerged in equatorial water – Alex took the Captain 'S', the senior naval officer of submarines, aloft. He was horrified to see how easily Alex could detect a submarine in those transparent seas, in time to warn the target ship by radio – and receive a laconic "well done!" in reply.

Alex found himself flying most mornings though he had his share of night flying. He made his first solo night flight in September 1938, the last hurdle between him and complete mastery of his new profession. Somewhere along the way he had mastered the art of surviving a tropical line squall. The trick was to gain height before it hit, to allow room for error; then, using the compass for direction, to set the throttle at cruising speed and concentrate on the airspeed indicator, immediately reacting to an increase or decrease – a change in airspeed meant the aircraft was diving or climbing – and ignore whatever drama was unfolding outside the window! Whatever the ups and downs of his life Alex was happy so long as he could fly – he could never have enough of it. So he was particularly upset by the grounding of the Singapores for six weeks in 1937 for mechanical reasons – those weeks were a low point for him. Again he was grounded for three and a half months from December 1938, this time because of a seriously damaged knee from playing rugby. In spite of having longed for a wooden leg as a small boy, his rigid plaster cast was itchy and hot and absolutely no consolation! Once it was off he bicycled furiously to build up his muscles, swearing off rugby for a year, lest he ground himself again.

A second silver lining was the relaxed duty schedule at the base and the sporting and fun-seeking atmosphere which reigned after hours. Before leaving England Alex had perused Air Ministry pamphlet #50, *General Notes for RAF Officers proceeding Abroad*. This distillation of imperial wisdom encouraged him to, among other things, keep his bowels open, keep his abdomen covered when sleeping under a punkah or fan, cultivate a respect for the sun and also the midday siesta, have his mosquito net put down at tea time, keep his quarters free of vermin (warning that Egypt is infested with bedbugs) and wash his hands before meals. He should also avoid drinking during the day, putting ice in his drinks and wearing shorts after sundown. Finally, if he really wanted to avoid sand flies, he should wear socks in bed with pyjama trousers tucked in and should smear his head and face with oil of citronella.

He was surprised to find that many of these items were normally observed – only 'mad dogs' (and no Englishmen) were to be found in the midday sun. Normal duty hours ran from 7:30 a.m. to 12:30 p.m. – period. Afternoons were siesta time when most people snoozed; social life picked up in the evening. This meant that there was plenty of time for sports and the enjoyment of this fortress city's amenities. The European community numbered about ten thousand, many of whom were in the Far East for a limited tour of duty, including all members of the armed forces. Social life for the Seletar mess began at the nearby Singapore Swimming Club or at the Tanglin Club – where you could cool off in the shade of palm trees, slip in and out of the pool, cast a practiced eye on the divers and watch the social scene over a long drink. Further away, the tennis club was another cool haunt; and there was the yacht club where an afternoon's sail with a reasonable breeze was a release from the stifling city, although dinghy sailors were in danger of heatstroke when the breeze failed.

Being young men they also played unsuitable sports like rugby. Already an enthusiast, Alex played regularly in spite of the temperature and hard grounds, sometimes captaining the team. Officers promoted and participated in all kinds of sport and there were plenty of opportunities for all ranks. In the course of a year Alex played field hockey, cricket (against a women's team which took cricket too seriously, he thought), soccer, tennis, squash, water polo (nearly drowning from exhaustion the first time he played), golf and badminton – and he ran the mile in a track meet which he helped to organise. He also joined the swimming club on the day he arrived and spent several weeks allowing himself to be coached by copper-coloured champions (mostly female) in the art of diving "without getting that sting-y feeling," – his euphemism for a belly flop.

His favourite sports were squash, rugby or sailing. He loved 'messing about in boats', was an enthusiast for anything that would float, would teach airmen or Boy Scouts to sail in the squadron whaler, maintained the sampan used for bombing practice and was never happier than when racing in a small 'pram' dinghy, when winning the round-the-island race in a 50-foot ketch or when defeating the navy's entries in a whaler race. His skills and enthusiasm were recognised and in demand; when a newly arrived squadron persuaded him to look after the whalers at their 'picnic', Alex commented: "I haven't seen quite such a large number of people who knew so little about boats before!"

The "gin-soaked, sin-cloaked, sun-drowned, Hell-bound, dead-to-the-core Singapore" of G. S. Richardson's *Singapore Soliloquies* also offered traditional pleasures. People went on from sporting events or clubs to cocktail parties, a sort of nightly ritual; these were followed by dinner, maybe at Raffles Hotel or the Coconut Grove, followed by dancing – with those who stayed the course often not crawling into bed before 3:00 a.m. Apart from being gradually poisoned by alcohol, anyone involved in the social round had to accept the dress code – no shorts for men after 7:00 p.m. and evening dresses for the women – in spite of the heat and humidity. They also must travel in cars, which Alex neither owned, could afford, nor knew how to drive, because travelling by bus or rickshaw was not permitted for officer-class *tuans*. For Alex that meant going in somebody else's car, keeping somebody else's hours, not being in control of his life. The bachelor lifestyle was celebrated by Richardson:

> "Jesus wept! Haven't slept.
> What a dump! What a CHUMP!
> Got tight last night,
> crashed car in Jalan Besar!
> Court tomorrow, trouble and sorrow!
> No money not so funny.
> It makes me sore, Singapore."

New officers found themselves trailing around the mansions of the rich, leaving calling cards to open doors for themselves. AVM Tedder wondered in his memoirs whether those enjoying the social activities of Singapore realised that they were seeing the last flickering lights of a way of life immortalised by Kipling.[10] Evenings had a dreadful sameness, talking chitter chatter to an endless supply of young white women whose main aim was to find a husband, as satirised by Richardson:

> "Sunday curry, no hurry;
> late tiffin, how spiffin',
> eternal sun, what fun!
> Mah Jong? Don't be long!

Sun tan, get your man;
that's him; let's swim!
I adore Singapore."

Alex remembers cruise liners, from Australia in particular, disgorging young female passengers onto the island at regular intervals. "Fishing fleet's in," was the mocking greeting between young men when there was a liner in port.

There were no Asians or blacks – unlike Dutch Batavia, Singapore had an unofficial colour bar and mixed marriages were taboo. Very attractive to women, definitely not interested in matrimony and too honest to string girls along for any other reason, Alex had had enough after living in this manner for three months. It was just not his idea of fun. Unsuccessfully at first, then increasingly successfully, he limited himself to one or two evenings of cocktails, dinner and dancing a month. He found that not taking his long pants to the swimming club meant that he could not go on. Instead he saw a large number of movies, dined at friends' houses or in the mess, played his 'squeezebox' for anybody who cared to listen or join in, wrote letters and went to bed in reasonable time, consequently being sufficiently awake to work or play sports in the afternoon. Or he describes spending a couple of hours with friends, sitting under the palms outside Raffles, listening to a regimental brass band concert. It was still a sort of Twilight of the Raj in which he was involuntarily participating but it was very enjoyable – and quite easy to live with if you could experience it in moderation.

The young women, however, were a constant presence and Alex was a very good-looking, charming and amusing young man. They seemed far more concerned with the challenge of persuading air force officers to pop the question than they were about the danger of war. When Alex was at a party he was usually the centre of the group having the most fun and the biggest laughs. Gordon Stilling told Agnes that Alex was popular with everyone: "In fact we married men didn't get a look-in with our wives when Alex was around!" But he remained unmarried, not involved in the serious dating game though he seemed at war with himself. On the one hand he had many girlfriends. He loved female company, especially if they were pretty, outdoorsy and willing to live fairly riotously. From time to time he would ask a girl to play tennis, go sailing or go to a 'flick'. They would have a lot of fun but he would cool down a relationship if either he or the girl showed signs of getting serious. He was so far from home and a foreign wife – or worse, a foreign fiancée – would make getting back to Canada all the more difficult. His confidence had been badly shaken by what he saw as his own lack of judgement in his affair with Daphne when he was eighteen. Consequently, he became cautious and did not trust his own emotions with regard to women, as he often repeated.

In letters home he called Singapore women artificial, predatory. He longed for a girl as natural as his own sisters whom, after several years' absence, he was probably imagining as more perfect than they really were. In addition he was determined to do a proper job of providing for his future wife. He said that no wife of his would have to go to work; Harold's example lay heavily upon him. He did not see a junior officer's salary as being adequate; choice of a wife would have to wait until he was out of the service and making a good salary flying for TCA.

Alex had astonishing self-control in affairs of the heart. Whereas most men are content to await Cupid's arrow, then act upon it, Alex, to corrupt a phrase, usually looked a gift arrow in the mouth. But there were chinks in his armour: during pre-war days in Singapore there were two women with whom he fell in love, two whose marriages surprised and upset him at the time and one for whom he had a yen long after she was married to someone else. The last one was, of course, Topsy – their month on the *Pindi* was such a shared paradise that it would always be a hot spot in his memory.

Muriel Fardel was one who surprised him. He had pursued her round the Pacific during his *Canada* years when they were both in their teens. At the time he cared for her very much, but they had last seen each other in Yokohama in the fall of 1931 and had lost touch. Suddenly, in March 1938 a belated Christmas card arrived, saying she was not married and wondering whether Alex was! He seemed unaffected, claimed he hardly remembered her. In the course of that year she married Commander Freddy Fellowes, RN, and the happy pair turned up in Singapore in September. When they met he certainly remembered his feelings for her: "It's a funny old world," he commented. He liked Freddy, thought they seemed happy and "enjoyed seeing her again very much." But after seeing her off he was "still getting used to the idea that she is married."

Then there was Mary Turner whom he had adopted as a pen pal at her brother's suggestion back in 1931. They had never met though they had been writing to each other for six years by the time Alex arrived in Singapore. Mary must have received glowing reports of him from her friend Anna on the *Pindi*. In May 1937 she wrote to say that she wanted to meet him, and Alex was quite keen. But, as 'junior bog-rat', he had no chance of leave immediately and was quite taken aback to hear, in August, that she was engaged. "I have expected it but always hoped I should meet her before she did decide. We have been writing now for 6 years – it does seem a bit strange!" She had definitely surprised him; Alex was quite upset. But he got over it. She married in May 1938 and still the two of them kept writing. Not until July 1940 did they meet; Mary and her American husband Len Everett were in Singapore en route to Rangoon, having fled Shanghai and then Hong Kong. She was a small person, natural and bubbly, and Alex was relieved to find that he really liked her face-to-face. He gave them a great time in Singapore, their send-off being the first Disney movie of *Pinocchio*. (Alex's favourite character was, of course, Jiminy Cricket, the puppet's conscience!)

Of the two women with whom Alex was in love, the first was Leslie Kealley, whom he met on the P & O ship *Ranpura*, travelling home to Singapore from Ceylon in the fall of 1938. Always on the lookout for congenial company, it was a reflex action for him to seek out the prettiest girl on board; within twenty-four hours he was inseparable from Leslie Kealley and her mother, Australians going home. For the few days of the trip he and Leslie had riotous fun but, without the supporting cast he had had on the *Pindi* to lend them credibility, some passengers just assumed they were inebriated! Ashore, he and Leslie climbed Penang hill by cable car, and then on foot, running into a troop of wild monkeys. In Singapore Alex squired the Kealleys around the base, lunched and dined with them at Raffles, but two days later they left for home. Alex, who saw them off, was downcast: "She was a real sport and ever so much nicer than the average female around here. I came to know them both quite well and now must get used to the idea of not seeing them again. It is amazing really; one shouldn't ever have to say goodbye to friends. Gawd knows, I should be used and hardened to it by now!" And the amazing thing about Alex is that he did get used to it, and soon. Their parting was made more bearable because their acquaintance had been brief – maybe a week.

The same could not be said of his acquaintance with Barbara Murray. The three Murray sisters – Elspeth, Barbara and Jan – burst into Alex's life in March 1939. They made him think of his sisters at home, "full of fun, real sisters and 100 percent more genuine than the average female here." At their first meeting he showed them around the base. "The results were disastrous – they dashed hither and thither, yelling and whooping and making noises like aircraft!" But for Barbara this was apparently the way to Alex's heart. She was exactly the right type for him – outdoorsy, gutsy, stunning to look at and full of fun. The fact that they clicked was obvious to both of them and to their friends. At first Alex resisted it. He took out older sister Elspeth in order to spread his favours. To escape, he went for a weekend in Seramban with planter friend Jack Lindsay.* But matchmakers took a hand. Alex was invited for the sailing trip of his dreams by RAF friends Geoffrey and Patience Francis – to sail a wishbone-rig ketch from Penang to Singapore. He accepted, of course, and arranged his leave – only to find that Barbara Murray was to make up the four-some. Alex and Barbara were to take the train to Penang to meet the boat, about

---

*There he attended a tea party in honour of a retiring planter. A Malay in charge of the gramophone and a pile of miscellaneous records unwittingly kept the old planters on the hop by casually playing "God Save the King" at frequent intervals, causing teacups to fly as they leapt to their feet at each playing!

which the Murray parents were not very keen. In fact they grilled him; he pointed out that it was not his idea and that he would be happy to find another way to go; so they sat on the fence and "did not forbid it!" It looks as though they, too, were anxious to see this knot tied.

The sailing trip was magical. The weather cooperated; they had a week of great winds and plenty of sunshine – while clouds and rain-squalls held off. There were two servants on board, rejoicing in the names of Ah Gee and Ah Wong, who looked after the cooking and the engine. All that the four of them had to do was to enjoy sailing the boat and have a good time. The Francises were the most discreet chaperones, leaving Alex and Barbara to make trips ashore in the skiff to native villages and to swim on huge lonely beaches in phosphorescent water. Alex had his squeezebox, the stars shone and they all had a most romantic time. They returned to Singapore with deep tans and smiles from ear to ear. And Alex and Barbara were as in love as you might expect.

At this point Alex's penchant for looking a gift-arrow in the mouth took over. The first night back he met Barbara for dinner; the question that Barbara found herself facing was not: "Will you marry me?" but: "What shall we do about it?" The answer they arrived at was not to see each other for a week, and then see! Singapore being what it was, that was rather difficult; they kept meeting at social events or at the swimming club. By the middle of May Alex reported that their feelings for each other were as strong as ever. They decided to go on meeting and went sailing again, only to try another cooling-off period in early June. Alex had written to Major Mayo soon after meeting Barbara in March, to enquire about a desk job with Imperial Airways. The letter was an attempt to find a possible future that would enable him to pursue her with a clear conscience and which might meet with the Murray parents' approval: a career at Imperial Airways headquarters, a house in Woking and a daily commute to Waterloo! But common sense already told him how Mayo would, and did, reply. At the same time the reasons he had for not marrying until later were hammering at his conscience – he had adopted Pinocchio's Jiminy Cricket. How could he propose to Barbara on a junior officer's pay? Incredibly, having lit the fire he was now trying to put it out without being unkind to Barbara. By mid-June he had convinced himself that he had succeeded; he reported to Agnes that their feelings towards each other were now just 'normal' – "I don't really love her, nor she me." He took her to the *Mikado* at the beginning of July and by midmonth he was only seeing her once in a while. After going together to a dance in the mess at Christmas, they went sailing again in June 1940 and her engagement to an army officer in October just rates a mention.

The opportunity for a change of scene, which happened in the course of

operational flying, was the third silver lining to this equatorial cloud. Within days
of his first arrival in Singapore Alex was off, as second pilot, on a trip to Batavia, to
participate in coronation celebrations for George VI. His 'boat' alighted at Tanjong
Priok. There followed two days of official receptions and parties when nobody got
to bed before 4:30 a.m.; after that, on their way back to Singapore, he and his first
pilot took it in turns to stay awake and fly. For the rest of 1937 he stayed close to
home. In the course of normal flying he became familiar with the coastlines of the
Malay Peninsula but made no further flights over the Dutch islands, as Britain was
scrupulously observing Holland's neutrality.

But fortune let him off the leash in February 1938. A squadron of Vickers
Vincents, the RAF's largest troop-carrying aircraft, arrived with ground crews and
spares for aircraft to take part in the annual 'defence of Singapore' exercise. While
these aircraft were at Seletar one second pilot was prevented from leaving. Alex was
ordered to fill the vacancy as far as Karachi, en route to the squadron's base in Iraq.
The Vincent was another large, obsolete aircraft, a twin-engined biplane with fixed
undercarriage, able to carry twenty-five to thirty soldiers at a cruising speed of

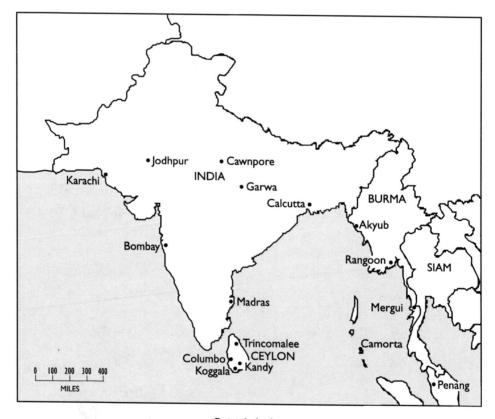

British India

120 mph – the land equivalent of the Singapore III though a little nippier. While the passengers were enclosed, the pilots sat in an open cockpit, as in a Tiger Moth or a Hart. In this museum-piece Alex was to fly a huge crescent across the heart of the British Empire, experiencing its sights and smells from 3,000 feet.

At first the Malayan coastline was familiar and Penang, their first refuelling stop, just as humid as Singapore. Like a happy spirit from a past life, Topsy appeared, with her policeman, to dine with Alex – as bubbly as ever and unchanged apart from being pregnant. Next day they flew over endless green water and white sand beaches to Mergui and then to Rangoon, in Burma. The smell of the air was different as they flew north and they came down in a drier heat, to be welcomed to their mess at Mingaladon by officers of the Burma Rifles – names from imperial romance.

After a day exploring Rangoon, it was of the books of G. A. Henty that Alex was thinking as they crossed paddy, then mountains, then desert on the way to Akyub. From there to Calcutta the air grew colder. They skimmed the muddy waters of the Ganges delta, startling white storks from perches on the endless mangroves, eventually seeing and smelling journey's end at the edge of a mile-high dust haze that hid the city. It had been a cold flight for the pilots and they were to spend two bitter nights under canvas on the field itself. Alex was better equipped than most, thanks to his Siwash Indian sweater. Next day, visiting Calcutta, he was repelled; compared to Bombay it seemed endless slum – the whole city filthy, itself a Black Hole.

From Calcutta they flew over cultivated lands, startling draft animals whose peasant owners paused in their ancient routines to shield their eyes and gaze uncomprehendingly skyward. After refuelling at Garwa they flew on up the valley of the Ganges, over more farmland and then desert, to Cawnpore. They dined at a club; it was cold, and after dinner they yarned around a blazing fire in a fireplace – for Alex, for the first time since leaving England.

The leg from Cawnpore to Jodhpur took them over desert dotted with walled villages; it was as if the Vincents were time machines, flying through the Middle Ages. Jodhpur itself, a mirage, a city of beautiful buildings and forts perched on rocks, seemed to rise up to meet them from the desert sand. Then the final flight to Karachi, across the wasteland of the Great Indian Desert and the great muddy waters and swamps of the Indus delta. Alex had flown over every landscape in every temperature. Luckily for him in his exposed cockpit, it had remained dry. It had been an unforgettable experience; the journey had taken seven days, including five in the air. That was military flying in 1938.

Bidding his new colleagues farewell he set off for Singapore, making haste slowly. He took ship on the SS *Varela* from Karachi to Bombay. On his second visit, Bombay struck him as a grand city, the London of India, and this time he avoided the slums. Having flown across India he now re-crossed it, at a narrower point, by train. First impression of his sleeping compartment was of a comfortable morgue; the upholstery of the seats was black, the windows deeply tinted and his companion a lugubrious doctor from the Argentine. However, once the glare of India replaced the station's shade, he appreciated the tinting and was able to enjoy the stately ride through the legendary hill station, Poona, then across the Deccan to Madras. The only disconcerting thing was the size of the knife which the doctor kept under his pillow. In Madras he dined, *à la* Phineas Fogg, alone and in some style at the Connemara Hotel before taking a night train down the east coast to Dhanushkodi. From there a ferry across the Mannar Strait and one more train journey took him back to Colombo, the city he had assumed he would never see again only eleven months previously. He had four peaceful days with Jim and Anna Cowie (Mary Turner's friend on the *Rawalpindi*) before sailing for Singapore on the P & O ship *Ranpura*, sister-ship to the *Pindi*. There followed his four-day shipboard fling with Leslie Kealley, referred to above.

The pilots and crews became familiar with the settlements up and down the coast of the Malay peninsula. At times they were sent to Penang or Kuantan or even across the South China Sea, to Kuching in Sarawak, to Brunei, or to Labuan in Sabah. Alex observed that he had as large a social circle in Penang as he had in Singapore. When staying overnight in these places, or preferably staying there for some time, officers would put up at the Club or, in Penang, at the officers' mess of the Punjab Regiment, and would be as comfortable as it was possible to be without air conditioning. In July 1938 Alex was to have gone on local leave with a friend, F/O Cave-Brown-Cave, up the east coast of Malaya and Siam on the coaster SS *Suddhadif*. A week before departure Cave was rushed to hospital with an infection. Alex visited him but the poor lad had become delirious and, with Alex and the CO at his bedside, died of blood poisoning. Alex was shaken but took the blow in stride as usual: following advice and his own inclination, he decided to go alone on what was, for him, a busman's holiday. It was a good decision; he had the time of his life in the most unlikely company.

His companions were as varied as Chaucer's pilgrims and none were young women. There were the Brooks, a married couple with two small children; there was Miss Brednor, the Scottish matron from the hospital, who seemed rather forbidding – in fact a battleaxe; there was Jack Lindsay, a rugby-playing planter a few years older than himself; and there was Yule, a ponderous Danish planter of immense girth. The captain was also a Dane as were the ship's officers and many of the planters they were to meet in southern Siam. A unique feature of the ship was a weighing machine in the saloon on which passengers were weighed before and after the voyage – presumably to measure its success.

At every port along this shallow coast the ship anchored far from shore while cargo was loaded and unloaded onto sampans. During the process sleep was impossible, because the sampan crews and the ship's crew shouted at each other without pause until the job was done. Yule left the ship in pitch-darkness at Kretay, the first port, rowed ashore by two oarsmen in a 20-foot *koleh* with a third man steering. Yule sat amidships, clutching between his legs a box containing $5,000 – wages for his coolies. He lived alone, eight miles from the nearest European. At Tunpat, the port of Kota Bharu, there were said to be only five Europeans; after visiting the town Alex and Lindsay called at the Club where all five were already in the bar. At most ports they did not go ashore and usually one sampan came off with cases of dried fish. They ventured ashore at the turnaround point, Tapli in Siam. Here the stink of putrid fish-oil overwhelmed Lindsay and Alex hurried him away lest a representative of the Raj be seen to lose control. On the return journey, as well as swimming off ten-mile golden beaches, they explored both Kota Bharu and Singora – neither place of any distinction but Alex would return to Singora in wildly different circumstances in 1942. European planters on this coast were grimly living out unromantic lives; most were lonely and delighted to see new faces.

Meanwhile, the company in the ship's saloon became more and more unbuttoned. By the time they docked in Singapore the captain had taken to calling Alex "that bloody Scotchman ... because you look like one"; and as Alex liked to give the impression that he was a reckless skirt-chaser, Mrs Brooks and Miss Brednor, having abandoned their customary reserve, were making ribald remarks about him and "the women," Miss Brednor even slapping her thigh and shrieking, repeatedly, in broad Aberdeen: "Aye, but ye are an awfu' laddie!" It was so unlike the formalities of Singapore society that nothing could have given Alex a better holiday. Lindsay remained a friend long afterwards and Alex's alliance with Miss Brednor smoothed his later rule-breaking stay in hospital with a rugby injury, ensuring that nobody seriously tried to stop him having a forbidden New Year's party with four other RAF patients, two Sisters and Canada Young – who brought the bubbly!

The same year Alex made two short trips to British north Borneo. The first of these was a formal one, escorting other aircraft to the opening of a new airfield at Kuching. But the second, when he was in command of two boats with Gordon Stilling and Canada Young in the company, was relaxing and enjoyable. Their task was to take air photographs and soundings at Brooketon, Labuan, Kudat and Sibu. As they were the first flying boats to land at Brooketon their arrival caused great excitement among the natives. After alighting, they were surrounded by dugouts full of ferocious-looking men, making manoeuvre difficult. Alex, unflappable and practical as ever, immediately hired some of the canoe crews for making their soundings. There, and at the other places, they found the Europeans friendly and relaxed.

They lived and ate aboard, played soccer and spent evenings listening to records on a wind-up gramophone belonging to an airman.

In July 1939 Alex had another change of scene. The background was the international tension of that summer, but the story of the tiger hunt might have taken place on another planet and reflects an optimism nurtured by isolation. Wing Commander Lang, CO of the squadron and a signals expert, had decided to fly north into Burma to examine the effects of sunspot activity on radio signals. Alex was assigned to take him north, spending at least one night on the way. The CO, who was short of flying time – in fact seriously out of practice – decided to fly the aircraft, but handed over to Alex when conditions became bad. On this particular day the clouds were low. Alex tells the tale in a scribbled memo he made at the time:

> "Clouds at 800 ft, blinding rain and a howling wind from a westerly direction, with the W/C 'navigating' and myself at the controls. Certainly most unpleasant flying and all the time wondering if it was clear at Penang. Visibility decreasing horribly.
>
> "Give me a course, please, W/C"
>
> "Hell, I don't know where we are!"
>
> "Here, you do this and let me have a go," and jump down to see if you can figure it out. "Yes, yes, gawd knows, but here's the best course for a while." No, no, you are heading out to sea. Come in a bit, in a bit more, more. How the hell does he expect to get anywhere like this. Now 120 knots. Oh gawd, look out, you'll stall and we're about 300 ft above the water. Here, push the stick forward. More revs! Come on, more, more! Oh Christ, he's going the wrong way now. Strewth, look at that top needle, as far around as the bottom and damn it, he's trying to fly without instruments when you can't see a damn thing. Land in sight! Hooray, now a course of 340 degrees and we're all set. Suddenly he sees land on his side and gets windy as hell and starts more of his turns, horrible ones at that.
>
> "Look sir, I think it would be best if we landed now."
>
> "Yes, yes; where's the wind?"
>
> "Northwest. No, no there, there!"
>
> "Lord, can't you see. Oh gawd, down we go, right across wind and we'll hit it hard, hellish hard. Look out! CRUMPH! CRUMPH! Hold her, don't do anything, just hold it. Thank God we're down and we haven't broken anything."

The flying boat came to a stop. They could see nothing except water and cloud.

Alison Maitland's design for the 205 Squadron's Christmas Card, 1938.

They threw out an anchor, to find they were in a few feet of water only. They had to wait for the weather to clear so bedded down for the night. In the morning they found the aircraft to be intact except for the loss of the trailing radio aerial; but, to their horror, they also found they had land all around them. The CO had landed blind in a landlocked bay; a few hundred yards in any direction and they would have crashed. This was Kuala Larut, it turned out, the only safe landing place for miles – and they had found it quite by chance. Alex's guardian angel was clearly at work. Trying to taxi to the narrow entrance they ran aground in shallow water and finally had to get a fisherman in a sampan to guide them.

After refuelling at Victoria Point, the southern tip of Burma, they arrived at Mergui, a squalid settlement of filthy huts surrounding a huge, gilt pagoda. They attended to their sunspot business, then returned to Victoria Point, where the CO had arranged for the local Resident to lay on a tiger hunt. There were to be two hunting parties, one for the CO and one for Alex. The CO grabbed the only reasonable rifle on the aircraft, a .303. "There you are, Jardine, you can have that," he said, tossing him a .22. Passing on the indignity, Alex exchanged his .22 for the Mannlicher carried by his head beater. The hunt was on. Without the traditional elephant to keep him out of harm's way, Alex the reluctant *sahib*, who had pooh-poohed the idea of there being tigers around, was suddenly feeling distinctly less confident. He clutched his rifle more tightly at each unexplained sound from the jungle and was comforted by the heavy feeling of a revolver on his hip. Fortunately for both hunters and hunted, after spending hours literally beating around the bush, neither party met a tiger. However, the CO was miffed to find that Alex had managed to shoot a barking deer, which was cleaned and hung in the cockpit.

On the way home they went ashore for the night – at least, the two officers did. The crew slept on the aircraft. When Alex returned to the aircraft in the morning, the decaying deer was by now "a bit high" and had brought a choking crew near to mutiny. So they continued south with the cockpit windows and all hatches open which, at 90 knots, at first made the smell tolerable – but meant cold breakfast because the Primus stove could not be lit in the draft. They landed at Penang to have a crew member with a bad laceration admitted to hospital, and, on takeoff, radioed Seletar to notify them. Later, finding the deer's smell intolerable in spite of the fresh air, they sent a further radio (RT) message requesting that a refrigerated truck meet the aircraft; the intrepid hunters were determined to entertain the mess to venison that evening. Murphy's Law ensured that the two RT messages became confused. As they taxied to the moorage they could see, instead of a refrigerated truck on the slip, a doctor and an ambulance waiting to receive a dead or dying airman. Needless to say the deer was past the care of a doctor, or even of a taxidermist. All that Alex salvaged were its feet, later made into an ornamental item which eventually became a trophy of war for some Japanese soldier. But that is to get ahead of ourselves. At the time, for lack of a photograph or a real trophy, Alex's story of "tiger huntin' in Burma, on *shikhari* doncher know, what!" was just not believed by his friends!

Alex's last trip before Hitler went to war happened a week later; he took Air Vice Marshal Babington to Kota Bharu where the AVM was to inspect a new airfield, one of several under construction. Alex now had a better look at the place from the air. It was an unprepossessing settlement straggling along both banks of a river, all mud and mangrove swamps, close to the sea. While the AVM and his aides were away from the aircraft, Alex was introduced to the Sultan of Kelantan and offered to take him up for a flip. The sultan eagerly accepted and greatly enjoyed his short flight, for the first time able to look down upon his land and palace. Alex discovered from his conversation that the sultan thought the aircraft had been sent from Singapore for that purpose alone, so tactful handling was called for. During the flight, to Alex's consternation as his attention was divided anyway between the aircraft and his guest, all four engines gradually slowed to a gentle tick-over; the nut holding the throttles in place had come away. "I had to hold the throttles forward whilst trying to fly with one hand. I got [second pilot] Canada Young to hold the throttles during the approach and landing!" Back on the water the sultan, who had noticed nothing amiss, was about to leave in his launch when he spotted the radio and insisted on sending a message of thanks to AHQFE. Not sure that HQ would approve of the flight at all, Alex was a little apprehensive when his operator sent the potentate's fulsome message. He need not have worried. British control of the Malay states depended upon the cooperation of the sultans; anything which cost nothing and kept one of them happy was a Good Thing. Within days Alex received words of praise and thanks from the Air Vice Marshal himself.

Singapore seemed idyllic for those who could easily escape it. John Gunther's view of Singapore included, "... on the one side, the glittering blue ribbon of the Strait of Johore, intersected by the wide causeway; ... on the other, the tawny hills and tropical jungle of the island." Noel Barber remembered "... palm trees, blinding white beaches, evening lightning flashing, the wet heat produced by hot sun and sudden rain squalls, monkeys at the bottom of the garden, above all the human zoo of bustling Chinese, languid Indians, doe-eyed Malays, and of course, the pink, perspiring *tuans*." He recalled "... city streets which drew the eye to ships shimmering on the horizon, liners and sampans and rusty old freighters all mixed up; also the Singapore river, full of sampans on which men, women and children lived and died." Its powerful smell – "... of drains, swampland, dried fish and unlanded spices" – was not unpleasant for him, though unforgettable.[11]

For Alex these idealised pictures were tempered by realities. He found the worst smells came from Malay cooking, burning rubber from the estates, and the stench of any river or harbour at low tide. As the gorgeous flowers which grew in profusion seemed to have no scent, there was little to counteract bad smells except for the wind. After six months on the island the three features of his Victoria home which he missed the most were the sight and smell of conifers, snowcapped mountains across the water and the singing of birds.

He nevertheless managed to find pleasure in his new home. Singapore was not convincingly urban – the concrete jungle never quite swallowed the green jungle that surrounded it. It still offered glimpses of attap huts, palm trees, broad green banana leaves, wild sago with its fronds like feathers, and frail papaya trees. Each sunrise came with the hot, wet smell of a new day in the tropics and each evening, at dusk, the cicadas and bullfrogs started their noises, somehow giving the impression of upcountry jungle far removed from any city. Alex spent leaves and some weekends with Batchy and Ann at their house on the beach. On fine days he liked to read in the shade of the palms on their east-facing verandah. Close inshore the water was such a transparent green that anchored fishing boats appeared to fly above it; further out, beyond the spidery poles of fishing *pagars*, the ocean darkened until it blended into the blues and purples of distant islands. In the strait, working junks moved slowly across the view with dark brown sails sharply outlined, while overhead cumulus ballooned into the deep blue. When the wind was blowing, which was most of the time, it sounded like rain in the palm leaves. When Alex was lying in bed before getting up, it was difficult to tell apart the sounds of waves, wind, or rain in the palms. It was all very peaceful.

Pre-war life in Singapore soon sank into a routine which encouraged neither thought nor effort. This was largely the result of the climate, the enervating effect of always feeling tired and sweaty in the middle of the day. Latin Americans have the same problem and their solution for it is *mañana* – tomorrow. Nothing gets done in a hurry; nothing much gets done at all. In Malaya and Singapore the saying is *tida appa*, which means essentially the same thing. For Alex it was at first disconcerting. Used to being decisive and vigorous he thought he must be sick when he felt himself to be neither of these things. It was some consolation to find that everybody had had the same experience, but it was not a nice feeling nevertheless. It reinforced his determination to resist late hours and afternoon snoozes, and made him anxious to live as 'normal' a life as he could.

He was rewarded by steady professional advancement. In July 1937 he was made temporary adjutant in the absence of the incumbent. October brought new pilot officers from Calshot – he was no longer the 'junior bog-rat'. In the same month he skippered a Singapore III for the first time with one of the new men as his second pilot. Clearly he was well regarded and this was confirmed when his application for a two-year extension of his short-service commission was accepted. Just after Christmas 1937 he was appointed permanent adjutant; as he explained to Agnes, he was now one of the essential cogs in the wheel of the squadron – a buffer between the CO and the officers and between officers and airmen, "arranging this and that and knowing what each person is doing and why." Normally the adjutant has no other duties but Alex was determined to do his regular flying as well – the last thing he would give up was flying hours. By working in the afternoons he was able to manage this balancing act for most of 1938. Status changes in the services are often heralded by a fog of rumour. Opening a letter from Gieves, the London tailors who had made some of his kit and who doubtless hoped he needed more, Alex found himself, *inter alia*, congratulated on his promotion to flying officer! Happily the rumour became official in May 1938 and in July the new flying oficer was appointed skipper of his own boat, Singapore III K6916, with the Australian P/O Gordon Stilling as second pilot. They were soon to be close friends.

His first independent command came in August, in charge of a detachment of two aircraft taking water-polo players, eleven people in all, for several days to Penang and Port Swettenham. This meant more responsibility but he only gave up the adjutancy in October, when the balancing act became too hard to support. By

February 1939, having been with the squadron for nearly two years, Alex wrote to Agnes: "These days I'm coming into my own gradually and like to be in the forefront of all that is going on; I'm senior Flying Officer and consequently involved in a large number of things – chiefly keeping tabs on aircraft maintenance and the general running of the outfit." The powers-that-be clearly agreed; in May, a year before he expected it, he discovered he was now a flight lieutenant – this time by reading the magazine *Aeroplane* which had beaten Gieves to the punch.

Alex had seen more of Japan than had other members of 205 Squadron. He cherished memories of New Year's Eve 1931 with Uncle Bill in Tokyo, where he had met and liked a number of Bill's Japanese friends. Although the Japanese were presumed to be a possible enemy in his course at Manston, he arrived in Singapore with few anti-Japanese prejudices. Japan was, after all, where Uncle Bill chose to live and work, and where his mother had been born. His attitude was to change radically; within months of arriving in Singapore he had become vehemently anti-Japanese. By September he was writing: "I am learning almost daily to dislike the Japanese more and more!"

The immediate cause of this change of heart was the 'China scare' of 1937; in July Japan had begun its attempted conquest of China and immediate rumours that the squadron was bound for Hong Kong focused attention on the brutality of events there. His information became personal when Mary Turner sent a map showing nearby houses damaged by the fighting in Shanghai. A city that he had known as "one helluva burg" was being blown apart by Japan. In January 1938 Alex could not figure out how "Uncle Bill can be so keen on the Japs." By February he was referring to them as "our one-time friends" and henceforth his suspicions were reinforced wherever he looked. The pilot, whose place he took in the Vickers Vincent, had been guilty of taking his snaps of the annual 'defence of Singapore' exercise to be developed in a Japanese-owned store; looking around, it was apparent that all camera stores were Japanese-owned. When Alex returned from his steamer cruise up the east coast in August 1938, his own negatives were mysteriously 'lost' by one of those stores. He was so aware of the Japanese as potential enemies that when Uncle Bill asked about RAF machines, Alex purposely did not tell him and replied in a plain envelope. In January 1939, in hospital, he read *Secret Agent of Japan* by Vespa; it proved his point about Japan; he wrote: "I can't imagine anyone wishing to say 'hello' to a Jap after this book!" Later that year he was furious when he flew over a Japanese cargo ship loading iron ore in (British) Malaya; he commented: "It's astonishing how much we are doing to help them in this rotten war!"

He knew, of course, that the world was becoming a more dangerous place; there was always a background rumour of war. They heard the radio, saw the Movietone News or read the British papers when they arrived weeks late, but in Singapore there was none of the apprehension and anxiety that people in England felt. In September 1938 Hitler seemed remote; nobody was digging trenches in Singapore as they were in Hyde Park. When Chamberlain went to Munich Alex felt confident there would be no war. Maybe his memories of the earnest Germans of Hamburg, who so deeply believed Hitler to be 'a good man', made him skeptical of the war-scare in spite of tightened security in Singapore. When the crisis passed he seemed justified. He had a realistic timetable for getting back to Canada and no tinpot dictator was going to wreck it!

His three-year tour of duty in the Far East would be finished in March 1940. At that time he would return to Britain via Victoria, BC, where he would spend the three months' home leave due to him. Reaching Britain in March 1940 he would have a year and a half to find a flying job in Canada before his 1941 release from the RAF. In fact, at the beginning of 1939, he was writing "coming home this year," and by July, more precisely: "I'll be leaving sometime in December for Victoria." He was convinced that the new fuss in Europe would evaporate. When he feared that heightened RAF readiness – after Hitler's seizure of Czechoslovakia and threats to Poland – might interfere with a sailing trip, he wrote lightheartedly to Agnes: "Gosh, I do hope that Hitler and Mussolini will keep quiet for a week or so, at least!" In August he was excited about the arrival of two squadrons of new Blenheim bombers at Tengah – "really fast and modern." Within days he found himself temporarily posted to Tengah, to train the pilots in navigation, reconnaissance and ship recognition – basically the course he had taken at Manston – and discovered that teaching was something he did well. His superiors were delighted with the results, demonstrated when the Blenheims became operational, and Alex was congratulated by the AOC Far East. But none of this caused him to see war coming – the reinforcement was, after all, long overdue.

As already mentioned, in March 1939 Alex had written one of his periodical letters to Major R. H. Mayo, his aeronautical backstop and now a director of Imperial Airways. He had asked him about the possibility of an administrative job with Imperial Airways when his short-service commission expired in November 1941. At the time he was contemplating marriage to Barbara Murray and hoped to sweeten his offer with acceptable prospects. Mayo's reply, written on the 21st of July, 1939, must surely rank as the third bucket of cold water during his career, as deflating as the previous ones from Captain Aikman and S/L Higgins.

Apart from offering no hope for an administrative job, Mayo told him to forget any plans to leave the service in 1941. In his words: "Whether we are embroiled in a war ... or not, it seems to me very doubtful whether the Service will be able to afford to release its short service officers by then." He assured him that with his present level of experience, he "would at once get a flying job with Imperial

Airways" when he did leave the RAF. For now, his advice was to grasp the nettle, sign up for a permanent commission and ride the promotion escalator that he could see coming. Whether there was war or not "the opportunities for fairly quick promotion to much higher ranks are bound to be good during the next few years."

Alex's personal plans had been called in question by somebody who knew what he was talking about. Alex had not seen Canada and home for four years; he had every reason to feel depressed, but seems to have treated Mayo's view of the international situation skeptically. In any case, the Singapore ambience wrapped itself around this new worry as an oyster smothers an irritating piece of sand; in no time he had ceased thinking about it. November 1941 was a long way off. There was the business of flying to be attended to; there were the constant invitations to parties. Reality was the hot sun and the rattle of palm fronds in the trade winds; it was men in sarongs and lazy times around the pool, joking with friends; it was the laughter of the young women who seemed to cluster around them. *Tida appa* to the rescue! Weeks passed. And so it was that Alex, along with everybody else, was quite unprepared when he found himself a member of a service at war with Germany.

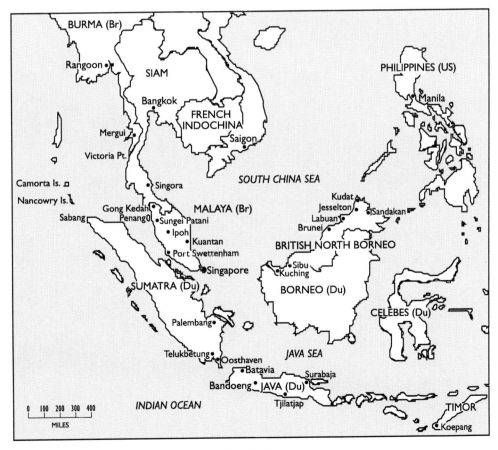

East Indies

6

SQUADRON LEADER

1939–DECEMBER 1941
In which the war with Germany traps Alex in Singapore; in which
he becomes Squadron Leader and second-in-command; and in which
he earns an AFC for outstanding and courageous leadership.

"So many things must now not happen"

If Alex still had a game plan in the late summer of 1939 it was to hang on in
Singapore until December, when his three-year tour of duty would be almost
complete. Then, after Christmas leave in BC, he would return to Britain to serve
the balance of his short-service commission. He hoped, in spite of Mayo's gloomy
forecast, to obtain his release in November 1941, head home to Canada and find a
flying job, preferably based on the west coast. After that he would marry and raise
a family, but only when his circumstances were better than those which his father
had managed. However, as Burns observed: "The best laid schemes o' mice an' men
gang aft agley." Before the actual declaration of war against Germany he and his
friends knew that something was afoot. In Alex's words:

> "First evidence of any real trouble was a signal by teleprinter that all
> operations rooms were to be manned. What a howl, what a joke, it
> seemed to me then!
>
> 'Jardine, that's your job, get cracking', so it came from the CO.
>
> 'Right, Sir.' The next few hours were utter and complete confu-
> sion. Sergeant observers making large scale maps, printing this or that,
> making signs and symbols. They must have thought me mad. Brown
> paper and coloured pencils the order of the day.
>
> 'Get cardboard!'
>
> 'Can't!'
>
> 'Then make some!'

'You Jones, print OPS ROOM. You Smith, another chart. You Jackson, information board.' And so it was. Brown paper, chairs, tables, notice boards all over the place. One could hardly move when the AOC arrived.

'Good afternoon Sir. Hope to have this working by 0800 tomorrow.'

'Right ho, Jardine.' Followed another day and then gradually out of chaos came order and we settled down once again to a more regular routine.

"Meantime Anti-Sabotage and Low-flying attack points had been manned. Coolies working 12 hours a day filling sandbags. Indian troops arrived to act as sentries: one's first shock at a shout meant to mean 'Halt!' in the middle of the night; the almost trembled reply 'officer friend!' and the 'pass friend' were the little things that brought home the fact of [possible] war."

He goes on to describe how news of the declaration of war reached them. His recollection has all the irrelevant detail of memories of once-in-a-lifetime events.

"We were walking along the road towards a small kampong five miles from the Aerodrome. Most of the day it had rained – a rather dismal, intermittent rain coming at times in extremely heavy showers and at others as a light drizzle. There were tall trees on either side and the rows of rubber trees in their customary lines at regular intervals. Low darkish clouds rushing overhead. To us they seemed to be moving a great deal faster than they actually were; ... one watched them apparently pouring into an unseeable funnel miles and miles away. It was hot and humid, though cooler than usual, thanks to the rain. Back to the mess, to find a circle of officers playing *you're a liar* for drinks. Then the remark from one of them who had been in the NAAFI listening to the radio: 'We have declared war on Germany!' That was at 6:20 p.m., local time. What a strange feeling of disbelief and a sort of numbness coupled with a feeling of resignation. So many things, that meant, must now not happen; hopes that had been accumulating for years here, striving to save money and not succeeding, but nevertheless knowing that when the time came I should find enough to get home. That, of course, was washed up.

"Funny really, I had always thought that war was impossible, just could not be. And because going home meant so much, not daring to

think that anything might happen to stop it. In retrospect, all the
things I thought of that might happen to prevent me going home –
now how very silly they seemed! Local leave too; no rest for over 6
months and then it was only a week. I had begun to feel that I must
get away.

"Now this, which meant we were 'gated', as the Wing Commander
put it, in that tiny mess, empty of everything but the barest necessities.
Followed days of 'when is the next news on?' And then the cry for
silence as the American stations came up with their 'Flash' and the
sinking of the 'Athenia', one of my company's ships, and no doubt
friends I sailed with on board her; wondering if they were safe, and
yet, because time had passed since I last saw them, the tragedy was not
so very real."

In fact, Captain Cook of the *Gracia*, who had given Alex a letter of recommendation, was skipper of the ill-fated *Athenia*. Though he survived, the least
fortunate of his shipmates and passengers were the first British casualties of the
European war.

"The announcement of war, on a Sunday evening to make it seem so
much less real; the Monday morning with the long message: 'Confirm
that England has declared war on Germany,' and then instructions
with regard to several administrative arrangements. Aircraft: six to be
at one-hour standby from dawn to dusk, bombed up and prepared
to leave as soon as possible. Those businesslike, sinister-looking
Blenheims on the edge of the aerodrome, for all the world appearing
to say: 'come on, let's get going.' Signals and more signals. Secret
letters and instructions. Likelihood all enemy merchant ships will
become Armed Merchant Raiders. Photographs of all German ships,
studying them to know their appearance, placing imaginary guns on
them, noting their speeds. Weird days of rushing here, there and
everywhere; then moments when nothing could be done, when so
much should be seen to. This was war, this *is* war, look! Read the
papers, people, friends, relatives are actually being killed. Strive as hard
as I'm sure most of us did at one time or another, the real stark reality
of it never was felt by a single soul. One cannot be living in sunshine
and billowy clouds, green and abundant trees, cooling breezes, natives
in their coloured sarongs passing by and believe that elsewhere in
another part of the world there's wind and rain and miserableness
and mud and bullets and shells and bombs.

"The days that followed: forcing home one's arguments to unimaginative and sometimes stubborn observers: 'You must!', 'Don't you understand, we're at war!', 'You can't?', 'Don't be absurd!', 'Do it!', 'Find a way!', 'Make it!', 'Of course you can!' I wonder how many times I said those words with all the forcefulness I could muster, willing, if such a thing *is* possible, people to do what I wanted and what I knew was right. Slowly and surely the 'answers' coming in, and the grandest satisfaction of it all as each one came in with the right answers. 'Yes sir, got it taped now.' 'Piece of cake.' The encouraging of those who couldn't make it; knowing, from bitter and often-experienced similar troubles, their feelings; temporary sympathy with jocularity and leg-pull and assurances that it would come out all right soon enough. Grand fun really and how I loved every moment of it!"

The RAF in Singapore were completely unprepared for war – witness the lack of an Operations Room. To be fair, they had been denied state-of-the-art aircraft for so long, had operated on such a shoestring, had been treated to such mixed messages from optimistic and naive politicians, that their complacency was understandable. But *tida appa* in Singapore had produced worse problems than complacency. In mid-September Alex wrote:

"During working hours for the last 2 weeks checking inventories. Aircraft that have been here 3 and 4 years, gear in the most incredibly chaotic state. No-one has done a really conscientious check for years, it seems. The result being aircraft with 5 engines when it should have four, on charge another three. Items which have never been seen; this, that and the next thing surplus; and hundreds, almost, of others deficient. 12:30 comes all too soon, down tools and hope for another day to enable a check to be done. At present the situation is nearly hopeless. No situation was ever completely hopeless; this, however, seems near enough to it. No doubt it will all straighten out. Simply have to, somehow or other. What is so aggravating is the knowledge that there are thousands of aircraft in the RAF where they can't and don't worry about such ridiculous items as 'spoons, tea' and 'knives, bread'. We have to, or make a show at trying to. Mistakes made by all branches, by people who have long since departed this Command, but you who have signed the inventory will pay for the deficiencies."

Life on the base was now much more restrictive.

"One-hour boat today, which means on the Station from 0730 until
0730, available at any time within fifteen minutes, ready to fly in a
Singapore III, empty of everything but guns and petrol and sometimes
a primus stove and a teapot. Enough petrol for 6 hours' flying, crew in
the Block and airmen ready to open the hangar to enable any extra
stuff to be found. Relieved for meals in the Operations Room, (where
this is being written). That means a hurried meal in the mess, a mile
drive in a Singer van with petrol fumes almost asphyxiating one. An
hour and a half of being eaten by mosquitoes, (tonight fortunately
there are none,) then back to the mess to spend the rest of the evening.
This Ops Room business is killing; nothing doing from hour to hour,
but ready should there be a flap. Usually when it does start there is
enough doing for twenty people. That however happens only once in a
blue moon and usually, again, at the most incredibly awkward times.
However, that's war here, one supposes. Dear knows, it's binding
enough."

However, life settled down again. If anything, the social pace quickened but for
Alex the interest diminished. In such a limited environment it was impossible to
find new things to do, new places to go. For someone active by nature it became
increasingly claustrophobic. He described the choices available.

"Singapore town and the people drinking, everyone does and no
small amount. A night out: have dinner after drinks at the Swimming
Club, where we sit in bathing costumes watching the lovelies go by,
they knowing, if they be half presentable, that they are being commented on. Sometimes a smile and a wave and more occasionally a
few words. The moment she's out of sight a table of 5 or 6 men will
bombard you with questions as to names, what doing, how long's she
been here and does she! Gradually, thanks to congenial company and
beer and the congeniality coming from the beer, one begins to feel a
little more alive to what's happening hereabouts. Then dinner at the
Airport or Raffles, if you're flush, or Cyranos or Café Wien; more beer
and the liqueurs that follow and perhaps a cigar. Now one of three
alternatives: to the Clubs or Hotels, to drink and watch people dancing – you have to be set on a boozy party for that; the cinema and you
pay $1 for a seat that's anything but comfortable; or crawl around the
low haunts, drinking warm, unpleasant beer and smelling all manner
and kinds of natives. This you do if you are really whistled and go to
wherever he who drives decides, usually ending the evening feeling

horribly tired, too much drink and its about 4:00 a.m. and you are on duty again at 6:30 a.m. That rubs no small amount. The awfulness of being unable to find the things one cares to do, that need not call for the company of others or a can of money, the really simple pleasures of life. Somewhere you can find a 'tang' in life, the desire to live and feel the nip in the air, not this nearly steaming heat, sickly, perhaps exotic, smells, coupled with horrible stinks of native quarters, warm winds laden with moisture, clouds, clouds, always clouds and a temperature every day of near enough 85 degrees."

Operations at least gave one the feeling that something was happening, that there was some point to life. And there was always the flying, the blessed escape into the upper atmosphere, that feeling of being in control for once. There was plenty of flying to be done. Alex's records contain one description of seeking out and photographing German merchant ships, which must have occurred in September 1939. Alex was flying Singapore III FVJ (K5916) and his crew of five included F/Sgt Williams, Leading Aircraftsman (LAC) Kendall, Aircraftsman (AC) Popple, LAC Herman and LAC Grant. On this occasion they were airborne at Penang at 0527, flying almost due west, over Pulau Perak to the coast of Sumatra, part of the then-neutral Dutch East Indies and prime hide-out territory for Germans. For once the weather was good and they could see for twenty miles. At the very northwest tip of Sumatra, in the harbour at Sabang, they found what they were looking for – no fewer than five German ships. Flying at a few hundred feet they were able to read the names of two of them – the *Lindenfels* and the *Verdenfels*. Making repeated passes, they snapped away with their 8-inch lens camera; then, with mission accomplished, they set a course back to Penang, reporting their discovery by radio at 0930. Because of censorship all Alex could say in his letters was that they were having plenty of flying – all day and every day – and most nights!

Militaries consider hardly at all the feelings and attitudes of those who have to 'do and die'. Consequently, military life is a mix of 95 percent idleness and 5 percent frenetic activity, activity which is itself often unaccountably countermanded before completion. Alex describes one such event, a trip to Nancowry Island in the Nicobar Islands, at the end of October 1939:

"Midnight 27/10:
'you are required in the Ops Room right away.' Oh lord, what now, some damn fool thing; they *do* choose the most incredible times to have people out. However, nothing else but to get dressed and doing. Arrived down about 1230 to hear that I was to leave at 0600

for Nancowry, staying away five days at least. Hooray, something doing at last. From 0100 until 0600 rushing here, there and everywhere; crew to be called, food arranged, petrol required at Penang; locating Sgt Graham. Time seemed to rush away, everything locked, everyone away. What an incredible time of day to arrange food for six people for five days! The F/B had no cruising equipment whatsoever on board. The rigger away and so someone else standing by for him; no keys; didn't know anything about what was on and what was off. Horrible shambles, made completely chaotic by the arrival of the W/C and then Signals organisation; where was this, have you got that?

"Finally away at 0630, half an hour late and I believe the W/C is not at all happy. Up to 1,500 ft.; low cloud at 2,000 ft. over Malacca and huge clouds piled high, one upon the other; climbing, climbing to try and get over; absolutely no way but to go through them. White, curling mist, bumping all over the shop, diving and climbing until at last at 9,000 ft., just on top of a sea of cotton wool, innocent as white snow on a hillside – but horrible inside. Followed an hour of dodging mighty towers of more cloud pushed up from the billowy floor; crags almost seeming to laugh at you: 'Ha, ha, ha! Keep away from me!'; flying between these castles, the sun shining white pure and clean on this sea of whiteness; we began to wonder if it was never-ending. As far as the eye could see, just nothing, and the four engines still roaring on. Breakfast being prepared aft – the grand smell of sausages and eggs, alas only to be served cold. The temperature was away down. Later a break in the clouds and the coastline, a welcome sight. So down again, engines idling and the nose pointing towards the land and the sea, all the glass faces of instruments misting over, caused by the sudden change in temperature. Ah, that's better, warmer now. 'Right you are, Sergeant Graham, take over whilst I shave.' Lumut beneath us, the hills around about capped with white clouds. Happy memories back again. Then in the distance the island of Penang, shrouded as it always seemed to be in its mantle of white, but clear as a bell at 1,000 ft. A prayer of thankfulness that the weather was fine, no snooping in through rain, trying to dodge hills. And then the memories of another trip when all in front was a wall of rain.

"No, not this time. Georgetown Glugor and the now familiar landing stretch of water, the speedboat speeding up the waterway, green flag flying, all clear for landing. Moored up and the refueller hissing to a stop alongside, thrashing the water up about its stern. 500

gals., then ashore for food. A Captain RN: 'Are you commander?' 'Yes sir.' A slow walk along the jetty, talking in whispers of the ships in the Bay of Bengal and the job I was on. Why on earth doesn't he stop and let me away? Oh please, I must get away. Into the town at last and the Cold Storage, rushing here, there and everywhere, fulfilling a hastily given order.

"Back to the aircraft and then away again, this time a course of nearly due west – out, out and into the blue. Good old engines, good old aircraft, everything grand; next stop 429 miles away, 5 hours or perhaps less, all being well. Clear, fair weather except for a darkish blue patch, which means rain and perhaps bumps. Maybe we'll miss it, let's hope so anyway. On and on, then on the edge. Up we go, up and up, but clear again at 5,000 ft. And then through it nicely. 2 hours to go.

"Then the return call to base before sunset! Oh curses, why, why can't they let us finish our job? No luck, turn 180 degrees and back for Penang. No interest now. Weather clear, so very lovely, everything could have been such good fun. Now tired, weary, that's all. Part of the game, I suppose, but it doesn't help. Arrive Penang. Refuel.

'Sorry old chap but we couldn't help spoiling your game of golf. War, you know.'

'Yes, I don't mind really.' Telephone to Singapore, request instructions. 'We can be back tonight.'

'Oh, why?'

'Saturday?'

'Yes, I supppose so.'

'Right ho, thanks. Cheerio.'

"Complete relax and the tiredest feeling ever. Stay the night in Penang. Arranging for accommodation for airmen and self. A whisky and soda aboard a friendly RNVR [Royal Navy Volunteer Reserve] patrol-boat. 'No, the job doesn't get much attention now!' This patrolling business is indeed practically full-time. Out to the aircraft; one airman to stay aboard, rest ashore for dinner and sleep. Up to the Golf Club; more whiskies and soda, tired and more tired. At last the Club and a glorious 'pour-over-me' with a dipper hot bath. Then the dash of cold water down you and so much happier. Dinner in the BC-wood-lined dining room. Soft lights, that lovely timber, excellent service, a tall glass of beer and a haggis. How very sweet and nice and good things are. Afterwards outside to meet a few people, but too

utterly weary to talk. So, half an hour later, bed. What a heavenly
place! Followed 9 hours of 'death' and an awakening at 0530. Breakfast on an orange and tea. Then away for Glugor, finally off the water
0700. Back to Seletar; the weather report said low cloud 2,000 ft., but
clear and fine along the whole route. We soon found it otherwise and
were more often than not at 100 ft., skimming treetops or wave tops,
though just a few feet below the clouds, through several rainstorms.
Luck again was in; when we arrived back it was clear and so landed
and ready for a few more weeks of stagnation!"

In November Alex was to spend three weeks away establishing a flying-boat
base on Nancowry Island in the Nicobars. As we can guess from the account which
he wrote of a similar job at Camorta Island a year later (see below), Alex loved his
three weeks in the wilderness. With him were Norman Birks, his second pilot, and
Gordon Stilling – both close friends; and he learned valuable lessons about
command of airmen and life in the tropics. It was "very near to the sort of thing I
should like to be doing all the time, with a little more work thrown in. Lumme, I'll
cop it one of these days, always wishing for more to do!"

Like his airmen he took advantage of the isolation to grow a beard, which added
to the crew's swashbuckling appearance on their private Treasure Island. Unfortunately, Alex's beard "itched like hell"; concerned that it might be concealing some
dreadful tropical complaint, he shaved it off bit by bit – just to check! Needless to
say his skin was fine – just objecting to its blanket; and the remaining Vandyke
looked so ridiculous that he took it all off. They were back in civilisation at Seletar
before Christmas. After a spell of constant activity, with much time spent away
from the mess, Alex actually enjoyed a brief resumption of 'boiled shirt' social life.
He took Barbara Murray, now just an old flame, to the dance which the single
officers of 205 Squadron threw for the marrieds.

He spent his fourth Christmas and New Year away from home in the cool of the
Malayan highlands. It was as if he were back in the temperate zone. After climbing
the 4,000 feet of Maxwell Hill, with a coolie carrying his suitcase on his head,
Alex's cabin had a fireplace, beds with blankets (!) and really cold water in the tap,
three things about which he could only dream down at the coast. Add amazing
views, crisp air and a feeling of being so much more alive and it is small wonder
that he and his friends had energy – when it was miserably, marvellously cold – for
eighteen holes of golf before lunch and twenty-seven after, or that they climbed
four different mountains in the week.

January 1940 brought the shape of things to come to 205 Squadron in the form
of a Link Trainer – an American invention for training pilots in instrument flying,

but which never left the ground. As senior pilot, Alex had to master the monster first, then put other pilots through it. It was popular, and not just because it brought more exciting aircraft nearer; being American, it was air-conditioned. Everybody wanted to spend their afternoons in the Link! As the Singapore III's instruments were rudimentary, the Link signalled that its days were numbered. It had been evident since the war began that RAF GR (General Reconnaissance) squadrons in the Indian Ocean area needed longer-range machines. Without the ability to visit its islands – almost all British and separated by thousands of miles of ocean – the RAF could not be sure that their lagoons and harbours were denied to German ships and submarines. Pilots had to be trained to fly a state-of-the-art replacement and at first that seemed likely to be the Short Sunderland, military version of the big Empire flying boats used by Imperial Airways.

On the 1st of February 1940 Alex became second-in-command of the squadron; by March he was flying a Sunderland, recording his first solo flights in the middle of the month. The aircraft was a Rolls-Royce compared to the Singapore's Ford truck. But Britain was hard pressed providing Sunderlands for Mediterranean, Atlantic and Coastal Command areas, where they were the main defence against U-Boats. For the time being, 205 Squadron operations continued to be flown in Singapores and this one Sunderland. Alex was away for extended periods three times between April and June; all these trips were probably to Nancowry in the Nicobars, from which the squadron was now patrolling the Bay of Bengal.

In spite of their hopes the squadron was to receive no more Sunderlands. In the beginning of August 1940 Alex flew their only one from Penang across the Bay of Bengal, to China Bay at Trincomalee in northeast Ceylon. He delivered the machine to a squadron already equipped with them and there spent a month of part-work, part-play, before returning to Singapore. He liked the drier heat of Ceylon and found the sea water cool enough to make swimming pleasurable. Pat Sowman tells a tale of Alex and others at a party at the Welcome Hotel, Trincomalee. Bored with the chitter chatter, Alex asked: "Hasn't anybody got a boat?" Johny Wheeler, the hotel owner's daughter, answered: "Oh yes, let's go down to the harbour." There were dozens of boats in the harbour. Sowman wrote: "I can see you now, whipping off your trousers, down to a pair of striped underpants, wading out and bringing a boat in for all of us to board. We sailed round Trincomalee harbour and you eventually moored the boat to its original moorings, all in moonlight. Wonderful fun!" The next day the president of the sailing club was about to complain to the RAF CO – which might have been unfortunate for Alex. Some fast talking by Johny persuaded him he would get faster results if he complained to the mess secretary, which he did. As this officer had been part of the boatload, they all had fun dictating a reply, telling the president that the officers concerned had received a severe 'ticking off' and that it would not happen again!

Before his return he and his friend 'Doc' were invited to spend a few days as guests of the government agent in Kandy. The occasion was the famous torchlit procession, bearing the Sacred Tooth to one of the temples at the Festival of Pera Kera. The procession was composed of elephants, drummers and temple dancers, a mix of sound, colour and stately movement. Alex was fascinated by the great pachyderms – so long-suffering and docile amidst human pandemonium. Next day he rode one; it was docile all right but it cured him of his fascination as he found it "a most uncomfortable brute!"

Disliking the formal or 'sticky' atmosphere in the government agent's mansion, the two of them thanked their hosts and departed. They spent some days enjoying the amazing hospitality of new acquaintances, first of tea planters at Nuwara Eliya then of other people at Matale, living very informally, playing golf in the rain at 6,000 feet, skinny-dipping in a mountain stream, enjoying the cool air and the great friendliness of their hosts.

At the beginning of September, after lunch with Anna Cowie in Colombo, Alex was homebound on the *Viceroy of India*. The reader will be right to suspect Alex incapable of making the four-day voyage without seeking out attractive female company! This time it was Iona Fraser, travelling with her mother to join her father, a navy captain at Penang. He does admit that Iona, a blue-eyed brunette, came close to his concept of the 'ideal woman'. If she attracted him we can be sure she joined him in his vigorous enjoyment of shipboard life and that they arrived at Penang breathless from laughing, having enjoyed their trip more than a little.

In the course of the normal rotation and of wartime expansion a remarkable group of individuals had by chance been assembled in the 205 Squadron mess, none of whom was afflicted with the upper class attitudes which had bothered Alex when he arrived. Far removed from his earlier status as 'junior bog-rat', by 1940 Alex was senior pilot and had seen each of the others arrive. As second-in-command, it was he who set the tone in the squadron. His friendliness, leadership and encouragement had greeted and guided them all and they responded warmly.

The Australian Gordon Stilling had been the first, arriving in July 1938 aboard a Sunderland skippered by Allan Ainslie of 'black troops' memory. That coincidence started Gordon off on the right foot and he was soon Alex's constant companion. Canada Young, a giant of huge strength, was next, arriving in September. At one time Alex's second pilot, he had been grateful when 'Jardo' had 'been a buddy' and not told others of the legendary hash he had made of a nighttime navigation exercise. Later he had bootlegged bubbly into the hospital when Alex was laid up, Canadian blood being thicker than water – or than bubbly for that matter. In 1939 the Australian Norman Birks arrived, another huge man, a businessman and boxing champion who could silence a hostile barroom with a glance, who was also soon to be Alex's second pilot. Like Gordon, he struck up instant friendship with the boss, strengthened by hospitality after his wife Pat came north to join him in 1940. For Alex, the Birks's house became a home from home, and as flying partners they always coincided at Seletar. The year 1940 saw the arrival of Dicky Atkinson, another Australian, and Terry Grieve, a Brit who adapted well to 205 Squadron's colonial mix. Atkinson had the sort of 'go' that made him Alex's automatic ally. Other 1940 arrivals were Jock Graham and Doug Shaw, both from Britain; Shaw, like all his namesakes at that time, was immediately and uncomplainingly rechristened 'Bernard' and Graham and Grieve were the 'drinking team' referred to below.

The squadron, headed by these eight pilots, was becoming a fine place to be. Whatever their assignments, eventually 205's pilots came 'home' to Seletar. Because of the uncertainty of wartime operations, each return was more enthusiastically celebrated. They were becoming a true 'band of brothers,' like Admiral Nelson's captains, each delighted to see the others. For example, in July 1940 the whole squadron was together for the first time in a long while; all were delighted to see each other. And after his return from Ceylon in September of that year, Alex wrote: "Arriving back here was awfully nice. I have so many very good friends here now." As time passed their lives intermingled; pilots on detachment together came to know each other well; married men kept open house for their fellows; and going out on the town had a new pleasure to it – they went in a group, let their hair down and had a lot of riotous fun. The festive season of 1940-41 found Alex and Atkinson at Glugor while Graham and Grieve were at Seletar. They exchanged telegrams. First, from Seletar: "To F/Lt Jardine Atkinson Penang: Probable repeat probable drinking team Jock Terry arrive assist bear White Man's Burden New Years' Eve STOP you claw back next day STOP Xmas greetings from Pertama to all at Glugor." The reply read: "To P/O Graham and George Grieve: The pipes will skirl and a dram awaits ye. A braw Christmas to all in Pertama di Malaya. signed Jardine Atkinson." The reunion happened: after haggis, with liberal doses of Scotch, six of them went on to a dance and "shook the local hotel quite considerably." This was not well received in Penang and Alex commented: "People out here are most peculiar at times and *very* sticky on occasions!" After another rowdy party in a restaurant in January 1941 Alex commented: "I feel it is the ideal occasion to let yourself go; how or why we didn't hurt each other, the menfolk, I don't know. What the poor Japs (the owners of the place) thought I don't want to know!" More recently Alex remembered: "Few people [outside the group] enjoyed the remarkable comradeship that developed between us. We simply loved each other, a horribly inadequate word to describe how much we cared for each other."

September 1940 marked another passage in Alex's life – the death of his father at the age of sixty. Alex had long since stopped expecting him to get his life on track and knew that he was extremely ill. His death was no surprise and hardly affected him; he wrote to Agnes: "I haven't said much about Dad ... I love to think of the early days with him on logging and camping trips, when he was so different to me than he was towards the end." His relations with Harold had been governed by two contradictory attitudes. First, from early days, Alex had been angry about the hardships which his mother had to undergo, the jobs she had to take, in order to keep his sisters and herself housed and fed – and ultimately this anger was directed at Harold. Paradoxically, he made every allowance for his father, refused to blame him for his lack of money, for losing jobs, for failing to make a go of things. He constantly encouraged him to stick with jobs, find new ones, be optimistic – in Alex's eyes the culprit was always his father's wretched luck.

Thus in January 1934, when he was still nineteen, it was his anger about his mother's and sisters' situation which made him intercept Harold in Vancouver, jobless and on the way back to Victoria from the Cariboo, to persuade him to stay away and not be another mouth for Agnes to feed. In doing so he was willingly carrying out the instructions of his mother, for whom Harold's recent lack of financial support had been the last straw. Alex explained to him that it wasn't only the money question – she wanted a break from him. At the same time, he argued Harold's case with Agnes – "Dad seems to have done everything in his power to keep above water, but fate or something has decreed otherwise ... It isn't possible for you to put up with it until the beginning of March?"

Harold's disarming charm made him a difficult person from whom to make a final break. He would arrive home with no money, but with something else which brought a lump to the throat. Once it was a gold nugget, which he pressed upon June. Another time it was a beautiful wooden cradle, no longer a useful item, but something into which he had poured hours of winter loneliness. In spite of Agnes's intentions, she and Harold managed occasionally to coexist until 1938. During the summers Harold found jobs but returned to Victoria, unemployed, in winter. Alex wrote to him from time to time and received replies, though they were both just going through the motions. However, as Agnes, who was determined not to go on relief, continued to accept low-paying jobs to maintain a decent home for her daughters, Alex became angrier and more indignant about her situation and less willing to seek reasons to support his father. For a proud man with little confidence, the knowledge that he could never please his family led him, in September 1938, to go and live with his sister Floss in Alberta. Alex offered him money to stay there and this must have further eroded his relationship with his father.

By that time Harold was ill: at fifty-eight he had the blood cell count of a man of seventy. In April 1939 he was in hospital and, once back on his feet, was employed by the hospital as an orderly. A year later he became ill again and died in August. Although his father's behaviour had made him angry, when it was all over Alex did not blame him; he preferred to remember the good times. But Harold's influence on him had been enormous. For Alex, his father's life was a cautionary tale. The example prevented him from marrying until quite late, until he was certain that he had the income and the control of his own destiny to take on the responsibility for a family of his own. And it enabled him to find good in everybody. It was quite a legacy.

The constant demands of wartime flying meant that none of the pilots of 205 Squadron spent long periods in Seletar. Alex, with his loathing of inactivity, was keen to fly anywhere, anytime and was always happy in the air or when living in informal surroundings. He had his chance for both these things on a trip through British north Borneo in October 1940. After a refuelling stop at Kudat the business of the trip began in Brunei where he and Norman were to attend the investiture of the sultan as Knight Commander of the Order of Saint Michael and Saint George, or KCMG. The actual investiture was done by a Foreign Office diplomat; by such flattery an overextended Britain managed to keep a tenuous grip on the loyalty of its empire. Alex and Norman and their Singapore III were present to symbolise British protection for the new Knight, a protection reinforced by precious little else. It was part of the huge gamble that the Japanese would not actually try to blow the house down.

After the ceremony there was a reception; perspiring in sticky uniforms, they toyed with inedible food. Then they climbed the palace stairs to admire the sultan's wealth and presents. Alex was impressed, on the one hand, by the tawdriness and, on the other, by the squandering of such wealth on useless trinkets – bejewelled boxes, swords and the like. It was a relief to leave Brunei, to work their way northeast along the coast to Labuan, then on to Jesselton and Kudat. In each place an RAF flying-boat moorage, previously established by the squadron or by the Navy, enabled them to visit at will. In each place, by their visit, they showed the flag, projecting power as Admiral Wylie East had done. Practically, they checked and improved arrangements for refuelling and minor repairs. More pleasantly, they visited scattered and tiny British communities. All sorts of entertainments came their way. In Kudat, for example, they were offered ponies to ride. Though tiny these ponies galloped like the wind; Alex reported that they "definitely put the wind up me; however, we arrived back safely, certainly hot, and rather sore behind." The final leg was southeast from Kudat to Sandakan. Here he and Norman stayed in the palatial residence of the Governor of Sabah. Alex's bedroom was so large that he kept losing his clothes. In spite of such surroundings they dined convivially, meeting Agnes Keith whose book about Sandakan, *Land below the Wind,* Alex had enjoyed. The place was later to have sinister significance for 205 Squadron, but in 1940 it was just their departure point for Seletar after three weeks away.

Back in Europe Britain was fighting for her very existence so there was little to spare for a part of the world not threatened by Germany or Italy. From letters Alex received from London, in which the writers made light of the nightly German raids of the Blitz, it was clear why there was no movement on the squadron's new aircraft. They would just have to make the best of what they had and, within a fortnight, Alex and Norman and their crew were once again headed for Borneo. We are fortunate to have Alex's notes on the outbound trip, made at the time. What is clear from his laconic description is the flying skill he had developed. Conditions which would terrify all but the very bravest did not seem to him extraordinary – were, in fact, all in the day's work. He shows the steadiness which was always commented upon by those who saw him on operations. His only unmeasured language is reserved for the foolish and the lazy, neither of whom he tolerated gladly.

"3rd November 1940:
Airborne at Seletar after takeoff with Pinnace and Powerboat. Unable to see green light from Pinnace so took OK from S/L in the PB [flying boat] alongside. A clear but horribly dark night. Fortunately stars were out so we were able to see which way up the a/c was flying. Occasional clouds at 3,000 ft. Not very bumpy. At dawn about 0545 all kinds of 'weather' about. Landfall St Pierre @ 2243. Arrived Kuching [SW Sarawak] under low cloud at 500 ft., 2400.
"4th November:
Of course! no petrol and we're in a hurry. Ashore to meet the S. D. O., Parker. [Colonial Office District Officer, the local dictator!] Fuel arrived about 0845 LT. More fun and games trying to get lighter alongside. Bloody place & nitwits! 915 gals. Airborne after takeoff 72 seconds 0249. Across the bay heavy and low cloud. @ 500 ft. across the land into more rain & cloud. Weather cleared at the coast for a moment. Then it cleared finally at 0430. Half an hour before Kudat 0750 violent rain & lightning cloud right down to the water. Visibility nil. Unable to proceed through as the coast was 5 minutes away with mountains to greet us. Turned parallel to coast & flew for 10 minutes when it cleared to North. Sighted Mantanani islands. Continued flying about 030 degrees. Finally, just 10 miles before Kudat, it cleared

beautifully though the bumps were very severe. Gliding down with engines throttled back we were thrown up 1,000 ft. on two occasions. 0825 Alighted Kudat [N. tip of Sabah] in fine weather."

A few days after this trip he was assigned once more the sort of task for which he was uniquely suited, being both democratic and practical. The job was to set up a second base for patrolling flying boats in the Nicobar Islands, tiny patches of tropical paradise in the Bay of Bengal. He had established a similar base the previous November at Nancowry Island. Although machines gave him plenty of trouble, this interlude of 'messing about in boats' was as good as a camping holiday for him. LAC Newman, a South African and sometime member of his crew, later paid tribute to Alex's skill and enthusiasm on patrols into the tropical wilderness. Often they had landed at small islands where he displayed a love of woodcraft and scouting and had shown his crew how to shift for themselves in the wilds. He loved every minute of the escape from routine and we know that he did an exceptional job because, for this and other similar jobs in the Indian Ocean in 1941, he was to be awarded the Air Force Cross (AFC), in the New Year's Honours List of January 1942. What follows are diary entries he made at the time; among other things, they illustrate the difficulty of living and working in such a climate and the calm with which he faced each problem.

"Monday, 18th November 1940: At Camorta Island. [Nicobar Islands]
At 0700 hrs GMT the following persons left the RAFA *Ann* and moved into the 'Other Ranks Hut' on Camorta Island:
F/Lt A. M. Jardine; D. Moore Esq, WD; P/Sgt Webb; Sgt Roberts, Armourer; Sgt Griffin, Sgt Fitt AG; Sgt Conley, F/Rigger AG; Sgt Williamson, WEM AG; LAC Rogers, F/Mech; LAC Brooks, W/T Opp.
"We disembarked from the local Doctor's launch & carried our personal belongings up to the Hut, some 600 yards of very muddy pathway. Throughout the morning and early afternoon there were frequent rainstorms, so that by late afternoon, due to many trips being made by natives and ourselves, the pathway was so slippery it could hardly be used. To ensure sufficient drinking water in the first few days, 7 buckets were filled with water from the *Ann* before she left.
"The Hut was barely fit to live in. One small room at the west end had loose boarding for the floor. The rest, some 75 feet, was mud. The small room we made the sleeping quarters. Camp beds &

Airmens' Biscuit Bedding with new sheets akin to canvas, & the Pillow a bag, I feel sure, filled with shavings and a rather coarse brand of canvas. The refrigerators ready for our foodstuffs and stores were placed on the north side of the building; eating tables and chairs in the centre. So far, that is for two days, the wind has been blowing steadily from the south and the downdraft from the open part of the walls is causing difficulty with the stoves (2) and refrigerators (2), all paraffin burning.

"Until tea time we attempted to achieve a little order in what seemed complete chaos. After tea the two W/Os, Griffin and self down to the jetty to go off to the aircraft in the outboard. Half an hour later decide to row the very long mile as the engine would not function. We borrowed the only and heaviest of rowing boats and with three oars arrived about 10 minutes late for the W/T [radio] watch. A long message from RAF Far East HQ [HQFE] imposing 5 watches now instead of the three I had hoped would be sufficient. One at 3:00 a.m. seems unnecessary & one at 3:00 p.m., and all we have is this decidedly temperamental outboard. The row back in darkness could have been most enjoyable!

"After arriving back at the jetty we collected a native from the Doctor's hospital with a lantern, who led the way back to the Hut. Our first meal was ready; Sgts Conley and Rogers were cooks. The menu: Tomato soup, salmon, all messy, and meatloaf with a taste, or rather no taste, of nothing. Wishy-washy potatoes and diced beetroot. Sweet was a mouthful of fig pudding. The food position is peculiar. All Army or RAF emergency rations. Decidedly *government.* The salmon is the cheapest procurable, likewise the spuds and vegs (Turnips and Carrots), Corned beef and tins and tins of pineapple cubes. Fortunately "G" [the identifying letter of another Singapore III] left behind some of the more eatable tinned foods & I managed a few bottles of sauce and one 'other' kind of jam from the *Ann.* The ration jam is Melon and Lemon.

"After dinner Sgt Roberts and self down to jetty with Sgt Williamson who is doing the night watch. Again no luck. The *Pearleaf* launch came alongside so the W/Op [radio operator] away in that. We continued with the outboard, finally gave up and came back. All turned in by 2200. Today threatened to be an anticlimax after a really hard week. We have all turned to at 0600 every day and knocked off at sundown. The work of building, carrying stores & cases up from the jetty, off-loading and loading 250 lb bombs, refuelling 64 gal drums from the *Pearleaf* has been real navvy work and especially trying in this climate. The airmen have all worked like heroes – granted they had no choice! We are most unfortunate in not having *Margay*, the powerboat from *Ann*, but then again luck has been with us in several ways. HMS *Durban* lent us 48 seamen on Friday last, to help carry the stores; they were a godsend – a beer to each man after the work was done. On the Saturday, a further 25 came off for 2 hours, and with the help of the Nicobarese finished the job. More beer for the seamen, but it was worth it. I can't think how long it would have taken us to get it all here from the jetty, especially as "G" left on Sunday morning. When the *Ann* left, all the coolies and the Chinese carpenters remained on board; wild horses would not keep them here. There is help from 10 Nicobarese, but its awfully uncertain. They love to just sit and watch. One really needs to show them exactly what's wanted by doing the job oneself; that rapidly palls as the day wears on, in addition to being very tiring.

    "Tuesday, November 19th, 1940:
Turned to after breakfast at about 0815. Sgt Roberts, LAC Brooks & self to get the outboard going if possible. Sgts Webb & Griffin down also. We left the outboard on the Hospital verandah overnight and the morning sun must have dried it up, as it started with hardly any trouble. Off to the aircraft for DIs [detachment instructions] and the 0850 W/T watch. Collected Sgts Conley & Rogers after their culinary duties. Sgt Williamson returned by Catamaran from the F/B earlier, this being much easier than trying to get over to him by outboard and saves the extra trip. Taxied the aircraft 1000; all okay. Back to the pier and now to get the Stuart Turner charging unit going, another obstinate piece of machinery. Everyone employed either on the engine or cleaning up around the house. Water pumps also a trifle obstinate. In the afternoon odd jobs, rather more of a standoff, though more attempts to start the Stuart Turner & the W/T watches to do. Conley, Rogers cooking. Lunch was Corned Beef, Potatoes, Turnip and Pineapple & always Tea. The Outboard was ok for both afternoon watches, though a trifle uncertain on the last trip. So arranged for a Catamaran for the night watch. All ended okay. Sgts Webb & Roberts cooks for dinner. HMIS [HM Indian Ship] *Parvati* arrived 1900.

    "Wednesday, November 20, 1940:
Turned to & breakfast over by 0800. Down to the outboard and Stuart Turner. Outboard went after much persuasion. ST still very

'dicky'. Morning W/T watch nothing for us. Gave the Varley refuelling pump a run. Started raining very heavily. At 1030 off to the *Capetown, Cricket* and *Pearleaf* in an attempt to obtain ice and oddments. *Pearleaf* moved off almost immediately so unable to see them about our requirements. Tiffin aboard HMIS *Parvati* which is here to erect a W/T station for the Indian Gov't. Rain continues and our pathway is once again very muddy. The outboard did not function in the afternoon. After tea Sgt Roberts attempted to make it go. They got as far as the a/c when it refused to function so as the rain was particularly heavy decided to remain on the a/c. Everything is wet and muddy. Supper: Waugh and I did a concoction of various kinds, finishing off with a jam pancake. Early bed for all hands. Little work could be done today as the odd jobs required working outside which was impossible in the rain.

"Friday 22nd:
Turned out at 0630. Breakfast over and the sun is shining. We looked forward to a long day of sun. 0900 down to the *Parvati* to get the chronometer checked. Brooks came off to say he had received part of messages, then the accumulator went down completely. Sent a signal to *Pearleaf*, asking if they will charge one of our batteries. They replied yes. Sent the battery off later. 1000 Williamson, Griffin, Brooks and self off to the a/c in a rowing boat. Against the tide it took us half an hour. Got through to base about 1200 & received check and repeat messages. Started raining again. 1300 back ashore in the Steam Launch. Rain continued throughout the afternoon. At 1200 I cancelled the afternoon W/T watch as transport was very difficult and arranged for the Steam Launch at 5:30 p.m. for the night watches. At about 6:30 p.m. the Chief Officer and 2nd Engineer of *Pearleaf* arrived with wine and potatoes & took some flour away to have bread made. The Doctor also sent up 3 chickens which will make a nice change for tomorrow. Most of the day spent in odd jobs about the Hut.

Saturday 23rd:
Turned out; breakfast over by 0815. General cleanup around and in the Hut. Afterwards collecting window frames for the mosquito netting and preparing the wire for the frames. Sgt Williamson remained on board until 1230. W/T watch has been altered to that time. The Doctor brought in 3 Pomelos. So far that is the only fresh fruit I have been able to persuade out of the islands. Each day I go through a little talk with the Doctor, saying that we will take any fresh

food the natives care to bring along. Sent off 6 buckets for fresh water from the *Parvati*. The water in the well is decidedly cloudy still and prefer to use the water from ships as long as they are here. At 5:00 p.m. the *Pearleaf* sent her launch off after *Capetown* was alongside her for a bath party. 4 of us enjoyed a long & hot bath. Away by 7:15 p.m. with Bread & meat extract. More work. Chicken for lunch and chicken broth for supper.

"Sunday 24th:

Turned out for late breakfast. Stand off today. The weather is fine and sunny and remained so throughout the morning. Washing clothes most of the morning. The Doctor has sent a Nicobarese as a 'Boy' to clean up. He started work today; goes by the name of Waiyal. After lunch Waugh and I went on a tour of inspection north of here. At 2:30 p.m. it started raining and continued until 6:00 p.m. 6:00 p.m. Captain Jones of *Pearleaf* invited Waugh and self for dinner. Back about 10:30 p.m.

"Monday 25th:

Turned to at 0745 and down to the jetty. Off in the Steam Launch at 0815 to the aircraft. Left moorings at 0900; slight rains, however attempted photography but unable to get good photo as the rain continued until about 1200. 2:00 p.m. fitting wire netting to the window frames. Knocked off at 4:00 p.m. Waugh and I bathed, very good too. Our day for the cooks' duties. The job is not nearly so unpleasant now, with the washing up being done by the native. Captain Jones called at 5:00 p.m.

Tuesday 26th:

Turned to at 8:00 a.m. and down to the Pier. One more attempt at the Outboard; still no good. Off to the aircraft to carry out various jobs. HMS *Durban* arrived at 7:00 a.m. Her Motor Launch came to the pier and fortunately towed us to the aircraft, saving an hour. Sent off signal for Stuart Turner spares. Three natives rowed me back at 0930. *Pearleaf* took off 5 water buckets and returned same with drinking water and a loaf of bread. 1230 Airmen returned from aircraft. 2:00 p.m. down to the outboard and Stuart Turner for another attempt. ST ok but outboard not. Remainder at mosquito netting on frames. No rain today, the first day for some time. Swimming in the evening. The Doctor sent up two cabbages from a trader (first fresh veg). In the evening Waugh on painting notice boards, self on painting the Visitor Box. HMS *Durban* & *Pearleaf* left at 1:30 p.m.

"Wednesday 27th:

Turned to at 0800 and finished off the mosquito netting on all doors
and windows for the building. HMIS *Parvati* left. Once again we are
the sole defenders of the harbour! The afternoon an easy one for the
Airmen as tomorrow will be a long and no doubt hard day. Doing
several odd jobs about the place which seem to take one's time up and
show little or nothing for the effort. A fresh fish was brought in by a
native; this we had for supper and was enjoyed by everyone. Tried the
well-water today. After boiling and treating, quite pleasant and a lot of
the sediment had settled, making it quite clear.

"Thursday 28th:

0730 turned to. Cleaning up around the Hut. 0900 off to the jetty
and across by Steam Launch to the aircraft. Then to the Fuel Dump
where we loaded up the 2 sampans with 9 drums. Had just completed
the job when "K" arrived with F/Lt Hallet & Sgt Lym; also reliefs for
Sgts Roberts & Brooks. The aircraft was loaded up with fresh food, for
which I am indeed thankful. Commenced refuelling at 1200 approx.
The petrol was filthy and frequent changes of chamois leather was the
only way to get any fuel into the a/c. Knocked off at 1:30 with 7
drums in. All ashore for lunch. Waugh had prepared a mighty stew of
all the meats and veg we had. It went down very well. 3:00 p.m.
turned to again to finish the refuelling. H. Hallet & self to check all
the stores for handing over. This took us till nearly 6:00 p.m., what
with the odds and ends of things he required to know. Quite dark
now. The Airmen arrived back, fuelling completed & bombs off "L"
[Alex's aircraft].

"25/11/40, RT message to "L" from 205 Sqdn:

'Relief arriving about 1300LT 28 Nov. HQFE will arrange for you
to keep interception watch. You leave a.m. 29th after handing over.
Go Penang then Seletar if can arrive in daylight. Your fuel ordered
Penang 1200LT 29th. Important'."

For the rest of 1940 and until the middle of February 1941 Alex was hardly in
Seletar; most of this time he was based in Glugor, Penang, occupied with patrolling
in the Bay of Bengal from the Nicobar forward bases. The job was routine and not
nearly as enjoyable as that of actually setting up the bases. He had spent enough
time in Penang for his circle of acquaintances to have become nearly as large as in
Singapore. Among those people was the family of Captain Fraser, whose wife and
daughter he had met on the *Viceroy of India* in September.

In spite of himself he renewed his acquaintance with Iona. A biographer might be excused for suspecting Alex of not sailing quite such a straight course as he proclaimed! His mother had been applying pressure on him to get married, as had friends in Singapore, especially Gordon and Beryl Stilling, recently wed with Alex as best man. "One of these days I shall marry just to keep people here quiet," he threatened. He went on to talk about Iona; "I met her and her mother on the *Viceroy of India* in September last." Although she approached his ideal for a wife, "I don't think she is *the* one, in fact almost certain she isn't!" (Why does Alex mention this if marriage was not lurking somewhere in his head?)

He made several excursions with Iona, including a walk to the top of the 2,600-foot Penang hill, where he had taken Leslie Kealley. After the hike he dined at the Frasers' house. Maybe Iona consented to such a venture in a tropical climate because she too was wondering whether Alex was *the* one. A mountain would give him an opportunity to propose. However, the question does not appear to have been put. Alex left Penang soon after and Iona does not reappear in his letters. But it seems as if he was thinking about Iona as a possible wife, if only briefly – why else the trial balloon to his mother?

In the 1990s Alex no longer remembers the incident: "Her name does not ring a bell in my mind." He believes that he may have had vague (!) intentions of proposing to her "but at that time in my life I was more concerned with flying and staying single!" And possibly of telling his mother the kind of stories that she obviously wanted to hear! If so, he soon hardened his resolve. A month later, in March 1941, he made it quite plain that he wanted no truck with marriage for the foreseeable future. He had offered Agnes money from his salary, and she was reluctant to take it, suggesting that he save it so that he could marry. He replied forcefully: "I'm afraid it is not in my nature to save money for the day when I'm likely to get married – because its a rather topsy-turvy world at the moment and I can't bring myself to worry about the future ... I still haven't met her and I hope when I do the whole world knows."

Writing home in wartime was frustrating, especially for such a frequent letter writer. Because of censorship he could say little about what he was doing. For example, he had not been able to tell his mother that he had been in the Nicobar Islands, nor why; and when he was in Penang or Ceylon all Agnes knew was that he was temporarily away from Seletar and Singapore. However, his letters of the 7th of March and the 12th of April 1941 were from Manila in the Philippines, a city he had last visited in 1931 on board the *Canada*. What he talked about in those letters was his excitement at finding a lunch counter where he could sit on a high stool and eat apple pie and ice cream. He was thrilled: "It tasted almost like I remember it in the Honey Dew or the White Lunch.* Are they still going?" Here was a

---

*in Vancouver, B.C.

Canadian whose homesickness was triggered by an American drugstore! What he could not tell her was that he and fellow pilots were visiting Cavite US naval air station to pick up PBY Consolidated Catalinas, up-to-date reconnaissance flying boats, which would greatly increase the range and usefulness of his squadron. With no Sunderlands in sight it was the Lend-lease programme to the rescue! While the RAF sold their Singapore IIIs to the Royal New Zealand Air Force (RNZAF), 205's new aircraft were to change the squadron's way of life, pushing pilots into more demanding flying situations which would take a toll of both men and machines.

The Catalina was greatly superior to the Singapore III. To start with, it was a monoplane, which brought it up-to-date. It was smaller and faster, with four times the range, at 4,000 miles. Its cruising speed was only 120 knots, faster than the Singapore but not by very much. Fuel capacity was 1,407 imperial gallons and the aircraft could be throttled back to a cruising consumption of only 56 gallons an hour – she could fly forever! Operationally it was not normally flown further than daylight would allow because reconnaissance was impossible in the dark and they had night-landing flarepaths only at Seletar. But this range gave 205 Squadron the ability to patrol the whole Indian Ocean as well as the South China Sea, greatly increasing the squadron's usefulness. And it was better able to defend itself in spite of RAF economies in defensive armament. It carried two Vickers .303 machine guns in the blister pods on the sides of the fuselage, a Lewis gun in the bow and another under the tail. Catalinas flown by the Dutch and Americans carried .50 calibre Browning machine guns, packing a bigger punch at longer range, while the Dutch Dornier flying boats were even better protected with 20 mm cannon. This was to prove a costly economy for RAF crews, as they would discover.

Because Alex's logbook was with squadron baggage lost at sea on the 6th of February 1942, it is difficult to be precise about the flying that he did. For the pre-war period his letters describe the sort of flying he was doing – such as bombing practice, air firing or antisubmarine patrols – but we have to guess about the frequency and duration of his flights. Details on most of his wartime flying have to be extracted from his letters or from contraband notes that he made at the time, like his description of the November 1940 Kudat trip. Norman Birks provided a general summary of the flying that Alex did with him as second pilot. However, his operational flights after the 25th of September 1941 are included in second pilot F/Lt Rob McVicker's logbook. Fortunately, Alex obtained a copy of this after the war to re-establish his own record of flying time – as significant for a pilot as the number of antler points are for a stag!

To compare his flying hours on the two types of aircraft gives some idea of the change to Alex's life brought about by the arrival of the Catalinas. Between mid-1937, when he arrived off *Rawalpindi*, and April 1941, Alex flew an estimated 700 hours on Singapore IIIs – approximately 200 hours a year. Flying Catalinas in the ten months between April 1941 and February 1942, Alex logged 835 hours – about 950 hours a year. Thanks to the greater operational potential of the Catalina, he was flying between four and five times as much! Many of these 1941 hours were flown over the Indian Ocean; Alex was leading a 205 Squadron detachment in pioneering new air links between British outposts, previously accessible only by ship.

In May 1941 Agnes received from him a telegram of two words: "Squadron Leader". The promotion meant more responsibility, more money and that he continued to be well regarded. To have made Squadron Leader in four years was fast promotion. Maybe Major Mayo had been right about the escalator. However, in spite of such good news, privately he was not very happy. He projected steadiness, unflappability, good humour – and was always friendly and thoughtful. But airmen in his crew might have been surprised to know that he would write: "This is definitely a crazy world, or else I am. As a matter of fact, there are times when I doubt *my* sanity. I have a perfect alibi, and that is being out here 4 bloody long years. I *could* go mental any day and no-one would be in the least surprised!" His frustration was never far below the surface. He felt trapped, doing something he would rather not do – fighting a war against an enemy who never appeared – and being powerless to stop doing it.

In May 1941 he asked to be transferred out of Far East command but his request was refused. He was needed in Singapore, as second-in-command of 205 Squadron and its senior pilot, since W/C Councell did not fly Catalinas. To Agnes he vented his frustration: "You voice my very thoughts when you mentioned that at times you would like to kick everyone and everything. I'm sure I shall, one day, just to see what it is like." Then his stoic self regained control: "However one must hang on," he went on. "I daren't think about all I want to happen – simply cannot. But I think and hope and pray for nothing else." Mountjoy must have said the same from his coal-pile.

On the 1st of May 1941, once pilots and crews were familiar with the new aircraft, Alex led a 205 Squadron detachment to set up a base at Koggala Lake, near Colombo, Ceylon. From that base, over the next two months, they started regular patrols over the Indian Ocean. They used moorages established by the Navy and the RAF auxiliary ship *Ann* at Addu atoll in the Maldive Islands and Sultan Island in the Laccadives, Diego Garcia in the Chagos Archipelago, at Victoria in the Seychelles and at Port Louis, Mauritius. They actually added the Indian Ocean to the RAF map and made Hitler's world smaller, by patrolling previous areas of sanctuary for German ships and submarines. Operating in the Indian Ocean was difficult and dangerous. First of all, refuelling at Koggala and the other new bases was lengthy and exhausting, as fuel was brought in and stored in 5-gallon cans. Furthermore, takeoffs had to be made before dawn. Such a takeoff was always tense and dangerous. As Alex described it:

> "Adrenal glands came into operation! One grabbed the two throttles over to one's right and pushed them hard forward, with the Second Pilot following with his hand; the First Pilot needed both hands on the 'yoke', as the Yanks termed the control stick – and it was a proper description! With both engines roaring, the heavily loaded aeroplane would struggle to get on the step; in anything like rough [weather] the windscreen would be enveloped in water." [The blinded pilot had to rely on his turn-and-bank indicator to keep to something like a straight line.] "We used 5-gallon drums with lights secured on poles to give us the wind direction for takeoff. Nearly all our takeoffs were at night, so that we could land at the Attols in daylight. There were no night landing facilities at the lagoons we flew to."

Sometime in May 1941, the arrival of Alex and his crew on the first aircraft ever to visit Mauritius was treated as a tremendous occasion. They were lionised – a not-unpleasant experience. The governor's American wife not only took a proprietorial interest in the aircraft but also organised a ball for the heroic flyers. At the ball, in one of the remotest spots on earth, Alex met and fell in love with Meg Ireland, the girl of his dreams! Apart from his original feelings for Daphne and those for his future wife, this was the only occasion when he admitted to this common human condition. They had a few days of whirlwind romance before Alex had to fly away. He could not be sure that he would return.

By the 9th of July he was back at Seletar. Two weeks later he received news of the squadron's first crash: on the 23rd, Canada Young, Terry Grieve and their whole crew were killed in an accident during a pre-dawn takeoff from the Seychelles. The crash brought them face-to-face with the danger of wartime military flying in a way that gentler experiences in Singapore IIIs had never done. In view of their extended responsibilities and dangers, it was likely that other deaths would follow, with or without enemy activity.

In spite of Alex's Mauritian love affair – or maybe because of it – Canada Young's accident firmed up Alex's resolve to stay single for the time being. It may also not be a coincidence that he spent his August evenings reading the *Letters of T. E. Lawrence*, a dead hero he had long admired and with whom, in his own self-imposed bachelorhood, he felt kinship. He recommended the *Letters* to Agnes when he wrote on the 1st of September, adding that "the impression in my mind will always remain." He went on, just months after falling in love with Meg: "I refuse the responsibility of a wife, with all its wonderfulness, unless she can be self-supporting – I mean with money of her own – so that she can, if she wish, beat it, leave me out of her plans. Then neither of us would feel that we were letting the other down. After this show I want to be responsible to no-one for my actions – at any rate to give that sort of thing a try."

In spite of long hours in the air he had found his Indian Ocean experiences exhilarating – "some of the most interesting work yet" as he stated obliquely for the censor. But he had been working hard and it showed. In September he was ordered to take some leave and spent two weeks at the Green Cow Tavern, playing golf at 5,500 feet in the Malayan highlands. He slipped down to Ipoh, for a couple of days with Topsy and her husband and child. Topsy was as full of life as ever – and joked that Alex only came to see her when she was pregnant – which she was once more. For two days it was like old times and he had fun playing with their child. Back in Singapore – from one old flame to another – Alex went sailing with Barbara Murray. She needed comforting as her army fiancé was a POW in Italy. They had an unexpected adventure and had to dive over the side when their becalmed sailboat capsized under tow. Barbara was okay but Alex became tangled in the mast stays and had a close call. One wonders who comforted whom!

Alex had no time to concern himself with minor injuries as there was news from Koggala that the Indian Ocean had claimed its second Catalina. On the 20th of September, flying out of Diego Garcia, FVS and FVY, in conjunction with three Royal Navy ships, had carried out a day-long search for a Vichy French convoy. FVY, unable to locate Diego Garcia on her return, had landed on the sea at dusk. The weather was stormy and the aircraft broke up and sank. There had been no survivors – Flying Officer 'Bernard' Shaw, Sergeant Thomas and a crew of six airmen were missing, presumed drowned. A replacement boat would have to go to Koggala and Alex would be flying it. As Norman was in Australia on sick leave, suffering from prickly heat, his second pilot was Rob McVicker. Before their departure on the 21st of September, Alex was the toast of the mess at a farewell dinner. The recent thinning of the ranks heightened the emotion of the occasion for the senior pilots, the surviving band of 'brothers', and Gordon Stilling jokingly called them the 'ten little niggers'*, of whom three were now gone. Alex wrote in a letter home that it was "the first time I've had to make a reply to a toast and have

---

*Title of an unpleasant but popular 1869 nursery rhyme by Frank Green; also of a best-seller whodunit by Agatha Christie, published by Collins (London) in 1939, which she adapted as a play in 1943. Both book and play are now entitled *And Then There Were None*. Apart from the racism inherent in any empire (enormous!) the term 'nigger' was value-free.

people singing 'Jolly Good Fellow' stuff. Made me feel very bucked and the world a rather good place to be in and a lot of very nice people about."

The trip for Catalina FVX to the 205 Squadron base at Koggala Lake in Ceylon started on the 25th of September, overnighting at Nancowry in the Nicobar Islands in the Bay of Bengal. They remained at Koggala for nearly two weeks, carrying visiting VIPs to and from the island air bases of Addu and Sultan. On the 8th of October they set off for a job in Mauritius, 2,500 miles to the south-south-west, planning to stop overnight at Diego Garcia in the Chagos Archipelago.

A look at the map gives some idea of the danger involved in this trip. There was little hope of rescue should they have to ditch; Bernard Shaw had demonstrated that. But Alex's ability to detach himself from disaster allowed him to exude a 'business as usual' confidence. They followed their established practice, taking off from Koggala before dawn. Once airborne they could relax and climb to their cruising altitude. As the sun rose they were heading on a bearing of 200 degrees over the vast sapphire emptiness of the Indian Ocean, with an emergency landfall possible at Addu after four hours. Otherwise they had only the specks of the Chagos to aim for, a full ten hours' flying away, well beyond their point of no return – defined by the hours of daylight remaining rather than the 4,000-mile range of the Catalina. "Diego Garcia, our first destination, was a gem of a lagoon, occupied by a chap who was responsible for delivering copra and coconuts. Also living on the island there was a man and his wife who had some sort of a job involving wireless communication. If I remember correctly he was of little use to us as he did not have our aircraft radio frequencies."

Next day they took off for another flight into the blue, with Mauritius itself the first landfall after eleven hours. This time they took off two hours before dawn, according to McVicker's logbook. Amelia Earhart had missed Howland Island, FVY had missed he Chagos Islands; if they missed Mauritius, their next landfall was Antarctica! It was an ultimate test of navigation, a flight to be undertaken only by the most competent. Alex made no mistake; eleven hours later, after a slow circle of the harbour to ascertain wind direction, they alighted at Saint Louis without incident.

Once in Mauritius there was work to be done. A Vichy French convoy was in the Indian Ocean, probably headed for Indochina. On four of the next six days Alex and crew were flying, spending nearly ten hours airborne each day. The log reads "patrol for Vichy French convoy" but Alex remembers nothing of the convoy. The patrols were uneventful, apart from foul weather, which kept them grounded on two of the six days. Although they searched a wide area they found no Vichy ships.

On the 18th their orders were to remain in Mauritius for the time being. They spent the next week among the palms and the sugar cane awaiting orders. For Alex those were bittersweet days. Here he was, on a tropical island with Meg, with whom, in an ideal world, he could imagine sharing his life. His heart was bursting but his head, as always, was in control. "Perhaps, if she had not lived so far away, perhaps because I was not keen to marry ..." He trails off. He had met the right girl in the wrong place and at the wrong time. They were but flies upon the wheel. Come what may he would not see Mauritius again. HQFE had promised him that once this trip was over, he would remain at Seletar until his imminent posting to Britain – via Victoria, BC!

Orders finally arrived, the wheel began to turn and the spell was broken. At dawn the following day FVX was already hundreds of miles north of Port Louis, en route for a job in the Seychelles. This involved an eleven-hour flight almost due north. The crew were becoming accustomed to the vastness of the Indian Ocean but the flight was as difficult a feat of navigation as previous ones, with the same attendant dangers. Once they had arrived they spent two hours next day taking aerial photographs of the islands for the local military, using the aircraft's reconnaissance camera. Those must have been among the most expensive air photos ever taken, for there followed a relaxing nine days on the Seychelles for McVicker and the crew, doing as little as possible, enjoying their escape from Seletar while once again awaiting orders. For Alex they were days of constantly seeking distraction or jobs to keep himself busy. He really did not want time to think.

Next came a brief African interlude. On the 4th of November, they were ordered to Mombasa, Kenya. It meant a ten-hour flight due west, but at least there was no danger of missing this landfall. In the next few days they flew south to Dar es Salaam, then to Lindi, both in Tanganyika. There, orders came to return to Seletar. Bad weather in the northern Indian Ocean kept them in the Seychelles for five days, waiting for it to clear. On one of those days they attempted to fly to their next stage in Diego Garcia but were ordered to return when only two hours short of the Chagos. Once the weather cleared and they were able to proceed, FVX retraced its route to Koggala, Ceylon.

On the flight from there to Nancowry, "about two hours out from Koggala we ran into a severe line squall. Line squalls reach up to great heights, always, it seemed to me, 'boiling' upwards from the sea surface. I decided we would be best at altitude, not relishing the idea of being thrown about near the surface of the ocean. We were thrown about in the most frightening manner; with no hope of being able to 'fly' the aircraft, I was just struggling to maintain what I hoped to be normal flight position. Instruments were quite hopeless – turn-and-bank indicators, artificial horizon, airspeed indicator, all simply out of whack! I have no idea how long we were in the storm; it was most unpleasant and unnerving but I am here to tell the tale! We eventually came out of it, in a not too steep angle glide".

They landed that day at Nancowry, eventually reaching Seletar on the 20th of November. As they were approaching it was reasonable for Alex to anticipate spending a week or two around the base in Seletar – then glorious release, the promised posting back to Britain with a stopover for overdue leave in Victoria. Only one thing could stop him now: he exhorted his mother to "pray God the Japanese don't put the kibosh on it!" As events unfolded, all of FVX's crew must have been grateful for their 'great swan' around the Indian Ocean before their world went mad: they had returned to a Singapore abuzz with rumours of a planned Japanese attack on Malaya.

The subject of the Japanese cropped up now and again in Alex's letters. His dislike for them, as explained in the previous chapter, increased with every month that he spent in the Far East. The Japanese he had known in BC as a boy had been fishermen. They had kept to themselves and had seemed no threat to anybody, although people at Toquart disliked them because they would work for a pittance. He remembered the *Mikado,* which he had seen with Barbara the previous summer, and chuckled to himself. Along with everybody else, he had no respect for Japan as a power, and absolutely no concern about their war machine. The word in RAF messes, based on a complete lack of accurate military intelligence, was that Japanese aircraft were small, old and slow. Like the rest of the Caucasian world, and in spite of his knowledge of the devastation in Shanghai, he was not aware of the degree to which Japan had been militarised by the events of the 1930s. He knew nothing of the Japanese battles with the Russians in 1938 and 1940, in which, while losing ground to Russian tanks, they had managed to defeat the Russian air force.

The fact that Japan had been attempting to conquer China on and off since 1931 did not seem evidence of Japanese military competence – rather the reverse. Everybody knew that the Chinese could not defend themselves! Alex remembered Shanghai – a colonial city like Hong Kong, only grubbier. He had walked through the park by the Bund with its famous notice: "No Dogs or Chinese Allowed!" If the Chinese could defend themselves why were there British police in Shanghai and British and American warships on the Yangtze Kiang? No, if Japan could not defeat the Chinese, there was no cause for Britain or the U.S.A. to be worried about them.

On the 18th of February 1941 Alex had commented to Agnes: "Japan *does* seem to be making herself a nuisance one way and another. I can't believe that she will be so foolish as to do something drastic in this part of the world. She'll end nowhere, and surely must be able to see that, though how incredibly blind people are at times." Three weeks later he brought up the subject again: "The Japs seem to be continuing their little hate against Britain. I do wonder how far they will go, the nasty so-and-sos. Certainly there is one thing not to be worried about; we have a very nice little reception all ready for them, a lovely one." Knowing what we know about the British state of readiness in the Far East, the only explanation for this confidence has to be a very low regard for the military ability of the Japanese.

Nevertheless, soon after Alex was back at Seletar, he was involved in training for war for the first time since September. On the 26th of November he was airborne for a two-hour, low-level bombing practice. In addition to second pilot Rob McVicker, he had on board two young officers, Pilot Officers McHardy and Garnett, whom he was training. Two days later he was engaged in night-flying practice for three hours, and the next week in an hour's formation-flying practice. But, as he was to say in a speech long after he had retired, in training for war in Singapore, "we never did, really, extend and exhaust ourselves."

Unfortunately, this was about to become the epitaph for a number of the pilots and airmen of 205 Squadron. Three days after the formation-flying practice, at 0820 on the 7th of December, Flight Sergeant Webb, his second pilot, Flying Officer Bedell, and their crew in Catalina FVY were flying patrol over the Gulf of Siam south of Cambodia. They were keeping an eye on an enormous Japanese fleet which the British hoped was heading for Siam. Without warning they were attacked by a Japanese reconnaissance aircraft which they managed to fight off. But at 0845 five Ki27 Japanese fighters attacked from several directions and FVY disappeared in a huge explosion.[12] There were no survivors. Across the dateline, the attack on Pearl Harbor was still twenty-four hours away but for 205 Squadron the war with Japan had begun.

7

WAR WITH JAPAN

DECEMBER 1941–JANUARY 1942

In which Alex and the RAF fight a desperate but losing battle
against the Japanese from their Singapore base.

"Well, I'm damned, the cheeky little so-and-so's!"
— OPINION OF 205 SQUADRON AFTER THE JAPANESE ATTACK

At 0100 on Monday the 8th of December 1941, minutes earlier than the attack on Pearl Harbor, Alex was woken by the CO: "Better get dressed, Jardine! Attack on the way!" Indeed it was; the first bombs caught him still struggling into his pants. Flying high and in the dark, the Japanese did well actually to hit the airfield. Alex's dressing was punctuated by a huge clump of dirt landing on his verandah. Dishevelled and half dressed, he jumped into a trench outside the door and waited. The bombers made another pass, dropped more bombs and then disappeared. The All Clear siren sounded and some rather stunned officers gathered in the mess. Most of them were astonished. It seemed almost unbelievable that the Japanese had had the nerve to carry out such an action. As Alex was to tell Agnes when reflecting on this event a month later: " I think the normal reaction was: 'Well, I'm damned, the cheeky little so-and-so's!' "

205 Squadron was not the only unit to be surprised. As a Japanese armada was pouring troops ashore just north of the Malayan border, Japanese bombers, mostly escorted by fighters, rained bombs on the northern airfields. General Percival wrote: "The rapidity with which the Japanese got their air attacks going against our aerodromes was quite remarkable ... the performance of Japanese aircraft of all types, and the accuracy of their bombing, came as an unpleasant surprise. By evening our own air force had been seriously weakened."[13] RAF dreams of winning control of the air disappeared on that day, not so much because of what their enemy had done – though that was very competent – as because of their own deficiencies. They had allowed themselves to be outclassed in aircraft, pilots and intelligence.

As far as fighter aircraft were concerned, the A6M (or 'Zero'), a candidate for the best World War II fighter, and its stablemate the Ki27, a top-of-the-line fighter which was as good as the German Me109, were facing the RAF's obsolete Buffalo, a stubby little chap which got easily out of breath. The Air Ministry had felt, nevertheless, that the Buffalo would be more than good enough to deal with a second-rate Asian air force. There was an equal disparity in bombers. The American B17 was the best bomber in the Pacific area but the RAF had none of them; the medium bombers that they did have in some numbers, Blenheims and Hudsons, compared poorly to the Japanese Ki21, which packed a bigger punch from further away.

The Japanese pilots were combat veterans. Japan had been fighting the Russians and the Chinese, on and off, for three and four years respectively. These men faced inexperienced RAF pilots, leavened only by a sprinkling of Battle of Britain veterans; Britain still felt too threatened to allow her own veterans too far away from home. And Japan had an intelligence advantage. While the RAF had arrogantly ignored whatever information it had on the quality of Japan's air force, allowing its unfortunate pilots to find out about Japanese strengths the hard way, the Japanese knew that their enemy was weak and exploited that knowledge from the beginning. The allied airmen's amazement and surprise gave the Japanese a huge psychological advantage.

If one adds to all this a lack of antiaircraft guns to defend airfields, the complete lack of training in defence against attack by aircraft, a tactical indifference to the dispersal of aircraft and a tendency to employ bombers and fighters in penny packets where they could be overwhelmed, rather than concentrating them for decisive blows, then one understands how this battle was lost before it began. The grafting of *tida appa* onto imperial hubris was producing bitter fruit.

All this was far from apparent to Catalina pilots at Seletar. Their confidence would take much longer to shake and in the first weeks of the war they had little reason to suspect that they would be unable to contain Japan. Within twenty-four hours of sitting in his trench, watching the bombs fall, Alex and his crew were out over the South China Sea flying reconnaissance and antisubmarine patrol for Admiral Tom Phillips and Force Z. This was composed of two powerful capital ships, the new battleship *Prince of Wales* and the battle cruiser *Repulse*, with a flotilla of screening destroyers. Phillips's plan was to use his 15-inch guns against the Japanese invasion fleet, at one blow putting an end to Japan's plans to attack Malaya.

Alex and his crew in FVZ were airborne at 0600; they patrolled northwards, in low cloud and rain, up the eastern coastline of Malaya into southern Siam. Just north of Singora they spotted a large number of Japanese ships landing troops. Radio contact with its ships was forbidden by the Navy so, instead of informing

Force Z by radio, they had to turn south and find the ships through gaps in the clouds in order to send the message in Morse code by Aldis lamp. At 1255 the great ships loomed out of the fog. FVZ quickly identified herself as friendly by firing a flare (which had to be the "colour of the day") – to avoid being fired at by trigger-happy navy gunners – and the message was sent and acknowledged. Now confident in his objective, Phillips continued northwards at top speed, having every reason to believe that his own position, course and speed were unknown to the Japanese.

Nevertheless, in spite of his Nelsonian determination, Phillips was leading his ships into danger with the ill-considered recklessness of the Earl of Cardigan in the Charge of the Light Brigade. Apart from Alex in FVZ there was no air cover for his ships. Phillips had been told that he could not expect air cover where the Japanese were landing but he never asked for it further south, nor did he inform the RAF of his position and course. Alex's job was to search for enemy submarines and deal with them but a single Catalina cannot protect its charges from an airborne torpedo and bomb attack.

On that day, the 9th of December, low clouds made life a little safer for everybody. They provided excellent operating cover for the flying boat, offering instant invisibility from Japanese fighters; they kept Admiral Phillips's ships invisible from high-flying Japanese reconnaissance aircraft, so the Navy was happy. But the benefits worked for both sides. The Japanese submarine *I-65* was also grateful for the clouds. Unknown to the British admiral and unseen by Alex and his crew, *I-65* had spotted the ships churning their way north and, having reported their position and course, was shadowing them at a considerable distance.[14] Late in the afternoon there was a slight clearing of the clouds; by nightfall, when Alex turned for home as he could be of no use in the dark, three enemy reconnaissance aircraft had appeared, at least one of which was last seen scurrying away in a northerly direction. Phillips could assume that the Japanese now knew his course and speed. Consequently, at about the same time that Alex and his crew landed at Seletar after fifteen hours of flying, Admiral Phillips decided to return to Singapore, realising that he had lost the advantage of surprise on which his venture depended.

While Alex and crew slept, Force Z steamed first towards Kuantan and then for Singapore. Dawn found them 150 miles north of that city. The sky was clear and blue, a good ship-sinking day. Japanese reconnaissance aircraft came and went. Observing radio silence to the point of the absurd, Phillips did not report his position or his predicament. Had he done so, Buffaloes could have been overhead within minutes and a full RAF effort would have disrupted the attack sufficiently to permit the big ships to escape. Instead, relying on the power of his ships' antiaircraft guns, which were indeed formidable, the Admiral gambled on being able to defend himself from air attack.

However, the air attack which hit him at 1115 was too much for any two ships; eighty-five aircraft, some carrying armour-piercing bombs, most carrying torpedoes, attacked in three successive waves. By the time the third wave had done its worst, *Repulse* was sunk and *Prince of Wales* sinking. In the event, the terrifying antiaircraft barrage thrown up by the ships had destroyed just three of the attacking aircraft. At 1320 *Prince of Wales* also disappeared, taking Admiral Phillips and 325 of her crew with her.

Reports of the sinking reached HQFE by radio from one lone Royal Australian Air Force (RAAF) Hudson, which had witnessed the whole sad event, surely one of the war's moments of truth. Unbelieving, HQFE ordered Alex and his crew into the air again at about 1600 on the 10th of December, being the only crew and aircraft available, with instructions to carry out antisubmarine patrol for *Repulse* in a given position, maybe hoping against hope that Alex would be able to wave a magic wand. They found patrolling in sunshine over the South China Sea a much less attractive proposition. "No fun in a Catalina when you know there are enemy aircraft about," as Alex remembered it. "On our way out we passed a Walrus aircraft anchored in a bay on the east coast, and circled to find out if he required assistance. All he said was, no, he was out of gas, and I recall remarking what a poor effort that was." They dropped water and Mae Wests and radioed for a warship to rescue him. Only later did they discover that it was *Repulse*'s Walrus and that the 'poor effort' was hardly the pilot's fault. He was Petty Officer Crozer who, with his aircraft, was subsequently attached to 205 Squadron.

"Then we passed two destroyers, loaded to the gunwales with people, we could not make out what kind, and assumed that they had evacuated some east coast port." In fact they were the 2,081 survivors of the big ships, 840 men having been lost. "Finally we returned to base with no *Repulse* having been found. I was puzzled and somewhat concerned and said so to my superiors. They replied that they feared that would be my answer, and that they had sent me out to confirm, in a way, that the two ships had in fact been lost. That was a dreadful day for us, quite unbelievable, as you can well imagine." Dreadful for him personally, too: as the Japanese situation worsened it became clear that they were now involved in a struggle for survival; thoughts of Meg, his home leave and his posting to Britain – all of them evaporated.

Alex and crew had by chance participated in one of the key events of the Pacific War, and further, of the collapse of the eastern British Empire as they knew it. An unquestioned assumption of superiority to the Japanese had been exposed as a foolish delusion by that nation's demonstration of aggressive military competence. To quote the authors of *Bloody Shambles*: "The effects were profoundly psychological as well as material, creating a feeling of hopelessness and a tremendous impression of total superiority of the enemy in all arms."[15]

The feeling of hopelessness did not immediately affect 205 Squadron. Demoralisation set in the closer you were to the Japanese; thus it first affected the air squadrons and military units in the north. The flying-boat crews tended to live in a world of their own. However, they were mystified by the events around them. As Alex was later to report: "The bombing of our base in Singapore continued, as did the advance down the peninsula and none of us could understand what on earth was happening." In fact, they saw their own world expanding in the next week, as their squadron was greatly reinforced. They received three Catalinas on loan from the Dutch to replace the three already lost; and others, which had been at Koggala, returned to Singapore. On the 12th of December the squadron boasted twelve serviceable aircraft, identified by the letters N, P, Q, R, S, T, U, V, W, X, Y and Z. It was 'high noon' for 205 Squadron.

Pilot Officer Sid Scales described his trip to the Dutch East Indies to pick up the three Cats:

> "Dec 10 1941 three skeleton crews flew to Bandoeng to pick up three Catalinas from Sourabaja. They were to be captained by F/Lt Stilling, F/Lt Atkinson and P/O Scales. From Bandoeng we travelled by train to Sourabaja and during the journey the news came that the *Prince of Wales* and the *Repulse* had been sunk by Japanese aircraft. On the train we Air Force men suffered some abuse from the Dutch for the RAF not downing the Jap aircraft. They were very panicky about it all. At Sourabaja, while we were familiarising ourselves with our new aircraft, the Dutch had a report of a Jap aircraft-carrier in the Java Sea. They immediately began to disperse their aircraft away from the moorings at Sourabaja. With Dutch pilots we flew our new machines to a Lake Serati (about three quarters of an hour away), where they were moored, nose to shore under overhanging foliage and the tails draped with branches and palms – very effective camouflage."

It was maybe their lingering but misplaced confidence that caused 205 Squadron to pay no attention, in spite of air raids, to the Dutch example of dispersal and camouflage of aircraft. Raids were frequent enough to be a nuisance though no more bombs had yet fallen at Seletar. In fact, it eventually took a serious attack on the moorage to convince HQFE that the Cats should be hidden at dispersal stations in Sumatra whenever they were not on operations. It was to be a case of shutting the gate after the horse has bolted. But this is to anticipate.

For the rest of December the Catalina crews carried out assigned tasks with professionalism and courage. This meant antisubmarine patrols, reconnaissance or ocean searches. Apart from the constant hazard of being attacked while they were doing it, it was not so very different from what they had done before. But it did mean spending up to fourteen hours in a slow and extremely vulnerable aircraft, in parts of the sky where, almost by definition, there were likely to be enemy aircraft. They knew by now that enemy aircraft with 20-mm cannon could destroy them from beyond the range of their own guns. And the more often they took off on patrol in disputed airspace, the harder it was on their nerves. The Catalina's guns were for use in emergency only. The trick was to avoid enemy aircraft completely by using the clouds, and there were usually clouds to use – blue days being rare during the northeast monsoon.

Alex demonstrated a canny ability to carry out his patrols without getting into trouble while his friend Dicky Atkinson seemed always to be fighting for his life against more nimble opponents. The first time Atkinson ran into trouble was on the 14th of December. He and Alex took off at dawn on separate patrols. Atkinson sighted six Japanese cruisers 200 miles south of Vietnam heading south but was unable to slip into clouds before being attacked by a twin-engined Japanese aircraft. His gunners fought it off, but not before the aircraft suffered some engine damage, and he had to return to base on one engine. The records do not tell us where Alex went; it would probably have been over the South China Sea or the Malay peninsula. We do know that he was airborne for ten hours and returned to base without incident.

The following day, the 15th of December, Alex and crew were again out on patrol, this time being airborne for thirteen and a half hours, returning at 2130, long after nightfall. After that they had two days off, probably because the weather was bad, but on the 18th both crews were again patrolling. Once more we know only that Alex returned to base safely, after a nine-hour patrol. Atkinson, on the other hand, was again attacked over the Gulf of Siam by a twin-engined G3M flown by Lieut Toshio Ohno.[16] Atkinson's aircraft got the better of the encounter: although one of his gunners, Sergeant Allen, received a scalp wound and twelve large holes were blown in the aircraft, seven below the waterline, Ohno of the G3M was killed, his aircraft broke off the engagement trailing smoke from its port engine, and it limped back to base flown by the second pilot.

We know that Alex was patrolling again on the 20th and the 22nd, airborne for six and a half and ten hours respectively. Both patrols were without incident. Other pilots were patrolling on these days, including possibly Atkinson, but we have no information about their patrols. But on Christmas Day 1941, Alex and Atkinson were airborne on patrol at 0600. Atkinson flew straight into trouble for the third time in ten days. At 0715, over the South China Sea, he spotted two Japanese cruisers and a destroyer, whose position he reported to base. He managed to avoid the flak from the ships, but was then attacked by a G3M flown by Lieut Yasuhito Koedaka. This pilot understood the limitations of the Catalina's defenses; he circled the aircraft at 600 yards, out of range of its machine guns, all the while pumping it full of 20-mm cannon shells. The Catalina caught fire and was forced down on the water.

Before they hit the water the radio operator had had time to report their situation to base. Consequently, as the crew was swimming away from the burning Catalina which did indeed explode, S/L Gordon Stilling was taking off from Seletar to come to their assistance. He had to search a large area of sea but was eventually led to them by oil and debris. He dropped dinghies, food and water. Unable to land because of heavy seas, he radioed for help and continued to circle until dark. From above he could see that Atkinson had had his nine-man crew hold onto each other in a circle. In fact Atkinson, in spite of his own burns, had given up his Mae West to a non-swimmer without one. Several others had burns or shrapnel wounds, and the circle allowed them to support each other and, if necessary, to fend off sharks. The exhausted airmen were eventually picked up by a Dutch submarine after nine hours in the water.[17] Atkinson was to receive the Distinguished Flying Cross (DFC) for his role in this action.

Meanwhile Alex flew a short patrol, learning about Atkinson's problems over the radio; he himself landed safely shortly after noon. He attributes the fact that his aircraft was rarely intercepted and attacked to Lucky Alex, but his safe patrol record and regular selection for the most important jobs indicate that he was not only senior pilot but considered an exceptionally skillful one. Although it was only later that he knew Alex well, Sid Scales was told "that in his logbook he had an 'exceptional' assessment – a rare distinction."

While Atkinson and his injured crew members, who included his badly burned second pilot Sid Scales, were recuperating in hospital, Alex went on flying. On Boxing Day he made a short afternoon patrol of four and a half hours. But life for him, and for other Catalina pilots, was about to change in a big way. Previously, the Japanese heavy bombers had operated from Saigon. Now they were established at several airfields in southern Siam, whence they were mounting increasingly frequent and effective bombing raids on Singapore. The RAF had to destroy these bomber bases if the peninsula was to be tenable. So Catalinas, which normally carried depth-charges, were pressed into service as bombers; these versatile machines could actually carry more bombs than any other aircraft available.

On the 30th of December two Catalinas from Seletar, flown by Alex and Stilling and loaded with fourteen 250-lb. bombs each, joined three Blenheims in a night raid on the airfield at Sungei Patani. The round trip took between seven and eight hours of night flying. Such night flights were relatively safe for most of the distance because night fighters were not yet very effective. But the actual bombing attack was a ten-minute hell of antiaircraft fire with the aircraft being thrown around by the nearby explosions of shells. On this occasion both aircraft came through the flak safely though Stilling's machine suffered slight engine damage. This did not affect its performance and he actually landed back at base an hour before Alex did.

Nobody flew on New Year's Eve, probably more on account of the weather than the celebrations. Really there was not much to celebrate although 205 Squadron, having lost just one Catalina since December 12, was in much better shape than any other RAF squadron. But it was to be back to bombing on the 1st of January 1942. Two Catalinas, flown by the same two captains, Alex in FVX and Gordon Stilling in FVS, were despatched on a bombing run to Gong Kedah. Again a long night flight; again the ordeal by antiaircraft fire. It had been decided that Stilling would go in first at low level while Alex was to bomb from 10,000 feet. The ride through the flak was rougher than on the previous run and at 0050 Seletar picked up these RT messages from the aircraft:

Alex:"report position, course and speed."
Stilling: "my pos'n E.QSP 1545; my course 170;
my speed 96 knots; one engine gone, other may not last."
Alex: "am returning to position ofFVS."

In fact, Stilling's aircraft had been hit by small-arms fire in one engine. It was losing oil so he shut it down. Alex remembers that they observed radio silence and that he was ignorant of the situation until he landed at Seletar. At such a distance memory is not reliable. As he had signalled he was doing, Alex must actually have throttled back to keep company with the struggling FVS. Stilling had climbed on his remaining engine while jettisoning everything he could to reduce weight. The round trip took them both the best part of ten hours. According to the RT log they landed within two minutes of each other at 0415.

The squadron learned subsequently that Stilling had been awarded the DFC for his efforts in nursing his aircraft and crew back to base. Curiously, two days later Alex was informed that he had been awarded the AFC. This was recognition for his leadership in the Indian Ocean in the months before the war with Japan. The citation states: "It is ordained that the Air Force Cross shall be granted to such officers and warrant officers of our said forces as shall be recommended to us for exceptional valour, courage or devotion to duty whilst flying, though not in active operations against the enemy." That sums up Alex's pioneering tour of duty in the Indian Ocean and seldom can an award have been so well earned.

Alex wrote to Agnes early in January, and his letter seems remarkably calm and normal when we consider what he had been doing and the conditions under which he had been doing it. On the 7th of January he told her: "We are now quite air-raid conscious and do not think very much [about it] but curse it when they disturb our night's sleep ... however we've had the pleasure of giving them a little of their own back, only about double, if not more, the quantity. When I say 'we' I can say that personally too ... subject to censorship so I can't say much about it. The big change is being completely blacked out."

What had actually been happening? According to the Seletar RT log, the Japanese had raided close enough to the base for air-raid sirens to go off on each of the first six nights of the month. The raid on the night of the 3rd had been close enough for the Take Cover to send them all scurrying to the trenches. During the same week there had been four daytime raids as well, on the 2nd, the 4th, the 6th and the 7th, with only the raid on the 2nd being close enough for a Take Cover. Blackout was not much fun on the equator. First, at that latitude there are close to twelve hours of darkness every night. Secondly the heat and humidity preclude more than a few blackout curtains, which would cut the airflow and be intolerable. Black-curtained rooms were possible for short periods – for mess dinner, for example – with electric ceiling fans to keep the air moving, but most air conditioning was provided by open, screened windows twenty-four hours a day. Consequently, people did much sitting around in the dark chatting – and went to bed early. That is why Alex considered it the big change – more so than the risk of bombs.

Actually, after the raid on the 8th of December, the Japanese had left Singapore alone for a while. Enemy bombing was directed towards chasing the RAF out of the northern airfields and supporting the victorious Japanese army. However, by Christmas they had achieved those goals, were well established on southern Thai and northern Malayan air bases and began a serious effort to reduce Singapore itself. When the sirens went in Singapore it did not necessarily mean that Seletar, or any other air or naval base, was being bombed. Often these alarms would be triggered by the presence of unidentified aircraft on one of the two radar screens in operation. Consequently, alarms were treated more as a nuisance than a danger.

This all changed in January. In the first week, as already mentioned, the Japanese bombed mainly at night, with only two raids requiring life to stop and everybody to find a trench. The second week was much the same, with five night and five day raids and only two Take Covers. But this pattern changed in the third week. Even when there were plenty of serviceable Buffaloes, these had had neither the speed nor the power to climb above the incoming bombers' top cover of A6M Zeroes before the raiders arrived. Spitfires could have done it but there were none. Consequently, time and again the Buffaloes were attacked from above and many were destroyed. By mid-January the Japanese had crippled the RAF fighter squadrons and had control of the air. This was signalled, in the third week, by no fewer than seventeen daylight raids with nine Take Covers. That meant that for considerable stretches of the day – usually the morning, when most productive work happens in the tropics – people at the base were in trenches, listening to bombs falling not far away and wondering how on earth they were going to get out of this mess.

To return to the beginning of January, life went on and missions were carried out without loss of life at Seletar. Alex had no flying jobs for ten days after his bombing run with Stilling on the 1st. Until the 6th, Catalinas were out on patrol, usually one or two a day. On the 3rd, FVX, the aircraft in which Alex had toured the Indian Ocean, was destroyed by an accidental fire while refuelling.* FVS, the aircraft in which Stilling had limped home, was being patched up but, with the exception of a few circuits and bumps, it never flew another operation. So the squadron was reduced to nine Catalinas from the twelve it had boasted in December. There were beginning to be too many crews with not enough to do.

The squadron was switched back to bombing on the 7th. Stilling in FVN and F/Lt Tamblyn in FVQ bombed Sungei Patani and Gong Kedah with eight 500-lb. bombs each; the weather was foul on the 8th and no flying was done by either side. The lull was temporary; when the sky cleared both sides decided that the 9th was a good bombing day. Alex and his friends were awakened by bombs crashing around them between four and five in the morning. Fortunately no damage was done to people or aircraft and that same evening the squadron replied with its biggest raid yet, sending out FVY, FVR, FVQ and FVN, flown by S/L Stilling, F/Lt Graham, S/L Farrar and F/Lt Tamblyn respectively. They were airborne by 1830, each aircraft carrying eight 500-lb. bombs and the target was Singora. 16,000 lbs. of bombs were delivered to the Japanese, all aircraft returned without major damage and there followed another two-day interval caused by the monsoon.

It appears from the RT log that there were alarms on both days, but nothing approaching a raid disturbed their enjoyment of the teeming rain – one of the few occasions when such conditions are really appreciated. In the mess the conversation must have turned to how the battle was going. From their point of view, things were not going too badly. Although they had no air photos of damage done by their bombs, they felt sure that they must have created havoc on the ground at the airfields they had visited. The squadron, after a month of war, still had nine serviceable aircraft and the fitters were doing wonders with repairing flak damage. What was needed, all agreed, were a few shiploads of Spitfires and Hurricanes, and the fighter pilots would soon deal with the Japanese bombers. The key was to regain control of the skies.

---

*see Appendix 3

Clear skies on the 12th meant that they had Japanese daylight raids to contend with, having to dive into trenches twice, once after breakfast and then just before lunch; but they were able to reply that evening when they sent out three Catalinas to bomb Sungei Patani and Singora – Alex in FVP, F/Lt Garnell in FVT and S/L Farrar in FVQ, all carrying 500-lb. bombs. These bombing operations were always a little makeshift; on this occasion, as Garnell was over the target, "his observer, Sergeant Bonnar, stood by the waist blisters, throwing incendiaries out by hand!"[18]

Next morning, however, the mood was sombre; Farrar and the crew of FVQ had failed to return and RT had failed to raise them. All morning Jock Graham checked periodically with the radio room, but by noon even he had realised that the squadron had lost an aircraft and a crew and they had all lost a good friend. Transmissions to FVQ ceased at 1310. In fact FVQ had had the misfortune to be intercepted in the darkness by a Japanese Ki27 fighter, flown by W/O Hideshima, who shot the flying boat down over the sea. There were no survivors.[19]

News from the army was bad and seemed to be getting worse. They had been pushed back down the peninsula towards Singapore and on the 16th HQFE sent a general order to all RAF squadrons with instructions for which type of bombs they should load in order to support the army. It sounded panicky: "Aircraft not detailed for reconnaissance to be at short notice from 0600, 17th of January, for support of army. Blenheims, Hudsons mixed 250-lb GP and antipersonnel; Flying-Boat squadrons and Albacores 250-lb GP; Wirraways antipersonnel; Glenn-Martins 100-kilos; Sharks 250 GP. First tasks may not be issued before 0450 on the 17th." For the next three or four days there was little flying activity; presumably the weather was judged to be too bad for night bombing. One aircraft a day went out on patrol but the rest were at moorings or on the slips being worked on. Each day there was an air-raid alarm but none amounted to anything and there were no attacks on the base. Then suddenly there was hope. Their wish had been granted: on the morning of the 17th there were Hurricanes taking off from Seletar! They had been landed in crates from a supply convoy on the 13th and two flights were now assembled and operational. Maybe, if there were enough of them, this war could still be turned around. In fact there were fifty-one of them, with twenty-three pilots; there were plenty of pilots in Singapore without fighters, so all fifty-one would be flown in action.

For 205 Squadron, however, the 17th of January was not otherwise a happy day. The skies were clearing and the air-raid siren sounded at 0410 and lasted just long enough to make sure that everyone was awake and unable to go back to sleep. A more serious alarm started at 0840, lasting for an hour, including two separate and bothersome Take Covers. When a third siren started at 1020, it was largely ignored and crewmen were working on the aircraft at the moorings. The raid appeared to be over when, at 1110, two Japanese Ki43 fighters, (described in the log as ME109 type) flown by Lt Kunii and Sgt/Major Omori, swooped down from their job of escorting bombers and made several passes, strafing the moored Catalinas in the anchorage. The results were catastrophic. FVP and FVY were set on fire by exploding cannon shells. The crews, who had been on board, escaped except for AC2 Edwards and Sergeant Arch on FVP. Arch grabbed the Vickers gun in the blister and returned the fire, raking the attackers when they were in range, and continued to fire as the aircraft sank. Both men were killed.[20] In addition, FVY sank, FVT was so badly damaged that she was a write-off and FVW took several days to repair. When the raiders had gone, the reality was that the squadron was down to three serviceable aircraft: FVR, FVU and FVV. Of the three unserviceable aircraft FVN and FVW would be back in service on the 19th but FVS would never fly again. There were now at least two crews for every aircraft and the squadron had a serious unemployment problem. In spite of the arrival of the Hurricanes, the optimism of the 11th had been badly shaken.

Belatedly the squadron was ordered to fly any aircraft not patrolling to dispersal areas in Sumatra, a few miles across the Straits of Malacca. There was now no alternative, as the Japanese ruled the skies over Singapore. There were twenty air-raid alerts in the third week in January and twenty-three in the last week. It had become impossible to run an air base; not much can be accomplished from a slit trench. The continued existence of the slip and repair facilities was entirely at the mercy of chance and the Rising Sun. The RT log records no further multiple-aircraft bombing sorties although on two occasions single Catalinas were loaded with anti-ship bombs for special jobs. For the next week, in fact, there was little activity; only one patrol was flown daily while the remaining aircraft spent their days camouflaged under palms in a Sumatran inlet, returning to Seletar at dusk.

This inactivity cannot have been because the weather prevented flying, as the Japanese were raiding between two and four times a day during that time; most likely it was to allow ground crews to set up engine hoists and other equipment at the dispersal locations. In fact there was only one day, the 19th, when there were no alarms. Presumably the weather was too bad for the Japanese – but not too bad for Alex who flew his last patrol from Singapore on that day, a nine-hour flight. On the 23rd and 24th the squadron was back in action; on each day three Cats were out on different patrols and FVR was off on a special job to Koggala.

By this time the Hurricanes were showing what they could do. Unfortunately this was not as much as had been hoped. These particular Hurricanes had been built for operating with the Eighth Army in the North African desert; they carried heavy filters on the air intakes and each was armed with no fewer than twelve wing-mounted machine guns.[21] The filters cut the speed and power and the weight of the extra guns made the aircraft sluggish. They were certainly more effective than the Buffaloes, but they were not good enough, nor were there enough of them, to turn the tide.

On the 25th of January Alex received a special assignment. The aircraft carrier HMS *Indomitable* was approaching Sumatra with two squadrons of Hurricanes on board. These forty-eight aircraft would bring the number of Hurricanes delivered to ninety-nine, and most people were willing to believe that *now* the Allies' luck would change. Surely the fighters which had seen Britain through the Battle of Britain would be able to see off the Zeroes. Alex and his crew in FVN had the job of flying antisubmarine patrol for the aircraft carrier and they made a five-hour flight to the Dutch Naval Air Service (DNAS) base at Tanjong Priok, the port of Batavia, to be closer to the approaching carrier. On the 26th *Indomitable* was still too far away, so Alex visited Headquarters in Batavia to make arrangements for the move of the squadron from Seletar to Java, for which orders had just been received. He never found dealing with Dutch officialdom easy but the most irritating thing was their attitude to air-raid sirens. When these sounded at Tanjong Priok, which they did less frequently than in Singapore in recent weeks, everybody downed tools and retired to the trenches – staying there for hours until the All Clear. To someone who had learned to live with them this was infuriating.

On the 27th FVN was airborne before first light and set a course southwest over the western tip of Java, then out into the blue over the Indian Ocean. It must have felt like a return to Diego Garcia and Mauritius. As they flew further from Sumatra they could relax for the first time in weeks, because an encounter with Japanese aircraft became less likely. Their main concern was searching for submarines. Navy radio silence made it up to Alex to find the carrier. His maritime instincts, knowing the general direction from which the ship would be approaching, led him to her without too much difficulty. Nevertheless, they had to fly for four hours before sighting her. He was familiar with *Indomitable's* appearance but it was still a thrill when she finally emerged from the haze on the horizon. She was travelling at 26 knots with her attendant Australian destroyers *Nizam, Napier* and *Nestor*, all four ships carving the sea as they narrowed the distance to Palembang airfield in Sumatra to within Hurricane range.

Alex did not know it at the time but he used up another life that morning. He and his crew came within an inch of being shot down by the *Indomitable's* own Sea Hurricanes. Sub Lt Hugh Popham and Lt Brian Fiddes had been scrambled on the approach of FVN. Popham wrote in his book *Sea Flight*: "... Brian and I were sent off on our first operational interception with our stomachs doing somersaults and our thumbs on the gun button – and that was one Sunderland [*sic*] flying boat that nearly didn't get home."[22] Presumably they were high and up-sun and Alex never saw them.

For four hours FVN flew a search pattern within sight of the ship; in strong sunlight over tropical seas you can actually see a submerged submarine at quite a depth, so they were happy to have nothing to report. Alex must have felt, as Popham wrote: "A ship at speed is beautiful, whatever its intent, and the sea it rides and the intolerable blue sky that arches overhead; and the aircraft that you fly has a beauty that supersedes boredom and loneliness and fear."[23] Towards sunset they saluted the ship with a dip of the the wings and returned to Tanjong Priok for the night.

They returned next morning. *Indomitable* had made good time overnight and they sighted her after an hour's flying. Now close enough to Palembang she had headed into the northeast monsoon to fly off the Hurricanes. It was a tricky operation: the pilots had never flown off a carrier and had to get it right first time. As the elevators brought up the aircraft they flew off the flight deck, some coming alarmingly close to the water, but one by one climbing quickly to circle over the carrier. Each flight formed up with one of a series of Hudsons, which then escorted them to Palembang. From above, the sight of the stream of fighters disappearing over the horizon was inspiring. The process took time but no sooner was it complete than *Indomitable* turned in a wide, foaming semicircle and steamed northwest at full speed. For a while they continued to fly with her, then returned to base feeling exultant that the operation had gone so well.

At Tanjong Priok they received their orders for the following day – to go back out to search for a ditched aircraft and its pilot. This turned out to be a long day. There was, of course, no sign of the carrier which was well out of range. They flew a search pattern from her position of the previous day to the coast of Sumatra, finding nothing after eight hours of searching. It transpired that no Hurricane had ditched but nobody had bothered to cancel the order. That was military life!

Once the distraction of the Hurricanes was over Alex had to get back to organising the reception of the squadron in Batavia. By the 30th FVU and FVV were on moorings in the harbour at Tanjong Priok. The Dutch were not willing to let them stay there so other arrangements would have to be made. However FVN's first task was to fly back to Seletar and help move squadron headquarters staff. The place, after only five days' absence, had an air of desolation. FVR was out on patrol and FVW on its way to Batavia. On the moorings there were no serviceable Catalinas, just FVS which had been cannibalised for parts and was to be abandoned.

As soon as Alex and his crew came ashore the aircraft was readied for the return trip; a pile of luggage and boxes on the tarmac was waiting to be loaded. There were two air-raid warnings that afternoon, and the sky twice filled with the contrails of aerial combat at 25,000 feet. The Hurricanes were doing what they could to turn this thing around, many of them operating from Seletar in spite of its cratered runway. Mercifully Alex was too busy to think too much about the four years when this place had been home. For him it held a lot of memories but when he and Rob McVicker had dinner with the CO in the mess, they were surrounded by boisterous Hurricane pilots, none of whom they knew and all desperately young. Seletar seemed to have forgotten them. He was not to see the place in daylight again. At 0434 FVN was airborne for Batavia carrying the CO and five other passengers. 205 Squadron had moved.

Tiger Moth at Hawkhurst, December 1935.

A Short Brothers' Saro Cloud amphibian, as flown by Alex at Calshot, 1936.

Alex with Topsy (Charmaine Jenkinson) on board *Rawalpindi*, 1937.

Some of the *Pindi* gang, 1937: back (l to r): Alex, Margaret Stevenson, Anna Cowie, John Boothman, Stella Vicarage, Jumbo Hills; front (l to r) Batchy Lewis, Guyler.

Pilot Officer Alex Jardine,
November 1936, aged 22.

An RAF Singapore III over Singapore island.

Inner harbour, Singapore.

Flight Lieutenant Alex Jardine,
1939, aged 25.

Barbara Murray with Alex, in the
squadron whaler, 1939.

All ranks of 205 Squadron at Seletar, Singapore, 1939.

At Nancowry island 1940; LAC Newman (2nd left), Alex (centre), LAC Grant (right).

A Consolidated Catalina long range reconnaissance flying boat, as supplied to the RAF.

Officers of 205 Squadron, Seletar 26 April 1941, just before arrival of Catalinas.
The war was still a solar topee affair.
Back, l to r: F/O D. Shaw, F/O J. Ingram, F/L J. R. Graham, P/O Brandt, P/O P. Biddell. P/O R.
McVicker. *Front, l to r:* F/L N. N. Birks, F/L S. G. Stilling, F/L A. M. Jardine, W/C L. W. Burgess,
F/L E. W. Young, F/L R. A. Atkinson, F/O T. Grieve.

(l to r) Doug 'Bernard'
Shaw, Dicky Atkinson,
Norman Birks, Jock
Graham, Terry Grieve
in front of the mess at
Seletar, early 1941.

Nancowry 1940. F/Sgt Tubby Williams refuelling a Singapore III
with 64 gallon drums.

Arthur Banks' painting of Alex's Catalina over Mauritius, 1941. The paint job and armaments are not accurate, nor the busy harbour.

Officers of 205 Squadron, mid-December 1941. Note the slung gasmasks and the tin hats, replacing those elegant solar topees.

Back, l to r: P/O F. W. Brandt, P/O J. F. Chester, F/O K. M. Whitworth, P/O R. S. McHardy, P/O Man Mohan Singh, P/O R. D. McVicker, P/O E. J. Garnett, F/O S. A. Tucker, F/O S. P. Wilkins. *Middle, l to r:* F/Lt J. C. Lowe, F/Lt H. Garnell, S/L S. G. Stilling, S/L A. M. Jardine, W/C R. B. Councell, S/L M. F. C. Farrar, F/Lt J. R. Graham, F/Lt H. Tamblyn, F/O A. T. Ingram. *Front, l to r:* P/O J. M. Barnes, P/O T. F. J. Crudden, P/O J. L. Kinsey, P/O R. E. Scott, P/O C. H. Keon-Cohen.

Back (l to r): S/L Pitts, unidentified officer; front (l to r): Hosh the Slosher (possibly), 'Slime' Kasayama, Gunzo 'Bamboo' Mori, Batavia 1945.

Squadron Leader Alex Jardine, still in
RAF uniform, late 1945, aged 31.

Robin Johnston and a just-arrived Alex
prepare to celebrate, 21 October 1945.

The Mustang flown by Alex for NRC tests at Arnprior, January 1948. Standing (l to r):
W/O Arnold, Bud Levy, 'Tim' Wood, Alex.

8

LAST STAND IN JAVA

FEBRUARY–MARCH 1942

In which 205 Squadron continues the fight from Sumatra, then Java,
eventually escaping to Australia; but in which, thanks to excruciating
circumstances, Alex is prevented from accompanying them.

"The outcome of this, one cannot try to imagine"

FVN landed at Tanjong Priok, the port of Batavia, at 0930 on the 31st of
January 1942. As Alex taxied through the moored flying boats towards the
buoy assigned to him by air traffic control he and his crew were greeted with a
welcoming wave by the crews of FVW and FVV. They had been in Java for a
couple of days and were on board their aircraft, attending to chores and keeping
out of the way of their hosts, the DNAS. Up on the slip was FVU, looking sorry
for herself with a damaged float, the result of a landing mishap on arrival. It was
scheduled to be repaired but obviously nobody had paid much attention to it.
Including FVR, on patrol out of Seletar but expected to arrive later, these five
aircraft were all that remained of the twelve that 205 Squadron had boasted in
December. It was a sobering thought, both for Alex and for the CO. Mind you,
they both saw it as a temporary situation. Although there were a number of
immediate problems to be dealt with, both men felt optimistic that they and other
squadrons could establish themselves in Java or Sumatra and that the war would be
turned around once all the promised aircraft had arrived.

All ranks were to be accommodated in Batavia for the night, some eight
kilometres away. Airmen were lodged at the Wielriders Club and the officers at
the Hotel Der Nederlanden. The 'extra' members of the squadron were already
installed in Batavia. The city was to be home for any airman or officer for whom
there was no aircraft to fly in or to work on. S/L Stilling was dispatched for orders
to General Headquarters, Allied Forces in Bandoeng. That evening he telephoned:
he would be back in the morning to brief officers about their new base.

Meanwhile, Alex had been busy at the repair station at Tanjong Priok. Because the Dutch had their own aircraft to worry about, it was clear that the repair of FVU would have to be done by 205 Squadron fitters. Besides, he had the impression that the DNAS were not exactly delighted to share their facility with the RAF. And to ensure that the repairs to FVU, and no doubt to other aircraft in the future, actually happened, somebody senior had to be at Priok to see that facilities were made available to 205 Squadron when the need arose. That person would have to be Alex, whose job as second-in-command normally included the supervision of repair and maintenance. It was time for him to brush up on his Dutch.

Next morning, the 1st of February, Stilling arrived from Bandoeng. The squadron was to fly across the Sunda Strait to Oosthaven in southeast Sumatra, where there were buoys for three flying boats and which was to be their permanent base. Just before the three aircraft set off, FVR landed at Tanjong Priok, piloted by Jock Graham. He was ordered to come to Oosthaven on the 2nd, to allow time to find an extra mooring.

As things turned out, a mooring was going to be the least of their worries. Without delay FVN, FVV and FVW, loaded with ground crew, some extra air crew and all the equipment they could carry, took off for the ninety-minute flight. What a surprise and disappointment awaited them! Oosthaven was neither a flying-boat base nor a military base of any sort. It was a fishing village, surrounded by tropical forest, with a sideline in coastal freighters. For servicemen used to having everything laid on for them, the only things that Oosthaven provided were moorings for three aircraft. Anything else they would have to find for themselves. From having been lords of the manor at Seletar they were now beggars at the gate.

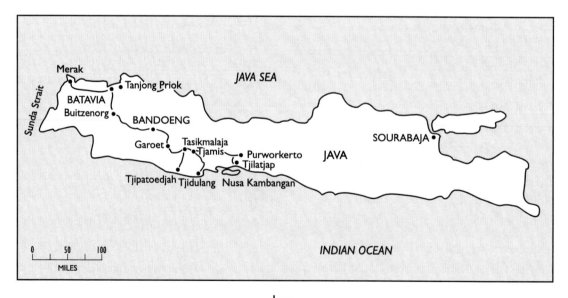

Java

Fortunately for them, Commander Schackel, a Dutch naval officer, was attached to the squadron to help with the language and the making of arrangements.

There was nothing available in Oosthaven. After many shouted telephone conversations arrangements were made for sleeping and eating in Telukbetung, the nearest town, about thirteen kilometres away. The thirty-three airmen were to be lodged at two hotels which had no restaurants. European-style food was to be provided, at a fixed price, in a Chinese restaurant – no bird's-nest soup to be booked to the Air Ministry! The ten officers were placed in a slightly more upmarket hotel and in two private houses. And that was it. At least there was a telephone in all these places but, apart from two RAF trucks miraculously produced – presumably from RAF Palembang, about 300 kilometres over the hills, other facilties did not exist. There was no officers' or airmen's mess, no repair facility, no squadron office or headquarters building – not even a squadron loo. And as you might expect in a fishing village, there was no hundred-octane gas for aircraft.

As an immediate means of meeting their military responsibilities, the CO and Alex decided that a 'strike crew' must sleep close to the aircraft, that boat-guards must be posted and that an RT operator must be aboard one of the Catalinas at all times to listen for messages. Meanwhile, they set about finding a place for the strike crew to sleep. Their eye fell upon the examination room of the customs house and the harbour master was asked to hand it over. The RT log says that he was "reluctant." No doubt he actually exploded at them in Dutch that no blankety blank "Englanders" were going to have his blankety blank customs house! It was just the body language that got recorded. To make up for his 'reluctance' the harbour master did agree to set out another mooring buoy and to provide them with a launch. Some success was also chalked up about fuel: RAF Palembang promised them 4,000 gallons in 4-gallon cans, which was a start. The physical separation between the moorage in Oosthaven, where the aircraft and the RT operator were, and the various hotels and houses where they lived in Telukbetung was the cause of endless difficulty and worry for the CO. He and Alex both spent time sweating up and down the winding connecting road between the two.

The following morning, the 2nd of February, Councell must have felt like a North American parent on a camping trip; the air was full of loud complaints about the food from the airmen. As these were airmen for whose morale he was responsible he had to do something about it. He cancelled the previous arrangements and entered into a signed contract with a shady character called Weng Kie – to feed the airmen for about twice the money promised previously. The following day his reward was still more and louder complaints about food. Because of the trickle of airmen who kept arriving, his calculation of the numbers to be fed had proved to be too low. As a result, he had to spend more time with the mercenary

Weng Kie over the next two weeks than he really wanted to. And it all fell to the CO because Alex had to put such mundane things behind him.

Flying back to Tanjong Priok with his crew in FVN, Alex had a list of problems which he needed Stilling to get some action on at Headquarters. These included the fuel supply, more boats and accommodation arrangements in a depot ship or in new buildings. Stilling must have moved mountains because serious amounts of petrol arrived by train the following day and a new building started to go up. It was just a shed but a shed was better than nothing. Meanwhile the squadron Ops Room was in whichever Catalina was manned at the moorings. Life at Oosthaven settled into a compromise which enabled pilots to obey orders and aircraft to patrol when they had fuel available or when they were not waiting for servicing at the DNAS station at Tanjong Priok. The fuel supply was uncertain, having to be trucked from the railway, and refuelling was slow and perilous, now done by hand pump from 64-gallon drums on rafts. Armaments had to be loaded in the same way. This was waging war the hard way, though it had one benefit: Oosthaven was sufficiently insignificant to escape the attention of the Japanese bombers.

With all of this Alex was only indirectly concerned. He was officer commanding (OC) the detachment in Batavia, with responsibility for repair and maintenance of squadron aircraft at Tanjong Priok. He lived in a fairly comfortable hotel in Batavia but his days were full of frustration. The main problem was the slow speed of progress on FVU. The aircraft was due for major overhaul as well as repair of the float. To get access to the repair facilities for his fitters he had to compete with Dutch requirements for their own aircraft. He also faced the absurd overreaction of the Dutch to air-raid warnings and their complete prohibition of night work. Alex remembers air-raid warnings as being frequent but has no recollection of actual bombing of the base. But he does recollect making patrols over the Java Sea to the north, although none are recorded in McVicker's log. Possibly Alex flew with another officer as second pilot. FVU took a back seat when one of the operational Catalinas came in for routine servicing. He even found it difficult to fit in their servicing and, on occasion during the first part of the month, one or other of FVR, FVV and FVW was flying patrols when it should have been in the shop.

Apart from this, transportation, or the lack of it, made his life difficult. Only towards the end of his time in Batavia did he manage to get hold of two fifteen-hundredweight trucks for his detachment's use. Before that he had had to rely on taxis, driven by enterprising but unreliable individuals who drove everywhere as though they had a Zero on their tail. In addition, as 205's 'man in Batavia', Alex was expected to fix all sorts of other problems for the squadron, marooned as they were on Sumatra. On separate occasions both F/Lt Garnell and F/Lt Tamblyn were sent over to "make representations" to Alex (as the RT log quaintly put it) to get some improvements in their conditions, as though he were some oriental potentate. On the 14th of February Alex flew to Oosthaven for the first time in twelve days to confer with Councell and find solutions for some of the problems, flying back again in the evening. He need not have bothered. By the next day the problems hardly mattered: the Japanese had provided them with a whole range of new ones.

On the 15th of February Japanese paratroops seized the airfield at Palembang; a major sea landing followed. Sumatra was suddenly too hot for allied air bases and besides, with the loss of Palembang, 205's fuel supply disappeared. Councell took rapid action. He sent F/Lt Lowe to Alex for orders (which Alex was expected to winkle out of their harassed superiors in Batavia or Bandoeng), packed all those not aboard one of the Catalinas onto the SS *Yoma* (a transport just arrived from Egypt and headed for Batavia), destroyed all stores which could not be removed and – last but not least – paid Weng Kie. Then, having heard from Alex that Tjilatjap on the south coast of Java was to be their next base, he shook the dust of Sumatra from his feet and set off, as an itinerant CO with FVW and FVV, in search of a new base. "Have aircraft will travel!" Jock Graham, in the third Catalina, FVR, was on patrol over the Java Sea and was to follow later – this was becoming a way of life for him!

While Alex soldiered on at Tanjong Priok and Batavia, the rest of the squadron had moved. Now they were all in Java, but an hour further away by air. Compared to Oosthaven, Tjilatjap was a dream come true. Instead of having to deal with a 'reluctant' harbour master, they were welcomed by Lt/Cdr Pratt, U.S.Navy, captain of the Catalina depot ship USS *Childs*. He rolled out a red carpet for them. Accommodation? Everybody was welcome on board his ship. Meals? Please be our guests. Refuelling? Just taxi over to the *Childs's* own bowser boat.

It was as well that good things happened to them on that particular day for the squadron was later devastated by the evening radio broadcast, full of news of the surrender of General Percival at Singapore. Only then, on the 15th of February, did it become clear to all that the war was being lost and that recovery was going to need more than replacement aircraft. A desperate defence of Java, the heart of the Netherlands East Indies and where they were now based, seemed likely to be the next battle.

Alex spent the 16th in Batavia and Tanjong Priok, attending to the airmen landed by the *Yoma*, which then left for India with civilian and military evacuees.[24] The airmen had to be temporarily housed in Batavia. No doubt he jollied them along, cracking jokes about Dutch drivers and sending them on their way by train. The airmen, as a result, would have felt that if "old Jardine" was still telling dumb jokes things could not be as bad as they seemed. Next day, the 17th of February, in spite of the still unfinished work on FVU, Alex flew to Tjilatjap in FVN to confer with Councell and help find new accommodation, in order to reduce the squadron's dependence on Uncle Sam. They arranged for officers and airmen to live in hotels and houses in Tjilatjap; refuelling arrangements were made, independent of the *Childs*, which included the replacement of the hundred-octane fuel already used; and they obtained the use of their own 25-foot boat, complete with unreliable outboard. Tjilatjap began filling up with so-called 'surplus' personnel, who were arriving daily by train and truck from Batavia.

Alex's arrival was a joyous occasion for his old gang of friends. For the first time since the Japanese war started they found themselves for a few days together again. By chance, on the day that Singapore fell, Norman Birks had landed in Tjilatjap on his way to a medical board in Bandoeng. The big Australian suffered terribly from prickly heat, torture in an equatorial climate and so bad that he was seeking a medical discharge or a posting to Europe. Dick Atkinson, recovered from burns suffered in his Christmas Day encounter with a G3M, was already back with the squadron and both he and Sid Scales had been passed fit for duty. On the 16th Gordon Stilling, who had been attached to HQ Bandoeng as squadron liaison officer, flew into Tjilatjap aboard a Dutch seaplane. He was carrying orders for the resumption of patrols but was to remain with the squadron, his sentence in Bandoeng over. So when Alex arrived on the 17th, 'the gang was all there.' Alex remembers no particular occasion, and besides, everybody's social life was on hold. On the 18th he flew a long patrol with Atkinson but by the 20th another squadron aircraft, TVW, was awaiting repair at Tanjong Priok. This caused him to return there right away, but they had had the opportunity to rub shoulders, if only briefly. Tjilatjap was not Singapore, the alcohol-free wardroom of the *Childs* not quite Raffles! It was as well; 205 Squadron as they knew it was melting away.

On the 21st, Atkinson and forty airmen boarded two U.S. destroyers for Australia. They transferred to the submarine depot ship USS *Holland* at Christmas Island. Stilling, with F/O Tucker, left on the freighter *Abbekerk* five days later. Both Atkinson and Stilling were to be killed during the war but Alex, luckily for him, would not discover this until after the war. Gordon Stilling, DSO, DFC, the bravest of the brave, as Wing Commander and CO of 11 Squadron, RAAF, at Cairns, continued to fly Catalinas into the lion's den. He paid the price eventually, being shot down over the Celebes in 1943. Dick Atkinson, DSO, DFC and bar, after bombing the Japanese at Rabaul with 11 Squadron, became CO of 20 Squadron before being posted to Britain, a trick which Alex had never managed. And thus it was that, as a Wing Commander, he was flying a Mosquito over Norway just before Christmas 1944. His mother told Alex after the war that her son was a victim of his own conscientiousness; his squadron had made its attack on the *Tirpitz* and was hightailing it for home while Dick chose to make another circuit of the fjord to observe the damage done. It was to be one circuit too many.

But again we anticipate. On the 19th of February, Alex wrote to Agnes: "The news about Singapore you know ... there have been some miraculous escapes and almost all our friends are safe here." He wrote about a recent telephone conversation, with her and his five sisters – he sounded excited about it and clearly it had cheered him up. It was as if he realised that his life had reached a crisis and he had taken the opportunity of phoning while such things were possible. He went on: "The outcome of this, one cannot try to imagine and so I'm not going to make any comments. So many odd things might happen, all of them so far have been happening which I for one never imagined would occur. The future hardly is there; day to day and hour to hour seems the only way. I wish it were possible for me to write and say something sensible but I cannot. I'm writing with coffee now! Pen has run dry. My bestest love to the girls, God bless you all always. Ever your very loving, Zander Myles." He signed all letters home in this way, a childhood corruption of his given names.

Orders were for the squadron to mount two patrols daily, one up each coast of Borneo. As the Japanese were well established in Malaya, Sumatra and Borneo, and had ships in the Java Sea, reconnaissance flights in that area were full of danger. That 205 Squadron continued to fly them successfully without major incidents speaks volumes for the courage and skill of the pilots and crews. On arrival on the south coast of Java the squadron still had four serviceable aircraft – three at Tjilatjap and a fourth, FVN, at Tanjong Priok with Alex. FVU was still in the shop. On the 18th the number was reduced to three. On that day Jock Graham, who had been there for the reunion on the 17th, was ordered to Ceylon with a planeload of VIPs. He was not expected to return because it was hoped to re-form the squadron at Koggala. He arrived safely and was subsequently attached to another GR squadron. Sadly he was to be shot down and killed by aircraft from the Japanese fleet while on patrol over the Indian Ocean in April 1942.

Alex flew a patrol on the 18th as already mentioned. He must have been desperately in need of operational flying after eighteen days struggling with DNAS officialdom. McVicker's log reads: "S/L Jardine, S/L Atkinson, self, 5 crew, patrol, 10.25 (hours)." It was not usual for two first pilots to be together on the same operational flight unless one was a passenger. Maybe it was a post-injury rehabilitation flight for Atkinson, a sort of 'aerotherapy'. More likely it was their way of arranging to have some time together while doing what they both loved to do. Alex cannot remember. February had not been much of a flying month for him – just a few flips between Oosthaven, Batavia and Tjilatjap and maybe a patrol or two northwards from Tanjong Priok in FVN, although not with McVicker. Let us hope that it was good flying on the 18th and, in so far as such a cloud-hugging, Zero-dodging affair can be, that it was fun; it was to be Alex's last wartime flight and his last flight in a flying boat.

To return to the squadron's operations, FVW had a misadventure on the 20th of February which is best told in the words of its second pilot, Sid Scales:

"On Feb 21, I was airborne as 2nd pilot to F/O Tucker on FVK* for a patrol in the area of Billiton Island and the west coast of Borneo. Taking off at first light we hit an uncharted reef in Tjilitjap harbour just as we were becoming airborne. It ripped a 3-foot gash in the hull but it must have bounced us up because we managed to stay flying. We continued the patrol with orders to land back at Tanjong Priok, if possible, for repairs. During this patrol we sighted survivors from sunken ships floating around on wreckage – no lifeboats. We circled and signalled Batavia the position, etc. Although the sea was calm we couldn't land because of the hole in the hull. We stayed with them until we had a signal that assistance was coming. As I recollect it must have been 100-150 miles from Batavia and we could see they were dreadfully sunburned as the sea was glassy and the reflected sun's rays off the water must have been terrific. We heard later they were all picked up by the three Dutch flying boats, 2 Dorniers and a Cat. There were, I think, nearly 100 people involved and some of the aircraft had to taxi all the way to Batavia because of their load. Fortunately it was a calm sea. Years later I can remember reading a story about it (possibly *Reader's Digest*) as one of the epic rescues at sea.

"But our problem was how to land at Tanjong Priok with a hole in the bottom. We stuffed it with mosquito nets and Mae Wests and blankets, etc., and had some of the crew sitting on the pile. The alighting area in Tanjong Priok was restricted because of shipping that had arrived to evacuate people and our landing was a rather rough stall which forced the stuffing out of the hole and scattered the airmen sitting on it. We started to make water quickly and as we sank lower we had to open up the throttle to keep her moving. Water was up over the bulkheads and the flame floats started to ignite. They were man-handled out of the blisters somehow, leaving a trail to the slipway, the location of which we fortunately knew. Eventually we grounded on to

*The 20th of February, I believe, and the aircraft was actually FVW !

the slipway at nearly full throttle. A big worry at the time were the depth charges we carried under the wings. They were navy depth charges that had been modified to hang on our bomb racks and had to be 'fused' or 'made safe' from a dinghy outside the aircraft when you were at moorings (there was a thing like a tap that had to be turned). Of course, we weren't in a position to do this – and they were set for 25 feet. Hence our hurry to get onto the slip. What we should have done, of course, was to jettison them at sea – bad show – but then it's easy to be wise after the event."

The immediate upshot of this story was that Alex had two Catalinas in a damaged condition to worry about. At the same time, life at Tanjong Priok was becoming more difficult as the number and severity of Japanese air raids increased. Meanwhile on the 21st, with only two serviceable aircraft, FVN and FVV, the squadron continued patrolling from Tjilatjap. The 22nd was not a good day. FVV, in order to prepare for a special job, was ordered to unload its depth charges and top up with petrol. The depth charges were fastened in the same way as those on FVW had been. F/Lt Jackie Lowe jettisoned them too low, at about seventy-five feet, and they exploded on the surface, hurling the aircraft up to about 600 feet and well over on a wing tip.[25] Lowe managed to regain control and land the wrecked aircraft near a sandbar, in spite of large holes in the hull and loss of fabric from wings and ailerons. The crew survived but FVV was a write-off.

The story had a sequel. F/Lt Tamblyn in FVN was then ordered to do the special job and, to avoid the possibility of his aircraft suffering a similar fate, unloaded his depth charges by dumping them from a considerable height. His action caused more waves than he knew; the U.S. cruiser *Houston* was approaching the port but, on seeing a Catalina dropping depth charges, assumed there must be a submarine at large. Immediately turning tail, the cruiser zigzagged at full speed back out to sea! Not for another thirty minutes was Captain Rooks of the *Houston* sufficiently reassured to resume his approach to Tjilatjap. By that time Tamblyn had refuelled and was on his way.*

This mishap meant that the squadron was down to one operational Catalina for the 23rd of February. Undaunted, Tamblyn went out on patrol. Next day he was patrolling again and, miracle of miracles, FVW returned. Alex had worked wonders at Tanjong Priok, the hole was patched and she was as good as new. One suspects that FVW was cluttering the slipway because she had been holed and

---

*The American end of this story appears in *The ghost that died at Sunda Strait* by W. Winslow, in which he gives the date as the 21st; the 22nd comes from the 205 Squadron RT log. Take your pick on the date; there is little doubt that the two stories refer to one event. C.C.

could not be moored; and that therefore the Dutch made her repair top priority in order to clear their working space. For the next few days both FVW and FVN flew patrols while Alex was straining every nerve to repeat the miracle for FVU, which had been at Tanjong Priok for nearly a month. During that time she had been cannibalised for spares for other machines, particularly magnetos and fuel pumps, according to Scales, so repairing her had been like trying to fill a bucket with a hole in it. However, although it was clear from intense air and naval activity that the war was reaching a climax, the missing parts had been assembled, work was progressing slowly and it looked as if Alex might have FVU ready to fly on the 1st of March.

On the 26th Councell sent off another group of airmen, some on the *Kota Gede* for Colombo, others on the *Abbekerk* for Fremantle. On the 27th the squadron said goodbye to F/Lt Tamblyn in FVN; he was dispatched to Emmahaven on the west coast of Sumatra with a military passenger and instructions to carry on to Koggala and join Jock Graham. That left FVW, flown by F/Lt Lowe, to alternate patrols on the west coast of Borneo and the Sunda Strait, which he did on the 27th and 28th. W/C Councell meanwhile concentrated on finding yet another ship on which to evacuate the rest of the squadron. There was no point in having trained airmen without aircraft hanging around in harm's way.

The 28th turned out to be doomsday for Alex at Tanjong Priok. All day the noise of a hellish sea battle could be heard to the north. Unknown to him at the time, in this Battle of the Java Sea the Japanese were in the process of destroying the combined fleet of Dutch, British and American ships, completing the job in the Sunda Strait that night. A Japanese invasion fleet could now land in northern Java without fear of interference and actually landed troops that day at Merak, on the northwest corner of Java, about one hundred kilometres from Batavia. The landing produced the crisis that followed, a day of pure hell which, in retrospect, made the difference between whether Alex and his 205 Squadron detachment would be able to fly to Australia in the repaired FVU, or whether they would become prisoners of the Japanese.

Alex, as second-in-command, knew that the squadron had been ordered to make its way to Ceylon or Australia to regroup; and that many, including Atkinson, Stilling, Tucker and Birks, had already gone. Obviously, if his detachment were unable to get away in FVU, the chances were pretty good that they would be too late to go with the rest of the squadron. To put it bluntly, it was either FVU or an extremely uncertain future. The story, in the words of Alex's report to the Air Ministry after the war, is devoid of the wrenching emotions that he experienced that day. In italics in what follows are what we might suppose those emotions to have been.

"On or about February 24th, RAF Headquarters in Batavia gave instructions that all personnel ... not urgently required ... were to leave by rail for Tjilatjap. Accordingly F/O Ingram and the majority of the personnel then in Batavia left. The following personnel were kept in Batavia in order to:

1) fly out the aircraft then unserviceable at Tanjong Priok; it was hoped that it would be possible to make it serviceable about the beginning of March;

2) have a maintenance party consisting of nine airmen with WO Sanders in charge, able to carry out any repairs or maintenance required without the assistance of a crew. The whole object of keeping these personnel was to ensure that maintenance work and repairs could be done by the Squadron without assistance from the Dutch.

F/O Whitworth, the Adjutant, his Orderly Room Clerk and LAC Sherriff also remained at Batavia in order that the Squadron Records, etc., could be maintained.

"The detachment consisted of:
<u>4 officers</u>: S/L Jardine, F/O Whitworth, F/O Scales, F/O Westcott;
<u>18 airmen</u>: WO Sanders, F/Sgt Bowdon, F/Sgt Stammers, F/Sgt Brett, Sgt Littlewood, Sgt Gamble, Sgt Tugwell, Sgt Allsopp, Sgt Freeman, Cpl Guérin, Cpl Wilson, LAC Hall, LAC McDowell, LAC O'Keefe, LAC Haslam, LAC Taylor, LAC Francis, LAC Sherriff.

"On the 28th of February 1942 the service personnel, British and Dutch, were being evacuated from Batavia.

1200: "During the morning I attempted to get in touch with Reconnaissance Group Bandoeng to obtain instructions – it was not possible to reach them ... *(Where the hell ARE these guys? What a way to run a bloody war! No wonder we can't seem to lick the Japs.)* ...

1300: "I also visited the Dutch Naval Headquarters to find out if they had any information as to the situation in Batavia. Only one or two officers were left and one of them told me that the Japanese had landed at Merak, to the west of Batavia along the coast ... *('Hello, anybody home! Helloooooa!' Where on earth are THESE guys? There's not a solitary Dutchman here! It's their bloody country, not ours, for Pete's sake! 'Oh, hello Sir! Squadron Leader Jardine, OC RAF detachment Tanjong Priok. Can you please tell me what in the heck is happening around here?' Japs in Java! My heavens, the little so-and-sos. How on EARTH did they get here? The little buggers are like weevils in hardtack! What in HELL is the Navy doing about them, with all that noise out there?)*

1400: "I then proceeded to Tanjong Priok Dutch Naval Air Service station, where I discovered that the station had been evacuated except for a skeleton staff who were busy laying wires and charges in order to blow up the hangars and the slipway ... *(Oh my Gawd, Priok's a ghost-town too. 'Mr Sanders, the Japs are in Java, tell the men. Do we ever have to get a move on; we need to get the heck out of here, and soon. Look at those guys laying charges – we'll be blown to Kingdom come!')* ... The starboard mainplane had been handed over by the civilian metal workers and was being placed in position on the aircraft ... *('Good job, good job you guys! It takes the RAF to keep its eye on the ball! That's the way, NOW we're getting the old lady shipshape!')* ...

1500: "I asked the CO of the DNAS if he could clarify the position for me ... *('I'm glad I found you Sir. Nobody at HQ is making any sense. YOU're the man I need to talk to. Maybe YOU can make some sense of things for me! What on earth is going on? How long do I have to get aircraft repairs finished?')* ... He stated that he was awaiting instructions to blow up the station and demolish all shipping in the harbour. He could not give me any definite information about what was to happen to the aircraft in the hangar ... *(Ye gods, we really DO have to get a move on! We've got to fly her out TONIGHT – tomorrow will be too late!)* ...

1600: "I then proceeded to the Port Captain, the senior Dutch naval officer at Priok. He and his staff were in a built-up slit trench ... *(My goodness me! Who ever saw a sailor in a trench!)* ... looking towards the west when I arrived. After some delay ... *(What the hell is the man DOING in that trench?!)* ... I was able to talk to him about getting the aircraft in the hangar away. He told me that his instructions were that nothing should be left afloat in the harbour when the order was given to blow. I asked him if he had any idea when this was likely to happen and he said it would probably be either that night or the following morning. He would not give me any guarantee that the aircraft would be left when the orders were given to blow up ... *(This man is in a flat spin! No concern WHATSOEVER about the fate of a perfectly good Catalina and 22 RAF types! Bloody nitwit, damned bureaucrat – of COURSE he could let me keep our small corner until later on; all he has to do is give the order.)* ...

1700: "I returned to the DNAS station ... *('Good, good, good – NOW she looks more like an aircraft. Good work, chaps, that's the stuff! Let's see if she'll run.')* ... and after putting a little petrol in the tanks, we gave the engines a brief run-up. The aircraft was then put into the water by the maintenance party and crew. Considerable difficulty was encountered as the surface of the water in the harbour was covered with fuel oil. The APC refueller was sent for and, after some delay, it arrived and fuel was taken aboard the aircraft ... (*Jardine, keep your fingers crossed – this thing might just work out. 'Take her out to the nearest mooring with the boat, Mr Sanders. Too bad about this awful mess; some of you will have to get dirty. Oh, and Mr Sanders, send someone in the boat to fetch the refueller. And look sharp, you chaps; it'll be dark in an hour and a bit, and God knows whether these people will let us go on working.'*) ...

1730: "When the only remaining marine craft returned to the pier (from the moorage), one of the fitters reported a serious petrol leak ... (*"What's wrong, a fuel leak? How bad is it? My heavens the fates are testing us today, O'Keefe. Can we fix it? You're not sure, eh: I'd better go and take a look. Jump in, let's go!"*) ... I immediately went out to the aircraft and examined the leak. It was decided that a temporary repair could be done, which would take (about) two hours, and I returned with the fitter to obtain necessary materials ... (*'We've got to do this now chaps or we won't get out of here at all! Let's go get what we need!'*) ...

1800: "On arriving at the pierhead from the aircraft, I was greeted with the information that the orders had been received to destroy the DNAS hangars and slipway and scuttle all ships in the harbour and that the Dutch required their marine craft immediately. I explained the position and pointed out that it was not possible to take off then, nor could I go outside the harbour until I had the means to make this repair ... (*'Now look, Sir, there is no other boat! I HAVE TO HAVE A BOAT TO GET TO THE MOORAGE, DON'T YOU UNDER-STAND? Why don't you send your men for supper while we finish off? The Japs CAN'T be here before tomorrow, at the earliest! We'll be done at 2000 – THEN you can blow the place up!' Damn, damn and blast! Damn this Dutchman. He wants the boat NOW; why can't he hang on for an hour or so? This is our LAST CHANCE!*) ...

1900: "I discussed taking off with this leak with the DNAS Engineer Officer and asked him if he considered it dangerous. His opinion was in accordance with mine, which was that there was danger of fire and possibly of an explosion as the result of petrol vapour forming behind the exhaust gases ... (*Nice chap, nice chap, the only one with a bit of sense round here. Now, if we could just get them to give us a little time, just a couple of hours, we might still make it)* ...

2000: "By this time the Dutch were insisting that they have the use of their marine craft in order to carry out demolition of shipping in the harbour ... *(Oh Lord, let them HAVE their wretched boat! The man's in such a spin he can't think straight. We'll just have to find some other way of getting out to the moorage! 'Send the men to look for anything that floats, ANYTHING that floats!')* ... I again asked if they would allow me to remain in the harbour to effect this repair. Their reply was that nothing was allowed to remain afloat; secondly that the showing of any lights in the harbour was forbidden and that orders were that any light was to be fired upon immediately ... *(We're done for, we're done for, we're done for! Jardine, what on EARTH can we do now? What a blasted bureaucrat! He can't bend a rule at a time like this! 'You know, Sanders, I believe the bastard would LIKE to shoot us!')* ... A few hours previously the CO of the station had stated that in his opinion the order would not be given to blow up until such time as the Japanese were from three to five miles away. Finally, I had decided when the small detachment was formed at Batavia ... that it should keep together if any question of evacuation arose; when this order to blow was received, a number of detachment personnel were in Batavia itself – a distance of eight miles from the station. It was not possible to get them down to the station in time to get away before the blow up, even if the aircraft had been serviceable.

"In view of the general situation as I then visualised it, which was:

a) the Japanese were 3 to 5 miles away;

b) the aircraft could not be made safe to fly without at least two hours' work;

c) that if I were to take off now I should have to leave a number of the squadron in Batavia without instructions;

I decided that the only thing to do was to have the aircraft destroyed and return, with the personnel then at Priok with me, to Batavia and leave from there for Reconnaissance Group at Bandoeng to obtain further instructions. I was naturally reluctant to put the destruction of the aircraft into effect and delayed it until finally the Dutch said I must leave the station with my airmen and that they would destroy the aircraft if I gave the order. By this time the situation at the station was such that, if I had remained, a serious incident may have occurred ... *('Mr Sanders, ask all the men to come over here.' 'Well, chaps, we did our damnedest, but it just can't be done. I'm sorry; you're great fellows and*

*you've all worked hard. But it JUST AIN'T POSSIBLE! We need light,
we need time and we need that damned boat. The Japs are round the
corner and these nitwits are going to blow the place to smithereens any
moment. Let's get the hell out of here before they shoot us! We'll let THEM
blow up the aircraft, and WE'LL go find the boat that the CO has for us!')* ...

2100: "Accordingly I left the station and proceeded to Batavia."

It was to be the beginning of a long trail. With his aircrew and ground crew
Alex roared back into Batavia. Knowing that every minute was important, they
rounded up the rest of the detachment. Having adopted an abandoned three-tonner
Bedford truck, they loaded it and the two fifteen-hundredweights with as much
baggage and stores as would fit in. With two motorbikes they had also 'found', they
set off for Reconnaissance Group headquarters in Bandoeng. It was a hellish
night drive, mostly uphill on a winding road – no danger of any driver falling
asleep. All night they were negotiating their way around Dutch and British
military convoys, none showing headlights for fear of aerial attack, going to who
knows where.

At 0930 on the 1st of March they reached Bandoeng. The streets were full of
military but of nobody else, as the locals were sensibly keeping their heads down
until the Japanese arrived or were defeated. They found RGHQ empty and
reported for orders to Air Commodore Staton at RAFHQ. Staton passed Alex on
to Air Vice Marshal Maltby, General Wavell's chief airman and a more than usually
unsympathetic type. He had recently incurred the wrath of the Australians by
venturing to accuse some of their airmen in Singapore of being "yellow" when they
were assisting the war effort in obsolete Buffaloes.[26] Now he further demonstrated
his lack of empathy with those who serve by sending the exhausted Alex, with his
men, back to Tanjong Priok to confirm that the Dutch had indeed destroyed FVU,
"as a punishment" for not having destroyed it themselves! By such ill-humoured
orders are the fates of men determined!

Alex took only the aircrew in the two fifteen-hundredweights, leaving F/O
Whitworth with the ground crew in Bandoeng. As the little convoy nosed its way
northwest out of Bandoeng at noon, their more fortunate friends and colleagues in
Tjilatjap, including F/O Jefferies with thirty-five airmen who had arrived that
morning by train from Batavia, were humping their baggage on board the *Tungsong*.
This broken-down old steamer had, by good fortune, arrived in Tjilatjap. In more
peaceful times, as the RAFA *Ann*, she had served as the 205 Squadron tender at
Nancowry and Camorta in the Nicobar Islands. Her skipper, Captain McNabb,
"promised to help to the limit of his capacity as soon as his boiler trouble was
remedied," according to the RT log. Tjilatjap was certainly the right port in which

to find a friend! Everybody boarded *Tungsong* except for the CO and F/Lt Birks, who had returned from his medical board and was leaving for Broome as volunteer third pilot on an Empire flying boat. In addition, F/Lt Lowe and the crew of FVW were still operational and patrolling out of Tjilatjap.

Alex found the road deserted. Military convoys had gone to wherever they were going and the locals were lying doggo. At any moment their two small trucks could round a corner and run into Japanese troops, for the invasion seemed to be unopposed. But their luck held. Hurtling back down to the northern plain, the journey took them just four hours. After the relative coolness of Bandoeng, Alex wondered how on earth he could ever have survived the sweltering heat of Tanjong Priok. Or what remained of it! You could say this for the Dutch – they certainly knew how to do a demolition job; the DNAS station was no use to the Japanese, hangars and slipways a mass of twisted concrete, girders and corrugated iron. Out on the moorage a forlorn tail section broke the oily surface at an angle, all that could be seen of FVU. Fuel storage tanks were still burning and the columns of sinister black smoke were visible for miles.

Without wasting time they drove into Batavia, restocked the trucks with as much canned food as they could carry from the deserted barracks, and headed for Bandoeng. The sight of the wreck of FVU, along with the DNAS station had been a real letdown. None of them had slept for thirty-six hours and all felt suddenly exhausted. They craved sleep. At 2000 they pulled off the road at Buitzenorg (now Bogor) where they spent the night.

While they slept, the order from RAFHQ Bandoeng to evacuate the squadron to Australia and re-form in Ceylon, if possible, reached W/C Councell. It was 0100 on the 2nd of March. Councell had already seen off the last group of officers and airmen on the *Tungsong* and assumed that Alex's detachment would reach Australia on board FVU. All that remained were the crew of FVW and himself. One presumes that he grunted and went back to sleep. *Tungsong*, however, had actually not left the harbour. She had run aground soon after sailing. Was it, perhaps, on the same uncharted reef that had holed FVW on the 20th of February? Luckily, McNabb extricated his ship during the night and had returned to his moorings in Tjilatjap to make minor repairs.

In the morning, at 0600 on the 2nd of March, Alex was pulling out of Buitzenorg, still en route to Bandoeng. At the same moment FVW, with W/C Councell on board, left Tjilatjap bound for Broome, Australia. Before leaving, the CO had presumably been assured by Captain McNabb that all was now under control and that he would be proceeding to sea with the tide.

Alex's route crossed the beautiful 1,500-metre-high Puncak Pass on a narrow, winding mountain road. It was cool and misty in the early morning. The sun

contrasted the brilliant green of tea bushes with the red snake of the road winding
up among them – and everywhere the red soil. All that remained of the forest were
tufts of hardwoods on ridgetops; these clung to the skyline on distant hills, giving
them an unshaven appearance. From the pass they jolted down into Bandoeng,
surrounded by high volcanic peaks with whose appearance they were to become all
too familiar in the years ahead.

At 1000 that morning Alex, for the second time in two days, reported to RAFHQ.
Air Commodore Staton had the grace to apologise for his superior's behaviour of
the day before and advised Alex to get cracking down to Tjilatjap to rejoin the
squadron. He did not tell him of the order to evacuate Tjilatjap sent to Councell
at 0100 that morning. To be charitable, it is possible he was not aware it had
been sent.

As things turned out it was to be a closer call than the facts so far would suggest.
Having collected the rest of the detachment Alex was on the road for Tjilatjap by
1330. Southeast of Bandoeng their route passed through a fertile stretch of hilly
countryside and volcanic peaks, then through the orange and tobacco town of
Garoet. Garoet is the central point of several volcanoes and the road, which was
narrow and winding, looped to the south around two of these. The way ahead was
clogged with military traffic grinding up the steep gradients; thunderstorms made
conditions really bad and by 2000 they had only covered the 120 km to Tasikmalaja
– in six and a half hours of driving – at an average of 18.5 kph! There were 150 km
of winding mountain road ahead of them, headlights were not allowed and, rather
than risk their necks in total darkness and maybe heavy rain, they decided to spend
the night at the airfield.

That evening there were, in fact, 205 Squadron men still in Tjilatjap, in spite of
Councell's belief that he was the last to leave. At about the time that FVW touched
down at Broome, Western Australia – 1500 on the 2nd of March – out of the
clouds above Tjilatjap had dropped FVN, flown by F/Lt Tamblyn, the same who
had been despatched to Sumatra and Ceylon. Tamblyn had either not understood
his orders or a message had gone astray. He was now attempting to rejoin the
squadron and was dismayed to find the moorage empty and no sign of familiar
faces. He did not have long to ponder what had happened; he had been seen by
Tungsong as she wallowed her way out of Tjilatjap. Either *Tungsong* called him on
the RT (most likely), or (less likely) put about yet again. In either case Tamblyn
discovered that FVW had gone to Broome. Having refuelled, probably courtesy of
the U.S. Navy, he taxied alongside *Tungsong* and took from her a second aircrew,
that of F/Lt Garnell and P/O Singh. Thus it was not until 2200, two hours after
Alex had stopped for the night, that the heavily laden TVN took off for the
thousand-mile flight to Broome.

They were, had they known it, no more out of the woods than was Alex. At 1100 next morning Alex's trucks reached Tjilatjap. As they rumbled down from the mountains they watched Japanese bombers methodically destroying shipping in the harbour, hardly opposed by ack-ack fire. They did not know it yet but they were thirteen hours too late to catch Tamblyn and a bit more than that to get aboard the *Tungsong*. Had Maltby not sent Alex back to witness the wreck of FVU he would have gained twenty-four hours. In that case those twenty-two men would have encountered Tamblyn and their story would have been different. But on that day, the 3rd of March, they were fortunate to have missed him.

Tamblyn had alighted at Broome at about 0700 that morning; at the moorage were fourteen flying boats, among them the Empire flying boat, a Quantas flying boat and FVW. There was general surprise at his sudden arrival but the CO kept to his original plan. FVW had a bullet through one of its propeller hubs which could cause failure at any time. Consequently both Catalinas were to follow the Empire and Quantas boats to Darwin. From there they would fly around the coast to Sydney. The four flying boats were fuelled and preparing to take off when, at 0950, disaster struck. Six A6M Zeroes with long-range tanks, from Koepang in Timor, appeared like avenging furies out of the northeast. They raked the taxiing flying boats with cannon fire; all four caught fire and sank. After destroying aircraft at the nearby airfield, all on the ground except one, the attackers returned to finish off the eleven other flying boats at their leisure. In spite of the Zeroes' parting shot, the strafing of struggling swimmers, most of those aboard the doomed aircraft survived; but F/Lt Garnell, P/O Singh (who slipped from under Tamblyn's arm in the water,) F/Sgt Ellerby, Sgt McKeirnon and Sgt Markland were killed. The raid had lasted five minutes.

The shocked W/C Councell had just seen his last two aircraft destroyed. In spite of the facts that the USS *Holland* landed Dick Atkinson and his draft that same day in Fremantle[27], that the *Abbekerk* arrived the following day with Gordon Stilling and another draft and that the *Tungsong* would also reach Australia safely on the 12th of March, it was the end of 205 Squadron as Alex had known it.

9

"SHIP ME SOMEWHERES EAST OF SUEZ"

MARCH 1942

In which, for five extraordinary days, Alex and twenty-one of his men
hunt for a boat; and in which they are betrayed by a general capitulation.

"No fighting in the hills!"
— SID SCALES

"The future hardly is there; day to day and hour to hour seems the only way."
The words were Alex's in his letter to Agnes; they applied more than ever
on the 3rd of March as he pulled his trucks into the shelter of roadside trees to
avoid offering a target to the raiders. Without wasting time he ordered all vehicles
to be camouflaged; he would go down into the town with a few airmen in one
fifteen-hundredweight. He had to find squadron HQ, if it was still in Tjilatjap,
and arrange to join the exodus.

He manoeuvred along the docks, skirting rubble and fires and the pathetic
chaos of ill-equipped firemen trying to douse the flames. Opposite the berth used
by the USS *Childs* he stopped for a look around. The *Childs* had gone; so had the
RAF Catalinas from the nearby flying-boat moorages. It was as if he had dreamed
that they were ever there. Things did not look good. Next, he went to the Dutch
naval barracks where 205 Squadron airmen had been billeted. "The series of large
bamboo barracks, each with its long attap sleeping platform, were deserted but
crammed with abandoned equipment – suitcases, kitbags, backpacks, wallets of
photographs, letters from home, a hopeless jumble indicating a hasty, panic-stricken
flight."[28] One last hope was the house which had been rented for 205's officers. He
had difficulty finding it; when he did, nobody was there. He went back to the
docks and the office of S/L Briggs, the RAF embarkation officer, to get news of the
squadron. Briggs told him that Councell and his last Cat had left for Broome, W.
Australia. He also told him of the previous day's comings and goings of Tamblyn
and the *Tungsong*. 205 Squadron had gone.

They were too late! Alex and his men were marooned. He had suspected as much but it was still a shock to hear it officially. He asked about the next ship and started to hand over a list of his detachment. Not so fast! Even in desperate circumstances, things could not happen like that in the Air Force. Briggs would have nothing to do with stragglers such as themselves until they had been fitted back into the chain of command. Although he certainly had RT and telephone contact with HQ, he instructed Alex to drive fifty kilometres inland to report to the ironically named Air Commodore Silly at a godforsaken place called Purworkerto. And Alex, as he had to AVM Maltby, saluted and obeyed, without a thought of questioning the order. It was in his blood, just as Mountjoy Squire never questioned why his wife should have her baby on Perim. It is only to our modern, unmilitary ears that such obedience to authority sounds odd.

Alex returned to the vehicles hidden among the trees. To prepare for the next visit of the Japanese, Sid Scales remembers, "we (had) mounted aircraft machine guns (1 or 2 Brownings or Vickers – I can't remember which) on the trucks" and there were also a number of rifles among the group. They were prepared for the worst. There was little point in disturbing them. Alex told them that the squadron had gone and whatever other news he had gleaned. Then he set off, with a couple of airmen, to find Purworkerto. As he was driving north he must have crossed a convoy of cars and trucks carrying the aircrews of 84 Squadron (Blenheims) into Tjilatjap, led by W/C John Jeudwine. Jeudwine had also been ordered to report to the embarkation officer. When he did so he was told, as Alex would have been, "that there would be no boat that night."[29]

They found Purworkerto without difficulty, arriving at 1300. The air commodore turned out to be more formidable than his name, or the behaviour of his superiors, would suggest. Here at least was an officer who considered fighting the Japanese to be their duty, if attempts to escape the island failed; he wanted to know what guns Alex's detachment possessed. Then they discussed how to arrange an escape for RAF personnel, which seemed to be their first duty. Alex was to return to Tjilatjap, find billets for his men, then find G/C Ridgeway and W/C Steedman who were looking for a ship. He wanted Alex, with his Second Mate's ticket, to take out any ship that they found. Henceforth, Alex would take orders from Ridgeway and would need that officer's authorisation for further plans.

He left Purworkerto at about 1630, reaching Tjilatjap again at 1800 as the daylight was beginning to fade. There had been another raid. Sgt Dave Russell of 84 Squadron remembered "waves of 27 'Betties' (Japanese bombers) ... wiping out the docks and godowns and the port installations without let or hindrance ... We took cover in the 'rubber' when the next wave of bombers arrived. Tjilatjap was in flames, the trees were on fire, the billets were burning, we were in the midst of disaster. It soon became obvious that no relief ship would ever hazard approaching the place."[30] Sid Scales had similar memories: "We were hunkered down in the trees, taking potshots with rifles at Jap aircraft which were circling low." The fact of actually being able to strike a blow or two, however poorly aimed, was a tonic for morale. Alex congratulated them and seemed as pleased as they were about it all, although he must privately have reached the same conclusion as Sgt Russell.

The next job was to find some digs. The barracks seemed a bad choice because it was a target for raiders. They returned to the house where squadron officers had been billeted, which was large, comfortable except for the mosquitoes, and dry. Now they appreciated the wisdom of stuffing the trucks with canned food – at least they could eat, even if the menu was predictable. Later, except for those on watch, they flopped down wherever they could; most slept at once, soothed by familiar noises – drumming rain on the tin roof and the monotonous rasp of cicadas. Even air-raid sirens were familiar and caused no heads to stir.

On the 4th of March the detachment turned to early. Alex instructed F/O Whitworth to return to their position of the previous day with most of the detachment, get the trucks out of sight and prepare to defend themselves. It was as well he did; Jeudwine remembered: "Japanese aircraft came over in force and concentrated on the oil dumps, set fire to them and did a lot of damage to the jetty."[31] With two or three ground crew, Alex set off in search of the two senior officers. Little that they saw in the harbour made them particularly hopeful that they would find a ship. The Japanese raiders had been thorough. Every dock had its derelict, sunk in shallow water with masts and funnels projecting.

Remarkably, Briggs had good news: his RT operator had managed to raise the base at Broome in Western Australia. The contact had not been a good one but he had passed a message for 205 Squadron that Alex and detachment were in Tjilatjap. This had been acknowledged before the operator lost the contact but he would monitor the waveband for further messages. Sid Scales only heard of this indirectly. He remembered that "we stuck around for a while in the hope that the Squadron might send an aircraft back for us in a sort of Dunkirk operation – there was still a bit of W/T contact – but nothing happened." There was no 'Dunkirk' because the squadron had no aircraft but, unaware of that fact, for a day or two they lived in hope.

G/C Ridgeway and W/C Steedman were interesting officers, cast in the same mold as A/C Silly. They and Jeudwine had discovered a small Dutch warship, "… her fuel tanks full and with ample stores aboard. She had only superficial damage from machine gun bullets but no damage had been caused to vital parts. Here was a ship that could and would have taken all our aircrew personnel to Australia." Alex refers to her as a corvette while Sid Scales remembers her as a tug.

They are probably both right – corvettes tended to attract insults! Jeudwine urged Ridgeway to talk to the Dutch about it. That officer was beginning to see light in the tunnel: "Why Jardine, you can skipper her – if only we can persuade the Dutch brass* to let us use her." There was only one way to find out and he asked to see the Dutch naval commander.

The Dutch navy had taken a terrible beating in the Battle of the Java Sea. Morale, which had been good, had collapsed and although it was not difficult to find the senior Dutch naval officer, his command had evaporated. At first he stone-walled them and "sent a message to say he was too busy to see anyone. The next day, the 5th of March, [Ridgeway] tried again. This time the Commander made a variety of excuses which included that the radio equipment had been damaged by machine gun fire, that the Dutch themselves were going to use the Corvette and finally that it had been decided to sink it in the mouth of the harbour. Nothing could move him from this non-cooperative attitude."[32] The officer they spoke to was a stoic gentleman who seemed to be the only one of his compatriots who was not, as Alex would have said, 'in a flat spin.' He probably had reasons for his obstructiveness apart from the ones that Jeudwine mentioned. If he had an engineer officer to fire her up why was the ship still at anchor in a harbour under enemy attack? He probably had no technical crew. His men had been with the fleet, many being now at the bottom of the Java Sea and the rest with the destroyers at Sourabaja. Alex persevered. He offered the mechanical skills of his detachment, some of whom had enormous experience with aero-engines. He himself was no stranger to engine rooms and would be willing to put his experience to the test. Could he, along with W/O Sanders and a couple of fitters, at least have a look at the engine room? The Dutch commander would have none of it; if the ship sailed she would be manned by his sailors, period. He thought it amusing that English airmen thought they could run his ship if the Dutch navy could not. Finally, he told them that there was a skeleton crew on board to man the antiaircraft guns. They would resist any attempt to board her and their orders were to scuttle her if and when the Japanese arrived, explosives having been laid for that purpose.

It had been a good idea but it was now dead. The only hope would be to find a naval engineer but the Dutch navy must have thought of that too. No, they would just have to find something else that would float. It was then approaching noon; they had six hours to search the harbour. Unknown to Alex, during the argument with the Dutch commander Jeudwine had made an important find – a small motor launch in working order, which he immediately commandeered for 84 Squadron. However, a search for a larger vessel seemed unlikely to succeed for two reasons. First, though northern Java is bounded by the sluggish Java Sea, Tjilatjap

*senior officers

is the only deep-water harbour on a south coast pounded by Indian Ocean surf; if there was no large vessel there, they were unlikely to find one elsewhere. Secondly, had there been a ship the Dutch navy would have found it and co-opted its engineer. But pessimism would get them nowhere and they would not know for sure until they had looked. They started at the west end of the waterfront and searched the whole of it in six hours. They found vessels which might have fitted the bill if they had had engines or were not badly damaged. The sampans which were normally clustered along the wharves were – absent! No doubt their owners had sailed them out of reach of the 'perspiring *tuans*'. Eventually, having reached the east end of the docks, they had to admit there was absolutely nothing to be had.

That evening the talk in the house was nevertheless optimistic. For Whitworth, Scales and their men the day in their leafy hideout had been uneventful. Instead of Japanese aircraft their distractions had been a troop of monkeys which had passed by and set up a disapproving chatter in the trees. When Alex reported all the day's developments most felt certain that W/C Councell would send a flying boat back. Alex was not so sure: he found it odd that there had been no RT message for him that evening when he checked with Briggs. Naturally he did not share his doubt; instead he determined to spend the next day extending his search for a boat to the coastline to the east of the town.

Thus, the 5th of March was another day of searching. Jeudwine reported: "I had been sent by the Group Captain to try to discover whether, by chance, any ships had been abandoned on the coast. I could not discover any." He travelled by car, as did Alex and the two senior officers who were doing the same thing. Alex does not mention Jeudwine – in fact, was not aware of him – so they certainly searched different areas. There was no coastal highway so the only way to search was to drive inland, turn east or west on the road and take any track back towards the sea. In this way they visited a number of villages, each at the mouth of a small river flowing out of the hills. As they stood in sunshine on a riverbank, sometimes they saw a squall approaching, a dark patch moving fast across the sea then up onto the land, tossing palm tops in drenching chaos before passing inland. At each village were many fishing boats, stranded on mud flats by the receding tide, waiting for rising water to restore their dignity; once refloated they lazed at their moorings or reared like thoroughbreds in one of the squalls. There were also dugouts on the beaches but there were no boats capable of carrying numbers of men. It was the same story as far as they went that afternoon.

Jeudwine had been told by Ridgeway, "that if we could make a getaway we could do so". Accordingly, his officers had spent the day in their motor launch, scouring the harbour from the water. From that vantage point they had made a second important discovery: two 30-foot lifeboats without auxiliary engines, still in the davits of a sunken KPM liner but invisible from the shore. When their boss returned, "we got our two lifeboats to the jetty then divided up our personnel. We still had the motor launch ... and into this we put five men, the other boats taking thirty each. The idea was to let the launch tow both boats as far as she could with her available petrol, then jettison her, her crew being divided between the two lifeboats."[33] Leaving a strong guard on their prizes, 84 Squadron men spent the next twenty-four hours scrounging and loading fuel and stores, including an unbelievable quantity of American beer.

Once again, Alex's detachment exchanged stories that evening. The RT operator had spent part of the day trying to raise 205 Squadron at Broome. Although he had contacted the control tower, the Australian operator knew only that 205 Squadron was no longer there and agreed to forward the message to W/C Councell, if he could contact him, but no other message had been received. In fact, unknown to them, Councell and those with him were at sea, en route from Broome to Port Hedland on the pearling lugger *Nickel Bay*. The main party in Tjilatjap had spent a dull day on the outskirts of town. A new worry was that some airmen were developing tropical ulcers, so it was decided to contact RAF medical staff next morning, even if that meant a drive to Purworkerto.

The 6th of March started like the day before. Those without jobs to do, or a visit to the medics, returned to their roadside hideout. As his expectations were not high for the third day of searching, Alex ordered the detachment to rendezvous up on the road and not at the house. This time the boat search went to the west; they needed a motor boat to search efficiently, but the only one afloat was in the hands of 84 Squadron. No modern tourist visits the industrial port of Cilacap (as it is now spelt) for its own sake, but the boat trip west from Cilacap west to Kalipucang is the highlight of a visit to Java's south coast. It takes a visitor across the lagoons of the Segara Anakan – a stretch of inland sea sheltered by the long island of Nusa Kambangan to the south, the feature that also shelters Cilacap itself. A motorboat would have taken them to all the villages – the Segara Anakan has a shoreline of several hundred kilometres, including all the bays and inlets. In each they could have assessed the likelihood of success without having to land. They might have returned along the north shore of Nusa Kambangan, in whose harbours, no doubt, any local with a boat to hide was doing just that. They would have passed mangrove swamps, fishermen in dugout canoes and their villages – clusters of thatched houses perched high off the mud banks on stilts, sheltered by palm and banana trees, with rice paddies, then jungle, at their backs.

Without a boat, they had to search in the same manner as the day before, once again meeting passive resistance. The nationalist Sultan Sjahir wrote that the Indonesians at first thought of the Japanese as liberators: "For the average Indonesian the war ... was simply a struggle in which the Dutch colonial rulers finally would be punished by Providence for the evil, the arrogance and the oppression they had brought to Indonesia."[34] As fellow *tuans*, Alex and his companions could hardly expect more friendly treatment. Nevertheless, as the afternoon thunderstorm was trying to dissolve them in an unbelievable amount of rain, they heard from villagers that the Japanese were approaching Tjilatjap from the east and were not far away. True or not, the rumour put an end to the search. They returned to Tjilatjap to find the roads clogged with Dutch military vehicles. The Dutch army, who had not only not resisted the Japanese invasion of the island but had not fired a shot since, were pulling out.

On the surface it is hard to believe that while the Dutch air force and the DNAS had fought so bravely to defend Singapore and Java, and while the Dutch navy had fought the heroic and suicidal Battle of the Java Sea, the Dutch army should have been so reluctant to open its account. Mountainous and forested Java is good defensive country; the army was numerous with some excellent troops. The Japanese had the handicap of any maritime invader: their supply routes were at the mercy of enemy submarines. If the invaders could have been checked by a tough defence in Java, eventually the tables would turn. So, why did it not happen? Probably, the answers are suggested by Sid Scales: "The Dutch military had a lot of Eurasians in it whose hearts were not really in the fight! The cunning Japanese had promised a degree of independence for the Javanese once the Dutch were defeated. There were stories of sabotage and 5th column activities. It is said that some of their crack troops like the Ambonese (likened to the British Ghurka regiments) were kept in barracks." John Gunther had suggested: "The Dutch appear to be rather suspicious of their own natives in military matters. The native troops, for instance, are not allowed to train with machine guns, and natives are not permitted to visit Dutch warships!"[35] Like many colonial armies, the army of the Netherlands East Indies was not designed for defence against an external aggressor; it was intended for use against the people, should they decide to challenge the Dutch, using the ancient strategy of divide and rule. So the Ambonese and Madurese were willing to crack the heads of the majority Javanese in Jakarta, in the same way that British-employed Sikhs and Ghurkas liked to crack the heads of city dwellers in Bombay or Calcutta. Meanwhile the air force and navy were almost entirely recruited in the Netherlands.

If the Dutch were leaving, so must the British. Orders came to rendezvous with A/C Silly at Tjamis, a mountain village on the road to Bandoeng. At 1800 Alex was preparing to lead the detachment out of town when the road was filled with the trucks and guns of a British antiaircraft unit, commanded by a Colonel Humphries, who had decided to have a go at the advancing Japanese, presumably with their antiaircraft guns over open sights, Rommel-style. The idea seemed suddenly attractive to airmen about to engage in yet another withdrawal. With the gung-ho support of his men, Alex offered to help. Humphries was a reckless man but he could see at a glance that this bunch of 'flightless' airmen, with their handful of rifles, two machine guns and eager faces, would be more hindrance than help. He politely declined Alex's offer. Disappointed, Alex set off in the wake of the Dutch convoys towards Tjamis.

It was the end of a sticky tropical day at sea level, a day of steaming sunshine punctuated by rain squalls. The last thing the detachment needed was a night drive without lights on a road being destroyed by rain and heavy vehicles. Japanese command of the air, however, meant that a daylight drive would have been suicidal. So bad were the conditions that it took them eight hours to cover the hundred uphill kilometres northwest to Tjamis. They reached this village at 0200 and, without reporting to anybody, pulled off the road and slept for a few hours. But Alex could not sleep easily; he had to find a way to get his twenty-one people off the island and back to doing what they had been trained to do. After a couple of hours of mosquito-punctured sleep in the cab of a truck, he scrambled out and went for a walk in the darkness, looking for a road south.

On the evening of the 6th, as Alex's detachment were beginning their uphill grind, the sixty-five airmen with Jeudwine cast off from the Tjilatjap jetty, left the harbour and put out to sea. In Jeudwine's words: "We soon found that the motor launch would not tow the lifeboats and we could not steer a course. Then we tried our sail but owing to the overloaded state of the boats again we were unsuccessful. So we decided to return to a cove to the south of the mouth of the river [in fact, an inlet] which leads to the harbour at Tjilatjap." That was easier said than done; in the darkness they wrecked the launch and one lifeboat in the surf on the south side of Nusa Kambangan, while the crew of the other lifeboat, wisely anchoring outside the surf, swam ashore. Everybody survived and the half-drowned would-be mariners held a council of war. A crew of only twelve was selected to continue the escape attempt in the remaining lifeboat, their departure scheduled for the following night.[36]

Meanwhile Alex had found a road. His find was a piece of luck because roads through the jungle of the hills were few and far between. Returning to the trucks he waited until the first hint of daylight loosened the sticky grip of night. Then, as the cicadas were falling silent, he roused his exhausted charges, had them consume a breakfast they did not really want and set off due south down the road he had found. It was a more travelled road than he had expected, leading towards Tjidulang on the south coast, a place about seventy kilometres to the west of Tjilatjap. Alex felt optimistic again because they would be far enough to the west of Tjilatjap for the people not to be aware of the search for boats – so there might actually be one. All went well for a couple of hours, then their hopes were dashed. Round a corner, at the foot of a steep hill, the road was blocked by a tree which had been dragged across it. In the middle of the road an Indonesian soldier of the Dutch army vaguely pointed his rifle at them, while others sat in the shade of the trees. The reason was evident; past the tree trunk, the bridge over a ravine had been blown. The soldiers explained in sign language that no one was allowed to proceed further and that Alex must turn around and return to Tjamis. To avoid an argument that is what they did – at least, until they were out of sight and earshot.

At the top of the hill Alex held a council of war. They could return to Tjamis and report to A/C Silly, to take their chances with the RAF command structure; or they could hide the trucks in the jungle and trek south on forest trails. If they chose the latter, they would hope to find a boat and set off for Australia, though there was no guarantee they would survive. The boat trip would be under a tropical sun for a distance equal to that from England to North Africa. A tough choice! They decided in favour of a return to Tjamis because they had sick airmen with them. These men would certainly get sicker without medical attention.

By 1200 on the 7th of March they were back in Tjamis. Alex reported to A/C Silly who ordered him to join his vehicles to his convoy. That afternoon each man was issued with a rifle and ammunition. The Air Commodore told them to be prepared for a fight; they were going to take to the hills and would give the Japanese something to remember them by. Alex, the man for all seasons, once again had the necessary skills – at least he had some dimly remembered exposure to army tactics from Army Cadet days with Lieutenant Waldo Skillings. He began to plan out rifle training for the following day and darkness found them still in Tjamis.

Sid Scales takes up the tale again: "It seemed a hopeless situation as most of us were ignorant of guerrilla fighting in jungle conditions or even handling a rifle. I remember it was raining and the convoy was static and we were sheltering in an attap native building. Some of our airmen had 'come across' some Navy rum in our travels and another bright lad had a portable gramophone and records that he had 'picked up' from somewhere. We proceeded to have a farewell party." As the rum had its effect the atmosphere must have been 'eat, drink and be merry for tomorrow we die'; let us hope they enjoyed themselves for it was to be their last drink for a long time. The party ended with the rum and all fell into an insect-harassed slumber. Unknown to them, some distance to the south Jeudwine and his crew of eleven were once more at sea off Nusa Kambangan, having left forty-three of their number on the island, with a promise of being picked up within two months.*[37]

"Early in the morning darkness after the night before, there was an alarming racket," Sid remembered. "It was a truck coming round to collect up again all the arms and ammunition. No fighting in the hills!" Silly had been overruled by GHQ who wanted no heroics by frustrated airmen to disturb an orderly surrender to the Japanese, though nobody knew that yet. "This was all very unsettling and an angry S/L Jardine decided there was no future in this convoy. There was a feel of capitulation in the air – but no hard facts. It was decided that, when the convoy moved again, we would take the first road to the left and head for the south coast to try and get off the island."

For those who would blame these RAF men for not making the tough decision to fight, in spite of orders, it is worth considering the experience of South African author Laurens van der Post, who made such an attempt. He had orders from Wavell to establish an evacuation centre for British and Dutch servicemen cut off by the Japanese invasion. He had a radio transmitter for communicating with allied submarines to arrange escapes. As a cover, and to ensure Dutch cooperation, he set up a base in the mountains of southwest Java to carry out guerrilla attacks on the Japanese. He was joined by about a hundred men, some Dutch, some Ambonese, but mostly the survivors of an Australian unit which had fought the invaders. Their presence tied down numbers of Japanese troops, who were uncharacteristically cautious about advancing into the mountains, but otherwise the mission was a failure. Unable to find an RT operator, Van der Post made no contact with submarines. Most of the men became sick from tropical diseases, Van der Post himself suffering repeated and crippling resumptions of the malaria he had contracted earlier in Ethiopia, and the unit's Achilles' heel was its dependence on villagers for food. The Japanese had only to threaten to kill the people of their supplying villages to force Van der Post to surrender. It seems likely that most of his men either died from disease or starvation, or were killed by the bandits who infested that region.[38] RAF men would have had even less chance of long-term survival because, as *tuans* with no Dutch, they would not have had the villagers' cooperation – indeed, would probably have been betrayed immediately to the Japanese.

At 0700 the convoy moved off, still in a northwesterly direction. The collection of rifles had dealt a deadly blow to morale. Alex fully intended to make good his escape from the convoy and for that reason the 205 Squadron detachment brought

---

*Miraculously Jeudwine's crew made it to Australia. After forty-four days at sea they would be picked up by a Catalina from USS *Childs* a few miles off Port Hedland on the 22nd of April. For his efforts Jeudwine received the OBE. The forty-three who stayed behind were betrayed to the Japanese and became POWs on the 20th of April. Had they been able to hide for ten days more, they would have been rescued by the U.S. submarine *Sturgeon* which arrived to pick them up on the 30th of April.

up the rear. Fifteen kilometres past Tjamis they reached Tasikmalaja where a road to the south branched off – they were to find it later in the month when they drove down it – but that morning nobody spotted it. They were discouraged and very tired and many were no doubt asleep as they bumped along the road. Even the vigilant Alex missed it. There was no other road to the left and by 1200 they had pulled into the shade of the orange groves of Garoet to await orders. They had not long to wait. A general capitulation was announced: all allied combatants were to lay down their arms and RAF units were to return to Tasikmalaja airfield to meet their Japanese captors.

Those sixty kilometres were not pleasant ones. So the war was over, they were 'in the bag'. Conversation touched upon what 'they' thought they were doing, surrendering without firing a shot. The mood was of disgust, despair and some degree of fear. What they knew of the Japanese – the machine-gunning of survivors in the water or on parachutes, for example – did not make them confident that they would be well treated. At Tasikmalaja the actual surrender took place between the senior officers present and a Japanese officer with a few soldiers in a truck. It was very much an anticlimax. The officer gave instructions that nobody was to leave the airfield – and departed! Their captors' only presence was a sentry on a motorcycle who circled the field outside the perimeter wire three times an hour.

In the corner of the airfield was an enormous new hangar, more or less undamaged. They drove over to it; everybody went inside and an area was claimed for 205 Squadron. Their fears and tensions had suddenly been switched off. The shooting was over, there was a roof over their heads, they were deeply exhausted and more than a little depressed. Alex, whose irrepressible energy and enthusiasm had kept them going for so long, was affected more than most. Without ceremony they collapsed in little heaps onto whatever they could find to lie on. They slept for twenty-four hours.

10

ON THE RUN

MARCH–MAY 1942
In which Alex and twelve others break out of their first POW camp in Java,
spending ten weeks in a second attempt to find or build a boat;
and in which they are eventually recaptured by the Japanese.

"... He thought it was a great joke that we had been trying to build a boat!"
— SID SCALES, SPEAKING OF THE JAPANESE SERGEANT

Alex was able to think a great deal more clearly when he finally roused himself during the afternoon of the 9th of March. He had needed that sleep after a week of frantic activity, most of it under great strain. These events were taking place in the tropics, where people normally stay in the shade and walk slowly to stay cool, where *tida appa* is the usual reaction to pressure and where work is confined to the morning hours. Noel Coward had it right: in the tropics only "mad dogs and Englishmen go out in the midday sun." Awake, Alex's immediate feelings were depression and relief: depression because he was a prisoner and the future a grey blur; and relief because, although he still had problems, the high-pressure ones had been shelved by the capitulation. For captivity removed both the possibility of escape from the island and the need to be constantly scheming. Decisions about eating and sleeping arrangements and squadron duties had to be made, but these were practical issues.

Both these feelings lasted about half an hour. A turn around the airfield revealed that they were almost unsupervised. Senior officers had agreed that nobody would leave the airfield, but the Japanese army was too busy overrunning Java to do more than assign a few motorcycle sentries to guard its many prisoners. Those who wished to escape the island had 'a window of opportunity'. It would not remain open for long so they must pass through it as soon as possible. Immediately, hope rekindled itself in his head and with it, all the pressures came flooding back. Alex was still responsible for getting those twenty-one men off Java.

Before the surrender Alex had asked Silly whether he and his men might make another attempt to get away. The answer had been 'no' at that time. Alex did not take that as final and felt sure of a more favourable answer once the former 'fighter in the hills' had had time to reflect. Meanwhile there was work to be done. In that hot and humid climate, good sanitation was vital for maintaining the health of the many RAF personnel interned at Tasikmalaja. All available hands had to be turned to designing and digging latrines and sewers – open ditches which could be flushed with water on a regular basis. The Japanese made no pretence of supplying food, so kitchens must be built and supplied with firewood, vegetable gardens planted and food supplies bought from local farmers and merchants. The work was welcome as a way of keeping the men busy and spirits up – to be improving one's situation is always encouraging. But the restless ones could not accept that they were to be stuck in the bewitching beauty of this godforsaken volcanic plateau for the duration of the war. Rather than wait for the second shoe to drop they were on the lookout for a way out.

The airfield had been a Dutch air base, though not a major one. It had been bombed and a number of wrecks littered the runways. Among them was a small bomber in apparent working order. What happened next is best told by Sid Scales:

> "Two airmen, whose names I can't remember, approached S/L Jardine and myself one night to see if we were willing to fly off this aircraft which they said they had refuelled stealthily during the darkness from drums of fuel which were still scattered round the airfield. They had checked the engines as well as they could without actually running them up. They had some mates they wanted to take with them and they figured that by packing some bods in the bomb bay, the aircraft would take ten to twelve people! The aircraft was a Dutch air force Glenn Martin twin-engined bomber and we eyed it warily in the daylight. It seemed in reasonably good condition – how the Dutch hadn't destroyed it I don't know."

Alex and Sid accepted the challenge. After dark, Alex climbed into the cockpit to familiarise himself with the layout of the controls. He also rehearsed how to start the engines and have her rolling in the minimum time. The aircraft was probably a Martin 139WH, of which the Dutch had bought more than a hundred from the American manufacturer by 1939. It was not much of an aircraft. It was designed to be flown by a crew of three, sitting one behind the other under a 15-foot canopy, who had no armoured protection, thanks to this observation dome approach to aircraft design. Worse, neither its range nor its bomb load was very great. Finally,

the long canopy turned the aircraft into a flying greenhouse under an equatorial
sun. However, it was an aircraft and it looked as if it would fly. There were other
pilots in the camp and Sid suspects that the airmen chose to ask Alex and himself
on the recommendation of 205 Squadron men. He went on:

> "Perhaps they [the other pilots] were approached too, but we were the
> only ones mug enough to take it on! We had a small scale map of the
> N.E.I., including the northern part of Australia (looked like it had
> been torn from a school atlas), and we figured the shortest distance
> from Tasikmalaja to Australia was to Port Hedland, about 1,200 miles
> SSE. Although not sure, we thought it within the range of the aircraft.
> So it was on – how desperate can you get!
>
> The problem was to get the aircraft shifted to the end of the
> airfield for the maximum takeoff run and to avoid any taxiing. To
> achieve surprise the pilot had to start it up first go, open up the
> throttles and hope for the best. There was a Dutch army officer who
> was in charge of clearing the field of crashed and unserviceable aircraft
> and bits and pieces, and S/L Jardine persuaded him to use his tractor
> to tow the bomber to the airfield edge of the heap, so we would have a
> clear run. We were to take off at night, trusting in some moonlight,
> and try to get clear of the land before daylight."

Unfortunately it had not been possible to keep the proposed escape a secret.
"There were mutterings about possible nasty reprisals if the attempt was successful
– there was still a bit of childlike faith that the Nips would abide by the Geneva
Convention." Senior officers were most unwilling to give the Japanese a pretext for
claiming that the surrender agreement had been breached, lest they respond
brutally against the remaining prisoners. Nobody yet had experience of Japanese
POW camps; maybe they would be chivalrous if not provoked or made to 'lose
face' by escape attempts.

"Anyway, a guard was posted on the aircraft to prevent anyone from interfering
with it." Alex remembers making a gentleman's agreement with the members of
the guard: the escapers would pretend to have surprised and overpowered them,
leaving them tied up with a few scrapes and bruises – to allow them to appear
blameless in Japanese eyes. But later, in the darkness, the guard lost their nerve
"and to protect themselves from possible assault by the would-be escapers, they
slashed the tyres!" When they arrived to make their do-or-die attempt, Alex, Sid
and their daring companions were furious about this treachery. Alex, in particular,
was beside himself – he had had enough of the pusillanimous gutlessness of the

brass of which this seemed the worst example. However, as Sid tells us: "Several months after the event, in conversation with Dutch pilots who were familiar with Glenn Martins, we were told that we could never have made it with that load and the runway available! I think I can safely recollect that – fifty-seven years ago – we were relieved!" He went on: "At this distance it sounds very melodramatic and I sometimes wonder if my memory is playing tricks on me!"

In fact, maybe the tire-slashing episode was another manifestation of 'Lucky Alex'! They could have met a nasty end in all sorts of ways: by wandering from the runway in the darkness, by clipping the trees at the end of the runway, by being shot down or by running out of gas over the Indian Ocean. If the aborted test flight of the Flying Flea had been Alex's first 'life', the slashing of the Martin's tires was another.

A footnote to the Glenn Martin saga was the meeting of the twenty-two members of the 205 Squadron detachment before the proposed takeoff. Sid wrote: "I think it would have been [Adjutant] Ken Whitworth [who suggested the meeting time and place], enthusiastically agreed to by us all." The escape attempt meant saying goodbye to Alex and Sid. The rendezvous was to be at 6:00 p.m. under the clock at Paddington station on the first 8th of March after the war. Sid went on: "I always remembered about it, and when I was in London (1948-1950) I went along – but nobody was there!" Sadly, there would be only ghosts under the clock; every one of the eighteen airmen was to die as a result of Japanese brutality. The four officers survived the camps but only Westcott and Whitworth were in Britain and, knowing the facts, neither had the heart to go.

Alex soon got over his disappointment and began planning a different escape. The south coast beckoned; he was anxious to resume the search for a boat, a search which he had had to interrupt a few days previously. The camp commander, his fellow searcher W/C Steedman, did not go so far as to forbid any escape attempt. He did forbid Alex to take anything which had been accounted for to the Japanese and fortunately that did not include people. The Japanese had, so far, no idea how many people they had 'in the bag'. It probably did not include the three-ton truck in which part of the 205 Squadron detachment had arrived. So Alex, with other 205 Squadron members, joined a group which was planning to break out.

Many airmen were understandably reluctant to exchange the illusory security of the air base for the horrors and dangers of jungle and ocean. The final party included five 205 Squadron members – Alex, F/O Westcott, F/O Scales, Sgt Gamble and LAC McDowell. The other eight were W/C Bell, S/L Shoppee, S/L Roberts, F/Lt 'Bombs' Charlton, AC Monk, AC Gascoyne, AC Deadman and AC Sheerin. Some had a particular skill which would be needed. For instance, Shoppee, an Australian and older than the rest, had been a bush pilot in New Guinea, had jungle experience and local knowledge; McDowell was a carpenter who had built boats; Roberts and Gamble were radio experts; Scales, a talented cartoonist, was also a draftsman; Charlton was a bomb disposal expert and a proverbial Mr Fix-it; the young Irish lad Sheerin was Bombs's 'Man Friday'; while the genial Bell had no skill other than a marvellous basso profundo. And Alex? He was their mariner and navigator, their outdoors survival expert. He claims not to have been the leader and Sid agrees that it was a co-operative venture. But he also remembers Alex's natural leadership; it was to him that others took their ideas. Bell was a more senior officer, but Alex's earlier requests to Silly and Steedman speak for themselves. Knowing his compulsion to be doing something about problems and his love of being busy, not to mention his popularity with all ranks, we can be sure he was the whipper-into-shape, the inspirer, the peacemaker, the supplier of energy and ingenuity and the spring which kept them all wound up.

They were setting off on a venture full of risks and uncertainty. Tasikmalaja itself is near the southern edge of the central plateau, an area of tea and rice and citrus plantations surrounded by great volcanoes, looming in and out of clouds. Civilisation lay to the north and southeast. Due south, where they were headed, was the least populated part of Java. Oh, there were people there all right, Java's population being as dense as that of eastern China. But there is no coastal plain to the south of Tasikmalaja. From just west of Tjilatjap the south coast bears comparison with the west coast of Vancouver Island – the same pounding surf, the same hilly and forested countryside, accessible only by forest trails over cliffs or along the beach at low tide. But the resemblance goes only so far; though cool at night in the mountains, it is extremely warm at sea level. Off the trails the tropical rain forest, the oldest and least cleared in Java, is impenetrable to a 'perspiring *tuan*'. Moreover, it was always unlikely that they would find a boat large enough to reach Australia. The people were fishermen, their boats small. There are few harbours and none capable of sheltering vessels of any size .

Those of the party with any experience of the rain forest would know some of its hazards, sufficient that they could imagine others. Their chief danger would not be snakes and large animals – such creatures avoid humans and would receive warning from so many pairs of feet. The most insidious enemies would be heat, rain, disease and innumerable, unavoidable insects. They faced human dangers too. Outside the camp they were outlaws, fair game for the Japanese. Though unarmed, there was every likelihood they would be killed in an encounter with Japanese soldiers, or, if captured, executed as guerrillas or spies. There were no rules for the game they had started playing. In addition, on the whole the Javanese preferred the Japanese to the *tuans*, whether Dutch- or English-speaking. Any 'honeymoon' with local people they might enjoy would last only as long as their money did or until the people heard of Japanese reprisals against those who helped whites.

Sid Scales described the beginning of this time of limited freedom.

> "We'd stocked a 30 cwt truck with provisions, bits of timber and tools acquired around the aerodrome, put white arm bands on with a red spot on them – the story being we were a work party sent by the Nips down to Simpang to help restore a bridge that had been blown. So when the Nip patrol drove past the spot on the perimeter where we'd parked the truck in the foliage, we cut a hole in the wire and drove out. We'd figured they used to go past every twenty minutes. Anyway, it worked and away we went towards the south coast. One of our party, S/L Shoppee, an Aussie, knew the way. We never sighted any Nips fortunately – in hindsight I don't think our story would have washed! At Simpang we ferried the truck across the river on a bamboo raft, the local Javanese being only too happy to accept our guilders. A bit further on we ran out of petrol, dumped the truck, made up packs and tramped the rest of the way to a little kampong at the mouth of the river, called Tjipatoedjah."

They had probably taken the road that Alex had missed on the 7th of March. The distances are not great, about 55 km as the vulture flies from Tasikmalaja to the coast at Tjipatoedjah. Simpang was halfway. The terrain would have been hilly, the road a winding, red-mud track and the need for low gear would explain why they ran out of gas. It would be interesting to know what people at Simpang made of their arm bands; had they encountered any 'Nips', these might have been just enough to get them all shot. Nevertheless, having abandoned their truck they must have been a fine sight, with packs topped by scrounged tools, tramping down the road to Tjipatoedjah – "Heigh ho, heigh ho," for all the world like the seven dwarfs.

At Tjipatoedjah, instead of marching boldly into the settlement, they bivouacked discreetly while Shoppee went to see a planter he knew. Once on this planter's property, some distance north of the kampong, they were secure from prying eyes but had no hope of keeping their presence a secret – it was impossible for so many *tuans* to have marched down a public road, after dumping a truck which they had had ferried across a river, without the whole district knowing about them. The situation begged two questions: how long would it be before somebody informed the Japanese and after that, how long until the Japanese arrived to round them up. They had time but probably not much – and if they hoped to leave by sea they had better get cracking.

Shoppee's planter friend turned out to be useful. First, he himself had no wish to be interned and wanted to come with them; consequently he made his resources available to them, including tools. He had a Ford 10 engine with a boat-propeller and a shaft, but needed a boat to put them in. Secondly, although he employed Indonesians he also employed Chinese and, while the Indonesians were reluctant to assist *tuans*, this was not true of the Chinese. They were considered equally alien by the Indonesians and, furthermore, had no reason to expect good treatment from the perpetrators of the 1937 Rape of Nanking, when Japanese troops had murdered more than a quarter of a million Chinese civilians. This planter lent them a cottage on the beach and, had they been on vacation, it might have been idyllic – falling asleep and waking to the thunder of surf, loud enough to drown even the cicadas. It was not exactly the Hilton, just a native hut with a dirt floor in which Bombs and Sheerin excavated a fire pit and made themselves responsible for cooking. But it was a roof.

Alex takes up the tale at this point: "From the cottage S/L Roberts, Scales and myself went to the east with the hope of obtaining a boat or finding a harbour suitable to launch a boat, if it became necessary to build. Nothing could be found and we returned." Alex had not been convinced that boat building would be necessary and had set off confidently with Roberts and Scales, with some advice from the planter about where and how far to go. Sid remembered that they made good progress on a distinct trail through fairly open country with scrubby vegetation. They encountered jungle only in river valleys. At night they slept on the beach above the tidemark. There were certainly no better rivers and they were disappointed to find no harbours.

At the end of their second day they came across the only village they were to find, a knot of thatched houses on stilts, shaded by palms, banana and bamboo, the whole like a timeless organism at the water's edge. All that mattered to the villagers were rice and fish. As V. S. Naipaul wrote of such a place further north: "To enter one of these villages was to find more than shade. It was to enter an enchanted, complete world, where everything – food, houses, tools, rituals, reverences – had evolved over the centuries and had reached a kind of perfection." Alex and his companions were curiosities – not many *tuans* came to visit. The headman was welcoming and helpful; he lodged them in the hospitality hut and saw that they had food and water. However, he held out no hope of better luck further east and besides, they had no wish to get too close to Tjilatjap, where the Japanese were known to be. Predictably the village had no large boats and the villagers, though friendly and willing to sell them food, made it no secret that they did not relish having them around. Realising there was no point in going further they headed back. For some of the way they were accompanied by village boys, laughing and joking as they marched alongside. The three stopped to re-examine a ship's lifeboat they had found earlier, wrecked on a beach. No amount of wishful thinking could make it reparable, however, and they were back at Tjipatoedjah by the evening of the third day.

Alex and Roberts spent a couple of days there before setting out again because there were decisions to make. The cottage had become an object of curiosity for the people of Tjipatoedjah, especially for children. It was not a good place for boat building as it was public and nobody could launch a large boat into that kind of surf. Their best hope was to launch their boat into the river from a new base upstream. Even that would have its problems: the beginning of April was the end of the wet season and the river would be shallower. On the other hand they would be out of sight and, more importantly, would by their presence bring less danger of Japanese reprisals to the people, whose attitude was changing perceptibly. The radio brought word of the liberating mission of the Japanese and there were more hostile stares and fewer smiles.

With the planter's aid a site was selected about three miles upstream on the west side of the river. They hoped to build a house for themselves and a slipway for launching their boat. Most of the group set to work cutting bamboo and hauling it to the site. As one or two men were sick with fever Sid decided to stay in Tjipatoedjah to work on boat plans with McDowell and allow Alex and Roberts to go off without him on the second boat-search mission. McDowell, the carpenter, had been interested in assembling boat-building materials from the start. He and Sid drew up plans for a boat and took them to the planter's house after dark. This was also inland from the village but on the east side of the river. There, Chinese workers were shown which tree limbs to cut and they began collecting materials. These would have to be transported to the river and towed across to the boat-building site.

Alex went on: "A few days later, S/L Roberts and myself went to the west about three days' journey in another effort to find a boat." With just two of them they probably travelled faster than previously. This search was as thorough and frustrating as the previous one. Alex remembers it as being less comfortable: one night darkness fell before they had made camp and they spent the night fighting off insects beside the trail. They found no boats and by the time they decided to turn round Alex had spent a total of ten days searching different parts of the south coast of Java – if you include his searches in the neighbourhood of Tjilatjap. We can be sure, when he tells us there was no boat to be had, that he knew what he was talking about and that their lack of success certainly had not been because of a lack of effort on his part. He concluded this description: "We were unsuccessful and it was decided, after we had returned to the cottage, that we should have to build a boat."

Immediately, they needed a small boat to use on the river but nobody is quite sure where they got it. Sid remembers that they bought a dugout canoe from the headman of the village for five guilders; Alex is sure that when he returned with Roberts from the west he was most impressed by a small dinghy built by McDowell and Sid. Maybe Alex just thought the dugout was something they had built. In any case, one of this vessel's first uses was for Bombs and Sheerin to investigate the mouth of the river to determine whether it would be deep enough for any larger boat they might build. Apparently they were satisfied that it was. Thereafter, others used it to travel upriver to their house- and boat-building site and also to tow across the logs they would need.

There was now an urgency to the boat-building project. By this time it was the middle of April, they had been on the coast for weeks and time was increasingly against them. Some of them were sick. Though they could buy rice, they had to ration it as their money was running out while the price they had to pay was quite high. Also, there was growing suspense as to when the Japanese would come looking for them. Obviously, they needed to build a boat immediately and leave. However, we know that they never actually began the boat. How could this be?

Alex remembered: "We built a bamboo framework house approximately three miles up a stream away from all habitation. The intention was to build a small boat." They must have spent several weeks building the house, while at the same time McDowell, Alex and Sid were trying to get started on the boat. Alex cannot remember what they did with their time – it seems an exhausting blur in retrospect. Doing physical work in the tropics is never easy. When you are also hungry and unwell it is like trying to climb Mount Everest without oxygen – a simple task becomes desperately hard to do and takes forever. Most of them were still at the cottage on the coast; it was easier to feed and look after the sick there and others were looking after them. The fit men spent much time on the river in the dugout, ferrying materials. This occupation was not without hazards: on one occasion Sid and Shoppee were approaching the bank in the dugout and Sid, in the bow, stretched out his hand to grab a branch. From the stern Shoppee shouted: "Don't move! Don't touch that branch!" Sid's first reaction was irritation until he saw he had been about to put his hand on a krait, the most deadly of the poisonous snakes. Shoppee had saved his life.

They just had too much to do for their available energy. Morale was beginning to slip in spite of whatever Alex could do to keep people hopeful. Sid, asked whether he had felt optimistic whilst at the coast, replied: "Yes, in the beginning; weeks later, when malaria, etc, had its effect we weren't so sure! We all got malaria, dysentery, dengue fever, etc. – [we had] no quinine. My overall feeling was – at least we were doing something." It sounds pretty grim; as their need to be working flat out on the boat increased, so their ability to do anything at all withered. Eventually time ran out on them. Alex recalled: "On or about the 7th of May, Scales, McDowell and myself established ourselves in this hut [the 'house' they had built at the point where they were building the boat] and crossed the river to collect some timbers for the boat which had been cut by Chinese labourers belonging to the English-Dutch planter. We were met by W/C Bell, who informed us that a letter had arrived stating that the Japanese had ordered us back to Tasikmalaja and that they were on their way down to collect us. The local native chief [the headman of Tjipatoedjah] was very concerned about this and implored us to leave. Finally, after we had returned to the cottage on the coast, Javanese police, armed with rifles, surrounded the house and forbade us to leave unless we took all our gear and proceeded for Tasikmalaja."

The letter, presumably from W/C Steedman, meant the end of the boat-building dream. Both the chief and the Tjipatoedjah police were seriously afraid of what the Japanese might do to them. The chief was quite desperate and actually told Alex that if they did not get away, the Japanese would burn his village and that this had become the normal policy of the Japanese where villages had provided help to whites. Just to make sure that they did leave, and maybe to impress the Japanese who would hear about it, there were shots fired around and at the cottage in the night. Fortunately, nobody was hit. Alex went on: "We decided that the best thing to do would be to make a show of leaving the next morning and, if possible, make a break into the jungle on our way inland." As they moved out in the morning, a very different-looking group from the one which had marched so jauntily down the road six weeks before, their speed was limited by the speed at which eight of them could carry two stretchers. The idea of making a break into the jungle no longer made much sense but the decision was taken out of their hands after they had been walking for only thirty minutes.

The scene that followed could have been everybody's last. One minute they were trudging up the road in morning sunshine, each man concentrating on his thoughts and his footing; the next minute a truck, which had been rumbling towards them, suddenly skidded to a halt. Staccato orders were barked excitedly in Japanese. Soldiers tumbled out of the back, filling the road and surrounding them at the double. As they ran the soldiers fumbled with rifle bolts which were noisily drawn back and slammed shut. In a few seconds, rifles with long bayonets were levelled at them from every direction. There was silence. Then a calm voice, in English, told them to stand still and put up their hands. A command in Japanese brought two soldiers running towards them; roughly they prodded the stretcher cases to their feet with bayonets, making them stand up with the rest. The atmosphere was electric. "TENSE is the word – we had heard stories of Jap brutality," Sid recalled. Alex remembered "... young Japanese soldiers, with bayonets as long as they were almost – bayonets as long as their arms – all very uncomfortable-looking," breathing hard and ready to kill them all on the slightest pretext. "The young officer, with his sergeant-major, began searching our equipment, mainly for weapons." After working in silence for a while, the sergeant-major reached Sid and read his shoulder flash. "Ah, New Zealand! I play rugby in New Zealand!" "Rugby," Sid shot back. "I play rugby. Who do you know?"

Instantly, the tension was broken. Sid remembers the "Jap sergeant ... thought it was a great joke that we had been trying to build a boat! He spoke very good English – was a Tokyo University graduate who had played rugby against a NZ university team way back in 1934-35. I had a New Zealand flash on the shoulder of my shirt, we were almost buddies!" They began exchanging names of players they both knew, amid shouts of delight and astonishment. "Taking a cue from their sergeant, the Nips produced cigarettes and ice drinks and treated us like human beings." The pleasant interlude was brief but had a happier sequel than they had a right to expect; instead of being made to march the hundred, or more, kilometres to Garoet, they were transported there by truck. Alex maintains that the rugby coincidence saved their lives. Without that stroke of luck, "... It's as likely as not that the Japanese would have done their usual – and that was bayoneted the lot of us."

The story of Alex's search for a boat and his efforts to build one is a sad and frustrating one. Alex would never have allowed himself the luxury of abandoning members of the party. Had they, in due course, put to sea with many of the crew already sick, their chances would have been slim. Perhaps the fact that he was prevented from making the attempt by the rugby-playing Japanese sergeant was just another part of Alex's luck! Perhaps the sergeant was right to laugh.

11

IN THE BAG

MAY 1942–OCTOBER 1943
In which Alex and his companions benefit from
the early leniency of the POW camps' administration.

"A Golden Age"
— LAURENS VAN DER POST

After the 'rugby players' reunion' the eleven able-bodied members of the expedition loaded the two stretcher-cases into the back of the truck, climbed in themselves and were followed by the soldiers. They were little men in battered khaki baseball caps, all buckteeth and eyeglasses, carrying rifles with enormous bayonets still fixed. There was a canopy on the truck and the soldiers sat by the tailgate. As the vehicle ground its way up the hill out of town they seemed to relax enough to chat among themselves. However, they remained wary and rebuffed efforts at fraternisation, as though suspecting these malnourished men in tattered uniforms, many slumped on the floor, of actually planning to jump them.

The journey took all day – back across the ferry-raft at Simpang, once again through Tasikmalaja and westwards on that winding climb up to Garoet, nestled among its volcanoes. For those of them who had thought about life as a POW, this journey was a precious time for savouring the 'outside'. Once in the camps the 'outside' would become a half-remembered place where a change of scene can be arranged, where people can make choices, where there is enough food, enough space, enough medicine. It was also where you can relax, lower your guard, forget about being one step ahead of the guards, where there is freedom from fear, from compulsion, from the smell of other people, where there is not only freedom from hunger but freedom to think about something other than food. Journey's end that day was a small schoolhouse and playground festooned in barbed wire. This was to be home for six weeks, cooped up with an Australian machine-gun battalion.

Chronology is not much of a guide when writing about a POW camp – of all

'Life in the Bag', cartoon by Sid Scales.

places its days tend to be the least distinguishable. However, we need to review the chronology that does exist. Alex claimed to have been a prisoner in the Garoet schoolhouse until September 1942. Actually he and all others at Garoet arrived at the XVth Battalion Barracks, Bandoeng, on the 22nd of June, where they rejoined the RAF types they had left at Tasikmalaja in March. Their arrival was noted, precisely, in Weary Dunlop's diary.[39] There they remained for more than a year. In October 1943 (according to Alex's Statement Concerning Claim for Maltreatment for the Canadian War Claims Commission), or November 1943 (according to Laurens van der Post in *Night of the New Moon*) they were moved down to Batavia – the so-called Cycle Camp according to Sid – on the sweaty coastal plain, but only for two or three months. They were back in Bandoeng in the Depot Camp in January 1944, where they again spent just over a year. In March 1945 the Japanese concentrated all their Bandoeng prisoners into the Boys' Gaol, built for 120 delinquents but by then home to 7,000 prisoners. This would be the crisis of their imprisonment for a number of reasons. Finally, after the Japanese surrender, they returned to Batavia on the 21st of August 1945 – Cycle Camp again, according to Sid – where, after a month dodging care packages from the sky, they were liberated on the 18th of September 1945. This meant that, with the exception of four months in Batavia, they did not have to fight the climate. Bandoeng and Garoet are on the central plateau where the climate is tolerable and where it is possible, now and again, to feel chilly.

Their imprisonment began with a Golden Age, when the camps were manned by the army and when treatment of prisoners was typically more neglectful than brutal. Later came the real ordeal, after their care had been transferred to the new prison camp guards, many of whom were Korean. During this later period brutality and unpredictability intensified. There was a transition period when the Golden Age was fading but Laurens van der Post identifies the dividing point between the two regimes as the 26th of November 1943 – the day when he felt it was too dangerous for him any longer to keep a diary. He buried it.[40]

To begin at the beginning, Alex's notes for a lecture on his experience give some indication of the casual awfulness. In their Garoet schoolhouse, already packed with Australians, conditions were very crowded. As latecomers his group had to bed down on the verandahs – beautiful on a starlit night but everything got drenched when it rained. Rain in Java is torrential, movie-set rain, as though the gods had a fire hose. It was a good thing that it rained often; they relied on rainwater to flush the open sewer from the latrines, along which other water only occasionally flowed. The Japanese sent in food but there was no kitchen at the school and cooking had to be done on makeshift stoves and ovens, when they could get fuel. And finally, there was no bath house, making personal hygiene, though essential for health, an extra difficulty.

They moved to the XVth Battalion Camp in Bandoeng in June after only six weeks in Garoet. Getting there involved a train journey over a mountain pass. They were herded into goods wagons and carriages with the windows shuttered over. If they could find a hole to peer through they were able to gaze once again upon the 'outside'. As the locomotive clanked and hissed over the high country where the tea plantings began "... the terrain became more rolling, like the long sweep of midocean waves. Flat-topped, black-green bushes rose and fell in patterned clusters against red earth, from the shadows of one mountain into those of the next. In the highest places this crowded island was empty of people except for the occasional clutch of women tea-pickers. In their conical hats, chest-deep among the bushes, hands quick as sparrows, they were pinching off the pale green youngest leaves."[41] For the prisoners it was a long, uncomfortable journey with hardly any water. After they arrived Sid remembers "... Alex and me staggering along a road with our gear on a bamboo pole between us, à la Chinese coolies, then arriving at Bandoeng camp and standing in a long queue, awaiting our turn at a solitary tap trickling cold water – COLD WATER!"

At 2,400 feet, the Bandoeng climate is relatively pleasant. Though warmer than up on the pass it is less humid and cooler than Batavia and the northern plain, though not markedly different from Garoet. "When it rained the dark clouds sneaked up from behind the mountains and streaked down to burst apart over the city which lies in a valley; in the wet season it rained every afternoon, in long driving gushes. Streets steamed, sewers gargled and plants hugged the ground. Those rains could quickly turn gardens into swamps and parts of streets into streams; their drum and clatter, as always, shrank the world."[42] You could shiver in the rain there, in Java a delicious sensation.

At the Bandoeng camp, Alex remembers, "Since I was one of the senior officers, I was appointed officer in charge of RAF troops." Was this the saddling of a willing horse? He was certainly not the senior officer but he was a good choice. Right away he discovered why others had declined the honour. He noted, laconically: "Some problem at first, in many [airmen] thinking officers had no jurisdiction during POW life [but] that was straightened out." Naturally, Alex did the straightening-out and in such a way that there were no further rumblings. One of his strengths was that he had served before the mast; as a former able seaman he knew what it was like to be at the bottom of the chain of command and had not lost Kipling's 'common touch'. His command style was considerate of those under him – the 'erks' in RAF slang. One recalls his willingness to rub shoulders with airmen in the Nicobars. At Seletar Sid remembers him being treated "with great respect and admiration" by all ranks. "I never heard a bad word against him." His recent willingness to risk his neck in the Glenn Martin, his hard work in the search for a boat and in boat construction, had added to his reputation as "a good bloke," in

Sid's memory. "He always cared for airmen under his command and worried about leaving the rest of his squadron behind when we made a break to the south coast." He continued to worry in Bandoeng, where there was no news of Ken Whitworth and the airmen. Ironically, although an outsider in the RAF, Alex's personal qualities, together with his skill as a pilot, gave him the respect from all ranks which made him effective in this tricky situation. No doubt he approached the problem from a commonsense angle:

> "We're all in the same boat. Our task is to survive this camp. If we keep a united front, fewer of us will have to have contact with the Japanese. Whether we like it or not, they think of us as military. If we don't command ourselves, the Japanese will do it for us. It boils down to who you want to get your orders from: me, or old bandy-legs over there? Besides, we're going to win this war, no doubt about it. It just may take a little time. Think who's against them: [ticking them off on his fingers] Britain, China, America, Australia, New Zealand, Holland, Canada – maybe Russia. When they run out of steam it'll just be a matter of time. When the war's over you'll want to collect your pay, I'm sure – with maybe a little extra for how these old darlings are treating us? That could be difficult if we stop accepting orders. Remember, we're going to win! Think positive! Don't let the bastards grind us down!"

Put like that, between puffs on his pipe, who could disagree? Alex made sure that he capitalised on his advantage. The airmen were listening to him; as far as possible, he began to bring life back to normal. He had parades and inspections – and competitions between units. His first parade was a comedy of errors which would have destroyed the authority of a lesser mortal. As a flying squadron leader, he had last given parade ground orders at Wittering. He faced his reluctant troops and, with stentorian panache, ordered them to "form fours" – a manoeuvre which had gone the way of the musket and the infantry square. There was instant chaos and a warrant officer had to restore order, getting the parade into the three ranks with which they were familiar. Alex took it in stride, endured being the butt of jokes and the incident passed. As nearly as possible, he aimed to get service life back to what they were used to. His notes conclude that this "helped a great deal to maintain morale." No doubt it did and mainly thanks to him.

If you have to be a POW, a large camp offers more possibilities for improving a prisoner's lot. There are likely to be more people with extraordinary skills. Van der Post, in *Night of the New Moon*, records the success that they had with their school.

"We created ... a vast prison organisation for the reeducation of
ourselves, a sort of prison kindergarten, school, high school, technical
college and university rolled into one. At one end of the scale we had a
British officer, Major Pat Lancaster of the 4th Hussars, teaching a
couple of splendid Australians [all Australians are 'splendid' to LvdP!]
from the Never-Never of their country to read and write. At the other
end was 'Don' Gregory – a don from Oxbridge, but committed to war
as an erk in the RAF – coaching people for their bachelor and master
of arts degrees. We had an active school of drama, as active a school of
music and an extensive faculty of arts and crafts.... One of their main
functions was to keep alive in our men their sense of continuity. The
greatest psychological danger ... was the feeling that imprisonment was
a complete break with their past and totally unconnected with their
future lives. This danger we overcame in such a triumphant manner
that, with exceptions which I could count on the fingers of one hand,
imprisonment for our men was transformed from an arid waste of
time and life into one of the most meaningful experiences they had
ever known."[43]

He becomes a little carried away, but we get the point. The classes were indeed
catholic in scope and from items in this chapter we know that they included
Russian, Spanish, Japanese (Laurens) and celestial navigation (Alex). 'Weary' Dunlop,
medical officer and camp commandant, summarised the school: "1,207 students,
30 subjects, 40 instructors, 144 classes per week!"[44] Alex has notes which he took
in a Chinese class, plus notes on Malay. They had the advantage of access to a large
library – at least initially.

Alex's notebook, from which he taught his navigation course, has miraculously
survived. It is homemade from recycled paper with Dutch printing on it. The cover
was made from a worn-out pair of military trousers. The inside cover has this
inscription, in pencil:

> "S/Ldr A. M. Jardine. P.O.W. No 9290.
> Notes from the book *Mathematics for the Million* incl.
> Haversine Table
> 1B Projections
> 1A Sine Table
> 1C Formulae
> all in connection with Spherical Trigonometry & Projections
> of Spheres."

To a nonmathematician and navigational ignoramus like the author, the contents of the notebook are meticulous and obscure. They include a huge amount of information, including the listed tables in full, written in ink in tiny, neat handwriting, with a large number of complicated geometrical and geographical drawings, accurately done without instruments. In his class, as in other aspects of life, no doubt Alex applied enthusiasm, common sense and rule of thumb to demystify erudite material and make celestial navigation comprehensible.

Both Laurens van der Post and Alex were very pleased with *Mark Time*, the camp newspaper. Both claimed paternity of the name. As one of those rare humans immune from self-glorification, Alex is perhaps the more believable. In addition, he claims to have been the first editor – for an afternoon only, until he discovered that editing meant something more sophisticated than he had given the *Gracia Gurgle*. He had accepted it as another job that had to be done. Fortunately there was a galaxy of talent and he became manager instead. During the Golden Age *Mark Time* appeared daily, tacked up on a wall like a Chinese newspaper. They had inherited a supply of paper from the Dutch garrison. When that ran out they continued on Japanese toilet paper – with which those fastidious people were more liberal than they were with their rice. In addition, POWs produced small quantities of a rough sort of paper of their own, made from waste paper and rags. *Mark Time* printed news translated from Japanese papers but with a slant which came from knowledge of the real news, garnered from secret radios. It was done subtly, the real message being obvious only to native speakers of English. *Mark Time* also built community spirit as each day more men were mentioned in articles about the life and work of the camp. Sid Scales and another artist were commissioned to make cartoons of the principal characters and these, including one of Alex, were published as part of magazine supplements.

Secret radios were essential to morale because they allowed prisoners to have realistic expectations of eventual release. However, the possession of a radio, if detected, meant certain death for those involved, usually by decapitation with a sword. Even in the Golden Age it was desperately dangerous. Sid tells a tale of one of the radios:

"In mid-1942 in our first Bandoeng camp, (the palmy days), Alex and I and John Westcott and Jos Cadell were sharing a native NCO's cottage with seven other officers.

Squadron Leader Alex Jardine as POW in 1942, aged 28. Cartoon by Sid Scales for the Memorial Book.

One of them, F/O Bill Phillips, a NZ armament officer with 488 Sqadron RNZAF, had fashioned a small radio from an old Philco set. It was set in a rubble bench in the cookhouse at the back of the cottage. Very cunning, it was in a box with salt and blotting paper to absorb moisture. It was completely buried, with tiles above linking it with the rest of the bench. The space between the tiles was mortared with peanut butter which exactly matched the real brown mortar in the rest of the bench. Hidden in the peanut butter were small plugs for aerial, power and earphone, plus a flexible drive for the tuning which Phil manipulated with a screwdriver through the butter. In case of search alarms the aerial, power and earphone leads were pulled out and any holes left in the peanut butter were smoothed over quickly with a thumb.

"One night, Phil had the set out of the bench and in the house to make some repairs. There was a search alarm and we had to get rid of the 'box'. Even the dumbest Nip guard could have seen it was a wireless. I had a dose of malaria at the time and it was decided that the 'box' should lie with me, under a mosquito net in my bed of pain! In due course a Jap guard wanted to know who was under the mosquito net. With much pantomime the others explained that the man was very sick with *sakit panas* (malaria). The Japs seemed to have a healthy respect for malaria (they sometimes wore face masks!) and they backed away and went into the next billet. I was really sweating and shivering! The set was duly repaired and in action again. Sharing of the news was restricted because of informers, but Phil relayed it to Van der Post."

Sid makes it sound like a bit of a lark but Alex found it less so. He remembers the radio as a source of great tension:

"Started a life of living on a powder keg. Each day we would expect a new development. We followed the course of battle and found little to give hope – [certainly true before Midway in 1942] – though it never died. Radios buried in strange places, in water bottles and in clogs and books. The Japs were always seeking them out. They would come in with no notice and everybody would parade. We were thoroughly searched while others worked on the sleeping places. By the time they had finished, often a whole day later, and we would be out in the sun standing, the houses and barracks would look as though Hurricane Hazel had been through for a prolonged visit."

Even Alex accepted that being a prisoner in Java made escape from camp impossible. This was probably the major difference when comparing their lot with that of allied prisoners in Europe. They could not hope to lose themselves among a physically similar population or infiltrate across borders as could the heroes of the Wooden Horse or Stalag Luft 13. As he had proved, getting off the island was virtually impossible. After all his efforts he commented, rather bitterly, about the eventual failure of everything they had tried: "The countryside was anything but hospitable; people, terrain and vegetation were against us ... An island, thousands of miles from any friendly country, where a white man is as easily seen ... as a light ... at night." There was no question that breaking out of camp would have courted immediate detection and swift execution – in any of a number of unpleasant ways. As a consequence everything possible had to be done to make the camp experience as tolerable as possible.

Which brings us back to the amazing Laurens van der Post. A South African by birth and descent, he had early developed a special affinity for the Japanese. As a young journalist in 1926 he had witnessed Japanese sailors being refused service in a Durban café because they were 'coloured'. He had taken the tray from the abusive waitress and had served the sailors himself, subsequently sitting with them and attempting to talk to them. The captain of the ship, Katsué Mori of the *Canada Maru*, invited him on board to thank him, at which point the invitation was expanded into a round trip to Kobe. There, Laurens was so impressed with the country and the people that he managed to extend the invitation yet again, eventually spending two years on his friend Mori's ship, during which he learned to speak Japanese fluently. When war broke out he was trained in one of the early commando units and helped organise revolt behind Italian lines in Abyssinia in 1940. He arrived in Java, by way of the Western Desert, Singapore and Sumatra and received his orders from Wavell's HQ.[45]

His experiences in Java have been described above. On one occasion his knowledge of Japanese saved his life. He was taking a sick Australian to a local hospital when they were ambushed by a Japanese patrol. About to be shot, he addressed the soldiers in Court Japanese, which stopped them in their tracks. Playing on their horror of disease, he persuaded them to let him pass with his sick soldier but was later compelled to surrender to save the lives of friendly villagers. Before appearing in the POW camps he had been held by the *Kempetei* (the Japanese *Gestapo*) in appalling conditions. Under sentence of death, he was forced to watch executions, including the use of live prisoners for bayonet practice. In POW camp he was a mystery man. His rank of Colonel and his languages – he spoke Afrikaans (Dutch) as well – made him a person of influence. Not surprisingly he was in everybody's confidence. He seemed to have contacts not available to ordinary mortals.

Laurens's most important contribution to the general good was his credit with Chinese merchants on the 'outside'. He pledged the credit of the British government on his own authority and, until the war ended, these merchants provided extra food and medicines 'on the slate'. The facts do not seem to be in dispute; the camp was better fed and was reckoned by inmates of other camps to have had a less harsh experience. He wrote: "We [the RAF CO, W/C Nicholls, and himself] both knew that our Bandoeng fortunes could not last and that by far our best investment was in proteins and cereals, to make our men as fit as possible for what we knew were long, lean years ahead." A complicated system of purchasing was worked out which was run inside the camp by Mr Tan, a Chinese prisoner, and two young RAF officers.[46] Chinese merchants accepted his credit and produced the food. There was always something in it for the Japanese and Korean guards, so everybody was happy. Although during the Golden Age they could grow their own vegetables and the daily rice ration was still 500 grams per man, it was at that time that Van der Post put in place the support network which would keep them alive later on.

At the same time he was in contact with Mr Kim, a Korean in the Japanese organisation. The contact with this man was out of the blue – the first move came from Kim and for a long time Van der Post was suspicious. He decided to trust him after various tests, not so much because he had proved his trustworthiness as because he had the name of a Kipling character. Ironically he was unaware that many Koreans share the name Kim.[47] Mr Kim kept them warned of all changes planned in their lives. Consequently they were never surprised by being moved to another camp or about work parties to be sent out of Java. The knowledge was valuable.

Alex always speaks of Laurens fondly and with respect. That in itself says much about him: a man of energy and action has no time for a slacker or a fraud. Sid Scales believes it was good for morale to know that, through Laurens, they had a contact with the 'outside'. Nevertheless, in spite of Laurens's admiration for Sid's work, the New Zealander had reservations about him. He observed: "There was a cloak-and-dagger atmosphere about him – a mystery man – there were some who thought he was a great bullshit artist." Sid's friends were probably partly right: he was certainly a romantic intellectual with exceptional vanity and a flair for the dramatic. However, to have done what he did makes him a brave man. His talents, courage and above all education and sophistication impressed the Japanese; this is what mattered the most for three and a half years. Alex and Sid were lucky they fell in with someone so useful to have on one's side.

A characteristic of the Golden Age was the malign neglect of the prisoners by Japanese soldier-guards. Van der Post put his finger on the two main dangers to the survival of the prisoners: the first was the food supply and he did what he could to improve that; but the second was much more difficult to guard against. It was, quite simply, the contempt of Japanese soldiers for their prisoners. They considered captivity a degradation of the male spirit and would take their own lives in the hundreds of thousands rather than endure the disgrace of falling into enemy hands. Their culture promoted belief in the insignificance of life on earth, that the life of an individual was of no more account than a feather. What made this contempt lethal was their seething anger against their charges, a race-hatred produced by centuries of Caucasian arrogance.[48]

To personalise things, Alex was reaping the whirlwind from seeds sown by Wylie East and Mountjoy Squire. Or, as Laurens van der Post remarked in *Night of the New Moon*: "One of our gravest dangers was that we were imprisoned at a moment when not just the chickens but all the pterodactyls of our history in the Far East had come home to roost."[49] British and Dutch attitudes of superiority became all the more infuriating as the war proved them to be hollow and unfounded. How DARE the British assume that Japanese aircraft could be contained by a few old Buffaloes, that Japanese soldiers would be unable to penetrate Malayan jungles, that two battleships could ignore the Japanese air force! The lack of serious land and air defences in Singapore was itself an insult not to be borne. Furthermore, the efforts of Alex and others to maintain morale among the prisoners, even to get something out of imprisonment, was insulting; where was the shame, where the self-abasement in prisoners who put on funny plays, who drew cartoons, who published newspapers, who liked to pretend that everything would turn out all right and that the allies would win the war? This anger within their captors they ignored at their peril. When it erupted in brutality and incoherent rage, it just had to be borne. It could only be minimised by playing the game meticulously by their rules – the bow had to be at 15 degrees and the eyes must be cast down.

During the Golden Age these Japanese attitudes produced more neglect than brutality. The guards concerned themselves with preventing escape and prisoners were able to improve their lives in all sorts of ways. For example, enterprising men grew peanuts, bought oranges cheaply and produced both peanut butter and marmalade. Local tobacco was available and could be bought or grown. In an interview with a Victoria, BC, paper after the war Alex described the tobacco as looking like hair and smelling like hay – no wonder it is not well known outside Indonesia.* However, now and again something would trigger a blitz, even in the Golden Age. Something or somebody had brought the anger in the guards to the surface.

---

*To demonstrate his POW skills, right there in the newspaper office, he pulled out flint, steel and dried moss and lit a cigarette – because, of course, matches were unobtainable luxuries in the camps.

A blitz meant being paraded for long periods in the sun, being punched, kicked, yelled at and beaten about the head and face with bamboo sticks. It probably also meant top-to-bottom searches and a good deal of destruction of beds and chairs and whatever other furniture the prisoners possessed. Sid recalled that these could be triggered by not saluting, smoking in the wrong places and not catching enough flies, among other things. Flies were an obsession with the guards in all camps. Ernest Hillen, in *The Way of a Boy*, describes how he would keep himself amused by catching his mother's fly quota as well as his own. They had to be presented and counted daily.[50]

The campaign to maintain morale involved a regular routine. The camp had its own reveille and the day began with a brief parade and inspection; this was an opportunity for announcements but was also a morale booster. Classes would happen during the cooler time of the morning. On work-party days there would be little daylight time in the camp, as it got dark regularly at 7:00 p.m. On days when there were no work parties the men had plenty to do looking after their own chores. The Japanese were extremely rank-conscious in their dealings with prisoners and did not include officers in work parties. To assist morale and to set an example, the officers formed gardening teams. Alex joined with Sid Scales, John Westcott, Pat Sowman, Ray Vincent and army major John Denman to produce tomatoes for general consumption. They continued to do so in subsequent camps whenever the camp regime permitted it.*

Cooking was done in local messes – for example Alex and Sid and their nine room-mates in the NCO's cottage would look after their own food. There was always house- and latrine-cleaning to be done. Most men possessed few clothes but these had to be constantly washed and patched – there was not a man with unpatched shorts. It was as well that many clothes were not necessary because drying space was scarce – lines strung under the ceiling in the barrack rooms being the best place. Nothing outside would do because of the almost-daily rain. Gardens had to be tended and vegetables harvested. Beans and peas were important as one of the only sources of protein. They could seldom get meat and when fish could be bought it was so far gone that, to quote Alex's 1945 interview with the *Colonist*: "The taste of a quarter ounce remained prominent in five ounces of rice!" Many people still owned shoes but they were wearing out and were of limited use because of the heat. Most had their leather cannibalised to make clog-straps, clogs in this case being wooden soles carved to fit the shape of the foot, fastened by one strap over the instep. In fact they were more comfortable than shoes, one of the few good things of the camp experience. The idea came from the Dutch, who called them *klompen*.

---

*All six lived long lives, remained in regular touch by mail and, apart from Ray Vincent who died in September 1999 in Tasmania, entered the new millennium with flying colours.

Their routine did not include regular sports. While Dunlop was commandant he calculated that the men received an average of 2,200 calories daily, enough for light work but not for strenuous exertion. Nevertheless, there was a sports day in August 1942 when inter-nationality races were run, shots were put and discuses thrown. There were also regular boxing and wrestling events.[51] These sports involved few athletes, who could be given special diets, but there was no energy to spare for rugby or soccer. Competitive impulses found outlet in endless games of bridge which became the main recreational activity. Men could be seen playing in any available space at any time and the manufacture of playing cards was a cottage industry.

Laurens van der Post hoped to put together a memorial book, to contain issues of *Mark Time* and as many pictures and cartoons as he could find. Sid and others were commissioned to make portraits, cartoons and scenes of camp life. The idea came to grief because, although writing and drawing by prisoners was allowed, no papers could be taken with them when they were moved. As a result, before the move to Batavia, of which Mr Kim had warned them, they hid writings and drawings for retrieval after the war. Sid remembers his cartoons were "generally combined with other POWs' stuff and put in a drainpipe wrapped in canvas, sealed with melted asphalt and buried. Arrangements were made with Dutch officers (Indonesia) to recover it after the war. I had one lot buried with Van der Post's papers which I got back in 1946; another lot were presented to the Imperial War Museum by Van der Post in 1988 and I've got copies. They were with his papers which G/C Nicholetts took to a senior officers' camp in Harbin (*Night of the New Moon*)." All of them relate to the Golden Age – such activity became impossible in the later periods of imprisonment – and not all were recovered.

Van der Post relates how he buried some precious stones given to him for safekeeping by a Chinese merchant along with a considerable quantity of written material, including many copies of *Mark Time*, deep under the carcass of a decaying pig – to throw the Japanese off the scent!? After the war he had a squad of Japanese prisoners dig the place up from end to end without finding a stone, a paper or a pig bone. Presumably the Japanese or Korean thief had been too compromised by his theft of the stones to consider making trouble for the buriers of the papers.

Among Alex's papers is a list of hidden treasures. He typed it in September 1945, probably for Laurens van der Post to retrieve them. A galvanised metal cylinder (Sid's drainpipe?), with belongings of Laurens, Sid and Alex, was under a flagstone below the window. A bundle, with Phillips's Russian notes, Sid's drawing book and Cadell's papers, was above the lavatory ceiling. A third package, S/L Benzies' logbook and Spanish notes, was between the tiled roof and the ceiling in the servants' quarters. Lastly, a sealed bottle belonging to their director of education, Gunner Rees, was buried between 2 ft. 6 in. and 3 ft. deep. Each position was indicated on a map, unfortunately missing from the file.

For the first eighteen months that Alex was a POW, although he was both alive and relatively well, Agnes remained in the dark as to what had happened to him. Her last letter from 'the boy', already quoted, did not help; it was from Tjilatjap on the 19th of February 1942. In it Alex had given his opinion that "... the outcome of this one cannot try to imagine," meaning the general situation and his own immediate future. Although he was a free man for another seventeen days, they were desperate ones, too desperate for him to have either the peace or the time to write a letter.

After the 8th of March it was too late. Prisoners were at first not permitted to write letters at all – the Japanese had not signed the Geneva Convention. For a long time Alex was unable to calm the fears that he knew his mother must have and throughout the Golden Age she could only hope against hope that Alex was a POW. She had no help from the RAF nor from Ottawa. A telegram from the RCAF Chief of Air Staff in June was negative – "Regret unable at present to state whereabouts of your son S/L A. M. Jardine – not mentioned in official reports or by escapees in Java as having arrived any command elsewhere." Her only comforts were letters from Alex's friends – many of whom did little to calm her as they occasionally talked of Alex in the past tense. Thus Gordon Stilling wrote in July 1942, reminding Agnes that Alex had been his best man, and concluding: "I was proud to be numbered among his friends." G/C Councell (ex-CO of 205), on the 17th of July, wrote that he had been sure that Alex would get away in a native boat, but concluded, more comfortingly: "I am confident that if there is anyone who can come safely through these dangerous times it is Alec ... as I knew him to be the most courageous, steady and efficient officer in the Squadron." F/Lt Bailey wrote on the 21st of August, from Washington, DC, that he "... really wanted to speak about Alex's wonderful work with us during these last five years."

On the 2nd of November 1942, neither of them yet having news of Alex, Gordon wrote again to commiserate with Agnes. "We too miss Alec a lot," he told her, gave her news of Alex's close friends, the old gang of Norman Birks and Dick Atkinson – but also mentioned that Jock Graham had been posted missing over the Indian Ocean. Consequently, she had some support in her misery. By this time, partly to take her mind off it all, she had taken a job in the Esquimalt naval shipyards as a riveter's helper. Though hard, such war work allowed her to feel connected to her son, about whom she worried endlessly but whose continued existence she never allowed herself to doubt.

Finally, in November 1943, Eustace Bidlake, who had done much investigative probing on Alex's behalf, received the wonderful news from the Red Cross that Alex was in a camp. Immediately he cabled both the Air Ministry and Agnes. Apparently, such a source was not good enough for the RAF, who still refused to classify Alex as a POW. At last, in early 1944, Alex was allowed to send a card home. When Agnes received it she must have felt twenty years younger. She immediately cabled the Air Ministry and also Bidlake. Incredibly, the RAF still dragged their feet. While they had admitted from the beginning that Alex was probably a POW they still refused to classify him as such until they received Agnes's news via Bidlake! They neither acknowledged nor acted upon her cable. It was as well for the Allies' cause that such heroes were employed well behind the lines.

The climax of the Golden Age was a Christmas concert in December 1942. Alex recalls the show as set in London, with a backdrop of a view across the Thames, painted by Sid. The costumes were miraculous considering their situation. Dressed in all sorts of London garb, the performers sang a series of funny songs which brought the house down. Alex and a friend did a two-man comedy routine along the lines of Amos and Andy. Thanks to one of the choruses, the performers were greeted for months afterwards with shouts of "TAXI!" by Dutch and Ambonese POWs who had enjoyed the show.

Soon afterwards, at the beginning of 1943, the axe fell. The signs had been there for months. In September the regular army guards were replaced by Koreans and Dunlop had written: "They are rather brutal and most of those slapped down do not know why."[52] In November Dunlop and 1,000 Australians left Bandoeng, the start of a journey that would take them to the infamous Burma-Thailand Railway. New regulations banned meetings of more than two people. Drunken guards trailing rifles with bayonets fixed, would wander through the barracks at any time. An atmosphere which had been verging on secure was destroyed over-night. As rice rations were reduced everyone was affected by a new feeling of insecurity. Alex's earlier metaphor of sitting on a powder keg was now felt by all.

12

SURVIVAL

OCTOBER 1943–SEPTEMBER 1945
In which the full horror of being a POW of the Japanese is revealed
and in which life, even for the 'lucky', becomes a struggle to stay alive,
at which Alex proves himself both adept and a leader.

"This bizz"

With the end of the Golden Age, POW life lost whatever lunatic holiday-camp characteristics it had once possessed and became an exercise in survival. Sid buried his cartoons at the XVth Battalion Camp in Bandoeng. After the move to Cycle Camp in Batavia, for him as for Laurens and his diary, it was too dangerous to continue to amuse friends at the expense of the Japanese, whose sense of humour now showed a negative reading. In the early months the Japanese had issued plenty of orders which the camp population had been able to take in stride. Many were based on reasonable health considerations. Thus, Sid had fun with the order for heads to be shaved. It must have been a relief to be rid of hair that was not only hot but also a breeding ground for lice. Sid shows men carving 'V' for victory, 'dot dot dot dash' (V in Morse Code) and 'USA' into the stubble on their scalps, visible to the 'bowee' when the prisoner bowed the required 15 degrees. Similarly, beards were restricted to the size of that grown by the Japanese Colonel Anami, whose miserable growth earned him the nickname of Nitty Whiskers and which was caricatured by Sid. Again, this order was probably not entirely unwelcome – beards and Java do not mix.

However, two orders which changed their lives for the worse were the restriction of meetings outside the billets to two people and the requirement that shirts be worn at all times outdoors. The first of these made it no longer possible to hold concerts or plays, although the Japanese seem to have permitted re-education classes to continue. Bridge became more restricted because it could now only be played indoors. For a nervous Japanese prison service, there might have been a security

Cartoon by Sid Scales.

reason for such an order but the shirt order seems to have been straightforward harassment. No doubt guards, made to wear uniform, resented seeing POWs looking more comfortable in the heat than they felt themselves. Whatever the reason it increased laundry requirements, reduced comfort, increased the smell of people and provided guards with another excuse to abuse prisoners.

Because of such restrictions the guards loomed larger in the prisoners' lives. From early in life Alex had been enough of a scrapper to look after himself and was used to receiving knocks. This continued in merchant seaman days, especially on the *Empress of Canada*. It is not surprising, therefore, that the actions of camp guards did not unduly distress him, including being knocked unconscious in one particular incident. After the war he would say: "I made a vow when the war ended that if anyone asked me whether it was true that the Japs did this, that or the next thing, I would reply yes. In fact, I do not think anyone could, in their wildest imagination, ever think up nasty things worse than those I knew the Japs to have done. Mind you, in the same breath I must add that I did not experience any horrible happenings, nor did I witness any really horrible torturings. But believe me, the most awful things were perpetrated by the Japs and their Korean guards."

As with his combat flying Alex appears, on the whole, to have led a charmed life in the camps and, once more, it is hard to believe that it was an accident. The charmed life extended to Sid Scales who also reports no trouble with guards. In spite of his portrayal of them all as figures of fun the only contact that he had with the worst of them, Sergeant (*Gunzo*) Mori, was when Mori questioned him about some drawings that he had done for *Mark Time*. "Fortunately," he wrote, "he was in a good mood and we had tea! He took great delight in telling me New Zealand had been "Boom-Boomed" by great Japan – complete nonsense."

Mori, good mood or not, was a sinister individual who, in spite of not having tangled with Sid or Alex, nevertheless committed crimes sufficiently atrocious for him to be hanged as a war criminal in 1946. This gentleman was their guard at various times during their imprisonment. Not only that, but because officers in charge of him – Nitty Whiskers and his successors – were weak men, Mori in effect ruled the camp. He had been one of the original guards in their camp, early enough for Sid to have done a fine job of portraying him as 'Bamboo' Mori. From the beginning he had a reputation for gratuitous violence, using his cane or *rottang* on the head and face of any prisoner who crossed him. He is the model for *Rottang* Hara whose story parallels that of the real-life Mori in Laurens's book *The Seed and the Sower*. Quite early on, presumably in 1942, Mori (Hara) was "put in charge of a draft of RAF officers and men and sent to build aerodromes in the outer islands. We did not see him again until near the end, when he returned with only one fifth of the original draft left alive."[53]

Laurens is more explicit in *New Moon:* his secret contact, Mr Kim the Korean, had informed him that

> "... a party of British POWs ... had been sent not long after the capitulation to build an aerodrome on the small island of Haruko ... hundreds of them had died through both the inefficiency of the Japanese system of logistics and the brutality of the Japanese military in command there ... The prisoners were coming back starved and dying, travelling in such terrible conditions that not many of them would survive the journey. He also warned me that the members of the Japanese prison staff responsible for the worst of the atrocities on Haruko would be returning with the party, to assume positions of high responsibility in POW camps in Java."

Kim was telling the truth: "The few survivors of an original party of some fifteen hundred men who came into the camp looked like pictures of the last inmates of Belsen." Laurens added: "Moreover the worst of their guards appeared on the staff of our own camp, like the unbelievable warrant officer *Gunzo* Mori and his Korean satellite ... who had adopted the Japanese name of Kasayama."[54] This was none other than the 'Slime' Kasayama of Sid's 1942 cartoon.

And what had Mori done? Well, if Laurens is to be believed in *The Seed*, it was Hara (Mori) who

> "beat dying men, saying there was nothing wrong with them except
> their 'spirit', their 'evil thinking', their 'wayward willfulness of heart',
> which made them deliberately ill in order to retard the Japanese war
> effort. It was he, Hara (Mori), who cut off the heads of three airmen
> because they had crept through the fence at night to buy food ... and
> after each head rolled on the ground brought his sword to his lips
> thanking it for having done its work so cleanly. It was he who day after
> day in the tropical sun drove a horde of men, ailing and only half
> alive, to scrape an aerodrome out of coral rock with inadequate tools
> until they were dying and being thrown to the sharks in the sea at the

Sid Scales' cartoon of Colonel 'Nitty Whiskers' Anami and the beard-trimming order.

rate of twenty to thirty a day ... Hara (Mori) himself appeared untouched by his experience ... He came back to us burnt black by the
sun; that was all. For the rest he naturally took up the steely thread of
command as if he had never been away, and drove us again with the
same iron hand."[55]

Laurens's informant on the Haruko atrocity was Blackwood, an RAF officer who
survived the ordeal. Another witness to the building of airfields at Haruko, Amahai
and Ambon was RAF Sgt Talbot Knight. He understood that survival in such
circumstances was largely mental. He remembered another sergeant, at the end of
a particularly bad day on Haruko, saying: "To hell with this – I'm packing in my
hand." The man was dead in the morning. In spite of the horrors, Knight and
others managed to find amusement and enjoyment in the midst of hell. At Haruko
one gang of POWs pounded coral into chips and loaded it into sacks. With two
POWs to a sack and pole, others carried these sacks to a second gang building up
the runway. Although pushed close to their physical limits under the equatorial
sun, chip-pounders and runway-builders held day-long quizzes, with sack-carriers
as messengers!

The background to this torment was an earthly paradise and Knight tried to
focus his mind on its beauty. He described a night spent by just-landed POWs on
the beach at Amahai: the kampong behind them was quiet, its swept streets lit by
tiny half-coconut lamps suspended from trees; in front of them the surf was gentle
and astonished POWs waded into the water to catch phosphorous sparkles in their
cupped hands. On Ambon, another airfield-building island, he remembered how
important to them were the sounds of reveille and last post – comforting fragments
of normality which they managed to maintain. He also remembered with gratitude
the normal consideration shown to prisoners by some of the Japanese, in particular
a *gunzo* they christened 'Jack Holt', after a movie actor. POWs were being forced to
run down a dock and up a beach carrying a 50-kg bomb between two or a 100-kg
bomb between three. Korean guards chanted: *"Itchi, ne, san, see"* to keep them at
the double and beat those who faltered. Most had reached exhaustion when *Gunzo*
'Jack' appeared; he sized up the situation and ordered the Korean and Japanese
guards into the workforce. The tempo immediately became tolerable and 'Jack
Holt' was always equally fair.

Knight confirmed the size of the death toll at approximately 80 percent and
believed that the most intolerable thing of all, which killed the largest number, was
sea travel. POWs were herded into the holds of freighters, spending unbearably
hot days anchored near shore to avoid allied aircraft, sometimes for days at a time,
with occasional buckets of water lowered to them when somebody happened to

remember them. When Knight's ship reached Java from Haruko in October 1944, of the 600 men who had sailed on her, all survivors of airfield building, only 292 remained alive. Those not immediately admitted into the primitive POW hospital were sent to the same camp as Alex, along with the notorious Mori.[56] Alex took on the task of delousing their clothing, his contribution to alleviating their suffering. To have avoided their terrible experience Alex and Sid were indeed lucky.

There was another case of a draft which ended in incredible and brutal tragedy. The draft, including Ken Whitworth and all the airmen from 205 Squadron, went to build an airfield at Sandakan in Sabah, North Borneo. Ken wrote to Alex, in November 1945, that after they had left Bandoeng "we went back to Singapore for a month or so and then on to Jesselton, Sandakan and Kuching and had a pretty tough time to take it all round. I'm much afraid that the rest of 205 who were taken with us have 'had it'. I was with them all up to August 1943, then left them at Sandakan. They were all well then, remarkably so considering all we'd been through at that period, but you have, of course, heard of the unspeakable 'death-march' at Sandakan. Only six men out of 1,800 survived it, and I'm therefore pretty certain that Sanders, Stammers and the rest of them went under in the march." Once again Alex and Sid had dodged the bullet. It probably happened that way because Alex, Sid and John Westcott had been listed separately after their south coast adventure, whereas Ken had been listed with the rest of the 205 men at Tasikmalaja. It may also have had something to do with Alex being part of the command structure in camp – who knows?

Unlike Alex, Laurens was transfixed by Mori and wrote a great deal about him. Partly because of his own earlier solitary confinement under a death sentence, he had come face-to-face with him and the two appear to have had a special relationship. His experience of Japan and ability to speak Japanese enabled prisoner and guard to talk freely. He was able to sympathise with Mori as a victim of his mediaeval background, with its lack of education, its warrior culture and its absolute faith in the justice of his Emperor's cause. Laurens claimed that Mori believed in the rightness of his own actions at Haruko, for example. His attitude – that Christ's request: "Forgive them, for they know not what they do," applied to Mori and other Japanese just as it had to Roman soldiers – was not a popular one with Alex, nor would it have been with Ken. He wrote, in his 1945 letter describing Sandakan: "God, how I hate those bloody Nips!" It was also probably one of the reasons for Laurens being considered a 'bullshit artist' by the New Zealanders.

In fact, there can be little doubt that Laurens was right. Japanese soldiers had a microscopic world view. Ian Buruma, in *The Wages of Guilt*, talks of a chaplain who questioned Japanese camp commandants, awaiting trial for war crimes, about their reasons for mistreating POWs. He discovered that: "They had a belief that any

'Sons of Hell', cartoon by Sid Scales.

enemy of the Emperor could not be right, so the more brutally they treated their prisoners, the more loyal to their Emperor they were being."[57]

Nevertheless, Laurens's empathy with their tormentor left Mori's daily victims absolutely cold while Mori still wielded his *rottang* over them; their ill-treatment was reality, not an academic exercise. The photograph of the three guards after their arrest shows an intense Mori (right) and an unnamed guard, who looks like Sid's Hosh the Slosher, sandwiching the more relaxed Kasayama. The latter is certainly tiny but hardly fits the rest of Laurens's description of him – "of unlimited energies, resource and variety of mood." Mori, on the other hand, looks the part. Laurens described him as being both short and immensely strong having extremely broad shoulders and little or no neck. With some allowance for artistic licence, that is he. His face, with its prominent chin, is the face in Sid's cartoon. Arrest and the removal of his belt robs him of dignity – he is preoccupied with holding up his pants – but in contrast to the vapid expressions behind him, his face seethes with strong feelings. Laurens offers this description of Hara in the *Seed*, surely the essence of Mori in the photograph: "He was indeed a terrible little man, not only in the way that the great Tartar Ivan was terrible, but also in a peculiarly racial and demoniac way. He possessed the sort of terribleness that thousands of years of littleness might seek to inflict on life as both a revenge and a compensation for having been so little for so long ... I have seen him beat up the tallest among us for no other reason save that they were so much taller than he."[58]

With guards led by such a man, Alex and his friends faced the uncertainties of the end of the war. Secret radios kept them informed of Allied victories and they certainly felt the consequences of the successful submarine campaign. By 1944 this had cut off Japanese-held islands from resupply by sea. Little by little their rice ration was cut – from the half kilo per man, per day of 1942 down to a meagre ninety grams. In spite of living in one of the world's breadbaskets, they were beginning to suffer serious malnutrition and its painful symptoms. One of these was burning sensations in the feet which could only be relieved by soaking them in water. It also weakened resistance to disease and reduced everybody's strength. In this situation the food supplied through Mr Tan and the outside Chinese made the difference between life and death. In Alex's camp nobody starved to death, though many came close.

The intelligence which Laurens received from Mr Kim now became very important. As well as warning of the arrival of the Haruko survivors, Kim also predicted the arrival of hundreds of POWs from other parts of Java; his dates were precise enough to allow them to husband food supplies in preparation. On another occasion he told them of an imminent Japanese demand for several hundred men to work on a project in Sumatra. They were able to pick their fittest people and, as much as possible, to 'fatten them up'. In due course the men left and, thanks to their good condition, most of them survived.[59]

After the destruction of the Japanese navy at the Battles of Leyte Gulf and the Philippine Sea in 1944, the news from Mr Kim began to sound much more ominous. His messages no longer mentioned communication by sea between the various islands. He talked as though the Japanese command in Java had begun to see the island as a fortress, to be defended to the death, both against allied invaders and the swelling ranks of Indonesian nationalists. Some of these had mutinied against the Japanese and were holed up in the same southern mountainous region which had been so inhospitable to Alex. He also told them that the Japanese planned to close down all camps on the north coast to concentrate their prisoners in Bandoeng.

According to Alex's 'Claim for Maltreatment' form, they were moved from the Depot Camp in Bandoeng to the Boys' Gaol in March 1945, where conditions were crowded and about to become more so. Laurens recorded this event as happening three months later. In *Night of the New Moon*, Japanese plans for their prisoners became more concrete after the surrender of Germany in May. At that time they moved all prisoners from the coast to join those in Bandoeng, Alex and Laurens remaining in their Depot Camp until June. In that month Mr Kim informed Laurens that there was to be a still greater concentration of prisoners.

BRIDGE AT ALL COSTS! —— EVENING SCENE IN JAPANESE P.O.W. BILLETS – JAVA.

Conditions in the Boys' Gaol, Bandoeng, 1945, cartoon by Sid Scales.

He also warned that it had been decided to kill all prisoners when the Allies began their assault. The first prediction came true immediately: in late June, managing to keep in step and in military formation, the weakened prisoners marched from the Depot Camp to the Boys' Gaol at the edge of the city. This was described by Laurens as being built for a hundred and twenty boys of criminal tendencies – into which "minute confines some seven thousand of us were somehow pushed and expected to live until whatever end to the war the Japanese had in mind."[60] Whoever was right about the timing, the tension of the next weeks and months provided good reason for either or both of them to be confused.

The crowding was so appalling that the Japanese agreed to provide truckloads of lumber for prisoners to build floor-to-ceiling bunks into every available sheltered space. Only by doing so was it possible for prisoners to keep dry and have a place to sleep. "We were the proverbial sardines," Talbot Knight wrote; "you can imagine what the feeding and latrine problems were." Their numbers were so great that all the time they were in that prison, men stood in line for latrines twenty-four hours a day. Further, in order to maintain some level of hygiene, men were assigned shifts around the clock, on a bucket chain taking water for flushing the latrines from an irrigation ditch in the camp. So successful was this measure that there was no epidemic and Laurens comments that the latrines were the cleanest place in the camp. Another good side effect of the latrine lineup was that it made conspiratorial conversations easy to arrange as it was perfectly normal for men from different barrack rooms to be chatting earnestly in the line at 2:00 a.m.

After a week in the new camp, and just as things were, amazingly, sorting themselves out, Mr Kim reported to Laurens that "unless a miracle intervened, a massacre of prisoners everywhere in Southeast Asia appeared inevitable." At this moment the secretive Laurens decided to take Alex into his confidence – or if not Alex, somebody who was his double. Laurens mentions no name. Alex is not clear on the detail, warns that Laurens loved to spin a yarn and that he may have elaborated the truth. Sid answered "maybe" to my question – "I wouldn't know for sure owing to the secrecy of VdP's schemes, but it wouldn't surprise me if he was [the squadron leader referred to in *New Moon*]! I do recollect discussions on how we could use stones in a 'do-or-die' attempt to resist Japanese 'ethnic cleansing' – making sure stones were loosened in the courtyard, etc." But that is to get ahead of ourselves. It would have been perfectly sensible for Laurens to choose Alex. He was the officer commanding RAF troops and therefore knew more prisoners than other officers did. Sid observed that Alex was always busy – he could no more abide being idle than he can now – was usually cheerful, concerned about his responsibilities to his men, was the life and soul of any group and was NEVER depressed. Nevertheless, the reader must decide whether Laurens refers to Alex. Laurens wrote:

> "I picked first on a Royal Air Force squadron leader, an officer who
> seemed to me fearless and physically almost immune to the conse-
> quences of years of malnutrition. He still appeared, if not as fit as at
> the beginning, far fitter than anybody else in the camp, and full of
> amazing energy. I told him then, under a pledge of secrecy even to his
> senior officers, all that I feared. The two of us made a survey of all the
> men and officers in the camp, and drew up a list of some hundred and
> twenty who were not only the fittest we could find but men whom we
> could trust."

Trust was important because of informers. It would be unwise, for example, to trust anyone known to have friends or contacts among the Ambonese or Madurese native prisoners; many of these made no secret of their desire for a Japanese victory. "We divided the camp into six sections and in each section picked the best possible platoon of twenty men, under the command of the fittest officer in the area."[61] Alex's advice in the choosing of the men would be important because what they were about was the setting up of an *ad hoc* self-defence force.

'An ode to a steak and kidney pie', cartoon by Sid Scales.

With his love for the dramatic, Laurens probably made the most of the story. In a nutshell, he and Alex appear to have planned a desperate defence strategy for unarmed men about to be massacred. It was certainly ingenious. They reasoned that the Japanese would attempt to kill the prisoners inside the prison; the danger of a large-scale escape increased outside the walls and they would need more men than they had. So their plan started with an early-warning system, already in place, to warn of surprise searches; in order to deploy their response it was important to know as soon as the guards came out of their quarters by the gates. The Japanese military, including camp guards, were a scruffy lot and gave ample warning when they were on the move. As Ernest Hillen, himself just a boy in one of their camps, observed: "Few of any rank seemed to have footwear that fit. Their dragging feet made a special 'sloff-sloff' sound."[62]

But what could the response of unarmed men be? It was here that Laurens showed signs of genius which definitely raise him above the level of 'bullshit artist'. He had seen stoning used with lethal effect by unarmed blacks against armed police in South Africa and decided that this would be their only hope. The problem was that the camp was nearly stone-free. However, a possible solution lay in the pools of standing water which formed whenever it rained.

It probably helped that the approach to the commandant was made by the senior Dutch medical officer. Playing on the Japanese fear of *sakit panas*, he told him of his concerns that mosquitoes breeding in the pools were a hazard to guards and prisoners. He then offered a solution: send prisoners out to scavenge stones in the neighbourhood of the camp, have them fill the indentations in the ground with these stones and then stamp them well in. No more pools, no more mosquitoes – problem solved, easily and cheaply. Believe it or not, the commandant not only took the concern seriously; he went along with the solution! Every afternoon for several days squads of prisoners were herded out of the prison to return with what they saw as useless loads of rocks. Many grumbled, blaming their officers for not preventing the Japanese from issuing such a useless order. Talbot Knight knew nothing of the plan but actually welcomed the working parties – "It was a relief to escape the claustrophobic atmosphere of the camp." The indentations in the ground and the pools they contained soon disappeared and the prison yard lay covered in potential ammunition.

Laurens, feeling that this might well be his last opportunity to feast his eyes on the world outside a prison, furtively used the rock-picking excursions as opportunities to appreciate the beauty of the valley in which their Bandoeng prison lay, the tension of the moment adding to his perception.

> "Immediately behind us there was the great volcano of *Tangkoeboehan-praauw*, which is a Malay name meaning literally 'the ship turned upside down' ... All around *Tangkoeboehan-praauw*, as far as one could see, stretched great terraces of rice descending to a plain full of geometric shapes of more and more paddy fields. On these terraces and in these paddy fields one would see the peasants of the island at work under their wide-brimmed hats of golden rice-straw, in the slow, patient, timeless manner of souls dedicated to cultivating the earth ... Wherever a patch of water in the paddies showed itself to the sky, it revealed ... as in a cool mirror, the ... reflection of the solemn, topless towers of clouds that were building up in the blue sky for another downpour of rain at night ... In the heat of the afternoon the clear air of the island over this high plateau ... trembled from the impact of the long lances of bronze equatorial sun ... To add to this ... there were millions of dragonflies ... darting ceaselessly over the burning paddy waters, until the brilliant atmosphere became ... sequined and crackling with ... a quick electric sparkle ... Finally, to frame this stirring canvas of our vision, in the far blue-satin west, as the perfect counterpoint to *Tangkoeboehan-praauw*, stood the other great mountain of the

plain: *Malabar* – always a Hindu citadel, purple and imperial
in the shadows cast from behind it by the long level light of the
sinking sun."[63]

It was ironic that in such a crowded situation, the plan was not just to
overwhelm the guards with numbers; but the presence of informers and spies among
them made this impossible because everybody would have had to know the plan.
Consequently, the survival plan involved a tiny minority of the prisoners and, as
it was never actually employed, it was tempting for them to write it off later as
half-remembered fantasy. However, Laurens was fairly confident during July 1945
that they had things as well under control as possible. It was not till the end of that
month that their world started to change unpredictably.

First, all links with the outside were broken. Messages no longer arrived from
Mr Kim, who had been reliable if not always reassuring. Contact with the outside
Chinese seemed also to have been broken; nothing the industrious Mr Tan could
do made any difference. For the first time in their imprisonment they were on their
own, with their tiny rice ration as their only nourishment. Secondly, there was
evidence that pressure was mounting on the Japanese guards. In *Night of the New
Moon* Laurens tells the story of a parade for all Dutch and British senior officers.
Mori had paraded them because none would admit to having men with technical
skills, able to help the Japanese in the munitions factory they had set up to supply
the army when the Allies invaded. After screaming at them for a while he began to
pull them out, one at a time, to be beaten. So out of control was he on this occasion
that he broke a wooden chair over the head and shoulders of the first officer before
him. He then used pieces of the broken chair to assault other officers, while first
Kasayama and then other Korean guards joined in. Laurens himself received a
terrible beating. It was after he had staggered back to his place that he saw a
machine gun being set up in the corner of the parade ground and decided that he
had better do what he could to end things. Recklessly, he marched back to the front
and presented himself for a second beating! Mori was so confused by this evidence
of his own apparent ineffectiveness that he left the parade, taking his satellites with
him. Only late in the evening, after an afternoon sweltering in the sun, did they
dare request permission from the camp commander to dismiss.[64]

Alex is not able to confirm or dispute Laurens's account of this parade, because
he never saw the end of it. As Mori's blows rained upon his own head and shoulders, memories of the Japanese naval cadets on the *Canada* must have passed through
his head as he, like his companions, stoically refused to cry out or flinch until
falling unconscious to the ground. Talbot Knight was also there. According to him
the whole camp had been paraded in a hollow square with senior officers in the
centre. Kasayama had started the parade by demanding names of technicians. Then

"suddenly *Gunzo* Mori appeared ... and we ... then witnessed a brutal beating up of all those officers as Mori went berserk ... Officers stood or fell with dignity ... as Mori proceeded to beat them ... in turn. At one stage he was using his sword complete with scabbard. Kasayama joined in with boots as any fell." In his account he included the story of the broken chair, did not mention machine guns, agreed that Mori and Kasayama finally retreated, leaving them all standing in the sun but did not mention Laurens's extraordinary action – though maybe he could see little detail as he was one of 7,000 prisoners and possibly quite distant.[65]

The third change to their world was when their secret radio broke down – just at the end of July when the war in the Pacific was reaching a climax. After several days 'in the dark' the fearless Kiwi Bill Phillips not only fixed it but did so with parts he had burgled at night from the radio in the Japanese commandant's house! We have to be astonished at the courage of these actions, for discovery would have brought instant execution. But Laurens and Alex and their friends had a working radio again, in time to hear the news of Hiroshima and Nagasaki. That news, stunning though it was, brought two contradictory consequences. Immediately, it gave the Japanese an opportunity to surrender – even the *Samurai* code would not compel the Japanese army to continue the struggle against such an overwhelming and inhuman force. Therefore, as prisoners, their chances of survival improved dramatically. But there was a corresponding negative. Japanese forces in Southeast Asia were commanded by an officer of the old school, Field Marshal Terauchi. When it became known that the Emperor had made peace overtures on August 12, it was also known that Terauchi, unwilling to accept surrender, was insisting on a fight to the death in defiance of the Emperor. So, in spite of the tremendous change in the situation brought by the atomic bombs, their fate was still in the balance.

Only the prisoners in the circle of the secret radio operators knew of all this – for there was at least one other radio. Those few realised that they must keep the information to themselves until Terauchi's headquarters had made up its mind and had conveyed its decision to the camps. Prisoners not in the know, such as Talbot Knight, could infer from the concentration of prisoners that "something was happening ... that things were building up to a climax." For their part, *Gunzo* Mori and the guards showed no sign that they were aware of the atomic bomb or of the Emperor's peace initiative. Their treatment of prisoners did not vary or become more lenient. In fact, Mori delivered a severe beating to Laurens in the last few days, after he had tried to protect a sick man from one of the Koreans. Meanwhile Mr Kim's messages to Laurens had started again, as mysteriously as they had stopped. Between the 12th and the 17th of August Kim was hinting that a massacre could still take place; Terauchi had not yet changed his mind, in spite of the mission of the Emperor's brother to Saigon to bring this about. Laurens and those around him, including Alex, were aware that one foolish act of celebration by the prisoners

THE ARMED MITE OF NIPPON.

Cartoon by Sid Scales.

could still provoke the guards to drastic action. For Alex these were tense days –
anything could happen and they remained on their guard.

By the 17th of August they were aware of the capitulation; still the behaviour of
the Japanese gave no sign that all was not as usual. On the morning of the 21st they
were observed to parade, as they had done on a thousand mornings, ending, as
always, with a ritual bow towards the rising sun. Yet on that day the world, as they
knew it, was to come to an end. In midafternoon Laurens, summoned by the
commandant, was spirited out of camp in a staff car to the villa at the foot
of *Tangkoeboehan-praauw* which had been Wavell's HQ. It was where he had been
given his own orders before his capture and imprisonment. He was informed, by
a meeting of Japanese staff officers, that the Japanese had "changed sides!"
With great presence of mind he gave them orders on behalf of their new
'allies' – presumably concerning disarming their own troops and the treatment of
their prisoners.[66]

That same evening, after the official announcement that the war was over, Alex
and his companions of three and a half years, carrying their pathetic possessions,
walked to the station to board trains for Batavia. There they would await whatever
arrangements were to be made for their journey home. Armed Japanese soldiers
escorted them, two to a carriage, sitting on jump-seats at either end – as if nothing

had happened. Their role was now to protect their former prisoners from the Indonesian nationalists who controlled the countryside. The train was crowded and many POWs had to stand. Suddenly one of the POWs tapped a soldier on the arm, made a motion with his head. The soldier stood up and the POW took his place. For those who saw this happen it was as if they had pricked themselves with a pin! They were not dreaming, the war was really over. Through the windows "it was a magnificent sight to see the green jungle valleys full of mist and the verdant mountain tops striking up on all sides as the train wove a tortuous course between them."[67] Beautiful though it might be, after years of confinement it was an environment from which most could not wait to escape.

They returned to the same Cycle Camp in Batavia in which they had spent some months in the middle of their imprisonment. The camp was still a military organisation, but now under their own authority. They were to spend another month there, this time without the likes of Mori and Kasayama, waiting for repatriation and gradually getting stronger as their diet improved. Alex, whose weight had been 150 pounds in 1942, tipped the scales at ninety pounds. Remarkably, in spite of his emaciation, he was fit, as Laurens had observed in *New Moon*.

Immediately, Alex was busy, this time working industriously to find out what had become of the men of his detachment in particular, but also of all other members of 205 Squadron. Among his papers is a truly sad little document, typed on the back of a discarded Japanese form. Alex had listed the names of Ken Whitworth and the sixteen detachment members who had remained at Tasikmalaja. As a second group under them Sgt Gamble and LAC McDowell, who had been on the south coast breakout with him; and below them three other airmen's names. He had checked the list with whatever records they were able to put together in the first days of freedom. Opposite Whitworth and his sixteen there was "NO" in Alex's writing in pencil; also an official purple stamp: "NO RECORD IN JAVA POW & INTERNEES CAMPS." Opposite Gamble and McDowell, in Alex's writing – "MALAYA." Opposite the final three, one was "No Record in Java," one was "Malaya" and the third was "Malaya or dead." He had here an inkling of the likely fate of his men and may have found other records which told him the whole story, although from the diary that he started to keep it does not seem that he did. The letter from Ken Whitworth with news of the Sandakan death march did not reach him until November. There is another list, written in pencil on yellowing paper, of about a hundred and twenty 205 Squadron names. Alex had been checking the POW lists for the names of all squadron members whose names he could remember. He drew a blank; all had escaped from Tjilatjap, in one way or another, back in March 1942.

His next task was to get the Canadians in Java back home. He typed lists of

names and fired off letters to anybody who might help. He interviewed all the
Canadians; for each he listed home address and number of years since last in Canada.
He requested travel by hospital ship for the sickest men. The plan was to get all
Canadians home, come what may, before any other obligation was taken care
of, such as reporting to a British unit. He wrote to the officer commanding
English-speaking POWs in Batavia, to the Canadian public relations officer (PRO)
in Singapore, to the Americans – even to the New Zealand public relations officer.
He soon discovered that Uncle Sam was not about to cooperate with flights to the
U.S. in spite of his own good relations with Lt Cmdr Donovan, Senior American
Officer, POW. There were to be no seats for Canadians, period! Americans, after
bankrolling the war, from long before they became combatants, were beginning to
feel taken for granted by their allies. Alex had suspected all along that his effort was
a lost cause. He ended his letter to the PRO in Singapore with: "Should it happen
that nothing can be done about getting us out early, we should all be very grateful
to see you here if you can manage a flip down. If possible, bring a bottle (or two) of
Canadian Club!!!"

During this time of waiting another concern was the recovery of buried
treasures. Alex typed the detailed instructions for Laurens which were alluded to
earlier. The simplest thing to have done would have been to borrow or steal a
vehicle and go and dig them up. However, with the Japanese confined to barracks
and the POWs and internees in their camps, waiting for transport out of Java, the
Nationalists, or 'Extremists' as the Dutch called them, ruled the countryside. They
were inclined to shoot at anybody, friend or foe, who was not Indonesian. The
journey to Bandoeng probably could have been made safely, as Ernest Hillen's
family proved[68], but why take the risk for a few papers? So Alex contented himself
with waiting and on the 8th of September began a diary. The first entry is not
terribly coherent – for once Alex allowed himself to express feelings and just rattle
on – but he had some good news to record.

> "Sept 8, 1945:
> Today at 0730 hrs GMT (approx) the camp was visited by a paratroop
> Major Greenhall. Three years and six months to the day since I last
> wore RAF Tropical Service Dress. Today marks the first step towards
> going home since March 26 1937 – indeed a historic one for me. The
> Major gave a short speech (Lancs accent?!) and told us we shall be
> some time, that Singapore POWs are very badly off physically – 1%
> able to walk or stand, 30% unable to move without hospital treat-
> ment. Astounding news. An HM cruiser is on its way from Ceylon
> today. He [Greenhall] left Trinco [malee, Ceylon] at 8:00 p.m. – 15 hr

trip in Liberator. Today means so much to me and I could go on and
on writing (drivel?) certainly in a way feelings unexpressed, over years;
fulfillment of my fondest hopes over so many, many years. Definite
information that there are arrangements afoot to move ME out of the
Far East. WONDERFUL DAY."

For the next ten days, time seemed to hang terribly. But each day had its 'first'
– sometimes several of them. Maybe this gradual reintroduction to normality made
Alex's return to the world easier in the long run, a sort of decompression chamber
for recently incarcerated pilots.

"Sept 9:
We had aircraft over, a huge white Liberator.
"Sept 10:
There were more.
"Sept 11:
Two twins (Mitchells?).
"Sept 12:
4 days have passed and each of 24 hrs. In retrospect, four months
seem closer to the mark. Long days and no visible change. Seeing the
Liberator was indeed a tonic and now we hear no more supplies to be
dropped. This [is a] time of uncertainty, especially when we hear over
the radio so much happening in other areas. We begin to wonder
whether our new Commanding Officer & news generally is really so
well informed as we should like to believe. Certainly, unless the POW
and Internee figure has really changed, they have the figures all wrong.
Political unrest outside is giving certain people here lots to talk about.
I cannot decide definitely for myself as to the seriousness of the
situation. I believe that it is not as yet very well organised or extensive.
The hospital outside had some bother last night. Shoppee is doing
well enough; saw Kinmouth today and sent a message out with him.
Rae is now unfit for duty and so I must find another.
"Sept 14:
I broadcast from Mirom the names of Canadians here. First time,
quite an interesting experience. I enjoyed every moment of sitting in
chairs with space around one – carpets, stairs and real coffee, finally
ending with a real meal, off china, and NO RICE. I found my knees
unaccustomed to stairs, smoked Gold Flake cigs and talked to some
people though they were Dutch. The Manager of Mirom, a Jap, came

in almost crawling, nasty bastard. Smoky Douglas, RAAF, over in a Mosquito; he dropped RAAF news. Mostly all Air Commodores, it appears!"

On this day Alex also wrote his first note to his mother, presumably his first opportunity as it was a hurried scribble in pencil: "Am fit and well and longing to see you all again."

> "Sept 15:
> 3 RAAF Liberators over, shooting us up and dropping parcels.
> "Sept 16:
> Admiral Pattison of Cumberland visited camp and spoke to us this morning. We were all so very pleased with the way he appears to feel about us. He told us nothing new. It looks like about the beginning of Oct before the bulk of us move off the island. A few days ago an RE Major visited us. He is part and parcel of RAPWE Org [the forces organisation for care and repatriation of POWs]. There are days when the radio and aircraft flying overhead drive one scatty. We have repeated reports of atrocity stories which *are* unpleasant. Maybe we can sit in a chair in front of a fire and hear that sort of thing with no qualms but one's people must feel the strain as we do, sitting here surrounded by irate natives and Japs. The aircraft give me a sense of frustration. I feel that I should be flying again."

On the 17th Alex wrote again because Sid Scales, his companion for three and a half years, was leaving for New Zealand and could mail his letter; for both it must have been a bittersweet moment. They would meet again but not for four years, although they kept in touch. Alex could give Agnes no dates for his departure from Java or arrival in Canada. His letter was similar to his earlier note, adding: "Sending this with Sid Scales. He has been a grand chap all through this bizz." It was maybe the most stoic understatement of his career and a phrase he would use again. "This bizz" was a code word, a euphemism for the 1221 days of hell which Alex was later to enter on the official Claim for Maltreatment in 1953.

Sid remembers an event on his RNZAF repatriation flight: "We stopped off at Labuan on the first stage of the journey. There was a field hospital there and I reported in on the off chance that there would be some casualty there that I knew. I found Ken Whitworth – just a skeleton; he'd had a very rough time and was delighted that Alex and I were still alive; and I was, too, that Ken had lived through it. So I wrote a message to Alex (S/Ldr A. M. Jardine, POW, Bandoeng) and gave it to a pilot returning to Singapore. Communications were still very chancy but I hoped Alex would get it. I can't recollect now if he ever did." In fact he did, and it made him just as happy. The next day, the 18th of September, he was flown in an American aircraft to Calcutta. 'This bizz' had ended for him too and he had survived. It was three years and seven months to the day since his last operational flight.

To put 'this bizz' in perspective, in late 1946 Alex was to receive a letter from the RAF, pointing out that fewer than half of RAF POWs had survived. It concluded: "You will no doubt be interested to know that Colonel Anami (Nitty Whiskers), Sgt/Major Mori and interpreter Kasayama were arrested and taken to Singapore in chains by S/Ldr Pitts, where they were subsequently tried. Colonel Anami and Sgt/Major Mori were sentenced to death and Kasayama to life imprisonment. It will be remembered that these three were in charge of the draft at Haruko and subsequently at the camp at Bandoeng, and no doubt a great part of the casualties on the attached list are their responsibility." In spite of the best efforts of Laurens on their behalf, these sentences were carried out.

13

RETURN OF THE EXILE

SEPTEMBER–DECEMBER 1945
In which Alex picks up the pieces of his life and returns to Victoria for
the first time in eleven years; and in which he decides to jump to the RCAF.

"Arriving just before or after lunch today STOP"

The aircraft over the camp in Batavia had made Alex realise that flying, more than anything else, was still what he wanted to do with his life. But captivity had ruined his 1941 career plan: the market would be flooded with demobilised pilots, thousands of them better qualified and more current than a thirty-one-year-old whose last flying hours were recorded on the 18th of February 1942. From the point of view of BOAC or TCA, Squadron Leader Jardine would seem like Rip Van Winkle. Understandably, they would rather entrust passengers to some lucky young blood with thousands of recent hours flying Liberators over Germany or Sunderlands over the North Atlantic. To get back to professional flying it looked as if Alex would have to stay in the service, either British or Canadian, or go out on a limb with his own aeroplane, as a bush pilot up north.

He left Batavia at dusk on the 18th of September in a Douglas C54 Skymaster of the U.S. Air Force (USAAF) Transport Command, fitted out as a hospital aircraft. The first of two USAAF flights 'tasked' to evacuate U.S. POWs had taken off with about forty passengers and, after a head count of the remaining Americans, Alex realised there would be space for others on the second flight. Encouraged by Donovan, Alex rounded up Canadians willing to travel to the U.S.A. in this way, and from there to Canada. When they boarded the aircraft things looked promising. A four-hour hop took them back to Singapore where they landed for a thirty-minute refuelling stop. Alex "did not dare risk missing the aircraft so stayed on board when everyone else left to visit the facilities available." Besides, it was too late to see anything and he was tired. They continued northwards through the night, arriving at breakfast time at Dum Dum airfield in Calcutta. There his hopes of a speedy return home evaporated in the hot morning sunshine. A conversation with the pilot about the Canadians continuing on the aircraft to the States was pleasant but not productive. Captain Joseph F. Chuse from Buffalo clearly had his instructions; reflecting the weariness of his countrymen, he politely pointed out that Lend-lease was over!

Once in Calcutta Alex had a spare day before reporting to RAPWI, the rehabilitation agency at Camp Belvedere. His notebook, a booklet homemade from stapled scrap paper, some with Dutch printing on it, shows us what he had to do: he contacted Captain Just, the adjutant at the General Hospital; he also contacted the American Hospital; he phoned Mr Buchan at the Hong Kong and Shanghai Bank; he phoned Captain Fortescue at the pay office. He had a dozen Calcutta numbers in his notebook; he was looking for old friends and trying to get his life in order. At some time he must have sat down with a copy of *Who's Who*, the London and Glasgow telephone books, or maybe with some service records, because his address book began to take shape again.

When he reported to Camp Belvedere on the 20th, they found him to be emaciated, though now chunkier than his original ninety pounds. Otherwise he was in remarkably good health. For a week he was tested for bugs and parasites and was fed meals which allowed him to start putting on weight. Even service rations would have been a feast. This was supposed to be downtime for patients, all recent POWs, who were not encouraged to be busy. Nevertheless from the 18th of September Agnes received a string of telegrams about Alex's whereabouts and health which only ended with his arrival home in late October. Aware that Australian POWs were arriving from Java, on the 19th Pat and Norman Birks wired Agnes expectantly from Adelaide: "Have you good news? Thinking of you. Had baby August 10, godson for Alec. Great blessings and love." On the 21st Alex managed to send his own cables – to the Birkses, to Bidlake, to Beryl Stilling, to his mother and probably to others. Cable offices everywhere were drowning in such messages of survival; not until the morning of the 24th did his reach Adelaide. Immediately, an excited Norman Birks wired Agnes: "Sept 24: Pat and I received cable from Alec Rapwi Belvedere Calcutta. We are both overjoyed for you that he is safe and well. Our love, Norman." There was more of the same good news that day from RCAF Headquarters in Ottawa: "Your son S/L Jardine has been recovered from Japanese hands and is safe and well in allied territory at Belvedere Camp, Calcutta." Eustace Bidlake in London wired Agnes that he had received a "cable from Alex Rapwi Belvedere Calcutta. Expecting go Canada soon." Not until the 26th did Alex's own cable trickle through to Victoria: "Arrived safely at Calcutta. Hope be home soon. Writing. Alec."

He wrote that same day and again from Karachi four days later. His concerns were characteristic: "This whole bizz must have been frightful for you, and because of you and the girls I have regretted that I was such a bloody fool as to be caught. As for me, I'm out now and in one piece, reasonably fit and anxious to forget everything but the friends I have made ... Please, please, let me know your sponduliks [money] position ... I do insist!" He was amazed and excited, though disconcerted, by changes that had happened in his own family in the eleven years since he saw them last. More particularly he was amazed by the changes during the three and a half years since he had last telephoned them. This had been from Batavia on the 3rd of February 1942, which eighteen-year-old Deirdre ('Babe') had described in her diary as: "The most wonderful morning in seven years!" He had carried in his mind's eye the image of five girls aged between eleven and nineteen, as they had been in January 1935 when the *Gracia* had last called at Victoria. Now he was going home to meet four married women, aged between twenty-four and thirty-one, with children and husbands, and one twenty-two-year-old unmarried woman whom he still thought of as a child! "Bestest love to the girls," he concluded, "the 'married women + Babe' perhaps I should say!! I can't visualise nor believe it! One thing you must do is write in answer to this to Lloyds, 6 Pall Mall, [his bank in London] and tell me the names of all my new 'relations', both by marriage and as a result of marriage!! I'm so anxious to know all about them."

But he had a more general feeling of being out of touch. He also wanted his mother's help with the "whereabouts of friends of the days of long ago. I'm horrified to discover I can't remember the names of so many of them. It was not possible to keep address books and the like in many of the camps and my mind has become 'woolly', I feel sure as a result of my being 'Too Far in the Long East' as we often remark ... I still find it a little difficult to absorb the knowledge that we are really free; there is so much to take in, one can't do it in one gulp!!" On the bright side he was thrilled by the contacts he had already made. He was delighted to have heard from Norman and Pat Birks and from Beryl Stilling in Australia, and to find that he now had two Australian godchildren – a goddaughter, three-year-old Robyn Stilling, and a godson, six-week-old Johnnie Birks. Maybe, after all, the universe would unfold as it should. He discovered that his mother had kept in touch with Pat and Beryl, that they had both sent her telegrams in March 1944, acknowledging her news that Alex was definitely a POW, and that Norman had been to Vancouver, had telephoned Agnes and had taken his youngest sister Deirdre out for a meal.

He told Agnes that he was uncomfortable writing about his feelings or his POW experiences; not surprisingly, he wanted to postpone talking about them until he reached home, as he found being in transit to be unsettling. This letter and the previous one give us a glimpse of his mental turmoil, his feeling that the world had passed him by and his frustration at having no influence to get things moving. "We are considerable in number – i.e. the POWs – and also they cannot consider individual cases, and for the first time in many years I'm no more than a name ... the Air Force has changed by the tremendous number of people in it. I don't know 'everyone' as I used to." He was casting about for familiar backs to slap and found, instead, only hundreds of unknown servicemen who just wanted to get home. To somebody who had been in command, with a reputation for humanity and courage and competence and sociability and humour, the anonymity of the transit camp was like one of those nightmares in which people pay no attention to you however hard you shout! To be a nobody was as bad as being Rip Van Winkle.

In spite of his earlier hopes, his journey home from Java took him thirty-three days. On every part of the route he travelled by air, but always the long way round. Although it might have been quicker and more pleasant to take a ship across the Pacific, he was dependent for employment on the RAF and the last thing he wanted to do was to upset them. After seven days in hospital in Calcutta his journey to Britain went relatively quickly. On the 26th of September he flew in an RAF Transport Command Dakota, a DC3, from Calcutta to Karachi with a stop for lunch and fuel at Allahabad. This was his first flight in a DC3, an aircraft with which he was later to become familiar. Only its reliability was impressive. Compared to a Catalina it was not much roomier, just as noisy and almost as slow. He had to cool his heels in Karachi for the 27th and the 28th. The province of Sind, part of India until 1947, was rural and mediaeval outside Karachi – itself still a small seaport. If Alex and others went into town, their bus honked its way through lines of stately camels, shimmering in the heat haze on the tarmac. But they had little opportunity.

Non-Canadians had no idea how far away BC was and he was taking no chances; he insisted, when collecting his travel document, that it be written from Karachi to Victoria, BC, and not just to Canada. His journey to Britain began on the 29th in a Transport Command Avro York, for him another new aircraft. Developed from the four-engined Lancaster bomber, the York (named by Avro in an attempt to keep everybody happy, a rose by any other name!) was even bigger – said to be 'elephantine' in one history of the RAF. Much more powerful than the DC3, it would reach England in four hops. Leaving Karachi in late afternoon, they made a nighttime fuel stop at Shaibya in the Persian Gulf, landing again in Cairo as sunrise was gilding the pyramids on the 30th. For 1945 that was fast travel, unimaginably faster than his Vincent flight of 1938. Wasting no time, the aircraft reached Castel Benito in southern Italy in midafternoon. There, after twenty-four hours of travelling, the passengers were given beds for the night – an exciting night for most, the last of their exile. A good night's sleep would have suited all of them, but it was not to be. Not to be denied its military arbitrariness, the RAF rousted them out of bed before four in the morning. The York left for Britain at 0422 on the 1st of October and, hours later, touched down at RAF Lyneham in Wiltshire. Quaintly, Alex's entry in his logbook reads "and so on English soil after 8 years and 6 months," a phrase worthy of that old imperialist, Wylie East.

He was to be in Britain for more than two weeks before he could leave for Canada. Although desperate to get home, this time was useful for picking up the pieces of his life, both socially and professionally. His first cousin Hugh Constantine, now very senior in the RAF, was at the top of his 'to see' list and Alex phoned him from Paddington Station. 'Connie' and his wife Helen insisted that he come and stay in their London house while awaiting the pleasure of Transport Command. Delighted, Alex wrote to Agnes: "It is not everyone, nor every day that one can stay with an Air Officer Commanding a Bomber Group! Air Vice Marshal Connie and Helen are going to a lot of trouble to help me." Apart from offering him bed and board and pulling official strings, they included him in their social life, and at Connie's farewell party for his staff Alex met three old friends. Connie also encouraged him to call on John Boothman.

Alex's notebook gives the reader some idea of the frantic time he must have had, dashing all over London on the desperately grubby but efficient Underground or struggling with the telephone system where the operators called him "Luv" and asked him personal questions. He had to accustom himself to a strange environment. The greyness of the skies and the drizzle were reminders of British Columbia, but London, with boarded-up bomb sites, where signs warned that "Bill Stickers will be Prosecuted," where everything was covered by a layer of soot, was a good deal grimmer. That was compensated for by the cheerfulness of Londoners and the pace at which life was led. This was extraordinary after functioning for so long in the world of *tida appa*. A fellow had to trot to keep up with most pedestrians. Of course, people walked fast partly because London can be cold in October. Which reminded this ambitious squadron leader that he had no clothes – at least, nothing that could be worn at an air base or on social occasions in either England or Canada. He had arrived wearing a shirt and a pair of shorts. In spite of himself, he began to miss the predictable warmth of the Far East!

Consequently, one of his first tasks was to make himself presentable. There is a cryptic scribble in his notebook – "Off Kit Rep at 72 South Audley Street" – no doubt an officers' kit replacement depot – the address sounds about right. Top of the list was a greatcoat, the most immediately useful item, but his list was a long one:

"2 uniform tunics and 1 pair of trousers,

4 Van Heusen service blue shirts,

8 collars,

4 pairs of black silk socks,

Mess Kit, including jacket, trousers and 3 waistcoats,

3 stiff shirts,

3 soft shirts,

8 dress collars."

He was certainly not anticipating postwar austerity – for Alex it was to be 'back to the good old days!' Then came:

"Tropical Mess Kit, including 3 jackets,

3 pairs of trousers, a cummerbund,

leather gloves and white kid gloves."

Sanity returned; at the foot of the list he has written: "Tropical Kit??"

So much for uniform; what about his 'civvies'? Alex does not remember where he got these or whether he had to pay for them. It was possibly at the same place. In any case, the well-dressed man just out of prison camp has his priorities. Top of this list is a dinner jacket with pants and waistcoat! Then came two three-piece suits, a light suit without a waistcoat, six shirts and a dozen collars. The omissions are striking: would he not need sweaters and something more casual than a suit? However, his list underlines social and sartorial changes in the last fifty-five years; it tells us, for example, that he expected to change his collar twice as often as his shirt and socks – as did everybody.

It was a good thing that Alex did not have to pay for his new finery, because wages in the British forces were very low. As a squadron leader, a rank with responsibility, he earned 12 pounds, 7 shillings and 6 pence in November, and 14 pounds, 3 shillings and 6 pence in December 1945. That represented between forty and fifty Canadian dollars a month at the 1945 exchange rate. His accumulated pay for three and a half years in prison camp was the princely sum of 465 pounds, out of which he had already arranged to send 500 dollars to Agnes in Victoria. To his surprise, while he was on leave in Victoria, the Air Ministry was to promise him a further 373 pounds, 10 shillings and 2 pence. This had been "deducted from his pay in respect of sums issuable to him by the Japanese" but, of course, never delivered.

Happily, his time in London seemed to fly. His first task was to report to the Air Ministry to regularise his existence. Although not generous with money, at least they were generous with their time; they gave him home leave in Canada for the rest of the year. This meant ten weeks without stress, something he needed in order to begin to come to terms with his recent experiences. Furthermore, home cooking would build him up physically, in spite of his insistence that he was fit.

Having made an honest man of himself, he had to attend to his future. He applied for a permanent commission in the RAF, offering a list of senior officers to support his application. These included Air Vice Marshals Boothman, Maitland and Lang (his tiger-hunting CO) and Group Captains Cox and Burgess. Most of them were nearby, but Lang wrote him a kind reply from his post in Washington, DC. He would be delighted to put in a good word for Alex, "... an opportunity of repaying the very warmly appreciated loyalty and the excellent work you did for me in 205 Squadron."

He asked questions at the Air Ministry about the men of his detachment in Java, hoping that some might have survived, in spite of appearances. A duty which kept him busy, although he saw it as simple friendship, was to get in touch with the wives and families of the men. In addition, he received a sad request from the Director of Personnel Services at the Air Ministry asking, on behalf of Sgt W. H. James's mother, whose funeral he had attended in the XVth Battalion Barracks camp, Bandoeng, whether he still had her son's personal effects. And although he knew about the 1943 fate of Gordon Stilling, nobody had yet told him about Dick Atkinson. He caught up with that piece of news at the Air Ministry, who put him in touch with Dick's mother.

He had better luck looking up Group Captains Burgess and Councell and his last second pilot, F/O McVicker, finding all three alive and well. The Ministry had not been very sympathetic about the loss of his logbook and McVicker was to be useful to him in helping re-establish his flying hours. To advance his career, whether in the RAF or in the RCAF, he would need evidence that he had flown up to 1942, when his logbook had gone to the bottom of the sea. McVicker's log established his flying hours in 1941-1942, at least. Beyond that, his previous second pilot, Norman Birks, provided him with a notarised summary of earlier flights.

On his list of 'people to see' Alex had Air Force officers with impressive ranks. Many had started with him, had not been captured, had survived the war and had served in the public eye. Consequently, like Connie, they had ridden the antici-pated wartime promotion escalator. It was not easy to renew such acquaintances without a good deal of RAF bonhomie over beer or gin and tonic. In his notebook Alex has the phone numbers and addresses of a number of places where he met such friends for lunch: the Wings Club near Sloane Square, the RAF Club in Mayfair, or the Royal Aero Club in Piccadilly.

There were also people he just had to see. Major R. H. Mayo, his sponsor when he entered the RAF and his adviser on career decisions, was hard to pin down; they played telephone tag for most of his time in London. He phoned his Aunts Ruth Black and DeeDee Constantine, mother of Connie, Ruth and Daphne. Both invited him for afternoon tea. DeeDee gave him copious instructions on how to find her at 21 Wetherby Gardens. In spite of his pre-war reluctance, it must have been pleasant for him to be fussed over among the sponge cake and gingersnaps – he had not had much of that sort of attention in recent years. He also visited Guy's Hospital to see Mary Johnston, who was nursing there. He was most irritated to discover that because Mary was on duty, she was not allowed out; what is more, because he was a man he was not allowed past a locked iron gate at the nurses' residence. He made his displeasure known to the world in a loud voice!

He also had to see Daphne. Now Mrs Harry Owen and married to an Air Force officer, she was living in Woking, outside London. By this time Alex was not the only cousin to have come under her spell; his boyhood friend and cousin, Robin Johnston, had also fallen for her when in Britain with the Canadian navy. The businesslike Helen had written Daphne's address carefully in Alex's book, noting that Woking was a "toll call!" Toll or not, Alex called her and invited her to lunch with him at Wings. They met there, at 12:15 on one of Alex's crowded days, probably in the second week of his stay. It was also the day he was trying to phone R. H. Mayo again, collect clothes which were ready for him in South Audley Street, go to the Hong Kong & Shanghai Bank in the city, meet Mr McGrath at Lloyds Bank in Pall Mall, phone Connie, meet Mr Eric Robinson at 2:15 at the Aero Club in Piccadilly, visit the NAAFI in Leicester Square, do something with Customs, pick up a watch and get in touch with Daphne's sister Ruth, who lived in Kensington and worked in Mayfair! With such an agenda one hopes for Daphne's sake that the Underground was having a good day, that Alex had made an early start, had visited the banks in the morning and was prepared to keep Mr Eric Robinson waiting while he and Daphne had a leisurely lunch.

On Friday the 5th of October Alex popped in to see Mr McAdam, agent general at BC House. McAdam had an avuncular interest in Alex and had generously offered him free meals in the BCH dining room during his stay in London. After he left, McAdam cabled Agnes in Victoria that Alex had been to see him and would be "spending a few days in the Midlands." One wonders what Agnes made of that; on the same day Alex, who seems still to have been playing catch-up, also cabled her: "Arrived UK, staying with Tom Constantine. Arranging passage home." No mention of the Midlands, or why he would be going there. In fact, because he had so many friends in high places in the RAF, he had managed to wangle a weekend in which he would take the controls of an aircraft for the first time since 1942. Connie had told him to phone G/C A. E. Taylor, CO at RAF Waddington near Kebworth. Alex arranged to spend the weekend on the base and on Saturday flew a Lancaster for an hour and a half; it went into his logbook as "familiarisation and 2-engined flying." Whatever the label, it was occupational therapy. Finally he was doing what he wanted to do most in the world. To feel the power of those great engines, as he roared into the sky over Leicestershire, was to know that he was really free. Afterwards he cabled Agnes again, this time from Kebworth. Once more he said nothing about flying; just: "Will know in few days when I shall leave ..."

Finally he heard that his flight for Canada would leave Prestwick on Thursday the 18th of September. This was good news because he had people to see in Glasgow. He took the train for Scotland at the end of his second week in London. His lunch with Daphne had been on one day that week. On other days he had to see the Red Cross about possible letters for him, inform the Air Ministry postal section of Agnes's change of address, visit His Majesty's Stationery Office to browse through publications on search & rescue and air navigation, visit the offices of ICI Ltd. on the Embankment to see Pat Young, and continue his efforts to track down documents in lieu of his sunken logbook. All this in addition to the inevitable social whirl stirred up by his reappearance. Before he took the train to Scotland en route for home, Alex made Helen give him a precise list of unobtainable treasures which he would buy for her in Canada; none were yet available in still-rationed and exhausted London:

"silk stockings (10 inch fully fashioned, nylon),
Revlon nail varnish (Mrs. Minerva Rose or Flagship or Action Red),
court shoe, medium heel, brown (shoe size 81/2 C),
hot water bottles." Even an AVM's house could be cool at night.

Once in Glasgow Alex's notebook is not so informative. He probably stayed with his old mentor Albert Black. He had the addresses and phone numbers of Donaldson Brothers, Baxter, Tierney, Dick West and David Lister – though he missed seeing West, who was in Vancouver, and Lister, still in the RAF. The highlights of his visit were catching up with news of his old shipmates at Donaldson Brothers' offices and contriving another flight for himself. On Tuesday the 16th of October he had a one-hour flight from Prestwick in a twin-engined Airspeed Oxford. His logbook talks of practicing approaches on radar and blind-landing control. The Oxford, used as a trainer, had a sinister reputation: it was virtually impossible, even for an experienced pilot, to get it out of a left-hand spin. No doubt Alex was characteristically cautious in an unfamiliar aircraft. Apart from the Lancaster, this was his first flight using radar and he found the instrumentation interesting. After the two flights he felt less of a Rip Van Winkle.

In a tragic coincidence unknown to Alex, the man who had beaten him in the search for a boat in Tjilatjap in 1942 also took up an unfamiliar aircraft three days later. Group Captain John Jeudwine, DSO, OBE, DFC was CO at RAF Little Staughton, Bedfordshire. He had only one hour's experience on the single-seater Typhoon 1B, which he nevertheless put into a slow roll at 3,000 feet. The engine stalled in the inverted position and the aircraft went into a left-hand spin from which it did not recover. Jeudwine was killed in the crash.[69]

On the 18th Alex took off from Prestwick aboard a BOAC Liberator. It carried a maximum load of fuel and was bound for Montréal. This was the shortest convenient Atlantic crossing and the first scheduled air service on the route. Civilians still preferred the big liners, the Queens and other surviving Cunarders, and were happy to spend five days on the crossing. Flying was still perceived as risky, noisy, uncomfortable and cold, only to be undertaken by people in a hurry. Alex spent thirteen hours in an unpressurised cabin between Glasgow and Montréal, including a fuelling stop at Goose Bay, Labrador. After a night in Montréal he was off again, across the country to Victoria, another thirteen-hour flight in a TCA Lockheed Electra.

On Sunday morning, the 21st of October, Agnes received a telegram from Lethbridge: "Arriving just before or after lunch today. Bestest love, Zandermyles." There were no further delays; the wanderer had come home after ten years and ten months. For a man who had spent his last three and a half years in a Japanese prison camp, the photograph taken by his sister Deirdre on their mother's lawn shows a remarkably relaxed and fit-looking Air Force officer. His cousin Robin, in naval uniform and standing beside him, was part of the reception committee. The only indication that the occasion is at all exceptional is their public display of intended drunkenness – Alex is cradling a bottle of whisky and Robin a soda syphon and Alex looks as if he just can't wait!

For a week or two life was a whirl of social events. Agnes, the proudest and most delighted mother in Victoria, could not see and hear enough of her son or his adventures. He was lionised by his sisters and their new families, whom he met for the first time, and his mother made sure that the whole world knew of his safe return. She arranged for him to be interviewed by the *Colonist* and the article brought letters and phone calls in its wake. It was a time when the mailbox filled up daily with letters from friends worldwide who had heard the news of his survival. Reading them was an emotional marathon, especially letters from those involved with 205 Squadron in Singapore or Java. From Norman Birks:

> "Thank God you have come through, as I knew you would … I saw
> quite a lot of Dicky [Atkinson] and Gordon [Stilling] in Australia to
> begin with [after the fall of Java] … They are both gone now and it
> looks as though we are the only ones left. When I look back on
> Gordon's tale of the *Ten Little Nigger-Boys** it isn't quite so funny,

---

*This then-acceptable phrase referred to the original pilots of 205 Squadron, the band of brothers referred to in Chapter Six. There had been eleven pilots in the April 1941 photograph (the 205 squadron Catalina originals) and seven of them were dead: Young, Shaw, Atkinson, Stilling, Graham, Grieve, Bedell. Also three of the six senior pilots who appear

continued

except that I always felt that you and I, of all of them, would talk about it afterwards."

If Norman's letter forced him to think of dead friends, Pat's must have left him confused. Wildly, she poured her feelings onto the page:

"My dearest Alec ... It's one thing to know inside yourself for so many years that someone you are thinking of all the time, knowing that he is going through hell and still knowing that he is going to come through in the end. But it's another to have to realise that he has come through and that hell is finished for him. There is so much to say to you I don't know where to start. It goes back such a long way. I was broken-hearted when I had to realise that you really were still left in Java. I prayed so hard that some miracle had happened and that you had got away to somewhere safe. I had a cable from Meg Ireland just after Java fell asking where you were and I answered that I presumed you were a POW in Java."

Some lines later she broke the news that she dared not keep from him:

"Klay Kames came back from Ceylon a couple of years ago and told me that Meg Ireland had married some man but I don't know who. I must tell you this because I should loathe to think of you perhaps hoping to see someone who just isn't worth you."

One imagines that Alex stopped reading at that point while he wrestled with his feelings. No doubt, in his usual cast-iron way, he soon convinced himself that these were once again 'normal', but he was to behave recklessly in the weeks ahead, as we shall see, possibly on the rebound from Meg's desertion. Another letter from Pat arrived within a few days. On reading Alex's letter to her family at breakfast, she had been unable to control herself and had burst into tears before finishing the first page. Norman had to explain to their astonished children: "Alex is a very good friend of Mummie's and mine and we have been so worried about him for such

continued from previous page

only in the January 1942 photograph were dead: Farrar, Garnell, Lowe – with P/O Singh making a total of eleven. The survivors were outnumbered: Birks, Brant, McVicker and Alex from the 1941 photo and only Whitworth for sure from the 1942 photo, Alex having lost touch with Tamblyn and Tucker – both OK in March 1942; nor has he information on the recently-joined P/Os in the 1942 photo. Of the three officers not in either photo, Scales and Westcott survived POW camps and Jefferies is an unknown. *See Appendix 2* long years and her tears were of happiness and relief." Pat went on: "Oh Alec sweetie, thank you from the bottom of my heart for the beautiful things you said. Somehow I never thought of us meaning as much to you as you do to us – we love you very, very much." The woman he had dreamed about so long was lost to him; and Pat, who truly loved him, was, as ever, beyond his reach.

For about the first time in his life he had a little money in his pocket and soon after his return in October he bought a green Model A Ford. This gave him independence and enabled him to visit friends, old and new, around Victoria. Since his return he had met Diana Jenkins, a woman a little older than his sister Deirdre. Like others in the past, she was dazzled by his Air Force glamour and sophistication, his good humour and exuberance – there are few like him and she had certainly never met one. He, after such a long time without female company, during which time and through all the awfulness he had preserved the image of Meg in his imagination, was swept away by Diana's youth, her looks, her liveliness, her undisguised regard for him and by their shared interests in sailing and the outdoors. In spite of an age difference of a dozen years Alex fell head-over-heels for her. Deirdre remembers, as only a youngest sister would who for years had idolised her brother from afar, that he was "besotted!"

In spite of this new interest, life at home soon seemed slow-paced. He was pondering his next career move. The prospect of returning to Britain after his leave and becoming reintegrated into the RAF – possibly to be posted overseas again – was not attractive. Transferring to the RCAF seemed a better idea. With that in mind, one November day he put on uniform and drove out to Patricia Bay to visit the RCAF station. "I met the CO, G/C Wally Wurtele. We yarned for a while and discovered we had both joined the RAF with short-service commissions. I asked him how he managed to be in the RCAF with his rank. Wally laughed and said: 'it was easy! We simply transferred – all Canadians in the RAF were given the chance to transfer by simply signing a piece of paper. Knowing that pay in the RCAF was much better than in the RAF we signed – and were immediately better off!' My response was the obvious: 'you lucky buggers!' Wally asked: 'why don't you apply?' Naturally I had to stop and think a bit, but not for long! My POW life had cut me out of the RAF. I was a 'nobody'. I had no particular ties in Britain nor to the RAF. I applied. A few weeks later I was told to report for an interview with the Air Officer Commanding Western Air Command, A/C J. L. Plant. When I walked into his office his first question was: 'what were you doing in the war, Jardine?' I replied: 'I was with 205 Squadron, Sir.' 'Good God,' he responded, 'my squadron, 413 Catalinas, took over your base at Koggala, Ceylon!' I do not recall if we had much more to say!" The deal seemed as good as done. One immediate benefit from this visit was a trip to Tofino to see his recently married sister Ruth, her husband

and two children – a new family for Alex to get to know. On the 19th of November he flew there in one of the station's Ansons which picked him up two weeks later and brought him back to Victoria.

The RAF had not finished with Alex, however. On the 17th of December, interrupting the first home leave that he had had in eleven years, he received a letter from the Air Ministry, dated the 5th of December. It required him to:

> "... submit to the Air Ministry by the 1st of January 1946 a brief
> account of 205 Squadron under the headings enumerated below:
>   a) outstanding events prior to the war in the Far East which
>   affected subsequent operations;
>   b) narrative of important events in Malaya during operations;
>   c) narrative of important events in N.E.I.;
>   g) any other outstanding events you wish to report;
>   h) the final destruction of your Flying Boat."

Naturally, the item over which Alex sweated a bit was h). He had prepared detailed notes for this while still in Java, so it was not particularly difficult to do – except for the typing. Although he did plenty of it, he was a member of the 'damn and blast' school of typing! Bearing in mind Alex's decision to transfer to the RCAF, this letter may have been a little less unfeeling than it appears. However, considering that Alex was due in London on the 1st of January in any case, it seems the sort of thing that gives bureaucrats a bad name.

After two months in British Columbia, it was time to make the long return journey to Britain soon after Christmas. Having been provisionally accepted by the RCAF he knew he would soon be back, but Canada is a large country. Being posted in eastern Canada, which he almost certainly would be, would keep him far away. So, after tearful farewells to all 'his women', now including Diana, he boarded a TCA aircraft at Patricia Bay on the 27th of December, promising a speedy return, bearing all sorts of messages for his aunts in London and a suitcase full of good things for Helen Constantine.

14

WINNING HIS SPURS

1946–1954
In which an unknown Alex practises self-denial while becoming known
in the RCAF, serving at Arnprior, RMC Kingston, Trenton and AFHQ;
and in which he is promoted Group Captain and CO of RCAF Rockcliffe.

"If I can't get a meal on a weekend my name ain't Jardine!"

The next part of Alex's story concerns his rise from the bottom to become an officer of consequence in the service that had refused to consider his application in 1935. For many years his quest for recognition took priority over all else – living in western Canada, leaves with his family, even marriage and family life. For him the consequences of the war were to be as difficult, in a different way, as the war itself had been. He had few illusions about the alternatives available to him. The old carrot of flying for the airlines had vanished and business scared him to death. In January 1946, when it seemed possible he might not be accepted into the interim Air Force even though the RCAF had permitted him to transfer, he talked of the "cold, cruel world" outside the service. A year later, having received his permanent commission, he wrote: "Business frightens me; I know I should have to adopt a cloak of hardness and indifference to cope with most situations." From the age of fifteen he had known nothing beyond the disciplined environment of the merchant service and then the Air Force. He loved the camaraderie and the "yarning" of a mess and felt disoriented whenever not among Air Force types, for he had yarned on a daily basis since 1935.

Once back in Britain, it took him just six weeks to turn his life around before heading westwards again. This time he sailed on the *Queen Elizabeth*, still a troopship in wartime grey, for a slower but more comfortable Atlantic crossing. When he needed it the most, fortune was kind to him and his introduction to the RCAF was cushioned by the best of all possible postings: after further leave, he reported to RCAF Patricia Bay, near Victoria on the 1st of April. From the 2nd he was flying

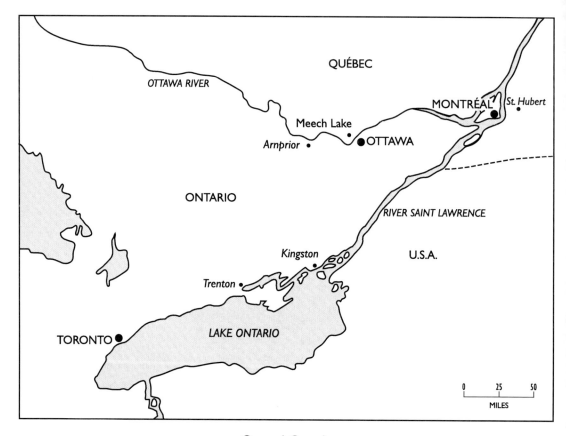

Central Canada

most days, as though making up for lost time. In his first two months he logged fifty-four hours in Ansons which was a therapeutic re-entry into Air Force life.

Meanwhile he had persuaded the Department of Education in Victoria to give him an 'Equivalency Certificate'. This solemnly declared that his courses and experience since leaving South Park were "equivalent to not less than four years of High School." Maybe as a result, on the 3rd of May he received the only news that mattered: he had been granted a long-service permanent commission in the regular Air Force – he was in! Exuberantly he buzzed Agnes and Babe from 2,000 feet in an Anson.

While at Patricia Bay he put in time in the Link Trainer, learned some new tricks of the trade, had one nostalgic two-hour flight in a Canso – the amphibious version of his beloved Catalina – and could go home on weekends to dig the garden. But that was not his only recreation: often he would drive the 'Green Hornet', as Deirdre had christened his car, to Metchosin to visit Diana. She was becoming increasingly important to him. His permanent commission brought a raise in salary and he convinced himself that at last he could afford to marry. He proposed to Diana and she accepted him. They did not settle on a date, but planned to marry when he had leave later in the year.

However, inevitably and immediately, the need to establish himself in the RCAF intruded upon his west-coast idyll. Still a squadron leader, lacking the skills to fly modern aircraft, with no recent flying hours and without Canadian connections, Alex was starting at the bottom in the RCAF. He could neither make his name in the service, nor provide his wife and future family with financial security, by searching for lost fishermen off Vancouver Island. Advancing his career meant going east, where decisions were made and where the action was. After two months at Pat Bay he was posted to Toronto. Never again, during twenty years in the RCAF, would he be able to dig his mother's garden on a weekend!

June found him living in a converted stable at the Eglinton Hunt Club on Avenue Road, Toronto. His #1 KTS was a conversion course for officers being absorbed into the RCAF; it would enable HQ to decide how best to employ them. Letter-writing, adjutants' duties and administration presented no difficulties to a former adjutant and it was a boost to his morale to pass out top with an 'excellent' rating. The CO asked him: "What next?" Alex applied for staff college, was summoned to Air Force HQ (AFHQ), Ottawa, for an interview and in due course was posted to the staff college course beginning on the 3rd of September. His campaign for recognition was definitely on track. As he well knew, without staff college he had little hope of an RCAF station command and, considering his age, the sooner he got it under his belt the better.

At the end of June he wrote to Diana to suggest that they get married during his leave in August, by then just five or six weeks away. He was hoping to buy a house in Toronto and to begin their married life there. Hardly was the ink dry when he wrote again. He had discovered that affordable houses in Toronto were impossible to find. Maybe they should revert to the original plan; he hoped Diana would have holidays in August so they could spend time together. There was silence for a week. Diana did not write. Then a letter came from Dr Jenkins, Diana's father. He thought Alex had made a tactical error in suggesting they be married sooner. Diana, almost certainly, had not realised the full responsibilities of being married; she was concerned about her ability to make him happy and was afraid she would interfere with his work. She had been sure when she had said 'yes' but, since, had developed a taste for solitude. Now, she was convinced that marriage was not for her. In a word, Diana had called it off!

It was a bombshell that failed to explode. Alex must have been having his own doubts for he took his dumping in stride. Tellingly, he accepted the situation and neither wrote to try to persuade her nor went to see Diana again. He just turned the page. Within a week, he told Agnes, his feelings for Diana were 'normal', though he confessed that at first he had been upset. As proof against self-pity as ever, he went out with Cecilia Milne within two weeks and, soon after, on a blind date with two girls, friends of a wing commander he had met on the *Queen Elizabeth* – not the behaviour of the broken-hearted!

That fall he received a reminder of his life in Singapore. After the war broke out he had not only put unwanted gear in cold storage in Singapore but had kept the receipts. These survived the war in the luggage he had sent home by ship and now he received his reward from the Air Ministry in the form of 27 pounds, 19 shillings and 4 pence compensation. It would be useful.

The staff college course challenged Alex a great deal more than K.T.S. There were thirty on the course, of whom twenty-two were RCAF, the balance being "Yanks, Navy, Army and RAF." He knew a few of them, including Wally Wurtele, ex-CO at RCAF Patricia Bay. He found the course interesting but the writing was hard work, so hard that in October he turned down an invitation from a new female acquaintance. His work came to a crisis point twice. On the first occasion, he had two written assignments and a twenty-minute talk all due just before Christmas. "The mere thought of it makes me feel quite queer," he wrote and it spoiled his fun in the first part of the festive season. The course culminated in a huge thesis which created the second crisis. This time he had learned a trick or two: he persuaded one of the stenos to type it for him. "She is supposed to work in the library but I reckon she hasn't enough to do anyway ... we keep quiet about it because she is paid by His Majesty's government to do his work, not ours!" Alex was demonstrating the gentle art of managing human relations in an institution – something that would stand him in good stead.

The course taught Alex important lessons about North America – a continent to most of which he was still a stranger despite his thirty-two years. No Canadian military course is complete without seeing how things are done south of the border and in November his group set off for Craig Field, Alabama. He was interested but not overwhelmed by the military things they saw. However, two cultural discoveries were most fascinating. The first happened as their aircraft was about to land for lunch at USAAF Luxborough. "One of the U.S. colonels on our course looked out the window as we were flying over and said – 'hell, this is a boogie field – I'm darned if I'm eating with niggers!' Roars of laughter when we discovered this was an all-darkie station – I for one could hardly credit it."

The second was provided by the U.S. military lifestyle. The mess at Craig Field, known as the Club, served 3.2 percent beer, no hard liquor and had a jukebox. After their welcome on the first evening Alex got to "bed about midnight, full of watery beer – most uncomfortable." Next day he was astounded by "a hurried and noisy lunch, eating out of tin trays divided into sections for different items of food." He provided a sketch of this astonishing phenomenon! "K.f.s. [knife, fork and spoon] held by some miracle in a part of the hand not actually holding other items. Arrive at cashier. Place all items on the counter and tables nearby, fish around in wrong pocket for $1.25, find it in the other, dash off having gathered all together again. Forget your change, place all down on nearest vacant spot at table, go back, collect change, return to table. Soup's cold, scoff it anyway, by which time meat and veg cold, scoff them as there is still a long line. Find that ice cream has melted and coffee is cold." Later, "Even in this climate when things should be done more leisurely there seems to be a frightful rush on. Can't think why ... anyway, it is a change and very interesting to see what makes the Americans tick."

On the 3rd of March 1947, when the staff college course was over, Alex flew home by TCA and immediately set off in the Green Hornet to drive back to Ontario. There he was posted to an instrument flying (IFS) course at Centralia from the 21st of March. The route chosen for 'Operation Model A arrive Toronto' took him through the States, to avoid Canada's snow and ice. As it would be their only opportunity to see each other Agnes courageously accompanied him as far as Sacramento, whence she returned home by train.

Driving in that car in winter was an ordeal: it had no heater, its canvas roof leaked wind and water and its wipers were Ford 'specials', which worked fine when the engine was idling but which cut out as soon as the car accelerated. When travelling uphill in second gear, Alex found that "the car makes a noise not unlike a large threshing machine; people would stop and stare and that does embarrass me!" He had to have the carburettor fixed on three occasions and the distributor gave up in the middle of snow-swept desert. Another day he found that he had "no brakes on the starboard side." Amazingly, he found repair shops easy to come by and received great service from a series of poorly paid mechanics. One of these remonstrated with him when he grumbled that the car would do little more than 50 mph: "And how much more were you expecting from a 1928 four-cylinder car?!"

His semicircular route took him from Sacramento to Toronto by way of Reno, Las Vegas, Albuquerque, Amarillo, Oklahoma, Tulsa, Springfield, St Louis, Indianapolis and Detroit. Everywhere, the variety of the United States surprised him. Amarillo, for example, was "definitely rough with all kinds of blokes in stetsons, with cigars, wandering about!" It did prove to be rough; the hotel bellhop offered him a "nice little girl" and there were bullet holes above the door of the next room. Travelling northwards he encountered the icy shadow of a Canadian winter for which, apart from driving extra carefully, he and the Hornet's tires were not well prepared. In Indiana he skidded through 450 degrees, ending up against an earth bank with a 'bonk'. It would take more than that to stop a Model A although, in a moment's inattention further north, he nearly repeated the manoeuvre into the Wabash River.

Potentially his most serious problem was the loss of his papers, including the Port Angeles entry document without which, he was assured, he would never get back into Canada. But he underestimated the uniqueness of the spectacle that he presented; in Windsor he was simply waved through! After 4,000 miles on the road, the frosted and filthy Hornet pulled into the staff college car park. The commandant's wife greeted him casually: "Hello, Alex. And where have you come from?" Alex nearly had to apply smelling salts when he replied: "Victoria"! It was a remarkable journey, as was its cost; for twelve days of ferries, gasoline, repairs, hotels and meals Alex paid just 200 dollars.

He had time to kill before the IFS course, so drove daily to the RCAF Radio School at Clinton. Days immersed in radar and other electronic devices continued the process of reawakening Rip Van Winkle. "Much of the equipment I had heard about from time to time when the other chaps talked about their operations in different parts of the world. I now know what they were talking about and though I have no practical experience I can operate the stuff after a fashion. It was all very interesting and most valuable for me."

Once the IFS course started, in April 1947, he was flying again. It was good to be back in the air, not having flown since leaving Pat Bay the previous June. In ten weeks he flew a hundred hours in Beechcraft – "smaller than an Anson but much faster, with no vices and really pleasant to fly." At first he found instrument flying difficult. However, once he had "weighed up all the newfangled gadgets," he made speedy progress and soon jumped another hurdle for ex-flying-boat pilots – his first night landing on land. With that and the course under his belt, Alex was at last employable within the RCAF. Agnes wondered whether he could get himself posted to Western Air Command, best of all to British Columbia. It sounded attractive but he realised it would not be a good idea: "As it is, no-one knows me in the RCAF, no-one in the top brackets, that is."

In fact, he was posted to the National Research Council (NRC) establishment at Arnprior, as OC the RCAF component. His year of schooling had made up for three and a half years away from aircraft and had also taught him how to run a base. To be OC Arnprior was a plum job for an officer not senior enough for his own station. He described the job as "any flying and odd jobs to do with the service that the NRC might require." It was a pleasantly informal situation, with Alex in charge of the Air Force element and Bud Levy, a civilian, in charge of the more numerous NRC people. A reason for his selection and for the choice of his subordinates, F/Lt 'Doc' Docherty and F/Lt George Lee, was that all three were considered to have the flexibility needed to work with civilians. It was a fortunate conjunction; not only were the three men congenial colleagues but Alex became a close friend of Bud and Peg Levy.

An example of the 'flying and odd jobs' was what Alex refers to in his log as MAD, acronym for Magnetic Airborne Detector. This instrument was being developed by the NRC, in conjunction with U.S. counterparts, as a cheap and quick method of making maps and geological surveys. Once airborne, the Anson lowered a bomb-shaped MAD by cable. Alex's role as pilot was to fly a predetermined checkerboard pattern along grid lines while maintaining constant altitude and a speed of 192 kph. This was difficult and not very exciting but the results of the experiments changed the way in which we make maps.[70]

In a preview of his later style of command, he got to know the locals, meaning not only the families of airmen and NRC people but also the citizens of Arnprior. Within days of his arrival he was on the golf course; lack of practice cost him a legendary five airshots on the first tee but he laughed them off, knowing that his game could only improve! He was a regular churchgoer, joined the United Nations Association, curled, played softball and managed the base hockey team. It had been losing and needed special motivation, so the manager shaved off his moustache, vowing to remain clean-shaven until they won a game. By season's end the moustache was back and the team in the finals! He involved himself in the social life of the base, chairing the children's Christmas party committee and spending a pastoral Christmas visiting airmen's homes and their wives in hospital. His year at Arnprior was also when Alex bought a 15-foot sailing dinghy and named her *Tida Appa*. A river ran through the town, wide enough for interesting sailing, and he did little else in his spare time in the late summer of 1947. Sailing was to be his most regular pastime for the next few years.

He frequently had to ferry NRC people to air stations in the course of the work, allowing him to become known in a new service. In fact dropping in on messes reminded him of flying-boat days and as a single man he was keen to fly anywhere, any time. Thus he became familiar with the Trenton mess, thanks to Wally Wurtele. Other trips took him back to Centralia, scene of the IFS course, where he was already known, or to Toronto where he was a regular in the staff college mess – as if he had never been away. Sometimes his visits coincided with mess dances, which he was always glad to attend and he was equally glad to accept kind offers of a bed for the night. He was a regular at Rockcliffe mess dances, at AFHQ mess events and, in May 1948, managed to arrive at Centralia on the day of their dance.

In fact, he invented a new recreation for the single officer – mess-crawling, as in pub-crawling! For example, on the 1947 Thanksgiving weekend he drove into Québec to see the fall colours. On the way he dropped into the Ottawa messes at AFHQ and Rockcliffe before calling at the RCAF mess at Lachine. Everywhere he met people he had known in the RAF, or on one of his recent courses; everywhere they introduced him to new people and Alex yarned his way through the odd pint of beer before continuing on his way.

Many away trips were weekend trips. Docherty and Lee, both married men, were happy to let the boss take such jobs. They were probably less happy when Alex managed to borrow a Mustang – and then insisted on flying it himself. It was an aircraft which had helped destroy Panzers just three years before and was still an exciting aircraft to fly. He told Agnes it was "the first operational single-seater I have flown and the whole thing was quite a thrill for me." The current NRC project involved subjecting test-objects to 4 Gs, four times the normal gravitational pull. This was achieved by pulling out of a 500-mph dive into a steep climb. He did not tell his mother about that part of it; to her he wrote: "One can get as much as 500 mph out of it in a dive; on the level it is good for about 300 mph, considerably faster than anything I have flown to date."

He took every opportunity to meet the 'brass'. In December 1947 he was delighted that AVM Campbell was a guest when he was dining with friends in Ottawa – "glad of the chance to meet him as it does no harm!" Air Force Day celebrations at Arnprior in June 1948 were a small triumph for Alex. By that time morale was high, largely thanks to him. The show, which involved both flying and ground displays, was attended by AFHQ brass and the media and went without a hitch. The press report was glowing and AVM James personally congratulated Alex; it was a feather in Alex's cap at a time when he was collecting feathers.

His discoveries in the States were not the only ones that this Canadian still had to make about the continent. Canada itself still had surprises in store for him. When delivering an aircraft to RCAF Greenwood, NS, he found he was a local celebrity and invited to the graduation dance at the high school. This turned out to be no ordinary invitation: his escort was the Apple Blossom Queen of the Annapolis Valley – to his own delight and the chagrin of male students who could only grumble about 'this old guy taking our girl'. It substituted for the high school graduation that Alex never had!

Less pleasant were his experiences in Québec, where a weekend visit left him dumbfounded: "Quite incredible the number of people in Québec who either don't know or don't care or don't like English as she is spoken in Canada. So cross-making when one is trying to find out something. I think it must be the first time I have come across people who just didn't seem interested whether you found out or not." It was a rude awakening to the French fact which he was later to take in stride when CO of a Québec RCAF station.

In other ways he knew his country better than most. After making a second transcontinental drive, this time in Wally Wurtele's car in March 1948, he called on his sister Deirdre in Calgary on the way back to Ontario and they dined at the Palliser Hotel. He had no need to ask who owned the hotel: "As soon as I tasted the soup," he wrote, "I recognised it as CPR!" His years on the *Canada* had not been entirely in vain.

His earlier determination to get married appeared to evaporate after the collapse of his 1946 engagement. For about a year married friends competed in promoting their protegées for his consideration and during this time he had no shortage of dancing partners. Three women whom he saw quite often were Cecilia Milne, Margaret Proctor and Marnie Murray; he liked them all but with none did he show much sign of getting serious. This situation lasted until he went to the IFS course at Centralia in April 1947 when even this perfunctory interest declined. Maybe Centralia was far enough from Toronto to make social commuting difficult, or maybe it was because Cecilia, whom he saw the most often, had graduated from nursing school and had left town, but in any case there followed six months when he had no romantic prospects on the horizon.

It was not until October 1947, when he was well established at Arnprior, that Peggy Lewis entered his life. Alex met the Lewis family through the Buchanans, RCAF friends in Ottawa. He and Dr Lewis liked each other at once and the Lewis house became a port of call whenever Alex was in Ottawa, which was several times a week. Peggy had been brought up with RCAF people, her brother Harry was stationed at AFHQ and she was comfortable in an Air Force environment. From the start Dr Lewis seemed to promote Alex as potential son-in-law; he lent them his new Mercury when Alex was collecting Peggy for their second evening out. Thereafter Alex's every letter was full of activities they had shared: with her he went to the 'flicks', visited the Buchanans, visited Bud and Peggy Levy, went to the AFHQ mess, went bowling, attended his own mess dance at Christmas and went skiing – she was a good Nordic skier and he a novice.

By January 1948 Alex sounded as if he would have liked to ask her to marry him but things were not that easy. He wrote: "Peg is a decided puzzle; I believe I could explain her attitude but it would be long and involved. Unless she changes her ideas radically, or unless she is merely putting up a front at present, there is not much likelihood of our becoming anything more than friends." Alex was the least possessive of men, always anxious to share his friends, so her attitude was not a struggle for freedom. Probably she found Alex, her father's friend, fun to be with but too old for a potential husband. He would have liked to marry her if she changed her mind but she seems not to have done so. Although they were to see much of each other for years, it became increasingly clear that their relationship was not leading to the altar.

Alex was back in British Columbia for a short leave in March 1948 and had another whirlwind romance, either there or more likely in Toronto, for in April Agnes questioned him about Joyce – surname not mentioned. Alex replied that he did not "expect any trouble there. I have made it clear that I am not keen on settling down, least that is what I think and we have left it that we are friends and that I will see her when I can. Anyway, the whole thing happened rather quickly and I think we both have calmed down a little. I would hope that once bitten twice shy, and having waited so long now I might just as well wait for what I think is THE best or not think about it at all. Women do baffle me anyway – just don't know what, when, how, why or where!!" He had set his cap at three young women in two years: Diana, Peg and Joyce. He had been bruised by the experience and was determined to be more careful. It produced quite a sea change in his attitude; henceforth he took to referring to himself as a bachelor and was adjusting mentally to a single life. In the same letter to Agnes he says he is trying to cool off "the Peggy thing"; and that summer will help by providing him with plenty to do with the boat. "Unless, of course, I meet another damsel who takes my fancy ... how happy this world would be if there were no women, or if I didn't really like them!"

The romance with Joyce died a natural death. She was a nurse in Toronto; he visited her twice in April, during weekends when he was flying NRC people to Buffalo and Hamilton. Thereafter there is silence regarding her. Peggy, on the other hand, remained in high favour. In spite of what he had said he continued to see her and her family continued most welcoming: "The setup has been ideal in many ways – a friendly family who expect you when you want, and at any time. Peg with friends in the Air Force who are also my friends. She, Peg, available to do what I want, when I want, without having to make arrangements ahead of time."

In March 1948 he heard he would be posted to the Royal Military College at Kingston for the September intake. In stages he and Peg, Tim Wood and his wife Rita sailed *Tida Appa* from Ottawa to Kingston, down the length of the Rideau Canal – quite an undertaking. They took turns to provide road transport home at the end of a day's sail. In this sort of enterprise the practical Peg was invaluable and Alex was still very attracted to her. In August, as though he had never mentioned the subject, he wrote: "Peggy I don't know about, except that at times we get on very well together." He added, ruefully: "There is, I think, no question of marriage as she is young and definitely wants her fling." Within the month she was living on the west coast, a lab technician at Vancouver General Hospital, and therefore temporarily out of his life.

Alex's time at Arnprior had been a valuable 'dry run' for a station command. He had earned the respect of subordinates and superiors, had become a competent modern pilot, had made a number of real friends in Arnprior and Ottawa and was beginning to feel that he 'knew everybody', just as he had in the pre-war RAF. The Royal Military College (RMC) at Kingston was to be a totally different assignment which he rightly approached with some caution. To be appointed Director of Military Studies with the internal rank of Associate Professor was a sweet irony, of course, which only he himself could fully appreciate. His thoughts must have strayed to S/L Higgins's refusal to consider him for a commission in the RCAF in 1935. Now, as an exemplary officer, he had been appointed to the staff of a university-level institution with power of pass or fail over those seeking commissions in the Canadian forces. He felt vindicated by this posting but it was not going to be easy.

First, he would be "away from Air Force chaps for the first time since 1935"; life without yarning would be a challenge. Secondly, he was going to have to teach and had not the first idea where to begin. To turn Bernard Shaw's dictum on its head, those who both CAN and DO usually find teaching pretty difficult! He approached the task methodically, of course, and was not too proud to ask for help. His Army and Navy colleagues at RMC, Major de Grandpré and L/Cmdr Nixon, had no more experience than he. So, having summarised the topics to be covered, he sought help from Ross Ingalls and Pete Fisher, academics on staff. Between them they put together a reasonable course outline. Alex immediately warmed to Fisher – " a grand head" as he called him, an expression he reserved for those of whom he completely approved.

Next he had to prepare lectures and ponder the process of lecturing and teaching. It was not an area to which he was a complete stranger; a mere three years ago, though it seemed like a different lifetime, he had been lecturing on celestial navigation to starving POWs. However, in early September before the cadets arrived, Alex spent a day in Toronto picking the brains of the chief instructor at the staff college about teaching techniques. When it came to it, the content of lectures and his teaching caused him no trouble. It was only at exam time that he became uneasy; in December he wrote: "The cadets are in the middle of exams and, for a change, quiet and not causing a noise. Tomorrow they write the exam we have set them. If they knew it, we, every bit as much as they, are interested in the results! Having never set exams before and not knowing how long it will take them to do and whether the questions are reasonable or not, we are also wondering how many of the things we have lectured about have sunk into their thick skulls!"

He found his RMC job tended to get on top of him, rather than him being on top of it. Apart from lecturing he was involved in the extracurricular side of life. He took yacht racers and squash players to Toronto and hockey players to Montréal and West Point, helped cadets with photo developing and enjoyed it all. Nevertheless, he soon wanted out. Quite early on he found that he had to keep the end result in mind to avoid frustration. In March 1949 he was feeling "unsettled," an expression that he had not used about himself since 1940; and by May he was unable to reconcile himself to what was, in effect, a desk job.

He had been making great headway in his campaign to become known in the RCAF. At New Year 1949 this had born fruit in a welcome promotion to Wing Commander. However, the new ring on his sleeve cut little ice in the semi-civilian and mixed-service world of RMC and made no difference to the way that the institution treated him. He felt shunted onto a siding and feared he would have to make his mark all over again once he was posted away. These feelings were in spite of his delight at a farewell party for the resident medical officer in March, "the first time we have had a 'hair let-down' party with all the staff present." He had hoped to be posted in 1949 because he had a theory that bachelors were considered more moveable. However, his efforts were appreciated at RMC and the CO, Brigadier Agnew, made every effort to keep him.

Physically he was not in very good shape during his first year at RMC, in spite of a few games of tennis, nor was he getting any flying. Both things may have affected his morale. Maybe unintentionally, he had begun to spend most of his spare time in non-aerobic activities. He had parted with the Green Hornet and bought a '46 Packard for 2,700 dollars just before leaving Arnprior. This made him more mobile, able to visit Montréal, Toronto or Ottawa – but less likely to go for a walk. Much of his time in Kingston was spent sailing in his boat *Tida Appa* or gliding – a new pastime into which he threw himself. There was an active soaring club nearby and after qualifying as a pilot, he became part-owner of a glider.

He discovered as time passed that RMC had one saving grace which perhaps made up for all the negatives that he perceived: even though it was Siberia as far as RCAF mess life was concerned, it was a great place to make your number with VIPs. He met some who were just interesting to talk to such as Field Marshal Lord Wavell, Field Marshal Slim, General Simmonds and General Sir Gerald Templar. He also met Minister of Defence Brooke Claxton, Australian Minister of Defence Sinclair and the Chief of Air Staff. In 1949, as things turned out, the Australian Sinclair was to be his most useful connection.

Alex had been thinking about Norman Birks. In December 1946 Pat had had a fourth child, her second son. Norman had originally thought it a "bum idea", but Pat had talked him into it. Maybe she had an inkling of what the future held. In the summer of 1948 Norman sent Alex a copy of *Forgotten Island* by P. G. Taylor, an Australian flying pioneer. It described his 1944 Catalina flight from Acapulco to Auckland by way of Clipperton Island, with Norman as his second pilot. Alex was brought face-to-face with the past: "Reading it I relived many incidents which occurred when Norman and I were together. My, but those days are far distant, and seem to belong to another person and life!" Only months later he heard that

Norman was seriously ill. When told of the symptoms, Dr. Lewis warned Alex that Norman had a brain tumour which would almost certainly be fatal. There seemed to be hope, nevertheless; Pat mentioned treatment, and no news for a few months seemed a good sign. However, in January it was clear that treatment had failed and Norman died in February.

At that point Alex began to think of going to Australia and of how and when he would make the trip. He decided to go as soon as he could get away from RMC after exams. It would be too late for Norman, of course; Pat wrote to Alex for his birthday and told him about the funeral, the largest ever seen in Adelaide. But Alex wanted to go to see Pat. In her six months in Singapore in 1940 Alex had spent many weekends at their house; to him Pat had become more than just the wife of a friend – with no suggestion of disloyalty by either of them to Norman, it is clear that in those months Pat and Alex developed a special bond. When she returned to Australia in November 1940, Alex was as dismayed as Norman had been. In letters exchanged in September and October 1945 it was clear that both Birkses had special feelings for Alex, which he reciprocated. Now that Norman was dead Alex wanted to be with Pat. What that might lead to was another matter but he was certainly aware that the topic of marriage might crop up.

Having decided to go, he found it paid to know the Canadian and Australian Ministers of Defence. He made his application to go to Australia early in the year and applied for military assistance with transportation. At one point he hoped that the USAAF might be persuaded to provide a transpacific flight. That came to nothing so he booked on Quantas. However, after visits to the Australian High Commissioner in Ottawa and thanks to the active support of the Defence Ministers, transportation in Canada was provided by the RCAF; and, once in Australia, all travel and most accommodation was provided courtesy of the Australian armed forces.

To make this work it had to be a semi-official trip. Before he settled down in Adelaide with Pat and her family, he criss-crossed Australia for two weeks on a number of visits in uniform – some at his request, some as part of his job. He went to see Parliament in session in Canberra, to the Australian RMC at Duntroon, to training stations in Melbourne with the Deputy Chief of Air Staff, to cadet colleges in Melbourne with the Director of Training, RAAF, to the British missile-testing range at Woomera. He had functions and official visits in Sydney and Brisbane as well. At one point, on the long flight between Adelaide and Woomera, he found himself alone on an RAAF aircraft with Canadian Lieutenant General Guy Simmonds, First Canadian Army commander in Europe after D-Day. Characteristically this little-loved gentleman behaved like a bear, refused to chat with a junior officer and resented sharing his aircraft! It was about the only occasion on the trip when Alex was not made to feel completely welcome – and by a Canadian. In fact, he had the red carpet rolled out for him everywhere he went; he was met and accompanied and handed over to his next handler like minor royalty. One can only suppose that it was the result of his personal impact on his seniors, especially the ministers; and one would like to think that it was also a way for the brass to acknowledge the service and rough wartime experiences of an admirable and trustworthy officer. Alex saw his good fortune rather more modestly: "Being on leave, yet ready to put in an official or semi-official word or two, plus knowing Sinclair, has really got everyone cooperating!"

By the middle of June 1949 he reached Adelaide and spent the rest of the month with Pat. To maintain the proprieties her younger brother Bill came to stay for the duration. It was to be a momentous two weeks which Alex was later unable or unwilling to describe. Although three or four years older than he was and the mother of four, Pat was an exceptionally attractive woman. Like all women of whom Alex approved, she was also energetic and full of fun. All his old feelings for her returned to him but he was not prepared for a house full of kids, two of them young ones. "How on earth Pat keeps going beats me. The two young ones are a menace, it seems. Surely we were not the trouble present youngsters are, or were we?! She has a cook-cum-maid and someone to look after the kids of an evening, just so long as I am here." The older children rather shocked Alex by the disrespectful way in which they treated their mother; the reality of domestic life with children was very different from the orderly single life to which he was becoming increasingly accustomed, and it was unsettling. He did not feel that the family had an internal happiness, comparing them with rather idealised memories of his own childhood, and possibly overlooking the effect of the sudden death of their father. Nevertheless, Alex adapted quickly and was soon leading the riot, as was his wont when visiting families with children.

At the beginning of July he wrote to his mother: "Staying with Pat and her brother Bill has somehow upset me. I can't really describe it, or perhaps I would rather not. I was accepted by everyone ... just as one of a large family. I have never been so utterly happy in what I realise was an absolutely artificial few weeks. I left yesterday, the 30th of June ... and all this looks absurd in writing and I shouldn't burden you with it. I have seldom, if ever, been so unhappy having to accept saying goodbye with no honest or real hope of seeing Pat again, at least for a very long time. I do hope you will not mind me leaving things as a blank for that two weeks."

Once Alex was back in Canada Pat wrote to him regularly for the rest of the year; she had not yet convinced herself that Alex was lost to her. For his part he passed on to Agnes snaps which Pat had sent him at Christmas, only asking her to return those of Pat herself. But as 1950 began to unroll, Pat, who had made enormous efforts to welcome Alex in June 1949 – by, for example, priming her Sydney friends to look after him and by making herself available for him the whole time he was in Adelaide – accepted his actions as a final decision and in September married an Australian. Only then did Alex let drop a few more thoughts on the subject: "At times, without a great deal of looking at hard facts, I liked to entertain the idea of being her husband. But ... having seen her in her own environment, meeting the children and her friends, I was happy to accept that such a thing would never, under the most ideal circumstances, work out as anything near a sensible proposition. So there is no doubt in my mind that all is for the best and I do not feel unhappy about it. Rather most happy, since she is happy and in a situation far more in keeping with her own life."

For this piece of reasoning and self-denial one can only be struck dumb in admiration for Alex's strength and unselfishness. Even more remarkable was his insistence on dealing with the situation alone, without discussing it with Pat. Apparently Pat was thinking about their possible future together while he was there; she tried to get him to talk, at one point asking what he thought of marriages between younger men and older women. In fact he usually disapproved of such alliances and her gambit seems not to have led to a more specific discussion. We know that he attempted to conceal his feelings from Pat – 'attempted' because the deed of flying halfway around the world to spend two weeks with a woman's noisy children was more eloquent than words – for in the same letter he asked Agnes to write to Pat but warned her on no account "for her sake, for my sake and general happiness, to say ... that I have ever dreamed anything but the fact that I am fond of her."

In other words he had never broached the subject of 'us' when he was with her. It was how Alex liked to operate; feelings were hard things to talk about, even to the object of those feelings. No doubt the alternatives open to him – of transferring once more, this time to the RAAF, or of Pat transplanting her four children to live in Canada – did not seem 'sensible propositions'. The discussion did not really need to happen because the choices were plain and he had clearly rejected both when, although desperately unhappy, he bade Pat farewell and flew away. Nevertheless, the first alternative might have been chosen by somebody more impulsive and less rational and the second by somebody more selfish and less considerate. He claims to have cared for Pat more than he did for anyone else up to the time of his eventual marriage. Most men in his shoes would have popped the question, sensible or not, and hoped for the best. But that would have left his future at the mercy of chance – something he was determined not to do.

In Sydney he had met Beryl Stilling, her parents the Barwells as well as Gordon's mother. He had not known Beryl as well as he had known Pat. He had been Gordon's best man; Beryl, like Pat, had kept in touch with Agnes during the war and was one of the first people whom he contacted once out of POW camp. The horrors of the losing fight against Japan in Malaya and Java and the subsequent death of Gordon, still flying a Catalina, in the Celebes in 1943, was a heroic nightmare shared by the three families. Now, with the sudden death of Norman, Alex was their only surviving warrior and his presence gave memories a special poignancy. Robyn Stilling, Alex's goddaughter, remembers his visit to Sydney; one morning she discovered a snoring man, smelling strongly of whisky, on her mother's living-room sofa. She reported this alarming phenomenon to Beryl who explained sympathetically that godfather Alex had been celebrating with his friends so late that the Sydney Club, that unreasonable institution, had locked him out and the poor man had had nowhere to go! Mrs Stilling, senior, later wrote that Alex reminded her strongly of her only son, a memory bolstered by his being godfather to her grandchild. Alex was aware that he had a special importance for a large number of people but eventually it was time to go.

Minister Sinclair and the RAAF had arranged a side trip to New Guinea and the Admiralty Islands for him, places with the appearance and climate of Java and Malaya. It was sudden immersion in his past – so complete, so stifling that it took his breath away. From Port Moresby he wrote: "In the real tropics again and not sure if I am really liking it. So much of my past seems around me in these places – all so hard to believe and take in." After this he would have liked nothing better than to go straight home, to have time to take stock of recent events before concerning himself with a new intake of cadets. However, he had earlier planned two weeks in New Zealand. Sinclair had talked to his opposite number and Alex found himself on a second semi-official visit. This time Bob McVicker was his RNZAF minder. McVicker managed to find a Harvard and a pilot for him so he could visit training facilities around New Zealand. He was busier than he wanted to be but stayed with both McVicker and Sid Scales, now a distinguished professional cartoonist* living in Dunedin. They enjoyed evenings of 205 Squadron yarning and painful POW memories. He was not back in Kingston until the end of July.

Alex's second year at RMC proved to be a different experience. His responsibilities for students had been lightened by the posting to RMC of some junior officers and the job itself was less of a challenge, as he had but to improve on his first year's lectures. Nevertheless, he was busy when he returned from 'down under'. In his usual manner he took material to the stenos for typing, on which they started work immediately. To his amazement he found that this aroused passions, "irate professors wanting to know why I should get preference! They maintained that the girls were afraid of us (the Service profs) and that is why! Little do they realise that

---

*Sid Scales was subsequently awarded the OBE.

stenos are as human as we and like to be treated in that way!" Alex, as he had at the staff college, found that charm and a little consideration carry all before them – with a few speechless exceptions.

In spite of this encouraging beginning, for Alex the year from July 1949 was in many ways a grey one, full of confidence-shaking events and serious health problems. The iron constitution which had carried him through three and a half years of malnutrition and abuse was finally showing signs of mortality. First, he spent part of December in hospital with jaundice. He was not completely recovered from that before the second shoe dropped, the discovery in May of a malignant cyst on his jaw. This put him back in hospital twice, first to remove the cyst and a piece of his jawbone and the second time to reconstruct the jaw with bits and pieces from his thigh.

When signing him off as fit in July 1950, the surgeon implored him to find a less violent way of taking exercise than playing soccer – Alex had organised and played in several games during the year, questioned him about his Java experience and declared him to be "a bear for punishment," with which Alex could hardly argue! It seems likely that even bears have limits and this bear appeared to have reached them. Nevertheless, having survived this worrying event, he was to be pronounced fully healthy with excellent eyesight at his annual Air Force medical in August. By then Alex had been posted to HQ Training Command at Trenton and it was probably no real reflection on the others when the MO there declared him the fittest Wing Commander on the base.

There were two events which, in retrospect, seem to have shaken his confidence in his longtime role of invulnerable playboy, able to flirt outrageously with anyone in a skirt. The first of these happened just before his bout of jaundice. He and Peter Fisher had taken out a nineteen-year-old Parisienne and her eighteen-year-old friend for a Saturday evening of pubbing and dancing. "To our consternation and astonishment on Monday the story was being bandied about the town of two *old* bachelors taking out two Queen's University coeds! We have taken an awful ribbing and I'm cursing because this was a dame that was different – brought up in Sacred Heart convents in Paris, Washington and Mexico, I think – altogether, well, you know ...!" At thirty-five he was learning that he would have to clip his wings if he was still to be perceived on the side of the angels, would have to be more careful on whom he focused his exploratory matrimonial telescope – a tough lesson for an innocent old roué!

The second event happened later in the month, when he was convalescing from jaundice and not permitted to drink. He went to a party with Bud and Peggy Levy where he met nearly everyone he had known in Arnprior. At the party was a recently divorced woman whom Bud had told about Alex's Packard and 'yacht' –

no doubt both embellished in the telling. "Result – she started chasing me AND she was not bashful! The party started as a well-conducted and orderly affair – by 10:00 p.m. it was a trifle out of control. I had the whole story of a sordid married life from this woman on my knee. She couldn't and wouldn't make any progress!" She gave up, temporarily, and told Bud "she couldn't get a peep out of me and the only reason she knew I was alive was from seeing me breathe! Bud said she was annoyed; she wasn't the only one – me stone cold sober making a small scotch last all evening, she quite the opposite! Bud and Peggy got a great laugh out of it, as did most people. Unfortunately she turned up at two other places we visited and continued to pursue. On parting she had decided that she wasn't my type – too right she were!" Alex related the story as a joke and claimed he had "never seen Arnprior with quite so much of its hair down – on the whole marvellous fun!" It must also have been a sobering experience for a man who believed that no holds were barred at a party. She had made him uncomfortable, maybe shocked him – women should not behave like that! Ahoy there, playboy!

In other ways the second year at RMC was a good one. Alex was the PMC – President of the Mess Committee – and at the beginning of the year was therefore MC at a staff corn roast. This event, designed as an icebreaker for new members, was conducted by Alex in the way that he thought all parties should be conducted: "Newcomers wondered what on earth they had come to!" Christmas was quite an occasion for him in spite of his convalescent state; he received sixty-five cards and five invitations to Christmas dinner, which bucked up his spirits. The silver lining of his jaundice cloud was that he drank no alcohol throughout the winter, only breaking his drought at a wedding in late April. And from the time in March when he had news of his posting to Training Command HQ at Trenton, he stopped worrying that his career had been sidelined. In fact the final months at RMC allowed him to make himself known to more senior officers. As PMC he had to look after AVM Plant, whom he knew and who had accepted him into the RCAF in the fall of 1945 in Western Command; also AM Curtis and AVM Slemon who was to be his boss at Trenton.

RMC gave a farewell party for him. The brigadier spoke about Alex, he replied and things developed to the point that the party was decreed the best ever – Alex's kind of party! Next morning he set off with much fanfare in *Tida Appa* and people thought: "Well, that's that!" But the wind was fierce; after a morning battling it with a reefed mainsail, he ran back into Kingston harbour for shelter – and up to the mess for lunch "much to the amazement and joy of the mess; everyone took it as a big joke, which it was, of course!"

The new job at Trenton, just a few miles down the road, dramatically restored Alex's enjoyment of life in the RCAF. 1950 was a historic summer. On the 25th of

June North Korea had invaded South Korea; two days later the Security Council called on UN members to send forces to South Korea. Immediately Americans from Japan became involved and on the 19th of July President Truman asked Congress for a greatly expanded military. Brooke Claxton made a speech the same day, seeming to indicate a general expansion of Canada's forces and the probable despatch of forces to Korea. As he spoke Alex was arriving at Trenton. The job involved planning for the whole RCAF – recruiting, training, equipment. Claxton had mentioned no limits to the expansion and as Alex touched the ground in Trenton he was already running; immediately he was into crisis meetings with AVM Slemon and other staff officers. Their first task was to introduce order into the chaos created by the Minister's announcement.

There was a Battle of Britain spirit in the air. Wartime airmen were signing on again, regretting having left the service in 1946. The press speculated that Korea was the beginning of the next war, that Stalin was using Korea as a diversion to conceal an attack in Europe. At the time nothing seemed too far-fetched. In fact, the cabinet had not reached agreement on what to do and Mr St Laurent would not announce the Canadian volunteer force until the 7th of August. But the decision was taken for granted by all concerned. In those weeks Alex was beginning his new job. On the 28th of July he was complaining: "Today has proved conclusively that I have taken over a job at a most unlucky time insofar as having a breather to look at what it all means is concerned. The number of things to be done is quite extraordinary. It is just bad luck, I suppose, that I did not take over either a month earlier or a month later."

By the 4th of August he had 'got his second wind' and would not have had things any other way. He had been up to Ottawa to discuss pros and cons; the newspapers had already written so much on the subject that nothing he could tell Agnes could still be considered sensitive. "You will know that the government decision [it would not be announced for three more days!] to send troop volunteers, and I think only army people, has had a lot to do with our work, since whatever is done we shall have to increase the size of the Air Force ... I should say that I am thoroughly enjoying every moment of it ... what I like the most is that I have to have a finger in most pies."

It had actually been a great beginning to a new job. It was perhaps a sign that Lucky Alex was flying again that his first real desk job coincided with a great expansion of the RCAF, caused by the dawning reality of the Cold War. Up until 1950 the Air Force, along with the other armed forces, had been winding down from their wartime peak. Korea was to change all that. With the expansion ordered in that year, in addition to the growing offensive capabilities of the Soviet air force, Canadian fighter bases became the front line in the defence of North America.

What had seemed a ho-hum assignment at Trenton was in fact buzzing with excitement and significance. It mattered that the new bases be completed on time, that pilots be trained to fly the CF100 jets, that the whole system be speedily linked with new and efficient radar stations. Alex was in his element. His work was absorbing from the beginning and more so when he began touring new bases in the building process. Gimli, St Hubert, Cold Lake and others came into existence at this time under his supervision. In the other direction he was visiting Greenwood, NS, and Summerside, PEI.

With the job his general enjoyment of life soared. In his spare time he struggled to bring *Tida Appa* to Trenton and at first made so little progress that people joked he would pull it into Trenton on the ice like a sled. By the first weekend in August he knew he had to finish the job; he rented an outboard motor and in two days completed the journey. He returned to Kingston by bus to pick up his car and dropped into RMC, hoping to get a bite to eat. "Lo and behold, they were just going in to buffet supper. I was hungry, very, and they all welcomed me with open arms. Without question I don't think people have ever been so nice to me as they are when I visit. They positively shout 'welcome Alex!' "

At Trenton he found his surroundings entirely to his liking: "Late breakfast this morning, then swimming and diving and sunbathing; later took G/C Carpenter and small son for a sail; back for a swim, then supper. Today, as never before, I have lead the life of a man at an expensive country club – really lapping it up! Glorious day – never could one wish for more in the way of pleasantness." He had social adjustments to make. As usual he took a while to make friends, in spite of previous mess-crawling. He was also finding the battle of the sexes quite daunting. Junior nursing officers or catering officers kept him at arms-length by calling him 'Sir' or 'Wing Commander' even on social occasions – a definite put-down for an ardent thirty-six-year-old! Alex commented: "I hesitate to change things myself" – presumably by saying 'please call me Alex'. Such are the mating handicaps for the single officer of senior rank! Meanwhile he relied on occasional descents on RMC and Arnprior to augment his social life.

In spite of these trials his morale remained high. In October he could not resist 'taking the mickey' out of Agnes, to whose paintings and cottage life at Shawnigan they had both devoted a good deal of paper recently: "Me mother, you know, she is an artist and always goes around with wrinkled stockings and her slip showing. Makes pots of money and we own quite a lot of land but really she is happiest in this awful hole. Do have a cup of tea me dear – no that is not dirt on the cup, that is paint. No teaspoon? Here, use the brush – no, not the furry end, the other end, you fool."

Alex always loved dress-up occasions; he burst upon the social scene at Trenton, at an August 'Hard Times' dance, in just a shirt and underpants, with a saying by Confucius pinned to his back – and some people were shocked. Later he persuaded a nursing sister to come with him to the Halloween dance. They went as Romans, dressed in sheets; it was a great party and he got to bed at 5:00 a.m., which was his idea of a really good time. But it was not until the end of September that he was invited to a bridge evening with the married wing commanders and group captains and he hoped that he might now have broken into the magic circle.

He used the opportunity of living on a base to get back to flying. It was a feature of his lingering youth that he could never get enough of it. To him flying would always be a spiritual experience: "Grand to be in the air again – still cannot explain why I enjoy it so." During two years at RMC he had taken to the air mainly in a glider and had flown only two and half hours in powered aircraft and those as second pilot. Now that all changed. From August 1950 Alex was flying on five or six days a month and sometimes for three- and four-hour flights. Usually he was flying Beechcraft but he also flew a Norseman float plane for short trips into the Shield and, occasionally, a Dakota. In his first year at Trenton he managed eighty-eight hours. He commented on a trip to Gimli: "Managed to persuade them to let me do the flying; a bit selfish but I get so little I grab opportunities and possibly make myself unpopular." It was a risk he had to take – in fact a remote one as he remained much respected. As the job became more demanding and his responsibilities heavier, so his time in the air diminished. In his second year at Trenton he managed only twenty hours, although that improved towards the end of 1952 and in those last six months he flew another forty hours.

Having a finger in many pies led to two benefits. Not only did he have a part in shaping much of what was happening but he was also involved with many departments of the RCAF. Senior officers in those departments had to make judgements about him. To a less-confident person this might have been intimidating. To Alex who, as the Pieman should have, only wished to 'show his wares', the opportunity was heaven-sent. Events played into his hands better than he could have hoped; as a bachelor wing commander he was swiftly elected PMC and was thus in the spotlight for two high-exposure events which came to Trenton in 1951: the presentation of the King's Colour and the Colour of the RCAF to Training Command, to be housed in the officers' mess and, more significantly, the visit to Trenton of the recently married Princess Elizabeth and the Duke of Edinburgh.

The first of these ceremonial events was in early June. Handling the Colours is an honour, as is the task of looking after them. Needless to say any informality or lack of smartness in parading or handling them gives offence. The need to get such things absolutely right puts great pressure on those involved. The Trenton event went without a hitch. Alex personally received the Colours into the mess from the hands of the Air Officer Commanding, AVM Slemon; the parade was flawless, the airmen's drill as smart as could be and the reception inside the mess for 300 invited guests went smoothly. Slemon was delighted. Score one for Alex!

Alex was due to hand over his PMC duties to another officer but Slemon would not hear of it. He insisted Alex remain PMC until after the royal visit in October. Alex wrote that the AOC "made a special point of saying that I have done and am doing a job which allows him to feel complete confidence in my judgement." He had intended to take leave in October and so had to change the dates. "Small feather in my cap, I suppose. The most interesting to me being his comment that we think alike on these matters – he with a definite Canadian background and me with your training, which I'm sure was different from his mother's; and my RAF training which again was a different background to the RCAF." After this Alex felt, finally, that he had 'made it' in the RCAF.

Having postponed his leave he left for the west coast on a routine tour of air bases. Agnes must have been startled by a telegram which reached her on the 5th of September: "FROM CANAIRTRAIN. PLEASED TO INFORM YOU THAT YOUR SON W/C JARDINE WAS NOT REPEAT NOT INJURED IN A CRASH ON TAKEOFF OF AN AIRCRAFT IN WHICH HE WAS A PASSENGER AT CLARESHOLM ALBERTA." He had been in the second pilot's seat but was not flying; the first pilot had made a normal takeoff but for reasons unknown the Beechcraft, after lifting off, never gained altitude and ploughed into the ground beyond the end of the runway. Lucky Alex's luck held once more and he and others on board emerged from the wreckage unscathed. At the end of October he made an official trip to Royal Roads in Victoria and squeezed in a couple of days' leave with his mother before returning to the east. Although his visit was brief, as he had to return to Trenton for the royal visit, at least Agnes could see that Training Command's telegram had told no lies.

Princess Elizabeth and the Duke arrived in Trenton on the 13th of October 1951 and the day was a personal triumph for Alex. He was entirely responsible for the arrangements and everything went according to plan, although two events nearly gave him apoplexy. The proceedings began with Alex delivering a briefing on protocol – what to do and say, how to shake hands (not too robustly), when and how to curtsy (!) and on keeping conversation informal – to the eighty assembled notables. The group included Vincent Massey (soon to be Governor General), cabinet ministers and MPs, Ontario MPPs, senior Air Force officers and local mayors, all with their wives or husbands. "In some respects I felt that I had some nerve telling such high-priced help that they should do things this way or that. However, it went off very well – many people congratulated me on it afterwards." He had kept the tone light and humorous without being flippant – a difficult trick.

After the briefing Alex was moving towards the front door of the mess to greet the Princess when a hurrying airman dropped a can of paint which splashed onto Alex's pants. This was his first apoplectic moment; he could see his guests' car arriving in front of the building while an airman was still dabbing paint off his pants! The panic passed; Alex was as unflappable as ever as the car doors opened, introducing himself with: "I'm Jardine, the PMC." The Duke, never overburdened by tact, asked: "What is a PMC?" "President of the mess, dear," the Princess cut in before Alex could say a word. After giving the royal couple time to themselves Alex took them into the anteroom to meet AVM and Mrs Slemon and G/C and Mrs Dunlop before meeting the assembled notables. Next came a receiving line, followed by tea and sandwiches. The royal couple stuck to tea – suspecting that the RCAF was better at flying than sandwich-making.

Alex had a five-minute conversation with the princess. "What are you doing here?" she asked him, presuming from his accent that he was English. Alex told her about his chequered career and after some talk about sailing, which they both enjoyed, he commiserated with her on never having the chance to get to know the people she met. The Princess agreed and proved the point by moving on. He continued the sailing conversation with the Duke. They were warming to each other, Alex had run his favourite line about feeling lucky to be paid to live at such a country club as Trenton and wartime yarns were beginning. Suddenly a rogue female guest interrupted with: "You look as though you need some help, Alex." She buttonholed the Duke about the IODE and the Duke of Edinburgh's Award programme "which the poor chap could not quite understand." The Duke looked startled and Alex apoplectic – for the second time that morning. He later complained: "We were quite happy and getting into some interesting topics."

The incident put paid to the conversation and shortly afterwards the royal couple took their leave. At the front door Alex was so preoccupied saying goodbye to them that three times he failed to notice Brooke Claxton's proffered hand. Nevertheless, the reception had been managed in a most urbane manner, the rogue guest apologised, the minister forgot the slight, the brass were delighted and Alex much congratulated. For him, a long-time defender of the monarchy, it had been more pleasure than duty: "I have no letdown feeling after all the effort, but rather the feeling of having been part of a show that has done something well, and we all now have a grand milestone in our lives."

Alex was now really enjoying life. The best indicator of this was his reluctance to take leave for anything but short periods. He wrote to apologise to his mother for his brief appearance: "You will know from years ago that I hate being 'out of things' and, as I have so often said, so much is happening of great interest that I don't really enjoy 'taking it easy' away from the Air Force." In his case the Chinese curse 'may you live in interesting times' had become a blessing; he had great zest for his work and found it exciting, especially as it held promise for himself of eventually getting command of an air base – the more air bases there were, the better his chances.

Underlying his excitement were always his worries about the reason for the RCAF expansion and about international events. In January 1951 he thought that "this peculiar situation could continue for a long time yet. He would be quite a chap who could tell with any degree of certainty the next move. Even old Churchill has not made any positive predictions to my knowledge." At the end of the year nothing had changed; he found he had little time to think of anything other than the job: "I feel the world situation most unsettling and know that we are going to have a pretty tough year in 1952."

In January of that year he was still working like a Trojan but his enjoyment of Trenton continued. He was involved in everything. *Tida Appa* was in the water from June to November in 1951 and to October in 1952; he sailed whenever he could with whomever was available and sometimes sailed and raced in other boats, including the RCAF's *Astra*. With swimming and diving thrown in he found it hard to enjoy summertime absences from Trenton and continued to see it as his country club. However, because of his seniority and bachelor status, he had no regular supply of sailing companions his own age; his refrain was his need for kindred souls – alas, most of them free spirits no longer. As for the younger men, for Alex it was "like when one gets near teenagers, one discovers that one is considered pretty old and not much good for anything else but being polite to (if they happen to have that sort of upbringing)." So his crew was definitely 'casual labour' – sometimes another officer's wife, sometimes a married friend and on rare occasions a girlfriend visiting from 'away'.

On one occasion he added to his own legend when sailing with two naval cadets; he was forward hauling up the jib when a sudden gust capsized them. After righting the boat and bailing her out, the cadets were roaring with laughter at the memory of Alex swimming in Lake Ontario with his pipe still in his mouth, like Popeye. He claimed he had nowhere else to put it! Alex's reputation for 'playing the giddy goat', occasionally displayed at fancy dress events, got him involved in a variety show. As well as producing it, he played an inebriate: "My nonsense hinged around a leaning act which was quite a gag because I had studs in the floor and special heels which allowed me to lean at a most frightening angle." He also became involved in an elaborate charade around a rumour that he had a Malay wife and children. He had been encouraging it quietly, but most people realised it was a joke. Eventually he received an invitation to tea from Mrs Slemon for W/C and Mrs Jardine. Encouraged by the AOC he composed a letter in Malay, signed by

Jasmin Jardine, regretting she could not get away because of her children, Marin Made and Roy Hayam Wuruk – Marin and Roy being the names of the Slemons. It was a great success and the Slemons dined out on it for weeks.

At this time, while he was so wedded to his work, Alex's romantic life hit a dry patch, as did the rest of his social life. In fact he had a serious love interest, a nurse called Louise whom he had met whilst in hospital in 1950. She had seemed a delivering angel at the time and afterwards they continued to see each other. In October 1950 she was working at the Army base in Petawawa and was first mentioned in a letter to Agnes when Alex went there to see her. They had planned to spend Christmas 1950 in the Laurentians but the idea fell through when she was assigned duty over the holiday and they saw little of each other in early 1951, when Alex confessed to working "like a Trojan". In March he discovered that Louise, now in Toronto at the staff college, was about to be posted to Whitehorse.

The news galvanised him. He shot off to Toronto to see her and even put up with a night in a hospital bed. Next week he took her to a mess dance in Trenton and the week after that spent a day with her in Toronto. He was prepared to break his single man's rhythm in order to be with her and she was obviously pretty special to him. Yet, after further visits to Toronto to see her he let her fly to Whitehorse, and effectively out of his life, on the 14th of April. They continued to correspond; he arranged to include Whitehorse in a tour of bases that he was making and she was thrilled about his visit. However, for whatever reason, the visit never happened and Alex did not report hearing from her again until March 1952. Then she wrote to say that she would be in Montréal in a couple of weeks.

Once again he dropped everything, including a high-profile event – the visit of the Italian Chief of Air Staff. He wrote to Agnes while awaiting Louise's train on a Montréal station bench: "I wonder what Louise looks like and what we shall do. One thing for sure, I must get some sleep so hope to do that this afternoon, though Louise is a tiger for having fun while she can, especially, I expect, now that she is back in civilisation for such a short while." For the first recorded time Alex was nervous about meeting a woman. He probably realised that he was being challenged to propose but we can only surmise what happened, for he made no further mention of her until August. Then, from Whitehorse, Louise announced her engagement to a soldier.

His success at Trenton, his job and his good relations with senior officers, especially AVM Slemon, gave him the confidence in 1952 to take the risk of refusing a posting. He had heard through the grapevine that he had been selected for the job of Air Attaché in Moscow, a considerable honour at that time, if true. The pantomime of rumour and counter-rumour in 1959, before he actually was posted to Prague, suggests this 1952 rumour to have been no more than a trial balloon floated by somebody at AFHQ. As Slemon was away, Alex made it known in unmistakable language to A/C W. W. Brown at Trenton that he wanted no part of the Moscow job. More than anything, he wanted back into the operational Air Force. Privately, he had decided to resign rather than accept a diplomatic sideshow! "Besides," he said: "I don't like Russians and their rotten vodka!" Somebody was listening because nothing more was said. Within six months he was posted to Air Force Headquarters in Ottawa, not what he wanted but at least it put him where future decisions would be made.

The last six months at Trenton were a sunny time. The pressure of work had eased and the planned expansion either in progress or complete. During this time Alex was very social, seeing plenty of his married friends – the Sproules, to whose child he was godfather, the Wurteles, the Newsoms and the new CO of Trenton, G/C Millward. As he said in July, socially he was enjoying a feast after a self-induced famine, it having been his choice to immerse himself in work to the extent that he had. The hermit of Trenton was now all over Southern Ontario and Québec. He attended the RMC graduation and danced until 5:30 a.m. He took a reappeared Peg Lewis to Montréal, stayed at her brother Harry's place and danced with Peg until 6:00 a.m., before putting her on a ship for England. He was out on the Gatineau in Ottawa, two days in a row at the same swimming hole, with "another chap and two dames." He danced into the wee hours with a friend's niece from Britain. He visited Tim and Rita Wood at Arnprior and golfed with Tim. He had a fishing weekend in Newfoundland and went to the Canadian National Exhibition with the Millwards and the Newsoms, all sitting together, rather grandly, in the Royal Box.

At the same time friends and relations from his past came to visit: Eustace Bidlake was treated to a mess dinner, then to a visit to RMC. He saw Aunty Floss, Harold's sister, and her husband Tom – she delighted in seeing him and reminiscing about life in Hollyburn with his parents before the First World War. And all the while he was sailing and flying as much as he could, aiming to be airborne by 5:00 and afloat by 7:00 every weeknight. In late October, returning from Montréal in a Harvard, he ran out of gas. He landed at Kingston, popped into RMC for a bite, only to 'discover' that it was a mess dance night. He went to the dance in borrowed clothes, claimed a bed for the night and had a morning game of squash before topping up the tank and flying home. Nobody believed the 'out of gas' story! At Halloween he 'played the giddy goat' at the dance, dressed as a Malay, staining his skin and gluing hairs on his chin. He heard next day that his boss and friend, AVM Slemon, had been appointed Chief of Air Staff – the first CAS to have an entirely RCAF background and, more to the point, the first one who knew exactly what a good officer he had in W/C Jardine.

Peggy Lewis re-entered his life before Christmas. She had returned from England, where she had enjoyed meeting the Bidlakes and the Bellamys. This pleased Alex – he was always delighted "when people I like like people I like." After a brief reacquaintance, when he had the opportunity to propose had he wished to, he put her on a train for British Columbia. Then, at her request, he pulled strings with Bidlake's brother, the Territorial Agent in the Yukon, to get her a hospital job in Whitehorse. Not only was he successful but history repeated itself almost exactly: as Louise had done before her, Peg announced her engagement within three months of her arrival there! Her fiancé was Ken McAdam, son of the former BC provincial agent in London. Alex, though possibly a little cast down, accepted the news philosophically, claiming that it was not a huge surprise. Peg later broke off the engagement and married a Dr Aubrey Tanner.

Now more than ever Alex seemed happy to live his life alone, as if on a high wire, but within reach of an ever-widening safety net of married friends of which Peg and her doctor became the latest mesh. He described such people as "very dear friends." All of them offered him more than ordinary friendship: the men because he was fun to be with and loyal and a very fine Air Force officer who enriched their lives; and many of the women rather wistfully, some even romantically, because they were attracted by him, mystified by his inaccessibility, aware of his vulnerability and hoping to protect him. He shared qualities with Pierre Trudeau, another long-time bachelor, of whom Margaret Wente wrote in the *Globe and Mail* that he was "terminally emotionally elusive." Within a month of Slemon going to AFHQ as Chief of Air Staff, Alex was posted to the same headquarters as deputy Director in the Department of Organisation and Establishment. His send-off from Trenton was huge and emotional. There were the usual speeches and presentation of clocks; then the women gave an enormous hamper of tins and bottles to their favourite bachelor. He moved into bachelor digs in the large Ottawa apartment of Colonel Spink at 223 Somerset Street West, seven minutes walk from the office and five minutes from the AFHQ mess, where he could eat. He took up his new duties on the 1st of January 1953. It was a different life. Pitched out of his live-in, 'country club' mess, with easy access to the water and to flying, he was plunged into city life with access to very little: no off-duty Air Force companions, no convenient place to sail or to fly – without making special arrangements. In addition, he soon began to dislike the job, by May even complaining that he hated it: "I am not built for it, I swear," but characteristically adding, "so it is good for me to have to do it!"

It soon became obvious that Alex would have a problem maintaining his sanity flying this particular desk and he began planning a solution immediately. On the 8th of January he announced he was thinking of getting a cottage in the Gatineau. As soon as the weather improved he went looking for one. On the 23rd of March he rented a cottage on Meech Lake in Gatineau Park. Its attraction for Alex was not just sailing and swimming within commuting distance of AFHQ; more importantly it was five minutes' walk from a cottage rented by AFHQ female messing officers, "so if I can't get a meal on a weekend, my name ain't Jardine!"

He found it so easy to enjoy female company on his own terms and when he had time for it, that his incentive to marry was becoming daily weaker. By April the cottage was opening up and women were competing to help Alex be comfortable – on one weekend the messing officers and Peg Levy all descended upon him with armfuls of linen, on the next somebody else organised a 'cottage shower' for him among her friends, following up with a decorating party when they plastered the inside of the smelly old outhouse with pictures of "scandalous femmes." There was not much doubt that they found him attractive, even if he thought it all a great joke.

But Alex's self-sufficiency was a two-edged sword, his own wounds coming from his repeated disappointments. He had refused to be pressured into making a commitment to Pat or Louise or Peggy and could never share their urgency. When he was with one of them the Peter Pan in him wanted to be doing things – sailing or skiing or raising a ruckus in a nightclub or just going to a party – but not looking soulfully into her eyes, talking about the future. It really did seem that he would never muster the resolve to decide 'this is the one for me'. His experiences with any of them left him confused and hurt; after he had tantalised them for months or years with his charm, each of them in the end relieved him of responsibility by marrying somebody else.

Alex now got to know an Ottawa widow of his own age, who had a young daughter. He thought they had a mutually convenient arrangement and a no-strings friendship: she seemed willing to be his escort when Air Force events required him to find one; for his part, he was able to provide her with invitations to functions and was available as her escort whenever she needed one. Unfortunately, the reality was quite different. The lady, not unreasonably, interpreted Alex's frequent companionship as commitment. Hearing about her often and knowing that he had no wish to marry her, Agnes was alarmed. She understood the danger of a misunderstanding when Alex told her that the lady and her daughter had accompanied him as his 'family' to the coronation celebrations on the Hill! Alex's antennae were not so well developed and regardless of his mother's warnings, he allowed the friendship to continue. In spite of resolutions to do just that, he could not bring himself to talk to his frequent companion about his lack of 'intentions'. Meanwhile, his politeness made matters worse: it compelled him to continue issuing occasional invitations in return for her hospitality – which he casually accepted.

Alex lived at the cottage during the summer of 1953. All he had to do was be there and the world came to his door. He was mulling over ways of fetching *Tida Appa* from Trenton when RCAF Rockcliffe phoned to say that they had her sitting on the tarmac and 'what should they do with her'! He had never imagined somebody would fly it up for him – Agnes was sworn to silence lest people talk. Starting in May, when he, John Levy and others put the boat in the water and brought in firewood in exchange for beer, he was overrun by visitors. It might be the messing officers and nursing sisters, or the Slemon children with their mother and father, or impromptu groups of young people from AFHQ – someone had said: "Let's go swimming at the winco's place!" Or it might be visitors from Trenton or Arnprior, or friends who stayed for a while like Bill Newsom and Wally Wurtele. People were in and out of the water, *Tida Appa* was busy whenever there was a breeze, meals were fun and chaotic and seven or eight for breakfast was routine. On some weekends a sort of feeding commune was worked out with the messing officers. "Having this place is wonderful, making the summer seem pleasant and long, almost a holiday," he wrote. Ottawa summers, breathlessly hot and humid as they are, are never pleasant and many visitors were envious of how he was living, just thirty-five or forty minutes' drive from the office.

Even his work became more enticing. His boss was away from May until the end of August and Alex was Acting Director of Organisation and Establishment; as his own boss he found the life tolerable. He was able to get away from the office, escorting USAAF officers around RCAF bases all over Canada. But most evenings would find him at home, cooking for himself, writing, working, sailing or chattering with his neighbours. Life was good.

At the end of summer 1953 he extended his agreement for the cottage over the winter but also rented what he called his 'garret' in town at 695 Cooper Street. By that time his boss was back, Alex's interest in the job had diminished and his mind filled with plans to go ocean sailing. He had been in correspondence with a Mr Sinclair who was building a yacht. Sinclair planned to sail from the Bay of Fundy to New York and needed a crew. That fall Alex thought of little else, telling Agnes: "I simply must get the thing out of my system." After accepting help from both the RCAF and the Navy in equipping *Sally*, he took some leave and finally got away at the end of October from Port Wade, Nova Scotia. He and John Levy sailed with Sinclair, who was seventy-seven and able-bodied but deaf and with poor eyesight. Alex, the Flying Tar of yore, was possibly a little surprised to be violently seasick in the Bay of Fundy. The passage to Boston was hampered by a misbehaving engine but, having had it fixed in Boston, they continued up Long Island Sound to New York. It was an adventure, especially as they had chosen to go in October, but it did the trick and Alex could move on to other things, after having delivered a slide show of the trip in the AFHQ mess to the Slemons and other friends.

In spite of spending Christmas 1953 in British Columbia, with his fortieth birthday approaching he was feeling that his life was out of control. Back in Ottawa he began a personal reformation. First he would cut back on the 'booze' – "I can't think why I do it!" At the beginning of March he made two more resolutions: to visit the YMCA gym for workouts and to start flying again – he had recorded no flying hours in 1953 and the realisation horrified him. In addition, he would become more involved in St John's Anglican Church. It was quite a programme, apparently successfully carried out. In March he was flying again – "Glad to say that I have not lost the art yet" – and he put in sixty hours between then and the end of July. In the same month he started attending the 'Y' three times a week. He also agreed to be convenor for the St John's men's tea – a charitable event for which he had to round up cabinet ministers and other worthies. The tea was even covered by *Time* magazine and was said to have been the most successful ever. He also became a sidesman and then treasurer – "I must be nearing the status of a pillar of the church, methinks!" 'Booze' does not rate another mention in his letters – and no news may have been good news.

On the 1st of July 1954 Alex was promoted to Group Captain and was inundated with messages of congratulation. Most pleasing were those from other wing commanders, men whose own promotion had just moved back a notch in a zero-sum game: W/C Edwards from Lachine congratulated Alex on his "big step into the RCAF hierarchy", W/C Cam McNeill thought it "couldn't have happened to a more deserving fellow", W/C Muss Mussels had "heard nothing but favourable endorsements." Senior officers generally praised his hard work and ability; only one struck a rather different note: Air Commodore Cameron, from the Embassy in Washington, wrote: "I do hate to see junior officers reaching the 'brass' when they have as little faith in their superiors as yourself. I remember distinctly trying to sell you a Group Captain's hat which was in very good condition at a time when you could have got it at a bargain price. But you didn't trust me. Fear, my boy, will never get you anywhere! And of course now that we both know that you need a Group Captain's hat, naturally I'll be asking a greater price for it!" Then, after regular congratulations, he went on: "I sincerely hope it doesn't go to your head and inspire you to any such serious undertakings as – for instance – matrimony."

Even had he been considering such a course, Alex would have found it temporarily driven from his head by the next piece of news he was to receive: finally he had his own RCAF station – he was appointed the new CO of Station Rockcliffe in Ottawa.

15

MISSION ACCOMPLISHED

1954–1959

In which Alex commands CF100 fighter squadrons at St Hubert in the RCAF's
Cold War glory days; in which he serves as ADC to the Governor General;
and in which a knight in a silver T-Bird marries his first cousin Ann.

"Do they think I would marry a dragon!?"

Alex's arrival at Station Rockcliffe marked the end of his apprenticeship and the beginning of his triumph within the RCAF. Rockcliffe, nevertheless, was a way station, the RCAF's maid-of-all-work and the capital's military airport. As CO there, Alex could neither strut the Air Force's stuff nor strike fear into the hearts of possible enemies, but it gave him the opportunity to earn a subsequent posting to the operational station on which his heart was set.

Rockcliffe was part of the RCAF's 'tail' rather than its 'teeth'. It brought under one roof six different elements: 408 Squadron, the Photo-Reconnaissance unit, equipped with Lancasters; 412 Transportation Squadron which operated Dakotas and one Comet; the Practice Flight which employed a variety of aircraft, including T33 jet trainers, to allow airmen stationed at AFHQ to keep their flying hours up to date; the Central Experimental and Proving Establishment; the Air Materiel Command Headquarters; and the Central Communications Headquarters. In addition, there was Alex's own station headquarters and a unit of army Otters, based at Petawawa but maintained at Rockcliffe.

Alex was to spend sixteen months at this station and in less than a year had made his mark as a station commander. In June 1955 he was complimented on his achievements by AVM 'Brandy' Godwin, who wrote: "I wish to express my appreciation of the excellent job you have done in improving Station Rockcliffe in almost all aspects of station administration and upkeep. It is a difficult station, consisting as it does of many 'lodger' units and your Command HQ sitting right on your tail. You have taken all the trouble in your stride and have performed in the very best Air Force fashion."

His job was soon complicated by a new one, that of honorary aide-de-camp to His Excellency the Governor General, Vincent Massey. His relationship with Massey dated back to the royal visit to Trenton. Since then Alex had attended Governor General's levees as an AFHQ officer and had had opportunity to chat with him on several occasions. His appointment as ADC came in December 1954. He was to hold the job for exactly a year, beginning and ending with the same annual investiture at Rideau Hall, when Scouts and Cubs received bravery awards. He regularly had to "don sword and trappings," as he did on New Year's Day 1955, and hie himself off to the Parliament or to Rideau Hall for an official function. When the Governor General travelled in Canada Alex would accompany him to the aircraft but did not have to travel with him, as Massey would be met by a provincially appointed ADC. However, on Massey's one overseas trip during 1955, Alex accompanied him to London and back, in 412 Squadron's Comet. The trip was unofficial so Alex had a few days' relaxing time with English friends.

He had kept the Meech Lake cabin through 1955 and enjoyed many great days there, on one occasion playing host to his Shanghai friend Mary (Turner) Everett, who came visiting with her husband and two children from Washington, DC. But the cottage had to compete with a new interest, a larger sailing boat called *Puffin*, which he bought in July in the Maritimes and which, with John Levy, he sailed through the reversing falls at Saint John into the Saint John River. Once he had taken over at Rockcliffe, however, he found himself too busy for the old relaxed life. As CO and a member of the Air Force 'brass' he began to experience a blurring of the social and official parts of his life. His time was no longer his own. One weekend in October, for example, he had a Friday evening drink with Trenton friends in the mess, where he later dined. After dinner he went to hear a speaker at the United Services Institute, unable to doze off because he had to thank him! On Saturday morning he was at the airfield at 6:00 a.m. to meet the Minister of Defence. Later he saw friends off, then visited the hospital. After lunch he was back to the airfield to meet the Minister of External Affairs. In the evening he played bridge with the 'younger chaps' in the interest of good relations. Duty finally satisfied, he fled to the cottage and, on impulse, spent the night and most of Sunday there – packing up, befriending a chipmunk and recharging his personal batteries. He needed to: the next week he was busy every day and booked to attend functions every evening.

He found there were so many official occasions for which he needed a female escort that the pressure to get married increased, though he resisted stoutly. At first he had to live in the mess; as an unmarried officer he was denied the CO's house by the housing authorities. After months of bureaucratic stonewalling, the AOC, Brandy Godwin, came to his rescue and authorised Alex to occupy the house. As if by magic, it was suddenly available! He wrote to Agnes about this development, concluding: "There is the easy answer to all the problems – get married. I have no really good reply except that I don't want to, thanks." His mother digested this news, together with her knowledge that Alex continued to see the friendly widow. As far as Agnes knew, that person was still in the dark about Alex's lack of intentions. So, killing two birds with one stone, she decided to accept her son's invitation to be his hostess in his new house. She arrived in January 1955 and stayed for most of the year, spending much time painting and only returning to the banana belt of British Columbia as another eastern winter loomed. By then Alex had only two months left in Ottawa before a posting to Montréal rather ingloriously solved his personal problem for him. Even Agnes had been unable to convey his lack of commitment to the unfortunate lady, who was left most unhappy by the way things turned out.

Provided he could find the time, it was not difficult to arrange his own flying at Rockcliffe. Nevertheless he only managed fifteen hours in the latter half of 1954; in 1955 he totalled seventy-eight hours, mostly tootling about in Beechcraft or Harvards, but including a little mild excitement in an Otter and his introduction to jets. He first flew the army Otter, which was fitted with skis, in January – and delivered it to Petawawa on the 4th of February. He put the nose down a little too far on landing and, as he stepped out of the aircraft, was unaware that any damage had been done. But he had damaged the prop, whose tips had bent back like banana peel, and it was severe enough for the engine to have to be changed! Maybe it counts as another 'life' for Lucky Alex – ranking alongside his dramatic first solo on a Saro Cloud at Calshot in 1937. In any case, his logbook tells us that once the aircraft had been trucked to Rockcliffe and repaired, he took it up for a test flight but that S/L Brown was in the 'driver's seat'. Alex also flew six hours on a T33 Silver Star jet trainer, an aircraft with a maximum sea-level speed of 600 mph or 965 kph.[71] On the occasions that he flew the jet that year he was on dual controls, the first time with G/C Don Miller, a friend and CO of RCAF Uplands. It must have been like learning to fly all over again. Circumstances conspired to prevent him from progressing to his first solo while at Rockcliffe; however, it was high on his personal agenda when he became CO at St Hubert and he returned to the T33 in June 1956. For a pilot who had received his 'A' licence on a Tiger Moth on the 10th of January 1936, the 3rd of July 1956 was a similar red-letter day, when he flew his first jet solo.

There were memorable incidents during his time at Rockcliffe. He heard that his old *Rawalpindi* friend, now Sir John Boothman and Chief of Air Staff, was visiting on RAF business. Alex persuaded Air Marshal Slemon to let him go to Washington on the aircraft that was to bring the great man to Ottawa. "He was, I think, both pleased and surprised to see me!" They had a marvellous opportunity to yarn all the way to Ottawa. Once there, Slemon invited Alex to dine with

Boothman and also to see him off the following day. "So altogether I saw more of Sir John than I had hoped to. He has not changed a great deal – a very dear person, I think." People might have been forgiven for thinking that Alex had an inside track with the CAS but it was really the reward of history, or fortune favouring not only the brave but also the long-in-the-tooth!

If such hobnobbing with the mighty caused him to be treated with extra respect by those he worked with, another incident certainly reinforced that respect. One day Alex walked into the Rockcliffe mess, to be greeted by a scene smacking of indiscipline and lack of respect. Accompanied by loud laughter and whistles, a female officer was standing on the shoulders of a male officer and, assisted by others in the mess, was climbing into the cage of the pseudo-baronial chandelier. The male officer's head was hidden temporarily by the female officer's skirt, as were the rings on his uniform sleeves as he steadied her ankles, when Alex roared at them: "And what the devil do you think YOU`RE doing?" There was a shocked silence. Then the officer's head emerged from the lady's skirt and Alex recognised him as his immediate boss, AVM J. L. Plant! The air vice marshal immediately apologised for leading a riot – to Alex, to the young woman and to the other officers. Alex gained kudos for taking him on but it was really less consequential than it might have appeared; Plant was the officer who had accepted Alex into the RCAF in 1946 and the two men had been on friendly terms ever since. In fact, later on he told Agnes that he had to introduce Plant as guest of honour at a dinner of the Civil Operators' and Pilots' Association, adding "so we shall have fun!"

Alex's move to Station St Hubert, outside Montréal, came at the beginning of December 1955. He was to be there nearly four years, his longest posting in the RCAF. The job was the greatest challenge of his RCAF career, maybe of his whole flying career. It placed him in the path of the hurricane during the most dangerous years of the Cold War, when Soviet bombers armed with hydrogen bombs could threaten North America with destruction, while this continent, unaccustomed to threats, was still developing a system of air defence.

In 1950 he had been posted to Trenton the very week that the Canadian government announced it would be expanding its forces to meet threats in Europe and Korea. From Trenton he had been in the thick of planning and setting up the system of air defence of which he was now the point man. St Hubert, where new construction began in 1951, had opened in December 1954, a year before Alex took over. It included Air Defence Command headquarters, the RCAF's Combat Operations Centre, was Canada's most important air defence base and was definitely the RCAF's 'teeth'. For an officer who liked not to be 'out of things', St Hubert was the place to be.

Alex's command included 423 and 425 Squadrons, until 423 left for Europe in February 1957, to be replaced by 416 Squadron. Each comprised eighteen CF100, twin-engined, all-weather interceptors. St Hubert was also home to 401 and 438 Auxiliary Squadrons which flew Vampires, and the Overseas Ferry Unit which flew F86 Sabres to Europe. A CF100 pilot wrote: "104 Communications Flight located further down the flight line housed the Electronics Warfare Squadron flying C119s. It also supported the C45 Expeditor transport aircraft and even a couple of Harvard trainers. It was an impressive airport to fly from and a busy one at times. It was a great time for aircrew and we seem to have had few restrictions on flying hours."[72]

When Alex arrived all was not well at St Hubert. As a new broom he introduced his own up-front style of leadership. Soon he was personally known to everybody working in his own headquarters. He instituted daily operational briefings with the aircrews, ensuring that they knew as much as he could tell them about the general situation, rather than dribbling out information on a 'need-to-know' basis. He would drop in on ground crews and the ready room at any time that he had a spare fifteen minutes – rather than occasionally and as an inspecting CO. He made himself part of the whole operation, learned to fly the CF100 and then maintained his 'green ticket'.* It helped that he was a workaholic. In April 1956, after four months in the job, he wrote: "We continue phenomenally busy. I always remember that it is much better to be too busy than not to have enough to do. In almost every respect things are improving and my staff are doing a bang-up job. The support I get is wonderful."

For those who did not live through it, it is hard to appreciate the atmosphere of the Cold War and the tension felt by ordinary Canadians and Americans, let alone by the air forces responsible for protecting this enormous land mass. The USSR had first emerged as 'the enemy' as a result of the Berlin Blockade. It became more obvious during the Korean War, when Soviet MIGs had engaged aircraft flown by the United Nations. The hostility worsened when the Soviets exploded their H-Bomb in 1953 and reached a climax in the fall of 1956 when Khrushchev threatened nuclear attack on Britain and France if they did not abort their attack on Egypt. President Eisenhower also vigorously opposed Britain and France's action. Consequently, the North Atlantic Treaty Organisation (NATO) was in disarray, with Prime Minister Lester Pearson using the UN to bridge the gap between Canada's two allies, Britain and the U.S.A. The opportunity for the USSR seemed too good to miss.

Alex's experience of 1939 and 1941 told him that such situations led to war. Two days after the Soviet threats and the day after Russian tanks attacked Budapest he wrote: "The tension in the world is having a reaction among us as you might

---

*A green ticket qualified a pilot to fly jets in non-VFR (visual flight rules) weather.

expect. I think it will be quite remarkable if there is not a flare-up, I'm afraid." A week later, when the Russians had defied a General Assembly demand for them to leave Hungary, Alex went on: "I feel that we should be preparing for war in a realistic manner, and we are in small things – really nothing more than clearing out the odd cobweb. Air Defence is still in the buildup period and that must continue in spite of the world situation. So we do tasks in a way – carry on 'normal-like' as the expression is – and at the same time keep an ear close to the ground for sudden moves and action if need be. All this may sound dramatic – I assure you it is not, but mentioned to explain the strange sort of life one leads today. Each day trying to consider it as normal and do the things which must be done, while in the back of my mind and in the minds of a few others we wonder 'what next'?" Alex and those his age sensed they were witnessing history repeat itself, in the same fatalistic way that veterans of the Great War had viewed events in 1939.

Although the North American Air Defence Command (NORAD) was not officially announced until the 12th of May 1958, the RCAF and the USAAF cooperated informally throughout the 1950s. While at Trenton Alex had escorted U.S. officers on tours of Air Defence Command bases. From the start of his St Hubert command he had U.S. four-star General Partridge in and out of the base; he arrived at the end of January 1957 with a huge staff, was back in June and again in January 1958 – prompting Agnes to wonder who was giving orders to the RCAF. Alex described the situation: Canadian Chief of Air Staff Slemon was in regular communication with Partridge, his opposite number; operational decisions which concerned North America as a whole were reached jointly, in consultation with AVM Wray, Alex's operational boss at AFHQ. Meanwhile, Wray regularly issued operational orders without U.S. participation.

The way that the U.S.A. and Canada cooperated was explained to the local public in the St Hubert Annual Directory and Guide, which Alex first had produced in 1958 to improve RCAF relations with the community. In the Operations Centre, Canada was divided into sectors for air defence; each was controlled by an Air Defence Command station with CF100 squadrons and a network of radar stations. Each of the seven ADC bases kept a number of aircraft in a state of readiness, armed with rockets and ready to scramble. From early on there had been cooperation between the sectors, including U.S. sectors which were similarly organised, with a degree of cross-coverage between sectors. NORAD just formalised a common-sense situation which already existed.

In the 1950s Canadian aircraft were state of the art and the development of the Avro Arrow was intended to keep them that way. The CF100, also built by Avro, had Canadian-built and -designed Orenda engines and gave Canada self-sufficiency in the air for the only time in its history. Its development was pushed by the government in the early 1950s at the expense of the development of an Avro civil jetliner but, while the two military jets were in service or in production, Canada still had the makings of a modern aerospace industry.[73] John Jackaman, a pilot in 425 Squadron, describes in his autobiography how the CF100s compared with their American counterparts:

> "In those early days, the USAF equivalent fighter was the F89 Scorpion. This was no match for the CF100 and we enjoyed showing off our aircraft to our brothers-in-arms to the South. On our big NORAD exercises we were often called upon to intercept the B36, B47 and subsequently the giant B52 ... The CF100 was designed as a long-range fighter and I know that the SAC* pilots were always surprised to see us stay up with them for long periods of time. The F89 had to use afterburner at the higher altitudes and had a limited fuel capacity and usually made just the one pass and returned to base."[74]

The pace of St Hubert took Alex's breath away. As at Trenton in 1950, he was running as soon as he touched the ground. With aircrews on ten minutes' standby and a large number of people, including ground crews, also on duty, he was unable to leave the base on Christmas Day. As he explained: "Life here is quite operational; we have so many people working round the clock, servicing and flying aeroplanes, whose hours of work are long and conditions not good, that I am morally bound to be on the job a lot more, just proving that I know about their conditions and jollying them along. It is demanding and interesting and testing." The atmosphere was actually best summarised in an advertisement which Avro placed on the back cover of the St Hubert Directory. Under the heading "Vigilance Pays" its text ran: "Twenty-four hours a day, the year round, Air Defence Command of the RCAF stands ready – ready to detect and destroy any invader. Its men and women realise to the full the importance of their work, and that constant vigilance is the price of safety."

Jackaman tells an amusing story illustrating the pace at which the station operated:

> "They were fun days in many ways and we often had some good laughs. There were periods when we spent ninety hours a week at work. We were either flying or on standby. Sure, we could sleep and relax but we were still at work and liable to find ourselves at 40,000 feet with just a few minutes' warning. There were times when the only

---

*U.S. Strategic Air Command

contact Joan and I had were with small notes left on the kitchen table of our apartment. I would return from work after she had left for her job and then be back at the Squadron before she arrived back in the late afternoon. On one occasion I had returned late, after night flying, only to be recalled to work in the early hours of the morning. We were subsequently scrambled and, due to awful weather in the Montreal area, were diverted to Wurtsmith AFB in Michigan. To ensure that Joan did not worry I phoned home collect to let her know where I was. When the operator asked her if she would accept a collect call from John Jackaman she replied, 'But he is asleep right beside me'. My response to the operator was, 'I don't know who that John Jackaman is, asleep with my wife, but this one is in Wurtsmith'. At this point Joan woke up fully and realized that I was not beside her and accepted the call. That's her side of the story anyway!"[75]

As the Directory explained, although 24-hour readiness was the main function of St Hubert, there was also a training programme happening all the time. This programme included practice interceptions, simulator training, day flying, night flying, clag flying* – in addition to surprise exercises sprung upon them at any time of the day or year to keep them constantly alert. For example, in January 1956 most of the base had been up all night flying interceptions against American B47 'raiders'; on another occasion, on a day when Alex had fifteen people invited for drinks at 6:30 p.m., a surprise air-raid practice started at 1:30 and continued until 5:30 – leaving him an hour to pick up drinks and food and be home ready to play the gracious host. A week later, on a day when he had flown back from Toronto at 3:00 a.m., a practice Saboteur Alert was sprung on the base, lasting for eight hours and allowing him finally to creep into bed at 4:00 a.m. the following day. In 1957 a surprise exercise was called during the station ball; most of the males and some of the females disappeared on the double to their respective duties and the evening was effectively ruined. Everything was sacrificed for station efficiency; on the 22nd of December 1958 Alex wrote: "Christmas holidays mean nothing to the higher authority around our business of air defence. This afternoon we had a practice with maximum number of fighters and another but less-complicated exercise tomorrow. I only hope they do not take it into their heads to pull some trick on Christmas Day; there is no good reason why they should not, seeing as how that is our business. Trouble is there is no letup at any time."

The only similar posting that Alex had had, with pilots on short-notice standby, was Seletar after the outbreak of the war against Germany – with the difference

---

*Air Force slang for foul-weather flying

that now he was not flying operationally but was responsible for everything that happened and everyone who flew. As in 1939 and 1940, so in the late 1950s, Alex was much respected by younger fliers. He knew from his experience with W/C Lamb – the tiger-hunting signals expert who had commanded 205 Squadron for a while – that an effective CO must be able to fly the squadrons' aircraft. Only thus can a CO know the conditions and difficulties facing his aircrews. For Alex this proficiency was harder to achieve than for most COs, as he had done no operational flying since 1942. So it is not surprising that he was airborne for an hour of night-flying familiarisation in a CF100 four days after arriving at St Hubert. Ten days later he did two hours' daytime familiarisation. That would have to do for a start.

In early July he accompanied the crews to Cold Lake for the annual Air Force exercises and competition. He had already flown a T33 ('T-Bird' in Air Force slang) to and from a course in Biloxi, Mississippi. At Cold Lake he flew more T-Bird hours, doing his first solo on the 3rd of July, as already mentioned. Then, seizing the opportunity of St Hubert aircraft being both available and not operational for a few days, he flew a two-day course on CF100s, including firing a full rocket pod – fifty-eight 2.75 rockets – and a back-seat landing, culminating in two separate one-hour solos on the 5th of July. He was elated. As he told his mother this was "a small ambition I have had for a long time, now realised." For the rest of his command he flew CF100s every few months to keep current and to show his pilots that he was not just a World War II fossil. Meanwhile, he took every opportunity to fly the T-Bird – in the four years of his command he flew 312 T-Bird hours – polishing his jet-aeroplane skills so that his less frequent CF100 forays just felt like borrowing the neighbour's more expensive car!

Jackaman described a crisis situation which illustrates Alex's style of command. It also gives an idea of the knife edge upon which they all lived. Jackaman's aircraft was out of control, he had decided to eject and had gained height in order to do so.

> "We had reached about 10,000 feet, and looking over the side of the cockpit we decided that it looked a long way down and I had second thoughts about departing the aircraft. By then my panic had subsided to the point that I could begin to experiment with power settings and speeds. I discovered that it was possible to control the aircraft at the lower landing speeds without elevator trim. By now though, our problem was compounded by two red lights indicating that I was down to the last few hundred pounds of fuel and that if I didn't get back to the airfield soon, the decision would be taken out of my hands. I set up a glide for base informing the Tower of my intentions.

Things settled down and I could hear Ron saying: 'It's okay Jackie, you can handle it.' By this time it was almost dark, but fortunately the final landing proved to be successful and we taxied in to the line with only three hundred pounds of fuel on one side and nothing registering on the other side. We were met on the flight line by Group Captain Alex Jardine who indicated he was pleased to see us and congratulated us on getting back safely.

"He became somewhat of a role model for Ron and myself. The only time we had seen the previous Station Commander was during inspections of our squadron facilities. They reminded me of my recruit days as this Station Commander seemed more concerned about dust and dirt than our operational capability. With the arrival of Group Captain Jardine there was an immediate change in thrust to our operations. We suddenly found that there were joint Operations Briefings every day and the Group Captain was very much in evidence. On occasion, during a practice scramble, I was surprised to see the Group Captain at the top of the ladder helping me with my straps. It was no surprise during our emergency to find the 'old man' waiting for our safe arrival right on the flight line.

"I rather suspect that the 'Kipper Crew', as we were known on our French-Canadian Squadron, the Alouettes, was a bit of a favourite with the Group Captain. He was still a bachelor then and subsequently got married during our squadron tour. In many ways he was a very traditional senior officer who understood his role and the leadership he could offer to a group of young aircrew. He could be a hard taskmaster and if you goofed he would let you know all about it in no uncertain terms."

Jackaman tells another story about this 'traditional senior officer'.

"... During this period ... I was awarded a permanent commission in the RCAF. PCs were hard to come by ... and very few young pilots were offered them. Group Captain Jardine had often indicated to me that I should purchase a proper Mess Kit for formal dinners. As a young married officer with two children I had little extra money and certainly not enough to buy a formal Air Force Mess Kit. I used to respond that if he gave me a PC, I would purchase a Mess Kit. Well, one morning I was ordered to the Station Commander's Office where a smiling Group Captain told me that he wanted to see a confirmed

order for a Mess Kit from my tailor later in the day. This was how I
found out that I had been offered the opportunity for a long-term
career in the RCAF."[76]

Only a pre-war RAF officer could have worked up a head of steam over mess kit!
Jackaman tells us elsewhere: "I often took my father-in-law to work with me ...
Dad loved to chat with my Station Commander ..."[77] When it came to yarning,
anybody with stories to tell would do: Jackaman's father-in-law or the Duke of
Edinburgh!

As Jackaman confirms, Alex gave top priority to the morale of those serving
under him, giving of himself and his time in an exceptional way. His command
included radar stations, located in strategic corners of eastern Canada, and he
visited them all to pump up the troops. They included one at Lac St Denis, seventy
miles north of Montréal, another a similar distance south of Québec City and a
third in northern Québec to which he travelled by train in January, a trip occupy-
ing the better part of a week. Alex was determined to be approachable; he hated the
barrier to human relationships created by senior rank which he had first noticed at
Trenton. How could he continue to be the most sociable officer in the Air Force if
younger officers, male and female, were going to call him 'sir' when helping to reef
the mainsail? How could he encourage them to treat him as a a human being when
off-duty situations made that appropriate? It was a dilemma which lessened his
enjoyment of service life and which he was constantly trying to resolve. This man
who loved nothing better than 'playing the giddy goat', who naturally befriended
both young and old, found the glass walls of hierarchy a cage. As he wrote to
Agnes, early on at St Hubert: "Well, I must away and be nice to a lot of chaps
and their wives and girlfriends; then tomorrow go and snarl at them during CO's
inspection for not cleaning up their place of work or something."

Some of his attempted solutions were decidedly unmilitary. In June 1956 the
base held its first Families Day; the idea was to provide fun and games for the kids,
but also to allow service families to wander round the base, poke their noses into
doors and see what their Air Force son or daughter, husband or wife did for a
living. It was a team- and morale-building effort and in it Alex saw an opportunity
to humanise the CO. A sign on his Operations Office door invited visitors to step
inside and watch the CO at work. At first, visitors assumed it was a joke and passed
by; but soon the door was pushed open to reveal a ghastly apparition. Behind the
desk was Alex – actually a dummy dressed in Alex's uniform but with a Frankenstein
monster mask! Shrieks of delight from children, who poked the dummy to see if it
was real. Reactions of adults were mixed; some were amused, others shocked to the
point of disbelief. Alex commented: "I expect some thought it was hardly the thing

to do for the CO to make fun of himself in that way. Not dignified, I admit, and hardly the right thing to encourage awe and respect!"

That was the point. He certainly wanted respect for his position, but wanted to earn it by example and not by the rings on his sleeve. To that end he was to be found everywhere on the base at any time of the day or night; it was not remarkable that he should have been on the flight line when Jackaman came in after his near-disaster. If there was an emergency on the base everybody knew he would be there. In September 1956, when he was entertaining Bill Walker (an ex-Java POW) and his wife, news of a crash off the airfield kept Alex busy all night and the Walkers had to see themselves off. In November, when a T33 was missing near Québec City, he left a bridge party to organise the search, was in and out of his office all night and left for Québec in a Beechcraft thirty minutes before dawn to carry out a three-hour search of his own. A month later, when two aircrew were killed in a crash, Alex deserted a visiting Laurens van der Post in order to comfort the widows and start an inquiry into the cause of the crash. It was not just crashes which had his instant attention. After returning home from serving the airmen's Christmas dinner in 1956 he just had time for his own meal – cooked by Jo Forbes and some friends in his house – when he left for a house fire in the married quarters, which kept him busy all afternoon.

The job of CO at St Hubert was extremely satisfying for him. At last he had an important task which absorbed his energies. It was surely the peak of his career and he enjoyed it with all his being. Although he might still hope to be promoted and retained in the service after the retiring age of fifty, nothing short of Chief of Air Staff could ever be so satisfying. The years of preparation were over and finally he could lower his guard concerning women and marriage. From early days in the RAF, whether learning to fly, climbing the RAF ladder, waging war or becoming known in the RCAF, he had felt that marriage would distract him from the job to be done. Without his determination to resist them, Alex's normal impulses might have led him into marriage on any one of a dozen occasions. How many ordinary men could have walked away from Jocelyn Thomas, the belle of the Wittering ball; or Topsy Jenkinson, the star of the *Rawalpindi*, engaged to her policeman but gorgeous and sparkling and available for a whole month; or Lesley Kealley, the Australian belle of the *Ranpura*; or Barbara Murray with whom he spent a week on a yacht off the Malayan coast; or Iona Fraser at the top of Penang hill; or the almost mythical Meg Ireland with whom he fell in love in Mauritius? His brief engagement to Diana Jenkins was a break in the pattern; it occurred during his re-entry into normal life after years in prison camps; once Diana had broken it off his single-mindedness reasserted itself. How many men could have spent so much time with Peg Lewis, have wistfully talked about marrying her, but have allowed her to walk out of his life; or have travelled to Australia to be with Pat Birks, whom he loved, and then have left without discussing the future; or have quickly suppressed his feelings for Joyce, with whom he had a mercurial relationship in Toronto; or have dated Louise, his life-saving nurse, sometimes driving hundreds of miles to be with her, but eventually have allowed her, too, to walk, unchallenged, out of his life.

Now that was all over. To be married would be an advantage, would make him a better CO. His many married officers were best led by a married CO and not by a bachelor. Furthermore, being 'traditional' was a handicap when dealing with women in service roles that Alex considered male by definition. He described a mess dinner in November 1956 as: "More fun than others we have had here because there were no women present. I have tried to get the women officers to realise they should leave about 11:30 and let the men be, but no! they reckon they have the right to stay – and of course they have – so they stay until the last dog is hung. I argue that if they were real ladies they would have the good sense to leave on such occasions." As he was fond of saying, he would never understand women. If so, what he needed was a wife as an 'interpreter'.

The only woman he was seeing socially was Jo Forbes, head of occupational therapy at the Université de Montréal, younger than himself but not inappropriately so. He would drop in on her in Montréal, go to parties with her francophone friends and invite her to be his partner at functions on the base. He had met Jo in 1946 when they sailed with his mother and sister Deirdre, from her Thetis Island home to Nanaimo. He had come across her several times since but, in spite of current proximity, the friendship was unlikely to become anything more.

In this state of mind he took two weeks' leave on the west coast after the 1956 Cold Lake competitions. He stayed with Agnes at Zanders, her Shawnigan cottage, with Ruth at Tofino and then with Ann and Robin in Vancouver. One evening, he and Ann went to *Finian's Rainbow* at the Theatre under the Stars in Stanley Park. The evening was a revelation. Ann had written two or three times earlier that year so she was already well established in his consciousness. Now, all of a sudden, he began to see her in a romantic light where previously she had been the kid cousin who, as a little girl, used to hug his legs and call him "my Alex." However, when his leave was over, although she had become more important to him, he did not discuss his feelings with her before climbing into his T-Bird.

From St Hubert he was euphoric about his holiday and, in an attempt to pacify Agnes about his flying, he described the experience: "Pink clouds, all colours of the rainbow about us at 40,000 feet; it was smooth and swift and we flew at 480 knots, about 550 mph." But he neither wrote to Ann nor mentioned her in his letters to his mother until October. Then he asked Agnes to give his love to Ann: "It is ages since I heard from them and wonder what she is doing now." Ann was obviously interested – why else the earlier correspondence? – but was not allowing herself to be strung along interminably, as other women had been. By not writing she kept the ball in his court – the more Alex wondered, the better! She responded to his indirect inquiry by sending a news clipping about Laurens van der Post. It worked. Alex must have written to her but not mentioned this fact in his letters to Agnes. It transpired that Ann had a job for the winter in the lodge at Sunshine ski-hill in Banff and Alex arranged to go skiing with her there.

On the 22nd of February 1957 he arrived dramatically in Calgary by T-Bird – the flight entered as cross-country training in his log. He drove to Banff with Deirdre and Bob and they stayed in the Timberline Hotel. Then events literally snowballed. On the first day's skiing Ann broke her ankle badly and was lodged in Banff hospital. The next afternoon Alex twisted his knee and gave up skiing for the duration. He devoted himself to full-time hospital visiting and things developed fast. By the 6th of March when he hopped back into his T-Bird, they were engaged.

He explained things to his mother: "I went to Sunshine especially to settle in my mind whether or not I wanted Ann, mainly to be with her on her own for a few days, sort of get used to her away from all the things we are each used to being with. The ankle break was about twenty-four hours ahead of me … The decision was not a sudden one but a growing one and I think that we both felt that me leaving Banff on this occasion without any thoughts or ideas of seeing each other again was close to being not acceptable." The break certainly dealt Ann a strong hand. Going away without making arrangements for the future had been Alex's trademark and had never seemed unacceptable to him before, but Ann's injury had helped to change that. "We both felt …" explains the rest of the story. Finally he had met his match – a woman willing, if not to pop the question, at least to prompt the popping.

What followed was a modern fairy tale. At St Hubert he was smothered in congratulations, "the best thing they had heard in years." Alex was uneasy about how his engagement to a first cousin would be received. He need not have worried; no less a person than Air Marshal Slemon had married a first cousin. He received no flak from his own family – both Ann's mother and his own accepted it as a normal turn of events. Robin, Ann's brother and his boyhood friend, agreed to give away his sister. Only from across the Atlantic was there a murmur of discord; while Daphne, probably enjoying the irony, said nothing, her brother Connie wondered, tongue-in-cheek, whether such a wedding was legal. Would Alex not have to "spend the first few years in jug?"

He was, of course, immediately plunged back into his responsibilities with little time to plan visits to a fiancée encased in plaster. He kept up a flow of letters, thanks to his secretary Margaret, who made sure that he wrote every day. Ann was still in the hospital on the 23rd of March and Alex could stay away no longer. On that day he flew a Beechcraft to Winnipeg, picked up a T-Bird ("my chaps had flown it to Winnipeg for me, bless them!"), parked it in Calgary, borrowed Deirdre's car, changed a wheel in the dark and was reunited with Ann in Banff. They had plenty to talk about, including wedding plans, and little time for the talking. Presumably the matron relaxed her visiting rules, for next day duty called him away again. He drove to Calgary, kissed his sister, jumped into the T-Bird and roared into the sky for a five-hour flight back to St Hubert. He touched down once, at Portage – maybe the justification for the whole trip. In the logbook there was no more pretence that this was a training flight.

It was to be an afternoon wedding at Christchurch Cathedral in Vancouver, followed by a reception at RCAF Jericho but, once back at work, he had no time to think about it. Eighty NATO officers, accompanied by the CAS, were descending upon St Hubert – the only Canadian base they would see. For the next few days alliance business kept him on the hop, culminating in an Army cocktail party for the visitors, at which Alex drank too much and had a hangover to deal with as well. Finally they left. Good news came from Ann: her cast was off but she was still at the hospital in a walking cast.

The knight errant winged back to Calgary on the second weekend in April. This flight was not entered in the log at all; we only know about it because he told Agnes he had done it. Once more he borrowed the car, fetched Ann and they stayed two nights at Deirdre and Bob's house. On Sunday he drove Ann back to Sunshine and returned to Montréal – again, right into the thick of things. This time the COs of the other six all-weather fighter bases descended upon him for their annual conference, with Alex as host. Meanwhile Ann continued to recuperate. At the beginning of May, urgent news from her: "Sunshine is closing – what do I do now?" Alex invited her for a preview of her future life at St Hubert and arranged for her to stay on the base with the MacCallums, the family of the Chief Administrative Officer.

Ann was thrown into the deep end of an Air Force CO's life; by the end of her ten-day stay both knew she could handle it because she had actually enjoyed the chaos. The first weekend set the pace. On Friday they were at a ball until 3:00 a.m. Up with the lark on Saturday, they saw friends off who had stayed the night, then went to an officer's wedding where a good deal of champagne was drunk. After a snooze they were out again, this time to the tri-service NCOs' ball, getting to bed at 3:30 a.m. Sunday offered no respite; at 10:00 a.m. they were at the Battle of the Atlantic ceremony, lunching afterwards at the Navy mess until 3:00 p.m. After that Alex had a date with local noise-complainers whom he showed around the base until 5:00 p.m. Then it was time for dinner at the MacCallums, followed by dessert and coffee somewhere else! Ann stayed, by popular request, for the station ball on the 16th of May. This was the event, mentioned earlier, when a surprise exercise killed the evening. Undeterred, Ann left for Vancouver with only four weeks in which to get ready for their wedding.

Alex was back in the air at the end of the month, arriving by RCAF transport for a 'recce' of Vancouver, for which he was kindly lent a car by Ann's cousin Derek Johnston. He met the Dean of Christchurch who would be marrying them – "a jolly sort of person" Alex thought – and made arrangements for their reception with Don Miller, his best man and CO of RCAF Jericho. After spending time with Aunt Marjory and Ann he disappeared to St Hubert again. He had two weeks to wait, two weeks when his time was, as usual, filled with the business of running the station. No time to think.

Six days before the wedding he set off once more on his silvery steed. This trip to Vancouver took seven and a half hours, justified by visits to Québec and Edmonton. Derek not only lent him a car again, but had arranged for him to spend his last nights of bachelorhood at the Vancouver Club – as comfortable a launching pad for matrimony as the city could offer.

And so the great day, the 15th of June, arrived. Alex entered the cathedral with his best man Don Miller who, having introduced Alex to jet aircraft, was now launching him on matrimony – though this time Alex would be flying solo! Ann, radiant in white, walked up the nave on Robin's arm. The sun shone, the cathedral organ thundered their chosen music, and some of their guests, being Canadian and profoundly unmilitary, probably found the uniforms and the gauntlet of crossed swords – through which the happy pair emerged – a trifle intimidating. No doubt they breathed easier downing champagne and nibblies on the smooth lawns of Jericho. In the distance the snow-capped mountains of Howe Sound shimmered invitingly in summer haze while the breeze stole the words of the speeches. In due course, when Alex had recovered from his shock at *not* being the best man at a wedding and had paused long enough to greet his guests, make a speech, cut the cake and have their picture taken, Ann and he departed in Derek's car, suitably vandalised for the occasion.

They drove to Eagle Crest on Vancouver Island, where they spent their first night. The next day, reluctant to dawdle even on honeymoon, Alex and his new wife were up early and back in Vancouver. At Coal Harbour they made the acquaintance of a well-known ex-rum-runner and his 35-foot launch, *Bonaventure II*. This ship with a shady past Alex had chartered; she would be their home for the next eight days.

After a belated start, their first day's cruise was modest: under Lions' Gate Bridge with the tide, past anchored freighters to Snug Cove on Bowen Island. Next day they were more ambitious, exploring Howe Sound and anchoring for the night at the north end of Gambier Island. The day after that, having explored Gibsons, they sailed past Sechelt to Halfmoon Bay. From there they pottered up the coast, reaching Pender Harbour the following day and then spending two days in Jervis Inlet. Spotting a float plane about to leave, Alex wrote a note to Agnes for the pilot to post. They were enjoying themselves: "I have managed with persuasion of all kinds to keep Ann with her nose to the cook-pot. So we eat well, sleep well, love well and as Ann says, even feel well." On their way back they ran into rough weather but, as ancient mariners, took it in stride. Ann wrote to Agnes, after they had returned Derek's car and were struggling with the uncertainties of RCAF transport: "I still need to pinch myself occasionally to make sure that your dear son is really and truly my husband." And so, by way of Arnprior and the Levys, they returned to St Hubert and a new life as a married CO and a new CO's wife – roles that would take a bit of learning for individuals accustomed to living autonomous lives.

Ann learned quickly that she would have no real life of her own while Alex was CO. It must have been quite a shock, though she knew how he liked to live before she married him. As long as they were in their house or on the base, Alex was liable to be called away at any moment. Rarely could they be sure of a weekend morning or afternoon to themselves, just gardening or puttering round the house. To have fun, she had to get him out of uniform and off the base. Whenever she managed this, the effect was miraculous. Soon after they returned from their honeymoon she managed to get him into shorts, his palm tree shirt with monkeys on it and a silly hat. They had a wonderful day as tourists in Montréal: "He just drops the CO business and becomes a happy lunatic! He keeps everyone, including me, wondering what he'll do next – and laughing!" At other times they went fishing – not one of Alex's usual pursuits, but good for a change. In winter they liked to go to games in the Forum where Ann, surprisingly, loved the fights – "It was great fun and right below where we were sitting!" And sometimes, at her suggestion, they dropped in on girlie shows at the Gay Paree, for a giggle! They could also have fun if they went far enough away: a flip to Ottawa in October 1957 gave Alex the chance to introduce Ann to his friends there.

Otherwise life imposed itself upon them. An example was the last week in October 1957: Monday, a dinner dance put on by Canadair; Tuesday, a guest for dinner; Wednesday, the usual tea party, then out with a guest; Thursday, a dinner party for two couples; Friday, the station Halloween dance, dressed as newlyweds; Saturday, to the Alouettes' game with the owner of the Club, then to the annual Polish RCAF/RAF ball and to bed at 2:00 a.m.; Sunday, chapel at 10:30, then visiting neighbours; the afternoon to themselves but in the evening Alex worked until 9:00 p.m.

Somehow, neither of them went mad and both kept a sense of humour. Alex waged a losing battle trying to protect the things he loved dearly – "old shoes and socks and underwear and such." He became indignant when guests unerringly detected a 'woman's touch' in the house – he claimed it was "just the cluttered-up appearance that prevails." Ann took some flak for her 'stone pie' – Alex's name for greengage pie – "The cook doesn't like it if you don't eat the gooey stuff around the stones! She is now looking rather cross at me and I shall have to feed her brandy and soda."

For her part Ann managed not to take the 'CO stuff' too seriously. When Alex was off on a four-day visit to ADC bases, flying himself in his T-Bird, Ann commented: "What fun Alex had, flitting about the country – he was so pleased with the whole trip." When Connie came to Montréal – he was then Sir Hugh and a big wheel in the RAF – Ann and her mother, who was visiting, lunched with him and Alex. Afterwards she took her mother shopping while, as she said, "the boys went off on their own business!" In one letter she gave a blow-by-blow description of home life with Alex: "He is working in his den – great gusty sighs coming out of there now, which probably means he is getting ready to give it up – now coughs – and here he is in person!" One day Alex looked at a photograph of himself and was horrified by the amount of white hair in his moustache, so he shaved it off. But humour has its limits. Ann kept looking oddly at him; that night she was not sure whether to get into bed with him, because he looked different. Within a week the moustache was back.

As Ann was to find out, Alex's absorption in his job was not just a bachelor's foible; he worked equally hard after they were married and, indeed, included her on the management team! Six weeks after their honeymoon, Ann found herself writing letters in their car at the foot of Mont Ste Hilaire; the mountain was on fire and Alex had spent half the night with a team of fifty airmen trying to bring it under control. But fire-duty was not really what Alex had in mind for her. Quite soon, he encouraged her to start her Wednesday teas which were to become a St Hubert institution. Ann would invite half a dozen officers' wives and Alex would then ask their husbands to pick them up and stay for a drink. This turned out to be the magic bullet that had eluded him – at one stroke he was able to meet and yarn with a manageable number of younger officers, most of whom he would have known only formally until then; at the same time their wives were amazed at how nice Ann was ("Do they think I would marry a dragon!?"); and many of them, who did not know the others, were grateful for this relaxed opportunity to widen their circle of friends. Over the months Alex met most of his officers in this way and word got around that the event was fun, especially the irreverent attitude that his new wife took to the group captain.

She certainly approached her contribution lightheartedly, talking of "telephoning the victims for next week" but learning to be a CO's wife was not problem-free. For example, Alex would just turn up for dinner with visiting officers. One Wednesday, early in their marriage, forgetting that Ann would be exhausted after her tea, he produced a wandering group captain for dinner; so they went out. On another occasion Ann wrote that Alex was "boozing at some male do he *had* to go to" and so she ate supper on her own. "Eventually he arrived home with two pals and a dog – naturally the dog was sick on the carpet – was I mad!" Then she and Alex, with the two pals and the empty dog, went to a party. Hardly surprisingly, Alex reported that "Ann was still a block of ice." She got over it and wrote: "How we have laughed! The owner of the dog was so upset – quite properly." Ann had her revenge the following night when: "One of Alex's old girlfriends, Betty Page, came for dinner; poor Alex, he was not very happy about it at first but I enjoyed it and really it went quite happily."

Alex not only attended all large social events at the base, especially all-ranks dances and events in the NCOs' mess, but also inaugurated 'Meet your Boss' night at the Corporals' Club, when he would spend hours yarning with the best of them. He had no need to put up a front of friendliness; he loved the human contact and came away invigorated. NCOs were crucial to morale; mostly ground crew, they tended to be overshadowed by the glamour boys of the aircrews but their jobs were equally important. Every Christmas Day saw Alex, in chef's white hat and coverall, carving turkeys for the troops with a skill developed over twenty years in messes around the world.

Alex also saw his job as a public relations platform for the Air Force. Inward-looking Québec ignored the military. Although Québécois had joined the forces in two world wars, conscription had caused bitterness and the services were still associated with old imperial wrongs. Alex was successful in changing that, at least locally. He did it by opening the base to its neighbours and rolling out the red carpet for local and provincial officials. Twice, in May 1956, he invited people who had complained about jet engine noise onto the base. Noise had increased since the opening of the ADC base and was the result of the replacement of single-engined by twin-engined aircraft and the twenty-four-hour nature of air defence. Many people were unaware of the reasons for the buildup! Few realised that themselves were being protected. Nothing convinced them more quickly than being taken into the ready room, having the air defence system explained and seeing how hard the ground crews were working to turn the aircraft around. Earlier he had briefed local mayors, fire chiefs and police chiefs, with similar results.

It was the start of a good relationship: on Air Force Day, 1956, 40,000 people came to St Hubert. In February 1957 and in subsequent years Alex invited the mayor and council of St Hubert to the all-ranks dance; they came and enjoyed themselves and Alex found that he got on well with the mayor. He welcomed the Lieutenant-Governor of Québec with a 100-man honour guard, showed him around and so impressed him that the great man promised Alex a silver medal with an image of himself upon it! "So gradually I am building up an interest in the RCAF in Québec, making them conscious of us and endeavouring to break down a natural barrier of antipathy to us," he told Agnes.

He made himself available for all manner of local events. On Remembrance Day 1957 he took the salute at parades held in Longueuil, St Hubert and St Lambert, as well as at the parade on the base. In December he answered, in English, questions put to him in French on a local TV channel. May 1958 saw Alex acting as Reviewing Officer at the graduation of Air Cadets at Laval College. He was modest about the impact of this speech – spoken in English to a French-speaking audience – and of the few words he did say in French "probably the pronunciation was so bad no-one would understand them either!"

Modest he may have been, but after the air show put on by his station for Air Force Day in 1959 he received an astonishing letter from the mayor, parts of which read:

> "... we have been deeply impressed by the Air Show and we firmly
> believe that the demonstrations of Air Power have the good effect to
> create in the minds of Canadian citizens a feeling of pride when they
> realise all that is done to protect them against enemy attack. Our
> salutations and thanks to all your officers who were very kind to us,
> and especially and more particularly our thanks and salutations to a
> very gracious Lady, Mrs. Jardine, lovely wife of a great and worthy
> Captain. To her and to you, Captain Jardine, our deepest respects,
> because you have already won the hearts of all those who had the
> privilege to know and meet you and all those who have learned about
> your successful accomplishments ..."

Alex sent his mother a copy of the letter with the comment: "Ann and I use it to boost our morale if it should get low!" And well they might; in spite of the letter's Gilbertian overtones, its subtext is simply 'mission accomplished!'

In January 1958 the doctor confirmed that Ann was pregnant. They had a few final flings before the baby arrived. In February they took a short holiday in Nassau; it was, of course, the coolest February for thirty years in that island paradise but they enjoyed their freedom in the sun and the wind, though the water was cold. In April they went to Ottawa for an old-style weekend in John Levy's flat, visiting endless old friends of Alex's and going for long walks. On the 8th of June Ann's mother moved in and two days later, as Alex was about to eat breakfast, Ann asked him to drive her to the hospital. Taking no chances, Alex flagged down a cop and asked him to lead the way – which he did, with siren and flashing lights, as far as the river. There his bailiwick ended and Alex was on his own, in Montréal's rush-hour traffic. At the hospital Ann was admitted to the labour room immediately, while Alex and Aunty Marjory, anticipating a long wait, resumed their interrupted breakfast in the cafeteria. He was contentedly wiping egg from his moustache at 10:15 when he heard that the doctor wished to see him. In his own words: "I duly reported, sort of ambling up the stairs, and his first remark was, 'Well, you are still the boss!' The doctor had not experienced quite such a rapid delivery before – 'just like a sixteen-year-old girl having her fourth' was his remark." Louisa weighed 5 lb. 9 oz.

They had another year at St Hubert after Louisa was born. While she was very small they took her to British Columbia to see her other grandmother, whose four-teenth grandchild she was. In September, refusing to allow this small person to cramp their lifestyle, the three of them toured the Maritimes in a camper. Back in Montréal, Ann was able to resume her role as CO's wife, including entertaining and evenings out, by adding a maid/helper to their household. Things went well and Ann, now and then, would be out at some wives' event, leaving Alex at home – which he did not enjoy very much.

Alex knew he would be posted away from St Hubert in 1959 and, as things turned out, he was ready for the change. His tenure had coincided with the Cold War glory days of the RCAF, when morale was at a peak and the future still held the promise of the C105 Avro Arrow and, with it, Canada's continued air defence self-sufficiency. The first cloud in this sky had appeared on the 23rd of September 1958, with the announcement by Mr Diefenbaker that: "In view of the introduc-tion of missiles [Bomarcs] into the Air Defence system ... the government has decided that it would not be advisable at this time to put the C105 into produc-tion." A hope remained: "Because of the tense international situation," he ordered the continuation of the Arrow project for the time being and promised a spring review of the decision.[78]

In February 1959 this hope was dashed when the government announced the cancellation of the Arrow. The military aviation industry's collapse, following Avro's firing of 14,000 employees, was not so much a 'crime' of the Diefenbaker govern-ment as it was a rebuke to the nationalist enthusiasm of Air Force officers and government officials. Opinions had changed since Canada, for the first time, had found herself in the front line of the Cold War. What they were asking for – a continued large military and an aviation industry which could compete with the traditional powers – was not something that Canadian taxpayers would pay for, once they had recovered from their initial fright. Alex was dejected at the news: "As you can imagine, it was to be the replacement for the CF100 we have here, so everyone is a little depressed about the future of the manned interceptor in Canada. These sort of things do help generate feelings of confidence and hope for the future. All we can do right now is carry on and hope that something will come up to solve these problems." In fact, with the government electing to buy Bomarc missiles as replacements, things soon got worse. The Conservatives were to make such a mess of air defence that the RCAF was humiliated by its lack of equipment in the early 1960s. For Alex it was time to go. One month after the news about the Arrow he discovered he was to be posted somewhere as an air and military attaché. This time he was ready; both he and Ann were pleased and excited. They waited impatiently to find out where and when.

He was to have a last hurrah at St Hubert. Just before the Arrow announcement Alex was appointed to be the military member in charge of the Queen's visit when she came to open the Saint Lawrence Seaway with President Eisenhower on the 26th of June. Both the Queen and the President were to come to St Hubert, from which the visit to the Seaway would begin and to which the President would return to fly home. This involved planning meetings in the spring and a trip to Washington concerning the President's visit. The day before the Seaway opening two things rocked the boat a little: Alex heard that his attaché posting would be to Prague, for which he would have to learn Russian; and that evening, the 25th of June, he and Ann went to Mayor Jean Drapeau's Ball for the Queen, at which 2,000 invited quests at one point seemed likely to mob the royal party. Life seemed a little out of control.

The big day began with a telephone call: "This is the White House calling; may I speak to Group Captain Jardine?" It was 7:00 a.m. and the group captain was in the shower. Wrapped in a towel, he heard a male voice ask what the weather was like. He described the clouds he could see through the window but the fellow wanted a Met. report, so he transferred him to the weather office. Once dressed, he walked to that office himself, in a shower of rain, to make the decision between the wet or the dry programme. Feeling a bit like Eisenhower himself before D-Day, he plumped for dry. It was going to be, he told himself, definitely the most exciting and historic day of his life. Or so it seemed at the time. Anyway, he had guessed right about the weather.

At 9:45 a.m. he and Ann were in the tent, a great white whale erected for the occasion near the flight line. Punctual to the second the royal motorcade arrived from *Britannia*, which was moored somewhere on the river. Alex greeted the Queen and the Duke of Edinburgh, introduced Ann and ushered the royal party into the tent. As usual, they both felt immediately at their ease in the Queen's presence. The Duke prattled about aircraft while the AOC, Air Marshal Slemon, and his wife, then Prime Minister Diefenbaker and Mrs Diefenbaker came into the tent to meet the Queen. Ann noticed that Dief's face had quite a twitch. There was a general mingling while they waited for the Americans; Ann had fun chatting to the Countess of Euston, a member of the Queen's household, and then to Mrs Diefenbaker.

Conversation was made difficult by the music of the RCAF band which was playing outside the tent, and by the sounds of approaching jet aircraft. Alex reminded the Queen of her visit to Trenton when she was still a Princess and he the PMC; he was a bit crestfallen when she had little memory of the occasion. The sun was now beating down on the tent, which was becoming unpleasantly hot. So, Alex had one wall of the tent removed and was about to remove another when the Queen stopped him – she thought that people seated on the nearby bleachers would stare in. In the circumstances, Alex graciously acquiesced! He was uncharacteristically flustered by the incident, however, and at one point called the Queen 'sir' by mistake. He calmed himself by talking to the Duke about aircraft and canals and ships and other comforting male trivia.

Several American aircraft arrived. From them emerged the press, various VIPs and Secretary of State Christian Herter. Alex made the necessary introductions to the Queen and the Duke. This was no sooner done than the President himself landed in *Columbine*, his more poetic version of the *Airforce One* favoured by his successors. Conversation was drowned by the thunder of guns firing a salute and the Queen and Mr Diefenbaker walked out into the sunshine to greet the President and Mrs Eisenhower as they stepped onto Canadian soil. The President inspected the Guard of Honour with Alex beside him; then everybody retreated to the shade of the tent while Alex ushered the American VIPs, then the President and First Lady, into cars. Mamie Eisenhower soared in Alex's estimation; of the four non-Canadian VIPs, she was easily the most relaxed and willing to joke and was obviously enjoying herself. "She struck me as a dear," he told Agnes. The Americans set off for the Seaway, followed exactly ten minutes later by the royal motorcade.

Everything had gone without a hitch. For the time being Alex and Ann were off the hook and went home to watch the Seaway opening on television. It had turned into a hot and humid afternoon and the elegant group captain stripped to his underwear and sprawled in front of the TV with a beer. They had some hours of downtime before Ann was scheduled to give tea to the President's social secretary, a Mrs MacCaffree, who was to create their only problems. First she was late for Ann's tea party – too late if she was to be on time for the President's return. Then she wanted to make a long-distance phone call, so Alex offered her his office phone, on which she talked to a friend in Toronto for twenty minutes. Alex went over to the tent to await Ike and finally had to send for her as the President was approaching. When the Eisenhowers stepped from their helicopter any worries that Alex might have had disappeared. He told Agnes: "My, the President was complimentary and they, he and she, were really very sweet!" The RCAF pipe band were playing their hearts out and, to the strains of "Will ye no come back again?", the Americans boarded their various aircraft and were gone.

It had been a great day and Alex, still glowing from the President's kind words, headed for the mess, fully intending to "get tight." There was a certain amount of backslapping and he downed a couple of Scotches, but realised, to his chagrin, that he was too wound up to become tight even if he swallowed a gallon of the stuff. So off home he went, to eat dinner and write to Agnes about it all while it was fresh in his mind. The events of the day, his new marriage and child and now this Russian business were swimming around in a genial, alcoholic blur in his head. "Dear Mum," he concluded, "what sort of a son did you bring into the world? At forty-five or so having to learn a strange tongue, with a cousin for a wife what he loves very much, a daughter that is more than a daughter, she is a joy; a greeter of Queens and Princes and Presidents and First Ladies, Secretaries of State and others of note!"

They had another month of normal chaos at St Hubert, during which they spent a day with their mutual cousin Connie, over for Canada Day as head of the RAF. Then, after a long holiday on the west coast, Alex handed over St Hubert at the end of August. Tears were shed at various ceremonies and parties but Alex had good memories and no regrets. He had had his opportunity and had made the most of it. It was somebody else's turn to sharpen Canada's teeth.

Alex playing a drunk in amateur theatre at Trenton, 1951. He was anchored to the floor by special shoes, allowing him to lean at this angle!

Damaged prop of an Army Otter – the only damage that Alex ever did to an aircraft, Petawawa, 4 Feb 1955.

Group Captain Alex Jardine, CO
at RCAF St Hubert, 1956, aged 42.

The 'CO' at work
for the June 1956
Families Day at
St Hubert.

A flight of four CF100s of 413 Squadron at St Hubert, 1955.

PM Diefenbaker greets President Eisenhower at St Hubert, 26 June 1959, under the watchful supervision of the base commander. The occasion was the official opening of the St Lawrence Seaway.

Coming out of the cathedral, 15 June 1957.   Ann on her wedding day, 15 June 1957.

Wedding day photograph, 15 June 1957. Back (l to r): 'Bee' Johnston, Derek Johnston, *Theo, June,* Robin Johnston, Ann, Alex, Marjory Johnston, Mary Johnston, Bill White. Front (l to r): Bob Mills, *Deirdre* Mills, *Ruth* White, *Agnes Jardine, Marjorie,* Evelyn Johnston, Val Johnston. (Alex's sisters and mother *in italics.*)

"We flew the CL-41R on 1 October 1963".

Penhold, summer 1964. The CO about to get his hat wet; "what we do for morale!"

Alex with Louisa and Marjory on *Wild Goose*, summer 1965.

Alex visiting locals as President of the RCAFA, 1967-69.

1999:Ursula Kasting, Alex, John Jackaman.

16

RELUCTANT DIPLOMAT

1959–1963

In which Alex learns Russian to become Canada's Air and Military Attaché in Prague;
and in which he experiences the dreary frustrations of a Cold War diplomat's life.

"President Novotny thinks Canadian chickens are good!"

In August 1959 the three Jardines moved into an apartment at 39 Mark Avenue, Eastview, Ottawa. Neither Alex nor Ann had illusions about the year ahead. Ann had scored low on a language-learning aptitude test, but Alex had been so low that, were he not assigned to a diplomatic post, he would not have been accepted for the course. They realised he would have to work extremely hard and would need all his time for studying. Consequently, Ann unselfishly elected to devote herself to child care and housework, instead of sharing these duties – their original plan.

His classmates at the language school were highly educated young linguists, eager to be Russian translators. By contrast, as he was to observe in a memo to AFHQ a year later, a forty-six-year-old with little knowledge of formal grammar and no recent familiarity with another language, apart from a few words in speeches, was not well suited to the immediate task. His selection for the posting may have owed itself to the résumé he had created when seeking admission to the RCAF. This had mentioned his POW classes in Mandarin and Malay, but an interview would have shown that little had stayed with him. Nevertheless, in the fall of 1959, he decided to tough it out.

The Russian classes were as difficult as anticipated; after three weeks he could see "no bright light to indicate real hope of mastering it." He soon became frustrated, finding his task daily harder, as he fell farther behind. Three hours' homework nightly made him comment: "It is not much of a life and nothing to relieve the boredom – no responsibilities, thus no spice to life." Stoically, he

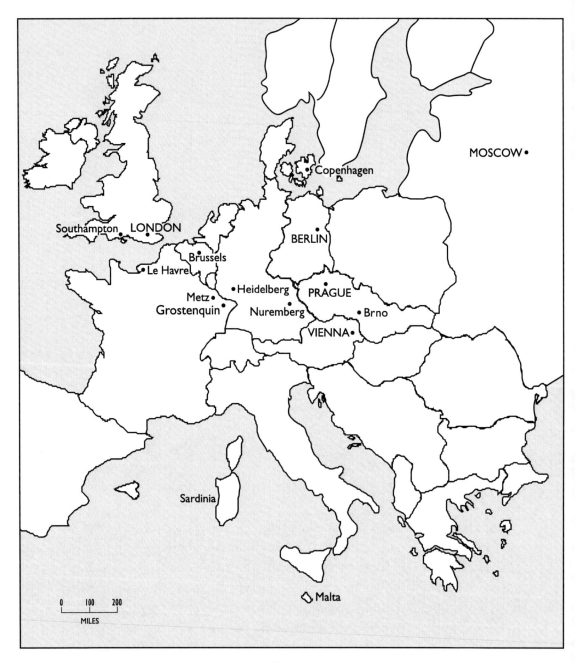

Europe

declared: "This is our year of trial." Had he but realised it, his life had become distinctly, well ... yes, Russian in its narrowness, an illusion borne out by their TV catching fire on two occasions. The gloom was lightened a little when he received a letter in mid-October from G/C Houle, his successor at St Hubert. "It would have done your heart good [in a recent two-day exercise] to watch the boys leap into the air for 101 sorties with only four aborts. St Hubert, as usual, outdid all the other stations … it indicates the state which Station St Hubert was at, at the end of August." It was satisfying to hear, but nostalgia would not solve current problems.

By late October he brought up reinforcements in the form of Captain Franks, a Russian-speaking ex-naval officer, who gave him conversational lessons. November dragged into December, still with no 'Aha!' experience to brighten his gloom. The moment of truth arrived with the Christmas exams, for which his classmates prepared diligently, but which were so far over Alex's head as to be irrelevant. At school he plugged along on his own, with occasional help from the teacher, but he had been abandoned by the class. He felt so discouraged that he found it impossible to make himself study over the Christmas break, devoting what time he had between social engagements to studying for his green ticket.

In the New Year the class formed a choir to sing Russian songs and went to watch plays in Russian. The plays were not a great success – while Alex could recognise about one word in ten, Ann understood none – but the singing went well. The choir director gave her instructions entirely in Russian with which Alex coped by keeping a close eye on his fellow choristers. "That's the way the Russian progresses," he commented. "I manage to understand some, some of the time." Once he had learned his lines he could sing probably better than his fellows, accustomed as he was to belting out Anglican hymns on a weekly basis. Consequently he was able to report, after they had sung in an Orthodox church, that: "One of our songs brought tears to the eyes of some of the people in the audience."

As spring rolled around, the Jardine family saw the Russian language as their cross. Alex soliloquised: "Many's the day I would gladly say to the authorities: 'sorry chaps, you have the wrong person doing this – I quit!' " However, he told himself, "reason reminds me that the RCAF has been jolly good to me and if I can't take this kind of a setback then they quite fairly can say I'm not playing the game. Besides, I don't think I was ever actually beaten and I never actually quit." Thus reinforced, he soldiered on, making unspectacular progress, bypassing another set of exams and continuing to practice his Russian well after the end of the course in May. He had relieved his own boredom in the last month of school by dressing up in a blue dress for his role in a prepared dialogue in front of the class. The instructor was not amused but Alex was received with "great howls of joy and laughter" by the students – causing other classes to wonder what on earth was going on. He was to set off for Czechoslovakia with the ability to talk and understand Russian if he had to, but with no real fluency. Considering his starting point it was quite an achievement.

Alex kept up his flying while he was in Ottawa. It was one of the things which kept him sane while he struggled with an intractable tongue. He flew forty-five

times in ten months from Rockcliffe, as many flights as he had had in the previous
year at St Hubert. In the fall he tried to fly in the evenings, as a way of blowing the
language cobwebs away. During the winter, when he had to pick his weather, he
flew at least once a week, usually in a T-Bird.

For a recently married ex-bachelor of forty-six, with no previous experience,
family life in a small apartment was an equal challenge during an Ottawa winter.
The 6th of October 1959 was a day when his difficulties suddenly increased: Louisa
took her first steps and the doctor confirmed that Ann was pregnant again. Ann
coped heroically through the winter, keeping Louisa out of her father's hair during
homework time, while Alex was the indulgent dad on weekends. His life did not
spin out of control until May, when Ann went into hospital, Marjory was born and
Ann remained in hospital for a hernia operation – ten days during which Alex and
Louisa were keeping house together.

Fortunately language school was finished. Alex fed, dressed, changed and amused
Louisa, now mobile and into everything. He discovered that time was precious
when she was sleeping; he would sneak out of bed early and tiptoe around while he
got things done. Letters had to be written standing up to avoid having to share
the paper. Things were impossible to plan for; as well as juggling babysitters and
hospital visits, he had to drop everything to fly to St Hubert for poor Wally Wurtele's
funeral, all in the same week that the car's fuel pump died. When Ann came home
with Marjory, Alex had a new trick to learn – running interference, as Louisa was "a
bit tough on the baby." They survived; Ann recovered quickly and took charge of
her small family. It was smooth sailing again until the beginning of July, when
Louisa picked up measles. This complicated their final month in Canada but
everybody was well again when they boarded the Cunarder *Sylvania* for the trip to
France and England.

They were travelling first class, had two cabins, stewardesses to look after the
children, nurseries available and both parents were looking forward to five days'
rest. Alex was right when he wrote: "Ann needs a rest badly – I think I do too!"
Nevertheless, in spite of his own exhaustion, Alex felt happier, with his wife and
small family, than he had felt in the five or six years before his marriage to Ann.
And true to previous form he was to spend all his shipboard time with the woman
of his choice!

The *Sylvania* docked first at Le Havre in Normandy. They watched as their
twenty pieces of luggage, marked "Not Wanted on Voyage," some of them large
crates, were unloaded onto the quay; at least they had got this far and French
railways should manage to deliver them to Prague by the time they arrived themselves. Then across the channel and into Southampton Water, passing close by
Calshot – Alex's point of departure all those years ago – the castle frowning squatly

on its headland, bereft, now, of its brood of flying boats. The boat train delivered them to London and the Vanderbilt Hotel. It was a hopeless place for children so they moved to the Princes Lodge Hotel which was a little better.

They spent some days in London before Alex left. They dined with Mary Johnston at the English Speaking Union, which Alex described, rather poetically, as: "Old, old with old, old people in it." He was disappointed by London which he had found so fast-paced in 1945. Now, except for the reckless speed of taxis and buses, everything appeared to happen slowly. Socialism and soot had taken off the gloss – London no longer seemed the centre of the world as it had in his youth. They visited Connie and Helen who were as hospitable as ever. Helen, a great lover of babies, just took over the little ones when they arrived. Daphne was there too, "looking and being as sweet as ever." She stayed for dinner and a long evening's chat among the four first cousins, each of whom Alex loved dearly though in different ways. He, maybe alone of the four, must have appreciated the sweet irony of the hand that life had dealt him.

Once sure that Ann and the babes could manage, Alex flew to Prague. Ann would stay in London among friends until he sent her word that Prague was ready for them. To his dismay, he found the attaché's house in shambles, with several rooms damaged by burst pipes, so he moved into the Esplanade Hotel until repairs were made. In spite of its faded glory, this hotel was far more comfortable than the Princes Lodge. Consequently, as soon as he had extracted the children's cots from the luggage he asked Ann to come to Prague, as repairs to the house would take ages. She had a horrible flight, with two children to look after on her own, but they soon made themselves at home in the Esplanade, with some of their own belongings.

Louisa adapted quickly to hotel life, becoming *persona grata* in the hotel kitchen. Alex wrote: "Whenever left alone for a moment near the dining room here, Louisa makes a beeline for the bread rolls and always succeeds in grabbing one. It is awful for the poor people at the table, this small human flea dashing in at the rate of knots, the tiny hand suddenly shooting out from under the table and, hey presto, the chap's bun has gone!" At first she was the only member of the family with Czech friends. While Alex wrestled with bureaucrats about house repairs, the while "possessing his soul in patience," which he had decided was the most necessary virtue in Prague, Ann and Louisa got to know Mary and Dagmar, the Czech women who were the cleaning staff at the house. In spite of the language barrier, they communicated by gestures and through the medium of Louisa, who became an instant friend to both. When Ann took her small daughter to a local park, Louisa started playing with Czech children without a backward glance. She made her parents look like real stick-in-the-muds!

First impressions of their new country were mixed. Ann found that ordinary people were not afraid to speak to her and that a surprising number had a smattering of English. However, everywhere there were signs of authoritarianism. In the hotel, for example, although they were kind to the children and willing to meet requests for food at odd hours, the elevator would only take guests up; the operator could not be persuaded to take one down, even if she was carrying a baby! The streets were swept by old ladies with handcarts and threadbare brooms, dressed in what Ann called "the most dreadful outfits." Only in Moscow could you see similarly wretched 'babushkas'. They took a drive to see fall countryside and found that they were followed, at a discreet distance, by security police, the STB.

Shops in Prague contained goods but shopping was inconvenient and time-consuming, with long lines common. This beautiful old city, which had largely escaped the fate of German cities in the war and which was full of palaces and mediaeval streets, was not at all convenient for a western family with children. Early in their stay they decided to rely on the American PX in Nuremberg for their needs. It became a regular feature of life to make the four- or five-hour drive. There they filled the car with groceries (including milk), drinks for parties and whatever else they needed. They also went there to have cars serviced or to visit the dentist or the doctor. On any such trip they would spend the night in the U.S. Army hotel before driving back. In addition, atmospheric pollution had made Prague almost unlivable: the air was grey with smoke from burning coal, used both for home heating and industry, as well as from choking vehicle exhaust. Here white shirts were dirty in hours, combs became disgusting and hair had to be washed three times a week at a time when such frequency was considered dangerous!

However, there were nice surprises. The city's zoo was one of these and a certain way of entertaining the children, who delighted particularly in the polar bears. In their first June they happened upon a brass band playing outside a pub quite close to their house. A crowd of people, many of them tipsy, were singing folk songs. They sat down and ordered beers for themselves; the scene sounds like one from a Peter Breughel painting and decidely uncommunist but, as their beer was watery, they did not stay long. There were other scenes which seemed to belong to bygone days. In Slovakia, later in their tour, they came across farmers, men and women, working in traditional costumes and it was common to be brought to a halt on even the busiest road by cows. Ann had "never seen so many cows in her life" and was also amazed by the numbers of geese being herded. Communism was also held at arms' length by traditional customs. Before Christmas, four children dressed as Saint Nicholas, an angel and two devils, came to the door and gave them food presents for their two children – this was *Svaty Mikulas* night. And on All Saints' Day they noticed that in Slovakia the cemeteries had chrysanthemums and candles on each grave. It was also a silent and tragic country with the occasional horror.

Alex found himself one day at Lidice, where Nazis had killed the villagers as a reprisal, then erased their village from the map. Ann visited a synagogue (used just once a year as only 2,000 Jews remained), which served as a memorial to the Jews murdered by the Nazis. "The sole decoration on the walls is the names and birth dates of these 72,000 – every wall is covered; it is positively eerie and as cold as death in there." After living there for two years Alex became indignant about the condition of the Czechs and their capital – comparing it with Nuremberg in West Germany: "The Czechs, thanks to a warped economy directed by warped men, have so little it is disgraceful and a tragedy."

As time went by they became quite isolated from Czech people. Casual chatter in the park did not translate into willingness to visit the house. One reason was the fact that Alex, thanks to a decision of his superiors and against his own protests, had spent eight months learning Russian, a foreign language to adult Czechs, though taught in schools since 1948. That made it difficult to communicate with Mary and Dagmar, with the gardener and with the only two couples whom they met socially.

The first of these were a retired avocat (lawyer) and his artist wife with whom they sat à quatre at a Yugoslav reception. Dressed in their best and apparently alone, they spoke a little English, were extremely hungry and ate an enormous quantity, wrapping up and carrying away what they had no room for. They were great drinkers, too, and brought to the table bottles of anything they could find, so that their conversation was punctuated by the clinking of glasses before every mouthful. The woman was keen to come and give Ann painting lessons but, as Alex suspected would happen, they never heard from them again.

The other couple they met at the Canadian ambassador's house; the man was a trade union official who had studied in Sheffield, England. Alex liked them but when Ann took the children to tea at their house, she felt uncomfortable with them. "I don't think I like them," she wrote; "too bad since they are the only Czechs brave enough to ask us – perhaps that is why I don't feel comfy with them." In spite of the man's job, they lived in a tiny apartment with various members of their extended families. Louisa was particularly unimpressed by their unheated bathroom; the coldness of the toilet seat made her want to go home at once.

After six weeks in the hotel they finally got the workmen out of their house. The children were thrilled. Alex complained bitterly because an excited Louisa woke at 5:00 a.m. for breakfast – "It's not fair on old parents!" It was a large house in a large garden, in a suburb of the city where the air was cleaner. They had a coke-burning furnace; fuel deliveries, though sometimes short, were made regularly, even when the rest of the city was suffering terrible shortages. There was also a pool and one of Alex's first tasks was to make and fit a chicken-wire contraption to prevent Louisa from falling in when nobody was with her. A mysterious old lady lived in the basement and came with the house! Nobody seemed to know who she was, what she did or why she lived there. Every now and then she could be seen flitting into the house and down the staircase like a ghost, but otherwise they hardly realised she was there.

Mary and Dagmar worked for Ann in the house; in spite of the language problem things were soon working out fine. When Frau Mary told her she was going to "*gerwashen*" the floor, it was not hard to catch her meaning. Dagmar came to work now and then but Mary came daily and was the linchpin of the household, becoming a firm ally of the children, whose runny noses she would absent-mindedly wipe with the washing-up towel. She introduced Ann to a custom that had 'always been done': the locking of all the doors off the entrance hall at night. Ann had a bunch of keys like those of a mediaeval castellan and the last one to bed locked up.

It was a marvellous house for entertaining, which they had to do quite often in the surreal society in which they now moved. For Alex's new job, as Air and Military Attaché, was about as far from the mess-crawling milieu that he loved as it was possible to be. Long before there had been a hint of his diplomatic posting he and the 'good heads' among his RCAF friends had guffawed over a pint about the 'attaché types', officers who actively pursued desk jobs and attaché postings and who seemed to prefer a diplomatic cocktail party to an air-base mess night. Now he was in that milieu and quickly found that he did not enjoy it.

As soon as they were both in Prague, Alex and Ann attended a Rumanian reception to celebrate Rumania's National Day. They shook hands with their hosts when they arrived, collected a drink and surveyed the company. The crowd was mainly Czech, uniformed or suited, and presumably connected to government. There were also Russians in uniform and a sprinkling of western diplomats and uniformed attachés. Nobody rushed up to them; when they walked around they heard conversation in Czech, a language that was no easier to understand here than in the hotel. They talked to some of the attachés in English but soon tired of that and went home.

It was an appropriate introduction to three years of the same. There had to be more to the job than drinking bad champagne and Alex had high hopes when he went off on his first week-long tour around the country, in company with the U.S. military attaché, a Lt/Col Hoagland. To go further than 25 km from Prague they had obtained a permit from the government. Hoagland was an old hand and Alex found him interesting and useful to travel with. Together they made a five-day trip, passing as close as they could to known military installations. The STB were always behind them so they were unable to get really close to anything. Nevertheless they made notes on what they did see, both Czech and Russian, and spent time making reports to their governments when they returned.

Alex's hopes of finding his new job interesting were dashed again on the day in November when he was invited to visit General of the Army Lemsky at his headquarters. He had hoped for a sensible discussion of military issues and was ushered into a room containing one long table and plenty of chairs. The *Good Soldier Schweik* might have been looking over his shoulder as he was asked to take a seat on one side of the table while Lemsky, another general and an interpreter sat on the other side. A major also sat on his side, a long way to his right, probably to take notes. Alex felt like a criminal up for investigation. The conversation was between Lemsky and Alex and, apart from the interpreter doing his job, the others said nothing. "The whole thing was terribly formal and uninteresting and stupid and unnatural. I stayed for half an hour then departed." He had learned nothing, the general nothing that he should not have known already. And both were paid to do what they had just done. That was the Cold War.

Alex was to make many more trips around the country, sometimes with other attachés and sometimes with his family. He also pooled observations with other Western attachés and his reports included whatever they had passed on to him. Only once did they slip their STB leash and that was during the tense days of the Cuban missile crisis in 1962. By prior agreement Western attachés left home at 2:00 a.m., to avoid their STB escorts, and fanned out to pre-assigned military and air bases within the allowed 25 km. Without the STB they were able to get closer to most installations but, even so, saw nothing of interest. Not surprisingly, the Russians were not doing much in Czechoslovakia while fully engaged with the United States. That information in itself was probably comforting to Western governments, so their efforts were not in vain, but the subsequent fury of the Czechs was predictable and had to be endured.

Otherwise the job entailed being taken by the Czech government to see objects of interest. The Czechs, of course, wanted to project themselves as a modern industrial country and the attachés went along, hoping to read military significance between the lines or, better still, hoping to witness events or installations which their hosts had not anticipated. Thus Alex and Ann found themselves in the company of the American and Italian attachés watching the so-called World Aerobatic Competition in Bratislava. Alex pegged it as a "good show," praise indeed from a stager of air shows, but they saw nothing of military interest or that they could not have seen at home. Less obviously palatable was the Brno Industrial Fair – where a visitor inspected rows of massive, pale-green machines of inscrutable function, festooned in triumphal red banners; or a trip to a brewery where the beer was good but the timing bad, at a point in 1961 when Alex objected to making friendly conversation with communists.

Both Alex and Ann were quite excited to be invited to sit in special seats at the

Czech Army Day parade. There were a large number of marching troops, trucks and "other stuff besides tanks – the sort of display we do not see in our countries. We were prepared to be impressed and thrilled but both Ann and I felt somewhat let down." The parade signalled 'quantity' rather than 'quality'. Of more interest to Alex were six large rockets, but the Western attachés believed them to be the same six displayed a week earlier at the Hungarian May Day parade in Budapest! The lowest of the low was a tour to a so-called 'military object', which turned out to be a hospital for members of military families with heart disease. Alex commented: "I swear they were pulling our legs, but don't think officialdom's sense of humour extends that far."

Apart from such excursions the job consisted of attending official receptions and unofficial cocktail parties on the off chance that somebody in the communist camp might choose such a medium for a contact with the West or, alternatively, became drunk and indiscreet. As Alex discovered, the attitude of the communist camp was largely dictated from the top. That meant that either everybody was frosty and unwilling to talk pleasantly or that they were all extra-friendly; there seemed to be no polite middle ground. It was the sort of charade which Alex found insufferable and quite early in his stay he made waves.

In the fall of 1960 a popular British attaché was going home and, traditionally, the longest serving attaché would organise a farewell gathering. This was the attaché from the United Arab Republic (Egypt/Syria), but the UAR official, firmly in the communist camp, was dragging his feet. So Alex picked up the phone and told him to get on with it. Such behaviour was unheard of and "diplomatic fur was flying in all directions for a day or two!" When the fur had settled Alex received a peacemaking invitation to visit the Egyptian in Egypt when the latter had retired; more immediately, he was quietly congratulated by some Western diplomats. It was to be the first of several run-ins that Alex would have with the UAR. No doubt his animosity towards that country was based on his identification with the RAF in their 1956 attack on Egypt and his loathing for Nasser who had rejected Canadian peacekeepers. Whatever he did, he had the luxury of knowing that it was unlikely to lead to the first Canadian-Egyptian war!

The USSR's allies, for their part, probably enjoyed a little Alex-baiting. Prime Minister Diefenbaker had tangled with Khrushchev at the United Nations over Soviet suggestions that Canada still had 'colonial' status. This made Canada temporarily a Soviet bloc target. A few months later, at a strictly soft-drink UAR reception, a Czech officer asked Alex, apparently innocently, what he thought of the 'colonial problem'. As Alex said at the time: "That was good for a few tense moments and we parted not agreeing about Dag Hammarskjold." No doubt the Czech officer was later quietly congratulated as Alex had been.

There were other bones of contention between East and West in 1961 of which Hammarskjold was just one; they included the Congo, Laos, Berlin, Cuba and Khrushchev's belligerence after his Vienna meeting with Kennedy. At some time in that year, or the first part of 1962, Alex reinforced his reputation for undiplomatic directness. He and other Western attachés were at a Soviet reception where their host, General Voloshin, made a speech berating the Americans and their allies. He spoke in Russian but Alex's 'year of trial' finally paid a dividend, for he knew what the Russian was saying before the interpreter had a chance to water it down. He put down his drink, marched up to the Russian, saluted, told him – in Russian – that his behaviour was intolerable, turned on his heel and marched out, closely followed by the other Western attachés. It was dramatic and as effective as anything could be in the circumstances.

It certainly made life more interesting and he grew in confidence in the dream-like mini-United Nations in which they lived. A little later he and Ann decided to break the mold. They had had several cocktail and dinner parties at their house, all conventionally formal with waitresses and a butler, dress 'formal or black tie'. May 1961 was a hot month in Prague; Alex and Ann sent out invitations for a cocktail party, dress 'informal or NO tie'. Not only that but they hired no help and passed the nibblies themselves, or their guests did. It was a huge success and, whereas most diplomatic parties broke up in the middle of the evening, leaving a homebound guest half-fed and wondering how to kill the hours till bedtime, their guests left at 1:00 a.m.

Alex's confidence did him no good. They went to another UAR reception in July, to celebrate Army Day. Alex mistook the Iraqi ambassador for the ambassador of the UAR. He told him, in a jovial dig, that he was glad he was present – so he could keep an eye on his military staff! It was Western-style humour anyway. "He naturally was somewhat nonplussed by my unnecessary and quite foolish remark. I think he twigged I had got me nations mixed up because he murmured something about 'I must go and say my greetings to the UAR ambassador'. I do wish I could keep my trap shut." The incident would have done his reputation with Soviet bloc Arab countries no good at all, but may have made him seem more of a guru to ignorant and inexperienced Western attachés.

This became apparent a little later at an Iranian reception in honour of the 'Shah in Shah.' "An American chap approached me and asked if 'Shah in Shah' meant 'son-in-law' or what! I had no idea and was on the verge of asking somebody else when Mrs Wails, wife of the American ambassador, appeared; she had been in Iran and was quite overcome when we asked what this 'Shah in Shah' business was. Apparently it is the equivalent of King of Kings and nothing to do with in-laws. Shortly after that the Iraqi ambassador appeared and one of the British chaps standing beside me said 'Congratulations on your National Day, sir'. [This was the same wretched man Alex had mistaken a few months before!] He looked a bit puzzled and said 'Yes, it is nice to celebrate one's neighbour's National Day'. Of course there was a rather long and awkward silence after the remark – what does one say when one has said the wrong thing to the wrong chap?!" Another page in the story of Alex in Blunderland, though this time he was not the central player!

The Berlin Wall crisis happened in August 1961. It brought tremendous tension to Eastern Europe and Alex was half convinced there would be war though it seemed too unrealistic. He wrote to his mother while American tanks were facing Soviet ones at Checkpoint Charlie: "Of course the Berlin situation is very much to the fore and we wonder what will happen. One always says and thinks that surely there cannot be another war." He had written almost the same words in 1939. "Blowed if I know what to think!" In their situation there was not much they could do if war did come, though no doubt they had a contingency plan for a dash to Nuremberg. In this same week, when wise people were stocking their bomb shelters, Ann's cousin Val Johnston wrote that she was coming from London for a visit! Alex was horrified; never one to put off a visitor, especially in their current isolation, he wired back to persuade her to choose a more peaceful vacation spot in the circumstances!

Val took a rain check and the crisis passed. Tanks went back to barracks but things on the diplomatic front reached absurd levels of frostiness. In October there was a reception given by General Lemsky. The full diplomatic corps was there but the Soviet bloc attachés dined separately. "We (the Western people) wandered round in three rooms and talked to ourselves. Did not meet or talk to any Czechs at all. A rather unfriendly sort of gathering, quite absurd really. Just as we were leaving at 10:00 p.m., out rushed General Lemsky, President Novotny and three Russian generals we had never seen before. And that was it – very dull and uninteresting." Khrushchev evidently agreed. In February he proposed a disarmament summit and, to give it a chance, a simultaneous diplomatic thaw.

At the end of the month the Soviet attaché held a Red Army Day reception. Lo and behold, not only were President Novotny and Prime Minister Shiroky present and circulating, but Alex had a pleasant talk, about nothing in particular, with both. He complimented Shiroky, his next-door neighbour but three, on the efficiency of the Prague fire department which had recently extinguished a fire in their furnace room. With Novotny he discussed Canadian agriculture, which the president admired. In particular, he wrote to Agnes: "Novotny thinks Canadian fishmeal-fed chickens are good." It was banal but it was the first time in Alex's year and a half in Czechoslovakia that the president had spoken to any Western attaché. The two leaders remained approachable and Alex was to meet them twice more, once in May 1962 and then at the Red Army Day reception of 1963.

The year 1962 was a dramatic one. It saw the space flight of Colonel Glenn which was capped by the Russian multiman mission in August, but the diplomatic thaw survived both events. The Cuban missile crisis in October brought back tension but, as the drama unfolded, in Prague the two sides kept drinking each other's champagne. President Kennedy announced his naval blockade on the 24th of October and a thousand young Czechs demonstrated outside the American embassy. As demonstrations go it was token. That evening Alex and Ann and diplomatic colleagues pushed through the protesting students to go to an American cocktail party, probably filled with Dutch courage by the drinks they had just downed at the Rumanian Army Day reception. It was the most extraordinary moment of a lunatic era: Khrushchev and Kennedy were playing nuclear chicken, Western countries were praying and preparing for nuclear Armageddon but in the puppet world of Prague, for friends and enemies alike, the word was: 'Eat, drink and be merry – as usual!' Alex was clearly in tune with his Prague colleagues. While Canada cowered, he could write: "Like the rest of the world we shall be happy when the Cuban nonsense is over. Fortunately it doesn't seem to mean very much here, just lots of garbage – communist propaganda – in the newspapers."

The cocktail circuit in Prague was right. Within a month the superpowers had not only agreed on Cuba but also on the peaceful use of space. The Soviets dispatched a new military attaché, "quite a man," Alex wrote, "very nice and making a point these days of being nice to everyone. That is the current Soviet policy." It was to last for the remainder of their stay and at the Red Army Day reception in February there was a huge crowd and a friendly atmosphere.

A wild card for Canadian diplomats in Czechoslovakia was the sort of hockey teams sent from Canada to play Czech teams. Some of them were just plain bad while others were violent too. Only one team while they were there failed to be an embarrassment. Alex and Ann would always go to watch these teams, hoping that their lonely voices would encourage them. In December 1961 the visitors were the Port Arthur Bearcats. On this occasion Ann and Alex had been given complimentary tickets. These had originally been supplied to the ambassador and his wife but that wise couple were otherwise engaged, or possibly just warned. The Bearcats lost 10 to 1, earned plenty of time in the penalty box and dropped their gloves to fight on any excuse. During the game the man next to Ann asked: "Is that the sort of sportsmen you have in Canada, Excellency?" Alex leaned across and asked him to keep his opinions to himself. Later Alex had to ask him to show some politeness. Ann, realising that the fellow thought Alex was the ambassador, started calling Alex 'Jack' in a loud voice and he called her 'Clare'. They had a lot of fun, Ann reviving her Don Cherry-like love of hockey fights, and they later told the ambassador about it. Alex said the ambassador found it funny – he thought.

If hockey can be called cultural (only in Canada!), ballet was about the only other type of culture on offer, to Alex's horror. During their first fall in Prague Ann dragged him to a performance of *Swan Lake*. He was put out by the casual appearance of the audience, none of whom were wearing evening dress in this workers' paradise – even the orchestra wore casual garb. He enjoyed Tchaikovsky's music but failed to appreciate the finer points of the performance: "Some of the chaps dancing about the stage put me off a little. But the women and girls, prettily dressed and good at their antics, more than offset the odd-looking males in the chorus!" Dégas could not have put it better. Later on, when Ann went to see ballet on film in a Czech theatre, Alex preferred an evening at home by the fire.

A few months before they left Prague he was upset when he discovered that an evening at the British ambassador's, already accepted, included a visit to the ballet and dinner afterwards. The night before the event they were discussing it and "Alex gave occasional deep groans!" He complained that it would not be so bad if it was just the ballet, "but to have to discuss it after – oh dear!" "What a laugh," Ann chortled. In the event, Alex hated *The Firebird* but loved *Petrushka* and the evening passed off without embarrassment. The ambassador must have admired his stoicism because at their eventual farewell party he delivered a speech so full of praise and admiration for them both that Alex found it "too blushing to repeat, but good for our egos!"

Alex maintained, long after he had left Prague, that it was the worst assignment he had had in the Air Force. For evidence of this, witness the fact that he took every opportunity to escape. He actually spent more time outside Czechoslovakia than did Ann and the children because, in addition to conferences and holidays in the real world, two or three times a year he would be 'Gone Flying'. For this he went to #2 Wing of the Canadian Air Division at Grostenquin, France. He was there for ten days as soon as he had Ann and the babies settled in their house in September 1960. While Ann was getting to know Dagmar and Mary, Alex was flying fifty hours in DC3s. His flying took him far afield, in fact twice to the RCAF detachment in Sardinia where a stopover allowed him to go swimming in the Mediterranean. When not flying he was mess-crawling again at the Air Division HQ mess in Metz – "I know so many at Metz it really is remarkable." Nobody was surprised! But he missed his little family dreadfully and no doubt felt guilty as he drove up to the frontier on his way home. Once through the checkpoint he sang out loud. "I don't suppose there are many Western people," he observed, "who have crossed into Czechoslovakia singing!"

On other occasions he flew to Brussels, Copenhagen, Malta, Langar (close to his old Wittering training field) and all four wings of the Air Division in Germany and France. Time spent in those messes was not wasted: "I just love being among the RCAF chaps again," he wrote. He was able to draw upon an enormous bank of goodwill, many of the officers having served with him at St Hubert or earlier. As he admitted, they spoiled him a lot. Deprivation of mess-life was his biggest problem with a diplomatic posting, as it had been with an academic one.

With careful planning they were able to combine flying with family holidays. In June 1961 they all drove to Grostenquin and waited for Alex to cram twenty-five hours of flying into three days. Then they drove, via the Dieppe-Newhaven ferry, to Hove in Sussex where they had borrowed #65 Errol Road. It was a small house with cheap furniture, threadbare carpets, a tiny fridge and no phone – but it was near the beach and it was home for a month. Ann remained there with the children, enjoying being a normal mother, with her children all to herself at the seaside, while Alex commuted daily from Brighton to London for a course.

Britain, in spite of Hitler, had changed very little. It was Alex's private museum where he visited his past. With Connie he went to Shepheard's, a pub they frequented in the 1930s. "It hadn't changed one little bit! We found it hard to credit one place should remain so unchanged in all those years." Unchanged, except for well-bred chatter where the tipsy voices of dead heroes had filled the air. Commuting on whining electric trains from Brighton brought memories of his 1933 train ride with Daphne. He took Ann to dine at the Royal Albion Hotel in Brighton where he had dined with Daphne and Nancy Preston. Later his course took him further afield. He stayed at the Haycock at Wansford, where he and Hokey had stopped for tea. He and Ann lunched at the Sherlock Holmes, near Trafalgar Square, an old haunt from *Aeropilot* days, and he reeled from pub to pub in Brockenhurst with a retired W/C Laurence Burgess, once CO of 205 Squadron. Reluctantly, Alex and Ann returned to Prague.

The following year they managed a short time in Heidelberg, leaving the babies in Prague with Sheila Booth, their much-loved English nanny. Plans for a summer holiday on the Adriatic were stymied by Alex developing infectious jaundice, which put him in hospital for two and a half months. He had originally been admitted to hospital in Prague where he had been well cared for. Isolation patients usually communicated with visitors by shouting from the windows; Alex, unwilling perhaps to draw attention to being foreign, would write letters and toss them down. The Czechs also lowered long lengths of string for hauling up food and mail.

In spite of his good treatment, it was Allied policy to look after their own and Alex was removed to the U.S. hospital in Nuremberg, first by U.S. ambulance and, once over the border, by helicopter. Fortunately, they had bought a camper; this meant that once he was out of isolation, Ann could move into a campground and take the children to see Daddy every day. Campground life had its shortcomings and Ann used to come into the hospital for a bath in Alex's bathroom while he and the children intercepted nurses who might object. For Louisa and Marjory it was quite a happy time. As well as seeing their father every day, they had a whole campground in which to make friends. By this time Marjory was as mobile as her sister and the two of them more or less adopted a baby in one of the other campsites, 'helping' the baby's mother for most of the day! Eventually Alex was declared 'ambulatory' and came to live with them in the camper for a week, until finally discharged.

By the end of August he had a clean bill of health and they set off on a camper holiday to Cavallino on the Adriatic, travelling via Vienna. It was September, the weather was good and the crowds gone – compensation for a trying summer. They extended their holiday by visiting Lausanne and ended up at Grostenquin in France. Ann wrote: "We are very happy here – Alex with his flying and his airforce, me with no-one to worry about except my own little family and able to go along to the station stores when I need to." They made a trip to Ramstein in Germany to visit Don Jackson, a Singapore friend, and his wife Irene. While there, they took the children to the base chapel and Marjory loved the organ music. As the sounds died away after one hymn, her little bell-like voice cried out: "Tell him to play it again, Daddy!" It was an improvement on her previous church behaviour; in the pause between hymn verses she could clearly be heard singing "Three Blind Mice." After ten days Ann wrote: "This has been a wonderful holiday and we should be able to go back to Prague and its multitude of frustrations and grin and bear it – but, oh dear, we wish we didn't have to!" Alex was more explicit – packing-up day was "depression day."

Vienna was an escape hole for them on several occasions. They spent a week there with the Levys from Arnprior and another later on with Alex's sister Marjorie and her husband Geoff. They also visited Vienna with Beryl and Robyn Stilling, who came calling from 'down under'. The first of these occasions saw a frustrated Alex behaving in his least-diplomatic way. Ann and Peggy Levy were having their hair done. It was a warm April afternoon so Bud and Alex decided to wait for them at a sidewalk café. The women were a long time, maybe an hour and a half, and the men had time for several drinks. When their wives returned, both men had definitely had too much but they insisted that their wives join them for just one glass. When they began to walk back to their *pension*, Bud was feeling sleepy while Alex, irrepressible as ever, was raring to go! They heard that the King of Sweden was expected shortly at the Opera and so decided to join a crowd waiting outside. Unfortunately, arriving streetcars blocked their view so, while Bud went back to the hotel to sleep it off, Alex leaped into the street and began directing traffic – much to the amusement of the waiting crowd. Ann was most embarrassed but determined to see the king. It was no good trying to dissuade her husband; instead she and Peggy pretended they did not know him.

Alex had found himself a perch on a traffic island "that was much closer than we were allowed to be." From this vantage point he was entertaining the crowd until a policeman "kindly asked me to move on," as he put it. He was crossing the street when a limo, flying the Czech flag, drove up to drop a diplomat at the Opera. Unable to resist it, Alex shouted, in a slurred, parade-ground voice, according to Ann, though he insisted it was all very discreet: "DOWN WITH THE CZECHOSLOVAKS!!" Ann refused to speak to him when he approached, so Alex, "crestfallen, went back and had a sleep." When Ann returned, she too was crestfallen and, in her case, literally; for the rain had ruined her hair and, although she had seen King Gustav, "it could have been anyone!" It was a memorable but not-to-be-repeated afternoon, though apparently it was; Robyn Stilling, now Mrs. Dangar, remembers that Alex changed completely once they were out of Czechoslovakia and had reached Vienna. The correct group captain started to "behave like a child, let his hair down completely and became uproariously drunk on Slivovitz!"

The news that Alex had hardly dared hope for came in March 1963, just after his birthday. He was appointed CO of RCAF Penhold from the 16th of September. He had prayed for a station command. Now, he not only had one but it was near the west coast and far from interference by the brass in Ottawa or Montréal. His last year and a half in the Air Force were going to be all right! He was counting the days in Prague and the last months passed quickly. Once his Russian came in useful. On the long, boring road to the border he was flagged down by a motorcycle policeman, obviously intending to give him a speeding ticket. Alex rolled down his window and loudly announced, in imperfect Russian: *"Yah nyeh ponimyo Chek; yah govoryo tolko po-Roosski!"* (I don't understand Czech, I only speak Russian!) The effect was dramatic: the officer snapped his notebook shut, saluted and roared off to persecute less influential mortals. At one of their final official engagements Alex tried out his Russian on a Yugoslav journalist. Not much communication resulted although "we did make some foolish remarks to each other" – perhaps a fitting burial for a painful linguistic project.

There were many farewells, both official and private, and it was clear that the Jardines had made their mark and had been appreciated, though perhaps not in their own corner. Jacques Roy, the second secretary, gave a party for them but of the ambassador there was no sign – possibly the incumbent, who had a reputation for being hard to work with, felt that Alex's brand of foreign policy was not his own! Regardless, Alex bought a new Rambler to pull the camper and they made plans for their withdrawal in easy stages. The only hard part was saying goodbye to Sheila, the girls' nanny. She was off to a job in Poland and when they said farewell in Nuremberg on the 12th of August, they all cried. The girls did not understand that it was a final parting, which was as well, and Marjory shouted out of the car window as they left that she would send Sheila a present.

They drove to Grostenquin, where Alex did four days' flying. Their next destination was Le Havre, where car and camper were loaded into the hold of the S.S. *Homeric*, in which their heavy baggage was already stowed. They had first-class cabins on the ship, which sailed on the 21st of August and docked in Montréal on the 28th. They visited Ottawa, for Alex to make his final reports to External Affairs and the Department of National Defence. Then they hit the high road to the west. This was not exactly the Trans-Canada Highway of today, but it was a road and it was Canada and they were going west. And, after Prague, that was all that mattered.

17

OUT LIKE A LION

1963–1965
In which Alex is CO at RCAF Penhold; and in which he retires
from the RCAF on the day before his fifty-first birthday.

"This was such a tails up and away we go sort of Air Force …"

Alex took over as CO at RCAF Station Penhold, Alberta, on the 16th of Sep-
tember 1963, and would spend eighteen months there before retiring from
the RCAF. In one way that year and a half was a sad time, in which he would be
hard-pressed to detect any progress or improvement in the situation of his beloved
Air Force. There was an anti-military wind blowing in Ottawa and Paul Hellyer,
Minister of National Defence, would begin the integration of the services in 1964.
Budget limits and rising costs also meant reducing the size of the services. Before
Alex retired he was to be saddened by the spectacle of the wholesale early retirement of many good people. Having lived the glory days of the 1950s at St Hubert
and felt the spirit in the Air Division messes in France and Germany, it was diffi-
cult for him to accept the need for such changes.

However, Alex was never despondent in tough situations. Neither prison camp
nor Iron Curtain had prevented him from approaching unpleasant reality con-
structively. He would always ask "What can we do?" rather than "What's the use?"
In that light, his last eighteen months were a happy time, when he buoyed the
spirits of those in his command, did what he could to contribute to the debate over
the forces and cheerfully, and in a spirit of exploration, planned for his own future
as an unemployed ex-group captain with wife and kids to support.

Penhold was a different proposition from Rockcliffe and St Hubert. Here he
ran a peaceful training station with obsolete aircraft while enjoying nearly
complete autonomy because, for the brass, Canada ended at Winnipeg. It was not
a demanding job for a CO with his experience. There was no need for the sort of
reorganisation which he had introduced at St Hubert. No twenty-four-hour flying,

Western Canada

no ready room, and no arming or disarming of aircraft meant that his life, and the lives of those on the base, was predictable and largely routine, weather permitting. The main training aircraft was the Harvard, whose square wingtips and deafening flat engine noise had been familiar to childish spotters during the Second World War. Now it was *the* global trainer, the 1960s' equivalent of the Tiger Moth. Both trainers were popular in their time because they were simple to fly and fix and were relatively forgiving when handled by the unskilled, though the Harvard with its maximum speed of 205 mph (330 kmh),[79] could do much more damage to itself and its crew.

After taking over the base and moving into their house, Alex and Ann took the children for a holiday at the coast. It seemed important to do this because, for most of his sisters' families, it would be their first meeting with Marjory, now aged three. What was more, five-year-old Louisa had been just two when they left Canada and remembered nothing of her British Columbia relations. However, this was an ill-starred venture for the children. Both had had as much as they could take. They had said goodbye to their nanny, Sheila; they had tossed for a week on the North Atlantic while their mother had been seasick and they had refused to eat; and they had travelled and camped their way across Europe and North America, from Prague to Penhold. The holiday on the west coast was the final straw. When Agnes came to stay at Penhold, after their return to Alberta, the girls behaved abominably – little terrors who refused to do as they were asked and were anything but polite to their grandmother, who fled back across the mountains. Alex had often complained about the behaviour of other people's children; he felt mortified and could not adequately apologise to his mother. The problem resolved itself, of course, as soon as the delinquents had settled down in their new house. He and Ann would not be the first parents, nor the last, to be punished by their children for treating them as animate luggage.

From the beginning of his command the future of Penhold looked grim. Alex hoped to include T-Birds, or their replacement, in the training programme. The RCAF had a new jet trainer, the CL-41R, now familiar as the Tutor flown by the Snowbirds, and he went to Moose Jaw to take one up for a spin, declaring it "a lovely aeroplane and most interesting." That was to be the closest he would come to having one on strength. He was soon informed that there would be no jets at Penhold. In fact the Tutor was the last jet aircraft that he flew – and Moose Jaw gave him a certificate to mark the occasion. To make matters worse, early in 1964 he was told that the Harvard training programme would stop in May 1965 and, as Harvard training was what the station was all about, that looked like the end of Penhold. An abandoned Second World War airfield, it had been one of the expansion projects which his department had planned while he was at Trenton and had reopened as a NATO training base in 1953, training French, British, Italian, Dutch, Norwegian, Danish and Nigerian as well as RCAF pilots over the decade. Now, it seemed, that was all over.

Alex had just digested this news when he had to deal with his own future. On the 23rd of March 1964 Air Marshal Greenway wrote to tell him that he "would be released with effect from the 16th of March 1965, with 238 days of leave on full pay." Alex wrote to Agnes: "So it has come and I'm sorry. It means a complete rethink about ourselves ... I have no fears. In a way it will be an interesting time, but what an upheaval! It has the feeling of being unnecessary or, to put it another way, thirty years at one job is a long time; to change to something else is not a small thing." There had been times in the past when she had expected him to be promoted and retained in the RCAF as one of the top brass. Alex had pooh-poohed such hopes, citing his late start and his lack of formal education. He had sounded both convinced and convincing.

His reaction to Greenway's letter, in spite of the fact that he had been discussing the when and where of retirement before Christmas, seems to show that he was indeed disappointed. He had secretly been hoping that his mother was right – why else would he be sorry? Why else would it feel unnecessary? These were the only hints he gave that things might not be unfolding as he had hoped. He did not complain. The final duty of old airmen, as of old soldiers, is to obey the order to fade away. The decision could not be changed, must be accepted with good grace and he must plan accordingly. Retirement, after all, was an exciting challenge. Moreover, as 1964 rolled by and news from Ottawa about the future of the services became worse, he understood that once again his timing had been immaculate. 'Lucky Alex' was getting out just when the Air Force was ceasing to be the one that he had joined and so enjoyed.

In March 1964 Minister Hellyer tabled a Defence white paper which intro-duced the idea of 'a single, unified defence force'.[80] Alex and most others accepted the idea at first, as a means of avoiding the duplication of 'tail' functions, thus freeing more of the defence budget for buying equipment. But when Hellyer put a bill before Parliament to integrate the three services under one Chief of Defence Staff,[81] Alex and many others balked. He wrote to Agnes in May: "Times in the RCAF are worrying indeed. I've changed my mind about 'integration' because of the way Hellyer is trying to do it. So I'm off to Winnipeg to talk to our AOC about it – don't know what the outcome will be." Having nothing to lose, as a respected group captain without promotion worries, he flew to Winnipeg and, predictably, achieved nothing. "I saw the boss-man and told him what I felt about a lot of things." It probably made him feel better to get them off his chest. "I realise there is not a lot he could do about it; however I did learn that I am not by any means the only one." Parliament passed the Integration Bill in June[82] and immediately the prospect of an integrated staff reduced the required numbers of Air Force officers above the rank of Squadron Leader. Before Alex himself retired he became angrier by the day because of the number of good officers, all much younger than himself, who were being pensioned off at short notice. He lamented: "This was such a tails up and away we go sort of Air Force. Now it is not and Mr Hellyer is responsible to a large degree."

Alex decided at Christmas 1963 that the Jardine touch was needed to restore morale at Penhold, which had been battered by rumours of cuts and by bad press received under the previous regime. On the 23rd of December the officers went over to the NCOs' mess, by traditional invitation, and lined up at one end of the room. Standing in front of them, Alex, the new CO whom nobody yet knew, began a forgettable and nonsensical speech about not drinking the first drink but giving the money it would cost to charity and moving on to the second drink, etcetera, etcetera! As he was speaking a warrant officer nearby noticed with horror that Alex's trousers were beginning to slip down. The poor man was torn between his concern for the CO's dignity and his desire not to make a scene, when the adjutant came dashing in waving an 'urgent message'. Melodramatically, he tripped and fell, clutching at Alex's trousers, which came right down, to reveal, in all their glory, Ann's scarlet leotards! In the shocked hush that followed the officers turned their backs, removed their jackets, then turned around together with a roar of "MERRY CHRISTMAS AND A HAPPY NEW YEAR," the letters of which were taped onto thirty chests. There was a shout of delight and surprise from the room and the party took off from there.

Throughout his time at Penhold Alex did his utmost to improve morale and was obviously successful. In spite of its looming closure, the station became a happy place. At the same time, he was doing what he could to raise the faltering prestige of the RCAF, and of Station Penhold in particular, in the eyes of the public, just as he had done at St Hubert. He gave interviews to the local papers and made a policy of always accepting requests for speeches, ribbons to be cut or salutes to be taken. To that end he agreed to speak to the Red Deer wing of the RCAF Association about his Czech experiences though, as he said, "my heart is not in it!" He enjoyed his evening with the vets and thereafter became a regular at their meetings. On New Year's Day 1964 the officers' mess held an open house for local notables – the mayor, the aldermen, the fire and police chiefs, with their assistants and families, more than a hundred people in all, to kick off his public relations counterattack.

He soon found himself on the chamber of commerce and service club lunch circuit and much in demand with Air Cadets. It was all grist to his mill; he had no audience among the public at large, but to these influential people he explained how the Air Force spent their dollars, why it was money well spent and why the Air Force needed their support. He devoted many hours to the Air Cadets, who of all people needed words of hope and encouragement, and Penhold hosted the annual provincial meeting for Air Cadet officers. In July the station float, proclaiming Penhold the 'Best in the West', won first prize in its division in the Red Deer Parade and Alex was one of the parade leaders, waving to the crowd in his enthusiastic manner from an open car. He led a group of three young fellows from the base on a much-publicised adventure camping trip in the steps of David Thompson up the Ram River and onto Kootenay Plains. Then in September, as the narrator, spent many hours recording and re-recording a TV documentary about the station called 'Best in the West', produced by Corporal Lord for the local TV channel.

He was not alone in his efforts, for Ann became equally involved with the community. She worked with the station wives, put a huge amount of time and her craft skill into the Protestant chapel bazaar in the fall of 1964 and was involved with the Red Deer Women's Guild, who presented her with a white cowboy hat in appreciation when she left. Considering that the Jardines and RCAF Penhold had by then only temporary tenure in the Red Deer area, with every excuse to plead 'no time', they made quite an impact in their eighteen months. They were to leave a well-respected and happy station.

Indeed, Alex had little time and in several letters claimed to be as busy as ever, though now not all of the busy-ness had to do with the station. For he had two new preoccupations: the RCAF Association and job-hunting. Years ago he had taken a dim view of the RCAFA. After attending a meeting in Trenton days he had privately tagged many of the members as "odd fish," to be approached with caution! Now his perspective was different; not only would he soon be a vet himself but he knew that he would crave the company of RCAF people. Besides, he was a man with a mission. Serving officers could not speak their minds on policy issues and only through the RCAFA could their interests be championed.

Typically Alex jumped in at the deep end. He was surprised by the lack of information he found about current issues when he attended RCAFA meetings. Consequently, in October 1964 he travelled to the national RCAFA convention in far-off Charlottetown to propose a motion encouraging local wings to set up aeronautical libraries and information centres. The convention passed his motion but the ball was then in his court, on the principle of 'put up or shut up'. Back in Penhold he found himself contacting all ninety RCAFA wings nationwide to get them cracking on implementing his idea – "some task," as he remarked.

Job-hunting was another matter. To begin with he was completely at sea, not having looked for a job since his 1935 ultimatum to the Air Ministry. He registered at the local employment office, chortling that he was the only unemployed group captain on their books. He sought advice on how to write a résumé from cousin Robin and from Ann's cousin Derek, bank manager and chartered accountant respectively. Having written one, he sent it with a letter of explanation to forty aviation-related companies in British Columbia – and waited. After a month he had received twelve to fifteen replies, all polite and wishing him well, but none able to fit him in or willing to have him parachute over their own employees.

Eventually, the letters produced two leads. The first was the BC Owners' and Pilots' Association, based in Vancouver, whose boss came to Red Deer to see him. Of their meeting he wrote: "Quite interesting but I don't think my cup of tea quite. We shall see; anyway it was interesting meeting him and hearing about his project." That idea does not recur but another offer popped up. Mr Stacey, owner of the Sidney Aviation Electric Company at Pat Bay, wanted to sell him the company. Alex was immediately interested, mostly because of the location. He asked John Levy in Ottawa to come in with him and sought business advice from both Robin and Derek. All three advised him to go slowly, while Stacey wanted to sell within a month. That in itself was a deterrent to the cautious Alex, thrilled though he was by the idea. Then he discovered that Stacey was not only the owner but also the technical brains and that he employed no other electricians. Without him Alex would be on his own. Reluctantly he turned the offer down. One non-aviation offer came up – selling life insurance. A local insurance man took him to lunch at the Ranchers' Club in Calgary and pressed him to join Canada Life. Alex was flattered when he found out that the Ranchers' Club was the Raffles of Calgary, but selling insurance appealed to him about as much as had selling Jeyes' Fluid. He filed the possibility away, for use only in a future emergency. And that was it. As time passed, and his departure from Penhold came closer, Alex worried less about employment. Having always had a horror of idleness, he had been more concerned about keeping busy than about earning a salary and his new involvement in the RCAFA looked likely to give him plenty to do.

Only in his last three months in the Air Force did Alex begin to show signs of the emotions he must have felt. His state of mind was affected by two external events to which he had to respond. The first of these, in the fall of 1964, was the retirement of the RCAF ensign in favour of the national flag, which was not yet the Maple Leaf. Alex was determined to maintain the separate identity of the Air Force. On his entire command, paraded for the lowering of the flag, he urged: "Remember our traditions. Our service is young by comparison with our brothers in arms but we have won, deservedly, renown in peace and war and where our ensign has flown, all men have learned to expect efficiency, friendliness and a will to help. Be determined that we shall never change!"

If his tone was Churchillian it was fitting, for on the 24th of January that old warrior died, and his state funeral was held on the 30th. Again Alex paraded the troops and again he was determined to pass on to them an idea – in this case, the message of Winston Churchill's life. He asked a simple question: "Why should we, a small group ... from so many lands, stop our daily task to mark the moment when Sir Winston will be buried?" Facing young people from many ethnic backgrounds, he had difficulty finding a simple answer for them. He told them why *he* would remember Winston, but he was of another generation and of British stock. His listeners were too young, too diverse, too modern to be satisfied by that; they needed an answer relevant to their own experience. Alex solved the problem by offering them the leadership of Winston's own words from June 1941: "The destiny of mankind is not decided by material computation. When great causes are on the move in the world ... we learn that we are spirits, not animals, and that something is going on in space and time, and beyond space and time, which, whether we like it or not, spells DUTY." It was a message that they badly needed to hear.

'Duty' seemed to Alex to be a concept which younger members of the RCAF did not understand. He kept a diary for a few days, really just random jottings, and was disturbed by his own entries:

"14 Feb:

an officer-cadet on a charge for damaging his aircraft while taxiing – $2,500 damage.

15 Feb (Saturday):

inspection of barracks poor, so ordered all to stay in and close the bar; an officer trainee taxied his aircraft into a ground control vehicle (horrors, horrors).

(Saturday night):

the officer-cadets have a spree in the barracks; another officer impersonates an RCMP officer; an officer-cadet forwards a redress of grievance.

17 Feb:

an officer-cadet is put in jail.

19 Feb:

five officer-cadets are on a charge. This is ... capped by one Chornenki's son who tied up a fellow 13-year-old in a game of Cowboys and Indians and father finds out $22 is missing. What has happened? I know not and am mightily depressed."

Thirty years ago, when he was an officer-cadet, such behaviour would have been unthinkable. He was witnessing a sea change that had occurred in the attitude of young people since he had last commanded a station, a change evident throughout the forces. These and similar problems elsewhere reflected a generation's rejection of authority; the imminent fall of the axe on Station Penhold probably had little to do with it, although it must have had its effect. Alex had written to Agnes on the 12th of January: "It snows, it's cold, it gets mild and we are not able to do much flying, with the result that we are getting behind. That, plus the fact that all things are geared to run down, with flying to stop by the end of May, makes life not much fun here and I think people are beginning to feel the strain."

Disturbing and incomprehensible though the poor discipline certainly was, Alex refused to allow it to depress him more than briefly. One hopes that he felt mollified to receive this letter from Air Marshal Clare Annis a few weeks before his retirement:

"I would like to take this opportunity of saying how consistently high has been the quality of your service to the RCAF and how very much our service and our country are indebted to you. I somehow doubt whether you yourself realise how very much you have done and how much it means. But it is the level of contribution which has built the RCAF into the finest 'little' airforce in the world."

The Air Marshal's letter, following the strange behaviour of cadets and officers on the base, may have encouraged Alex to work on a letter of his own. Even on his final day in the RCAF he was determined to offer guidance to these young people, based on his experience. He was under few illusions that it would be heeded by all, but if it strengthened some it was worth doing. His letter was dated the 15th of March 1965 and addressed 'To my officers and airmen':

"Tomorrow I am 51. To many of you that's pretty old, thus there is a risk you may not heed what is written in this letter. But read on, knowing that it is sincere and meant to be helpful. I suggest my 35 years as a sailor and airman in many parts of the world, in a great variety of circumstances, must have shown me a way of life, a philosophy that is worth your attention.

These maxims I give you:
1 Always believe you are a member of a team and act accordingly;
2 Meet the times set and demand of your team-mates the same;
3 Consider others, especially those who are junior to you;
4 Be particular, be gentlemanly, be proud and never, never be afraid;
5 Accept any task given with the determination that you will give it your best;
6 Never dodge an issue but face it square and deal with it;
7 Except where duty is concerned practice moderation;
8 Keep fit;
9 Do all things as though you meant it;
10 Fear God; honour the Queen."

Someone unfamiliar with Alex might dismiss this as hypocrisy from an old rogue. However, the reader will be able to think of examples of each maxim from the story of Alex's life and will realise that he actually lived by them, though they were not articulated until the day before he retired. They are based upon unfashionable beliefs – in discipline, self-denial, respect for authority and duty – that were current in his boyhood. To him they were self-evident. In them we see a partial explanation for his own success, not only in seizing career chances but also in the almost universal regard in which he is held. His serious purpose in March 1965 caused him to overlook two other maxims which had guided his life: 'Nothing is too serious to be funny' and 'Laugh at yourself'. To borrow from the economists, his career also demonstrated the theory of the trickle-down effect of having fun.

The first two weeks of March 1965 were a benevolent blur, during which Alex received gifts, tributes and goodwill. He went to Winnipeg as a guest of the AOC for a mess dinner at Training Command HQ, to Edmonton for lunch with General Rockingham, his boss under the new dispensation. The airmen's mess threw a party for him, as did the administration wing and the technical wing. At the officers' mess party he received presentations from the officers and also from the mayor of Red Deer, the Air Cadet League and #4 FTS. He was fêted by the Red Deer Rotary Club and by the Red Deer wing of the RCAFA, where each of the four Alberta wings made a presentation. At each of these events he came away laden with gifts, all of them inscribed. "Never," he decided, "has a CO been so well treated, it seems to me." It was true, and it was clearly deserved. As was apparent to the least disciplined of his airmen, this Group Captain Jardine was no ordinary man. Indeed, one of his last actions in the RCAF, when ordinary mortals would have been preoccupied with their own problems, was to contact the superintendent of the Red Deer School District to create a scholarship for a student interested in a flying career.

On the 15th of March the handing-over parade took place and Alex's letter was distributed to every man. The family slept the night of the 15th in Penhold, probably not very well. Everything had been done and said and all they had to do was to drive away. In the morning of the 16th, Alex's fifty-first birthday, they loaded the car with a few bits and pieces – the heavy stuff had gone with the movers. Alex and Ann, the children too, felt both sad and excited. For him the temptation to feel very sad was strong, but he controlled it.

There was somebody at the door, several people actually, each with birthday wishes or some little item for the journey. He knew he must resist the temptation to go on saying goodbye. Everything had been said. They got into the car and drove slowly towards the camp gate for the last time. People were standing in little groups; they waved and clapped or cheered as the spotlessly polished Rambler drove out of the gates past the guard, who saluted as though their lives depended upon it. They waved out of the windows, Alex gave a toot on the horn and they were gone.

Alberta stretched in front. They went south, down the four-lane to Calgary, then west to Banff. In the end they had made no plans – they would see how things turned out. Alex's pension would be enough for them to live on and the Department of Veterans' Affairs would give them a 4.5 percent mortgage on a house. He was fifty-one, a young man, with half his adult life ahead of him and the world his oyster. It was a great feeling. Cecil Rhodes's words popped into his head: "So little done, so much to do!" He laughed out loud in anticipation. Quite soon they entered British Columbia, singing.

18

EPILOGUE

SINCE 1965
In which some aspects of Alex's subsequent life are touched upon.

This book set out to tell the story of Alex's extraordinary career. That story ended with his retirement from the Air Force, but such a man was unlikely to do a good job of fading away. This brief chapter attempts to anticipate the reader's questions about the next thirty-five years.

On arriving in Victoria his first task was to put a roof over the heads of his family. Veterans' Affairs would produce a loan but, to be eligible, the house had to be on a minimum of one acre. The original idea of settling veterans on enough land for them to be self-sufficient had been abandoned. Their chosen house sat on slightly less than an acre on Salisbury Way and a practical-joking official amused himself that summer by forcing Alex to measure and re-measure the lot in order to meet this obsolete requirement. The problem was overcome and they moved in, in time for Louisa to go to school in the fall.

For the first three years of retirement Alex was much involved in the RCAF Association. He was elected President in 1967 and was the first president to serve for more than a single year – in his case for two years. As he explains it, he had no plan to become president; it just happened. His Information Centre project had made him prominent nationally and it was suggested to him, after he arrived at the 1967 convention in Montréal, that he stand for election. He thought about it and agreed. As he tells it, he had a built-in advantage over the competition. He had recently held a Montréal command and was thus well known among the more numerous local delegates. He was known throughout the wings of the Alberta association thanks to his public relations activities at Penhold and, after two years in British Columbia, was also known there. In fact, of course, this Johnny-come-lately in the RCAF was well known even outside these three provinces, not only for his Information Centre work but also for his love of mess-crawling and yarning. Still "the friendliest youngster" that Daisy Swayne had ever seen, he was just a few years older. Besides, being well known is not necessarily a recipe for electoral success – ask any politician. His election must be attributed to the numbers of those who both knew and admired him enough to advise friends to vote for him. In any case it was a sweet result for this airman who, in mid-career, had felt such an outsider.

In his two years as president Alex travelled all over the country in the manner to which he had become accustomed, by service aircraft. Part of this activity was related to the push by his own Victoria wing for a stronger Air Force. In one way this was wasted effort; the government was moving away from the idea of Canada as a front-line Cold War player. But the leadership was vintage 'Alex'. He had always felt that effective organisations, be they squadrons or Air Force associations, are made so by a common sense of purpose instilled by visible and accessible leadership. And that he certainly provided: in two years he visited nearly every one of the ninety wings of the RCAFA. For him it was a marvellous swan song, a last glorious opportunity to be with airmen, tens of thousands of them. For them, they saw that their organisation was in vigorous hands and that their ideas were valued.

Inevitably, once he had handed over in 1969, he became less involved in association politics, though he has remained a lifelong supporter of the things that old airmen do. He never misses an opportunity for a reunion or a Battle of Britain or a Remembrance Day ceremony. Later, he was the first president of the Aircrew Association when this British organisation, open to all commonwealth flyers, formed a branch on Vancouver Island. To this day he corresponds regularly with many wartime 'chums' and contributes photographs and memories to those writing books. He is a very active veteran.

While still president of the RCAFA, in 1968 Alex served as honorary ADC to Governor General Roland Michener. The closest that he came to a job was his 1970s association with the magazine *Wings*, whose editor, Andy Leguilloux, he met at the Abbotsford Airshow. This was a magazine about flight and Alex was soon the western Canada correspondent. His task was to submit articles on flying on the west coast and he started with an article on flying out of Tofino. For a while Alex was absorbed in this form of journalism.

In the course of his research, he became interested in air-cushion vehicles and persuaded Leguilloux to allow him to produce the *Air-Cushion Vehicle Review* as a *Wings* supplement. This, naturally, led to his being invited to ride in a hovercraft and his enthusiasm evaporated as soon as he heard the appalling noise of its engine and experienced the vibration of its interior. His association with *Wings* was to last until Leguilloux retired in the mid-1970s. He continued his efforts to promote flying by teaching a one-year Aviation Ground School course at Brentwood

College, in which the students learned navigation and meteorology among other necessary skills, for which he probably dusted off his POW notes.

While his own children were at school, first at Cloverdale Elementary and later at Reynolds High, both Alex and Ann were involved in the PTA and Alex was the president of the PTA at the elementary school. Both parents were also induced to put their musical talents on the line and participate in a parents' band at the high school. Ann played the clarinet and Alex the trumpet – apparently there being no call for his barrack-room squeezebox. By this time his energies were being drawn into Project North, an ecumenical organisation which started the push for justice for Native people. Consciousness of their rights and how their wishes for nation-hood and self-government might be achieved was dawning among many of the northern peoples and Alex's contribution was often the practical skill of chairing meetings. He travelled to the Dene at Fort Fitzgerald, among others, to act as a facilitator. Later he was involved with the Nisga'a and spent time among them when Project North people were working to get the British Columbia government to take their claims seriously. At one point, when secret talks were being held between that government and the aluminum company about a smelter project on land claimed by the Nisga'a, Alex even launched a new career as a spy. Dressed in a suit and tie, he strolled into the meeting to find out what was being decided. He managed to blend into the other 'suits' around him for a while, but was eventually rumbled and expelled. Of more practical benefit to the Nisga'a, Alex allowed their dancers to live in his Victoria house during the Commonwealth Games, when these were held in Victoria in 1986.

Alex was always fit and loved nothing better than to pit his strength and skills against the ocean or the wilderness. In 1979 he accepted a serious challenge when he joined a group planning to hike the route of the future West Coast Trail, now promoted as one of the toughest. In that year the trail had not yet been created. He trained himself for the exploit by mowing his lawn wearing a pack full of bricks. Once on the hike all went well, except for breakfast on the first morning which Alex, the cook, managed to drop into the fire when about to serve it. After a week wrestling with the rain forest Alex came out of it on "a high you would not believe." Not bad for a sixty-five-year-old.

For the first ten years after he retired he owned *Wild Goose*, a 34-foot Nova Scotian schooner, ideal for family cruising holidays on a coast that was still fairly deserted. He sold it after rot began to appear and when the girls started to develop other interests. Later, he became a business partner with the inventor of Triaks, which are kayaks with outriggers and sails. He owned one himself and enjoyed paddling the waters around Vancouver Island in it. Commercially, however, it was an idea which refused to take off – maybe because assembly was complicated and time-consuming.

Sadly, Alex lost his beloved Ann in November 1991. Her illness was unexpected and brief; her death while he still enjoyed rude health was something he could never have anticipated and for many years he was restless. Ann had been a master gardener, taught by the Van Dusen Gardens in Vancouver. She and her brother Robin had created a memorial garden for their parents at the Horticulture Centre of the Pacific in suburban Victoria and this led to Alex's interest in horticulture. He volunteers at the Horticulture Centre, weeding and doing odd jobs, and looks after Ann's garden there. Another recent interest has been the Arion Male Voice Choir. He has been assiduous in attending practices and has accompanied them on tours within the province.

Alex has also travelled widely and often. Among other journeys, he and Ann had 'revisited the scene of the crime' in Singapore and Malaya. They found the mess building at Seletar strangely different and converted to civilian use. Alex did not enter the building but stood outside with his memories. Likewise Malaya was not even close to what he remembered but the climate allowed Ann to understand what effort it must have taken to work in such an environment. He stayed with Laurens van der Post in London in 1995 for the celebration of the fiftieth anniversary of VJ Day, though he chose not to march in the parade. He had been staying with friends in Scotland before travelling to London by bus, and he broke the journey overnight with people he did not know in York. He had telephoned his York host from Scotland: "I'll wear my RAF blazer and tie so you'll know me." What he did not tell him was that he would also be wearing shorts, hairy stockings and hiking boots. He telephoned from York to report safe arrival: "Most amazing thing," he enthused; "he knew me right away, can't think how!"

He has difficulty understanding his own uniqueness. He bought a mountain bike for city riding in his late seventies and sold it when he turned eighty. Undaunted by technology, he branched into computers and opened an e-mail account when he was eighty-six. In 1998 he fell in love with Ursula Kasting, sister of Jo Forbes, whom he used to see in Montréal all those years ago and had known on Thetis Island as a child. On Valentine's Day 1999 he took Ursula out to dinner and behaved like a sixteen-year-old. They are a happy couple, keeping their own homes and commuting between. On his eighty-fifth birthday his daughters organised a party for him at a Victoria golf club and about sixty or seventy people came, many from afar. Louisa and Marjory thought there should be speeches; they and their cousin Lionel did their best, then invited the birthday boy to address the gathering. Alex was still wiping traces of cake-cutting from his fingers as he strode to the microphone. He was delighted to see so many of his friends and made some appreciative remarks. Then, he looked around at the sun shining on the golf course and concluded, with that wide smile of his: "Well, you didn't come here today to listen to me so I'll shut up and let you all get the hell out of here!"

APPENDIX I

ALEX'S FAMILY TREE: SQUIRES, EASTS AND JARDINES

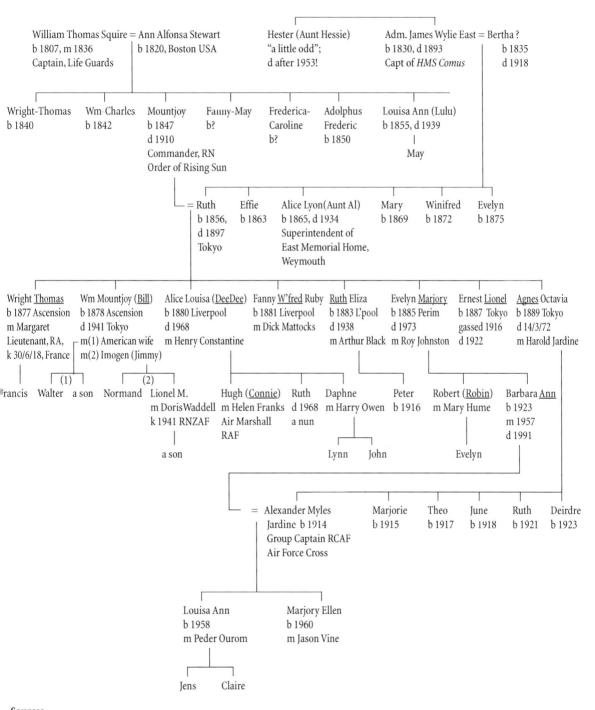

Sources

Notes made by Ann Jardine; Extracts from Burke's Landed Gentry of 1858;
London *Times* obituaries of Admiral East and Commander Squire; 1881 British Census on CDRom.

APPENDIX 2

205 SQUADRON OFFICERS

PHOTOGRAPH AT SELETAR, APRIL 1941 *(in photo section after page 140)*

F/Lt	Norman Birks	incapacitated by prickly heat; left Tjilatjap as 3rd pilot Empire FB, March 1; died 1949 from brain tumour.
F/Lt	Gordon Stilling*	on board *Abbekerk*; shot down, killed, Celebes1943
F/Lt	Alex Jardine*	POW, 8 March 1942
W/C	L. W. Burgess	posted to AHQFE
F/Lt	E. W. Young	killed in accident, Seychelles, 23 July 1941
F/Lt	Dick Atkinson	survived Dec 25 crash, on board *Holland*, 3 March 1942; shot down, killed, attacking *Tirpitz*
F/O	Terry Grieve	killed in accident, Seychelles, 23 August 1941
F/O	Doug 'Bernard' Shaw	unable to find Diego Garcia at dusk, 20 Sept '41, force-landed in sea, all drowned
F/O	J. Ingram*	on board *Holland* or *Tungsong*
F/Lt	Jock Graham*	shot down, killed off Ceylon, 6 April 1942
P/O	F. W. Brant	on board *Holland* or *Tungsong*
P/O	P. E. Bedell	shot down, killed over Gulf of Siam, 6 Dec 1941
P/O	Rob McVicker*	on board *Holland* or *Tungsong*

PHOTOGRAPH AT SELETAR, DECEMBER 1941 *(in photo section after page 140)*

F/Lt	H. Garnell	killed in strafing on landing at Broome, W. Australia, 3 March 1942
S/L	Max Farrar	shot down, killed over Singora, 12 Jan 1942
F/L	H. Tamblyn	flew FVN to Broome, 3 March 1942
P/O	Man Mohan Singh	killed in strafing on landing at Broome, W. Australia, 3 March 1942
F/O	K. M. Whitworth	POW, but not with Alex; knew about fate of airmen at Sandakan
F/O	S. A. Tucker	hospital in Batavia with dengue fever, Feb 19/20 1942; left Batavia for Tjilatjap before Feb 28; on board *Holland* or *Tungsong*
F/Lt	Jackie Lowe	flew FVW to Broome, 2 March 1942
W/C	'Boosey' Councell	on FVW to Broome, 2 March 1942
P/O	Keon-Cohen	on board *Holland* or *Tungsong*
P/O	Crudden	on board *Holland* or *Tungsong*
P/O	McHardy	on board *Holland* or *Tungsong*
P/O	Wilkins	on board *Holland* or *Tungsong*
P/O	Chester	on board *Holland* or *Tungsong*
P/O	Scott	on FVN or FVW to Broome, 2 or 3 March 1942
P/O	Garnett	on board *Holland* or *Tungsong*
P/O	Barnes	on FVN or FVW to Broome, 2 or 3 March 1942
P/O	Kinsey	on board *Holland* or *Tungsong*

IN NEITHER PICTURE:

F/O	Sid Scales	survived Dec 25 crash, PoW, 8 March 1942
P/O	John Westcott	POW, 8 March 1942
F/O	Jefferies	on board *Tungsong*, arrived with 35 airmen from Batavia March 1

NOTE: underlined definitely survived the war, *appear in both group photographs

APPENDIX 3

A RECORD OF 205 SQUADRON'S CATALINAS
FROM 23 JULY 1941 TO APRIL 5 1942

	Serviceable Aircraft ID letters	U/S	Serviceable/ Detached	Destroyed
July 23	?	?		U crash on take-off, Seychelles: <u>Young, Grieve</u>
Sept 20	?	?		Y broke up in force-landing, unable to locate DG: <u>Shaw</u>
Dec 6	NPQRSTVXZ		9	W shot down on patrol: <u>Webb, Bedell</u>
Dec 12	New (Du) UWY +NPQRSTVXZ		12	
Dec 18	NPQRTUVWXYZ	S	11/1	
Dec 25	NPQRSTUVWXY		11	Z shot down on patrol: Atkinson (survived)
Dec 30	SUVWXY	NPQRT	6/5	
Jan 2	NPSUVWXY	QRT	8/3	
Jan 3	NPQSUVWY	RT	8/2	X petrol fire on slip, Seletar
Jan 9	NPQRSUVWY	T	9/1	
Jan 10	NPQSUVWY	RT	8/2	
Jan 11	NPQSTUVWY	R	9/1	
Jan 13	NPSTUVWY	R	8/1	Q shot down at Singora: <u>Farrar</u>
Jan 14	PRUVY	NSTW	5/4	
Jan 15	PRTUVWY	NS	7/2	
Jan 17	RUV	NSW	3/3	PTY strafed on water, Seletar
Jan 18	RUV	NSW		
Jan 19	NRUVW	S	5/1	
Jan 20	NSVW	RU	4/2	
Jan 22	NRSUV	W	5/1	
Jan 23	N(R)SUV	W	4(1)/1	
Jan 24	N(R)VW	SU	3(1)/2	
Jan 25	N(R)UV	SW	3(1)/2	
Jan 26	(N)UV	RSW	2(1)/3	
Jan 27	(N)RVW	SU	3(1)/2	
Jan 30	N(RV)UW	S	3(2)/1	
Jan 31	N(R)VUW		4(1)/0	S abandoned at Seletar, probably cannibalised
Feb 1–18	(N)RVW	U	3(1)/1	
Feb 18	N(R)VW	U	3(1)/1	
Feb 20	NV(R to Ceylon)	UW	2(1)/2	
Feb 22	N	UW	1(1)/2	V DC accident, Tjilatjap
Feb 24	NW	U	2(1)/1	
Feb 27	W(N to Emmahaven)	U	1(2)/1	
Feb 28	W(N)		1(2)/0	U destroyed by DNAS, Priok
March 3			0(1)	NW strafed on water, Broome: <u>Garnell, Singh</u>
April 5			0	R shot down, Bay of Bengal: <u>Graham</u>

NOTE <u>Pilot underlined</u>: pilot and crew lost

ENDNOTES

1   The Times, London. *Obituary of Rear-Admiral J. Wylie East.* June 24(?) 1893
2   Johnston, Robert W.S. *conversation with Alex Jardine.* February 2000
3   The Times, London. *Obituary of Commander M. Squire, R.N.* 1910
4   Gunther, John. *Inside Asia,* 1938
5   Slessor, Sir John. *The Central Blue.* London: Cassell, 1956, p74
6   Lord Tedder. *With Prejudice.* London: Cassell & Co, 1966, p6-7
7   Dixon, Norman F. *On the psychology of military incompetence.* London: Jonathan Cape,1976
8   Stofer, Ken. *Dear Mum.* Victoria: Kenlyn Publishing, 1991, p142
9   Shores, Christopher, Brian Cull & Yasuho Izawa. *Bloody Shambles.* London: Grub Street Press, 1992, p50
10 Tedder, p6
11 Barber, Noel. *The natives were friendly so we stayed the night.* Anstey, Leics:Ulverscroft, 1979
12 Shores, Christopher, Brian Cull & Yasuho Izawa. *Bloody Shambles.* London: Grub Street, 1992, p77 (note that Shores states F/O Bedell to have been the Captain of FVY; in fact this appears to have been a rare case where command was not in accordance with rank.)
13 Ibid, p97
14 Ibid, p110
15 Ibid, p125
16 Ibid, p151
17 Ibid, p154-5
18 Ibid, p294
19 Ibid, p294
20 Ibid, p309-10
21 Ibid, p297
22 Popham, Hugh. *Sea Flight.* London: William Kimber, 1954, p96
23 Ibid, p101
24 Charpentier, Alain et al. *Global Warrior, the story of G/C Jeudwyne.* Eastbourne: Kall Kwik, 1999, p22
25 Campbell, Hugh. Appendix to his history of the 'Tung Song'
26 Shores, Christopher, Brian Cull & Yasuho Izawa. *Bloody Shambles.* London: Grub Street, 1992, p349
27 Campbell, Hugh. *Letter to AMJ* 8 Oct 1999
28 Charpentier, Alain et al. *Global Warrior, the story of G/C Jeudwyne.* Eastbourne: Kal Kwik, 1999, account of Sergeant Dave Russell. p32
29 Ibid, W/C Jeudwine's report to Intelligence section, Western Area HQ. p39
30 Ibid, Russell. p32
31 Ibid, Jeudwine. p39
32 Ibid, p40
33 Ibid, p41
34 Storey, Robert et al. *Indonesia.* Lonely Planet series. Victoria, Australia: Hawthorn,1992, p21
35 Gunther, John. *Inside Asia.* New York: Harper and Brothers, 1939, p329
36 Global Warrior, Jeudwine. p42
37 Ibid, Log of the 'Scorpion'. pp22 & 26
38 Kriek, David. *43 Special Mission.* http.//www.icon.co.za/~pjclarke/miss00.html c.1998

39   Dunlop, E. E. *The War Diaries of Weary Dunlop*. Melbourne: Thomas Nelson, 1986, p53

40   Van der Post, Laurens. *The Night of the New Moon*. London: Hogarth Press, 1970, p18

41   Hillen, Ernest. *The Way of a Boy*. Toronto: Penguin Books, 1993, p198

42   Ibid, p98-9

43   *The Night of the New Moon*, p10

44   *The War Diaries of Weary Dunlop*, p85

45   Plomer, William. *Double Lives, an Autobiography*. London: Cape, 1949 edition, p 213

46   *The Night of the New Moon*, p53

47   Ibid, p41 et seq.

48   Ibid, p35-6

49   Ibid, p37

50   *The Way of a Boy*, p157

51   *The War Diaries of Weary Dunlop*, pp61, 75, 79-80

52   Ibid, p87.

53   Van der Post, Laurens. *The Seed and the Sower*. London: Hogarth Press, 1963, p22

54   Van der Post, Laurens. *The Night of the New Moon*. London: Hogarth Press, 1970, pp41-2

55   Ibid, p42

56   Knight, Talbot. 18 page memoir addressed to Mr Mathieson, 13 Oct 1983

57   Buruma, Ian. *Wages of Guilt*. London: Jonathan Cape, 1994, p173

58   *The Seed and the Sower*, p13

59   *The Night of the New Moon*, p43

60   Ibid, p49

61   Ibid, p55

62   Hillen, Ernest. *The Way of a Boy*. Toronto: Penguin Books, 1993, p28

63   *The Night of the New Moon*, p61

64   Ibid, p70-7

65   Knight, Talbot. Eighteen-page memoir addressed to Mr Mathieson, 13 Oct 1983

66   *The Night of the New Moon*, pp84-112

67   Dunlop, E.E. *The War Diaries of Weary Dunlop*. Melbourne: Thomas Nelson, 1986, p114

68   Hillen, Ernest. *Small Mercies*. Toronto: Penguin Books, 1997, pp9-18

69   Charpentier, Alain et al. *Global Warrior, the story of G/C Jeudwyne*. Eastbourne: Kall Kwik, 1999, p133-4

70   Bailey, Ralph. *Canadian Aerial Magnetic Surveys (M.A.D.)*—NRC 1852. National Research Council of Canada, 1948. p527

71   Taylor, John W.R. *Jane's Pocket Book of Military Transport and Training Aircraft*. NY: Collier Books, 1974, p167

72   Jackaman, John. *Autobiography*. Unpublished, chapter 28

73   Solandt, Omond. 'Industrial Research and Development' in *Canadian Encyclopaedia*. Edmonton: Hurtig, 1985

74   Jackaman, chapter 28

75   Jackaman, chapter 27

76   Ibid

77   Jackaman, chapter 28

78   Globe and Mail, 24 Sept 1958

79   Holmes, Tony. *Jane's Historic Military Aircraft*. London: HarperCollins, 1998, p198

80   Morton, Desmond. "Armed Forces" in *Canadian Encyclopaedia*. Edmonton: Hurtig, 1985

81   Ibid.

82   Ibid.

BIBLIOGRAPHY

Bailey, Ralph. *Canadian Aerial Magnetic Surveys (M.A.D.) – NRC 1852.* National Research Council of Canada, 1948.

Barber, Noel. *The natives were friendly so we stayed the night.* Anstey, Leics: Ulverscroft, 1979.

Bowyer, Chaz. *History of the RAF.* London: Hamlyn Publishing Group, Ltd, 1977.

Broek, Jan O. M. *'Java' in Encyclopaedia Britannica.* Chicago: Benton, 1966.

Buruma, Ian. *Wages of Guilt.* London: Jonathan Cape, 1994.

Campbell, Hugh. *Appendix to his history of the 'Tung Song.'* Unpublished

Campbell, Hugh. *Letter to AMJ, 8 Oct 1999.*

Charpentier, Alain et al. *Global Warrior, the story of G/C Jeudwyne.* Eastbourne:Kall Kwik,1999.

Church of Jesus Christ. *CDRom:1881 British Census.* Salt Lake City: Family History Dept, 1999.

Dixon, Norman F. *On the psychology of military incompetence.* London: Jonathan Cape, 1976.

Dunlop, E. E. *The War Diaries of Weary Dunlop.* Melbourne: Thomas Nelson, 1986.

Globe and Mail. 24 September 1958.

Gunther, John. *Inside Asia.* New York: Harper and Brothers, 1939.

Hillen, Ernest. *The Way of a Boy.* Toronto: Penguin Books, 1993.

Hillen, Ernest. *Small Mercies.* Toronto: Penguin Books, 1997.

Holmes, Tony. *Jane's Historic Military Aircraft.* London: HarperCollins, 1998.

Jackaman, John. *Autobiography.* Unpublished.

Jardine, G/C A. M. Letters to his mother; documents and photographs deposited in BC Provincial Archives, Victoria; interviews with author 1999 and 2000.

Knight, Talbot. *18-page memoir addressed to Mr Mathieson,* 13 Oct 1983.

Kriek, David. *43 Special Mission.* http.//www.icon.co.za/~pjclarke/miss00.html c.1998.

Lamb, W. Kaye. *Empress to the Orient.* Vancouver: Vancouver Maritime Museum, 1991.

Morton, Desmond. *'Armed Forces' in Canadian Encyclopaedia.* Edmonton: Hurtig, 1985.

Naipaul, V. S. *Among the Believers.* London: André Deutsch, 1981.

Plomer, William. *Double Lives, an autobiography.* London: Jonathan Cape, 1949.

Popham, Hugh. *Sea Flight.* London: William Kimber, 1954.

Scales, Sid. Various written accounts; also interviews with the author, 1999 and 2000.

Shores, Christopher, Brian Cull & Yasuho Izawa. *Bloody Shambles.* London: Grub Street, 1992.

Slessor, Sir John. *The Central Blue.* London: Cassell, 1956.

Solandt, Omond. *'Industrial Research and Development' in Canadian Encyclopaedia.* Edmonton: Hurtig, 1985.

Stofer, Ken. *Dear Mum.* Victoria, BC: Kenlyn Publishing, 1991.

Storey, Robert et al. *Indonesia,* Lonely Planet series. Victoria, Australia: Hawthorn, 1992.

Taylor, John W. R. *Jane's Pocket Book of Military Transport and Training Aircraft.* NY: Collier Books, 1974.

Tedder, Lord. *With Prejudice.* London: Cassell & Co, 1966.

Thomas, David. *Battle of the Java Sea.* London: Pan Books, 1968.

Van der Post, Laurens. *The Night of the New Moon.* London: Hogarth Press, 1970.

Van der Post, Laurens. *The Seed and the Sower.* London: Hogarth Press, 1963.

Williams, Neville. *Chronology of the Modern World, 1763-1965.* London: Penguin Books, 1966.

Wilson, Stewart. *Zero, Hurricane and P-38.* Fyshwick, Australia: Aerospace publications, 1996.

The most-used source was the collection of Alex's letters to his mother. These, in addition to diaries, collections of memorabilia and letters from other sources, are housed in the BC Archives, Victoria, as the papers of Group Captain A. M. Jardine, AFC. His weekly letters, with a gap of the three and a half years of his incarceration in Java and of one or two other gaps when his mother was staying with him or he was on holiday in British Columbia, run from 1929 to 1965.

INDEX

ISBN 155369054-0

9 781553 690542